Fashionomics

Donna W. Reamy
Virginia Commonwealth University

Deidra W. Arrington
Virginia Commonwealth University

PEARSON

Boston   Columbus   Indianapolis   New York   San Francisco   Upper Saddle River
Amsterdam   Cape Town   Dubai   London   Madrid   Milan   Munich   Paris   Montreal   Toronto
Delhi   Mexico City   Sao Paulo   Sydney   Hong Kong   Seoul   Singapore   Taipei   Tokyo

Editorial Director: Vernon Anthony
Acquisitions Editor: Sara Eilert
Editorial Assistant: Doug Greive
Director of Marketing: David Gesell
Senior Marketing Manager: Harper Coles
Senior Marketing Coordinator: Alicia Wozniak
Senior Marketing Assistant: Crystal Gonzalez
Associate Editor: Laura J. Weaver
Production Manager: Laura Messerly
Senior Art Director: Jayne Conte
Manager, Rights and Permissions: Mike Lackey
Cover Designer: Suzanne Duda
Cover Image: Hawa Stwodah
Full-Service Project Management: Mogana Sundaramurthy
Composition: Integra Software Services, Ltd.
Printer/Binder: Edwards Brothers Malloy
Cover Printer: Lehigh-Phoenix Color/Hagerstown
Text Font: 9/15 Helvetica Neue

Credits and acknowledgments for material borrowed from other sources and reproduced, with permission, in this textbook appear on the appropriate page within the text. Unless otherwise stated, all artwork has been provided by the author.

Library of Congress Cataloging-in-Publication Data

Reamy, Donna W.
    Fashionomics / Donna W. Reamy, Deidra W. Arrington.—1st ed.
      p. cm.
    Includes bibliographical references and index.
    ISBN-13: 978-0-13-210981-9 (alk. paper)
    ISBN-10: 0-13-210981-6 (alk. paper)
    1. Fashion merchandising. 2. Clothing trade. I. Arrington, Deidra W. II. Title.
HD9940.A2R428 2013
338.4'774692—dc23

                                    2012006887

10 9 8 7 6 5 4 3 2 1

ISBN 10:   0-13-210981-6
ISBN 13: 978-0-13-210981-9

Contents

Preface

Fashionomics gives students a fundamental understanding of economic principles and their direct application to the rationale and decision making of the fashion industry. This textbook is directed to fashion courses with a business and economic point of view.

The textbook takes the reader on an exploration of economic concepts and their implications for textiles and apparel. The journey begins with the impact of the industrial revolution on the fashion industry followed by economic principles such as supply and demand. Various topics such as the stock market, mergers and acquisitions, tools such as economic indicators, the monetary policy used by industry professionals to plan business activity, the importance of the difference between the domestic and international consumer, and the role the government plays in the fashion industry are examined. The textbook concludes with the discussion of various trends in the fashion industry, many based on technological innovations.

The first two chapters of the text set the foundation for an essential understanding of fashion. Chapter 1 begins the book with a historical perspective and Chapter 2 studies the fashion vernacular. The remainder of the book emphasizes the modern-day fashion industry from a business perspective, both domestically and internationally.

Chapter 3 introduces the economics of fashion by discussing important economic viewpoints and using fashion examples to illustrate scarcity, the spillover effect, marginal analysis, marginal efficiency, and the interaction of supply and demand in the marketplace.

Chapters 4 and 5 delve into fashion from a retail perspective, looking at traditional (department stores, discount stores, and specialty stores) and contemporary (pop-up stores, kiosks, and franchising) retail models. Chapter 5 underscores

the workings of the fashion business from a buyer's perspective through a discussion of product pricing, the six-month merchandise plan, and the characteristics of a buyer.

Fashion is a profoundly competitive business and Chapter 6 examines the competitive forces of fashion based on the competition model developed by Michael Porter, a Harvard professor. Fashion companies study the macroeconomic environment along with historical sales followed by the microeconomic factors to make decisions about strategy and direction. This chapter establishes that a company can do everything right, but if consumer confidence is low, causing a decrease in spending, then the company's potential to earn a profit is decreased, resulting in the decline in the value of the company's stock prices. Through an examination of the stock market, students learn how the stock market works and the measurement of the financial health of a public company using the annual report.

Chapter 7 reveals the government's involvement in the fashion industry. For example, it defines and explains the monetary policy of the United States and how it is used to control economic conditions, such as unemployment and inflation, which affect consumer's discretionary income. Discretionary income is critical to the fashion industry, as that is what consumers use to purchase fashion items. Students gain knowledge of the implications, both positive and negative, of governmental policies for the fashion industry in favorable and adverse economic conditions.

Chapter 8 imparts to students an understanding of how the fashion industry is grouped by classifications or segments such as women's wear, menswear, children's wear, intimate apparel, cosmetics, accessories, and home fashions. The chapter discusses how the government keeps

statistical information on each classification for reporting purposes. Also applicable for students is the understanding of how each segment operates in different, yet similar, ways.

Chapter 9 examines domestic and international fashion consumers. Understanding consumers and their preferences, behaviors, and motivations is vital to the success of manufacturers and retailers of fashion products. This chapter identifies the demographics, geographics, and psychographics that lead to consumer decisions.

Chapter 10 identifies the four major fashion centers in the world and examines the history that led to their importance in the global fashion arena. It discusses the economic impact of the fashion centers locally and globally. The chapter defines the fashion show as more than a tool to promote fashion, as it serves many purposes from both a fashion and economic viewpoint.

Chapter 11 presents the world of fashion on a global scale to students. The international business of fashion occurs 24 hours a day, 7 days a week, throughout the world, and in this chapter, students grasp the organization of the international fashion industry. The discussion on trade preference programs and trade support programs and agencies promotes a deeper understanding of fashion on an international scale.

Chapter 12 identifies the top trends effecting contemporary fashion from an economic perspective. Issues ranging from social media, to the changing American physique, to the conservative consumer clearly exhibit the dynamic nature of fashion.

An Instructor's Guide and PowerPoint slides are available online to assist faculty with ideas for lectures, guest speakers, and student activities. The Instructor's Guide includes tests for each chapter.

Download Instructor Resources from the Instructor Resource Center

To access supplementary materials online, instructors need to request an instructor access code. Go to www.pearsonhighered.com/irc to register for an instructor access code. Within 48 hours of registering, you will receive a confirming e-mail including an instructor access code. Once you have received your code, locate your text in the online catalog and click on the Instructor Resources button on the left side of the catalog product page. Select a supplement, and a login page will appear. Once you have logged in, you can access instructor material for all Prentice Hall textbooks. If you have any difficulties accessing the site or downloading a supplement, please contact Customer Service at http://247.prenhall.com.

Acknowledgments

This book would not be possible without the people who have supported and encouraged us throughout this process.

Our thanks go to our wonderful fashion students at Virginia Commonwealth University who challenge and inspire us. They continue to feed and cultivate our love for what we do every single day of our lives. It is because of them that we wrote this textbook.

A huge thank-you goes to Pearson, Inc. Your faith in us, along with your continued encouragement, made this lengthy process bearable. Special thanks go to Sara Eilert and Laura Weaver, whose positive attitude and patience helped us every step of the way.

We owe a debt of gratitude and thanks to the following people contributed their knowledge and time to our textbook: Tom Gresham, public relations specialist, Virginia Commonwealth University; Nate Herman, vice president international trade, American Apparel and Footwear Association; Karen Videtic, professor and former chairperson, VCU Department of Fashion Design and; Holly Alford, associate professor, VCU Department of Fashion Design and Merchandising; Rose Regni, assistant professor, VCU Department of Fashion Design and Merchandising; Hawa Stwodah, fashion illustrator and adjunct professor, VCU Department of Fashion Design and Merchandising; Jacqueline Mullins, fashion historian, Valentine Museum; Dr. Dennis O'Toole, retired professor, VCU School of Business; Julia Pietras, Adrian Brinkley, Elizabeth Clancy, and Nadim Sudic, fashion alumni, VCU Department of Fashion Design and Merchandising; Sarah Yurow and Taylor Wilhelm, students, VCU Department of Fashion Design and Merchandising; Bree Reamy and Laura Catherine Williams, models; Taylor Francis, photographer; Claudia Chan Shaw, Australian fashion designer; David Levine, economist and distinguished professor in the Department of Economics, Washington University in St. Louis, MO; George Bridgforth, buyer, Stage Stores Peebles Division; Bill Wakefield, president, Wakefield's Inc., and the Apparel Strategist, premiere business journal.

We would like to acknowledge the following reviewers for their comments: Crystal Green, Art Institute of Charlotte; Carol Harris, Savannah College of Art and Design; Jennifer Roberts, Missouri State University; Leslie Simpson, Philadelphia University; and Neily Tejeda, Keiser University.

Dedication

This book is dedicated to

My family, Gil Reamy, my husband for his time and patience, my two wonderful children Michael and Bree
who had to endure listening talking about my project for years and my mother Patricia Wainscott
for always encouraging me.

DONNA REAMY

My loving and supportive husband Steve, my family and friends.
Thank you all for tolerating years of "book" talk. I love you all.

DEIDRA ARRINGTON

Fashionomics

A FASHION HISTORY

OBJECTIVES

After reading this chapter, you will be able to:

- Evaluate the importance of fashion
- Demonstrate a definition of and perspective on fashion
- Examine fashion from the nineteenth century to the twenty-first century

Fashion is important because it is in almost everything.
—ALFRED H. DANIELS (1951)

1

Mr. Daniels's statement remains true; fashion is everywhere, in everything we touch, and in some unlikely places such as science, mortuary practice, and business management. Fashion cannot be limited to costume and adornment, for to do so is grossly inadequate in characterizing its scope and impact on society and everyday life (Miller, McIntyre, and Mantrala, 1993). Paul Nystrom, author of the book Economics of Fashion, wrote, "Fashion is one of the greatest forces in present day life." Nystrom's work, which was published more than 80 years ago, has proven that fashion continues its prominence and significance in society.

Sproles (1979) defined **fashion** as "a way of behaving that is temporarily adopted by a discernible proportion of members of a social group because that chosen behavior is perceived to be socially appropriate for the time and situation." More simply stated, fashion is the prevailing manner of dress, usage, or style that is accepted by the majority of a population for a specific time. Fashion is our expression to the world about what we are, to which groups we belong (see Figure 1.1 for examples of different groups), our place in society, and what we are comfortable with and consider moral. From the cars we drive to the way we decorate our homes to the clothes we wear, fashion has an impact in all facets of our lives.

Fashion is important because of its effect on consumer behavior caused by societal influences. It is human nature to form groups and to be attracted to people in certain groups while at the same time avoiding those in other groups. Therefore, individuals will

FIGURE 1.1 *Fashion is our expression to the world about who we are (Source: Shutterstock).*

strive to become members of the groups they admire and avoid the less desirable groups. By adopting the styles and symbols of the esteemed group, we communicate to the world our membership in the group. The converse is also true: By rejecting the fashion and likes of the disdained group, we communicate our distance from that group. Fashion is dynamic and a way of expressing our self-image, position in society, and our feelings toward others that we hold in high regard.

Fashion is art, conceptual in nature. Some analyze fashion like a beautiful piece of sculpture. Figure 1.2 shows a dress by Japanese designer Yohji Yamamoto from his fall/winter 2008–2009 collection. "Oversized," "free-flowing silhouettes" are words used to describe Mr. Yamamoto's designs. The same words could also describe a sculpture. One may study the design, fabric, and details of a garment as he or she would an exquisite painting. Figure 1.3 shows Issey Miyake's spring/summer 2009 collection. Mr. Miyake uses many design concepts perfected by Madeleine Vionnet, a fashion designer described as the "queen of the bias cut" (Baudot, 1996, p. 82). If the dress were on a canvas hanging in an art gallery, one would view it as art rather than a fashion garment. The work of Mariano Fortuny is another example of the embodiment of the concept of fashion as art. Francois Baudot noted in his book, Fashion: The Twentieth Century, "It seems in a way ridiculous to use the term fashion to describe these works of art, which are rooted in notions of symbolism, memory and an idealized vision of the future, united by a sense of virtuoso plasticity."

FIGURE 1.2 *Yohji Yamamoto dress from his fall/winter 2008/09 collection (Source: Alamy).*

FIGURE 1.3 *Issey Miyake's dress from the spring/summer 2009 collection (Source: Newscom).*

Historical Perspectives on Fashion

Throughout history, fashion has been the expression of social, economic, cultural, and political movements.

> Social, political, and economic trends, cycles of war and peace, all link with one another, influencing and illuminating our cultural patterns and the fashions of the times. That is why we say that a sense of history is an integral part of every business enterprise and that there is wisdom in investigating and understanding the past. (Klein, 1963)

To understand the fashion industry and its economical magnitude, it is important to look at how fashion has evolved over time as clothing went from practical to lavish, symbolizing wealth and status.

The Industrial Revolution

Prior to the **industrial revolution**, textiles were handmade. A number of inventions during this time, including the cotton gin, the power loom, the spinning jenny, and the sewing machine, helped to speed the production of textiles.

Eli Whitney in America invented the cotton gin, designed to remove the seed from the cotton, in 1793. The following year, James Hargreaves invented the spinning jenny (Figure 1.4) in England. Hargreaves noticed that an overturned spinning wheel continued to turn and this led him to develop a machine that spun several threads at one time and improved the horizontal loom (Little, 1931). Joseph-Marie Jacquard invented the jacquard loom, enabling the manufacture of intricate patterns. Edmund Cartwright, a clergyman, invented the power loom in 1785, the first of its kind, to power the hand loom by steam. The very first functional sewing machine was invented by Barthelemy Thimonnier in 1830 and later improved upon by Elias Howe, who received the first American patent in 1846. It was not until Isaac Singer created the foot treadle for the sewing machine that people started to purchase sewing machines for home use (see Figure 1.5). Additionally, in 1870, less expensive, colorfast, synthetic dyes were launched, replacing plant-based dyes, which were hard to get. Table 1.1 highlights the inventions and discoveries that have helped to speed production to meet the demand of consumers for fashion.

These inventions took the manufacturing of fashion out of the home and into the factories. This transition led to the standardization of sizes, the homogeneity of the tastes of the American public, and the acceptance of ready-to-wear clothing. In addition, as clothing became more readily available, the time it took a garment to go from the state of introduction to obsolescence increased in speed.

The Nineteenth Century

THE EMPIRE PERIOD 1800–1830

The **Empire Period** followed the French Revolution of 1789. Prior to this period, French society and wealth characterized and dictated European fashion. After the French Revolution, the cotton dress became very popular. The high waistline and straight skirt were a direct

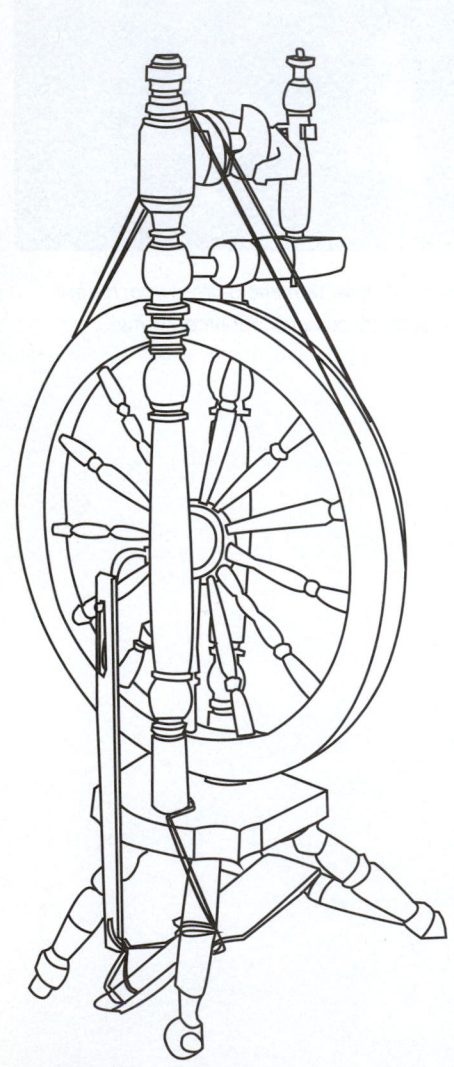

FIGURE 1.4 *The spinning wheel was created by John Hargreaves in 1794 (Source: Hawa Stwodah).*

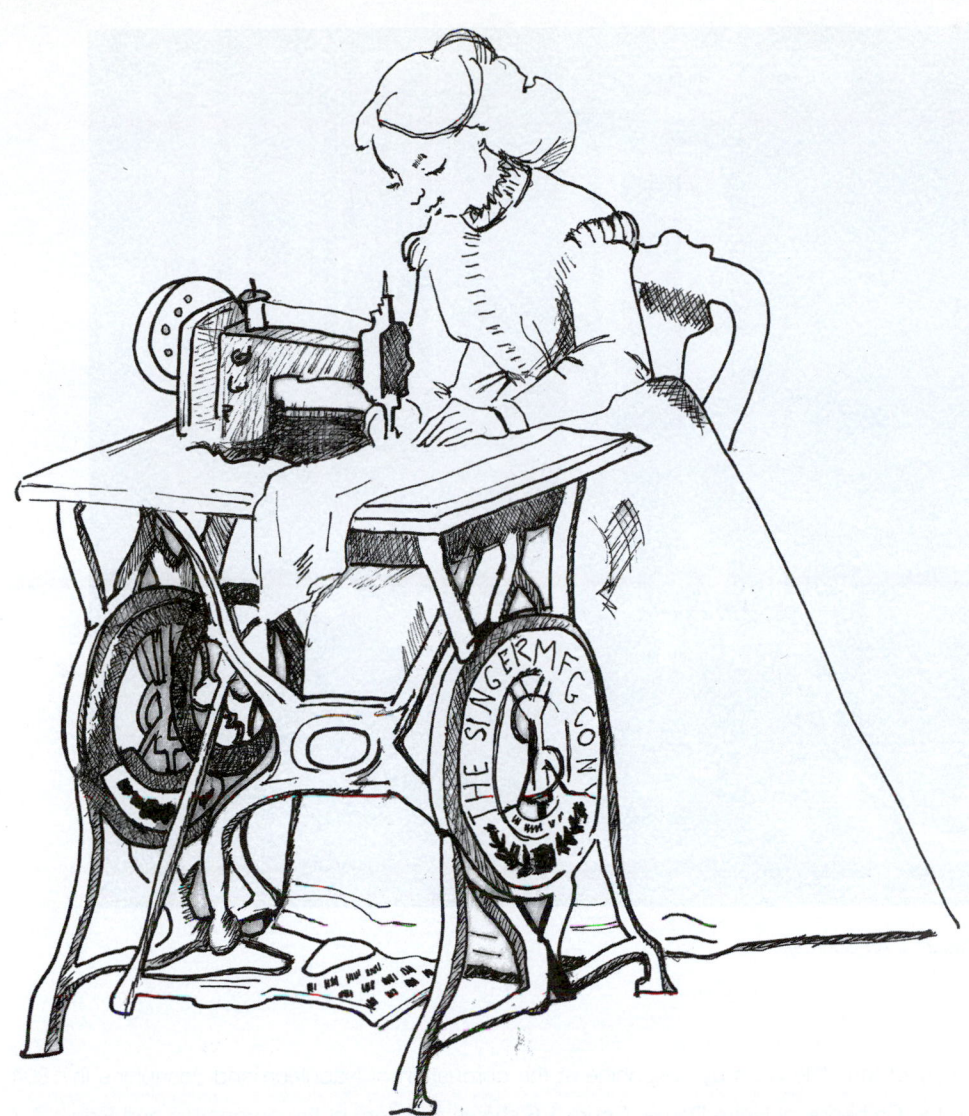

FIGURE 1.5 *Isaac Singer created the foot treadle for the sewing machine (Source: Hawa Stwodah).*

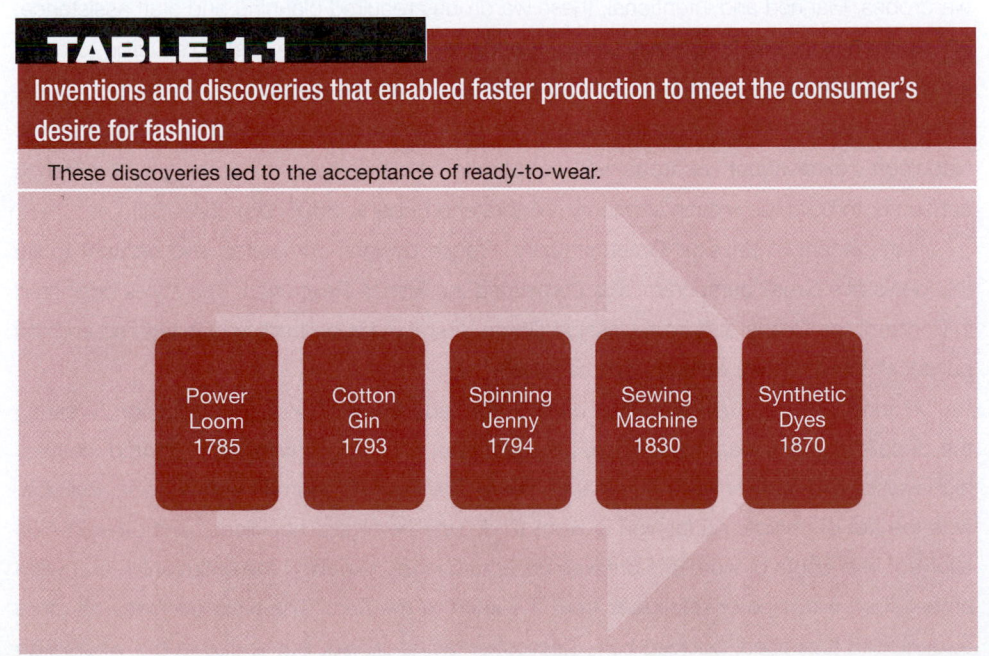

TABLE 1.1

Inventions and discoveries that enabled faster production to meet the consumer's desire for fashion

These discoveries led to the acceptance of ready-to-wear.

Power Loom 1785	Cotton Gin 1793	Spinning Jenny 1794	Sewing Machine 1830	Synthetic Dyes 1870

FIGURE 1.6 *The coronation of Napoleon and Josephine (Source: Art Source).*

copy of the style worn by Josephine at the coronation of Napoleon and Josephine in 1804 in the Cathedral of Notre Dame. Figure 1.6 shows a picture of the coronation and Figure 1.7 shows a cotton chemise dress that was a direct copy of the coronation gown. As major fashion influences of their time, Josephine and Napoleon owned sophisticated and organized wardrobes. Planned and intentional, these wardrobes required planning and staff assistance. A note from Napoleon to General Duroc, the Marshal of the Palace, instructs Duroc to order a highly detailed wardrobe of at least four dozen shirts and handkerchiefs, 24 pairs of shoes, and other various items. Josephine owned over 600 winter dresses and 200 summer dresses. Napoleon's extravagant wardrobe was intended to create demand for clothing by the French consumer to build the French economy (Tortora and Eubank, 2005, pp. 264–266).

Reminiscent of classical Greek statuary, French designs dominated and brought to life the ideals of a Greek democracy that dominated the French Revolution. The styles originated in England, the Orient, and from classical Rome. A softly draped bodice was favored and the painful and constricting **corset** became passé.

Around 1800, women's apparel used lighter fabrics with rounded décolletage. Wearing the décolletage low was acceptable. Dresses were floor length with short, puffed sleeves, high waists, and sometimes with separate trains. The bonnet, adorned with ribbons and lace, was the hat of choice. As fashion is wont to do, the hemlines, necklines, and other details evolved. The length of women's dresses became shorter, exposing the entire ankle and were embellished with lace or appliqués from the knee to the hem. The waistline became more evident with a cinched, buckled belt. Sleeves remained puffed, but ended at the wrists with adornment. While bonnets were still worn, larger hats with wide brims and decorations of flowers, feathers, and ribbons were also in fashion. By 1830, bodices remained close to the body but sleeves were very bouffant to the wrists and fastened in a tight cuff. Skirts, too, were full and puffy from the petticoats underneath. Figure 1.8 is a representation of women's attire in the 1800s.

Men wore high-waisted, cut-away coats with tapered sleeves that puffed at the shoulders and trousers called **pantaloons** with a beaver top hat. Wearing **cravats** and ruffled shirts under the cut-away coats was typical. Shirt collars were high, reaching the cheeks of the wearer's face. Men wore several types of coats. Coats in the Beau Brummel fashion had skirts that formed a square-cut tail on the coat. A **surtout** (a type of greatcoat) was a single-breasted coat padded from the shoulders to the chest. **Frock coats** were also popular and were either single- or double-breasted. Figure 1.9 depicts the typical wardrobe of a gentleman in the 1800s.

In addition, by the early 1800s in America women were beginning to contribute to the household income. While some women worked in the comfort of their homes as seamstress and laundress, others would go outside to work in dry goods stores. Producing clothing in factories for both men and women was a sign of the times. Purchasing clothing for lifestyles and events, ladies and gentlemen needed clothing for socializing, working, churchgoing, and everyday tasks.

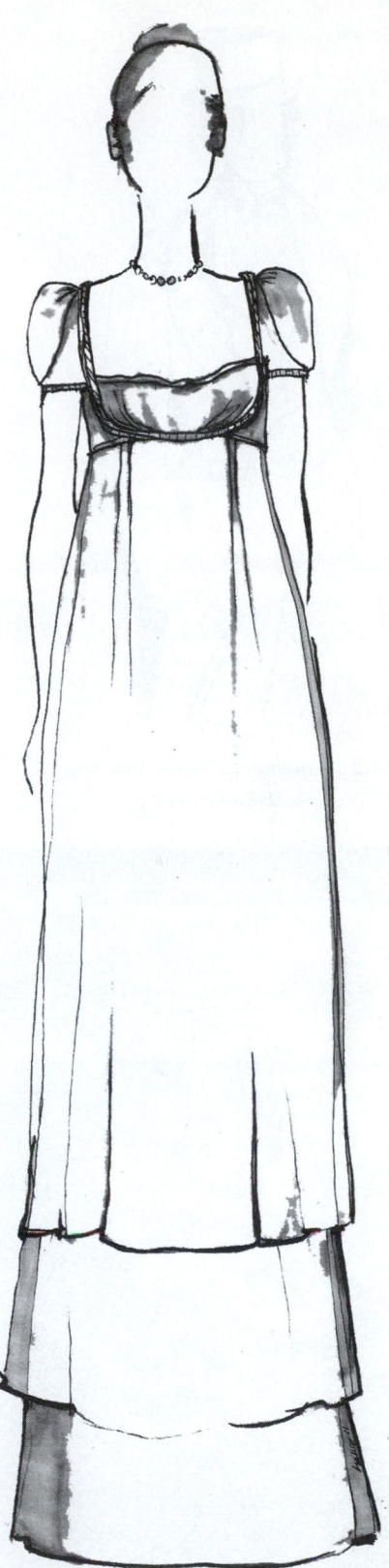

FIGURE 1.7 *An illustration of a cotton chemise dress similar to the one worn by Josephine at the coronation (Source: Hawa Stwodah).*

FIGURE 1.8 *An example of women's attire in the 1800s (Source: Shutterstock).*

THE ROMANTIC PERIOD 1825–1835

This was a crucial time in history. Fashion began to change at a more rapid pace and was distinctive from any other time in history. Baron François Gerard's famous painting *Cupid and Psyche* was an influence on fashion during the Romantic Period (Figure 1.10). While the subjects in the painting are barely clothed, they depict the feeling of timeless love that epitomizes the Romantic Period. The use of pure white for the faces and bodies influenced the trend of pale, porcelain-like skin, devoid of rouge.

For women, the emphasis was on the waistline, creating a renewed demand for corsets. Sleeves were close fitting with **gigot** (leg of mutton) shoulders. Figure 1.11 is an example of a gigot or leg of mutton sleeve. Skirts were ankle length and full, from the petticoats worn underneath. Embellishments decorated the skirt from the knees to the ankles.

In addition to fashion designers, entertainers of the time influenced fashion, evident in more costume-oriented designs. The demand for fashion increased both in Europe and in the American colonies, as did new methods of raw materials production. Trimmings, such as lace, were manufactured using advanced methods. With the exception of corsets and other undergarments (purchased in dry goods stores or through mail-order catalogs), the production of most of women's apparel took place at home.

FIGURE 1.9 *An example of men's apparel in the 1800s (Source: Hawa Stwodah).*

FIGURE 1.10 *The famous painting* Cupid and Psyche *by Baron François Gerard during the Romantic Period (Source: Alamy).*

FIGURE 1.11 *The leg of mutton sleeve was very popular during the late 1800s (Source: Alamy).*

Men's fashions did not parallel women's fashions. In Europe, men wore tight-fitting trousers held in place with leather straps fastened underneath the foot. Men also wore an outdoor garment known as a frock coat or **redingote** (Figure 1.12). Fitted at the waist using a belt, redingotes had tight sleeves, a flared skirt, and a velvet collar. The **petersham frock coat**, double-breasted, short, and full with tight sleeves, was another popular style during the Romantic Period. Shirt collars remained high, touching the cheeks of the wearer. Waistcoats were sleeveless garments worn under the outer coat. Men would dress in the **sack coat** for sports or work. Hair was kept longer than in previous times, which was unusual considering the top hat was fashionable. Seen as more elegant than the bow tie, a jewel pin held the ascot in place.

Clothing needs for men and women in the American colonies were different from those of their European counterparts. The men and women settling the land of America, called **pioneers**, dressed in less elaborate clothing than the Europeans did. They wore denim and other clothing suitable to farming and exploring. The economic impact of the clothing industry began to increase as the needs of people changed.

Originating in Europe, the demand for fashion moved quickly to the American colonies. Both European and American governments took advantage of the fashion industry's growth by protecting and promoting their own industries through the implantation of tariffs on goods. As America was building its economy during the mid-1700s, the government imposed tariffs on imported goods such as wool and linen to encourage the homespun industry. The homespun industry throughout America and Europe wove thread into fabric. The economics of fashion was beginning to globalize paralleling the **globalization**, the connectivity of world economies through trade and cultural exchanges, of the European economy.

FIGURE 1.12 *The redingote was a man's outdoor garment also known as the frock coat (Source: Alamy).*

1825–1850

Royalty no longer influenced the public as it had in the past. A new class of wealth emerged based on the new industrialism. New industrialism led to economic change and provided new inventions, such as the railway and the use of steam as a power source, that were important advances in transportation and manufacturing. Industrialization gave birth to the industrialist, a middle management position that allowed men to acquire finer things, such as suits and shoes. The industrialist became an aspirational figure for others. Sewing machines increased clothing production and the increased number of garments were distributed throughout Europe and the United States. As a result, masses of ordinary people were able to demand and afford fashion.

Ladies' dresses continued to be ankle length with frills from the knee to the hem of the garment. Sleeves were puffed and hats were decorated with feathers, ribbons, and flowers. Necklines were high with large collars that sometimes resembled capes. It was fashionable to cinch the waist with a belt. Around 1830, the necklines dropped but skirts remained full with petticoats underneath. Women wore skirts gathered at the waist; however, the popularity of the adornment of the skirt from the knees to the hem, popular from the early 1800s, waned. Sleeves were very **bouffant** and bonnets were in fashion. By 1850 the **basquin bodice** appeared. (The dress in Figure 1.13 is an example of a basquin bodice.) Sleeves were bell shaped and skirts were full to the ground. Ladies also wore bonnets and gloves.

FIGURE 1.13 *Example of a basquin bodice (Source: Hawa Stwodah).*

Frock coats, redingotes, petersham frocks, and waistcoats were still fashionable for men and tails on coats were common. Trousers became fuller at the waist, tapered down, and were strapped underneath the foot. However, tight-fitting trousers remained in vogue. Shirt collars still touched the cheeks of the face and top hats were in style. About 1840, beards and mustaches gained popularity.

1850–1900

Women's skirts were getting wider and wider by the end of the 1850s. In Nystrom's *Economics of Fashion* he says,

> A typical outfit for women consisted of long drawers, trimmed with lace, a flannel petticoat, another petticoat, then a wadded petticoat, wadded from the waist to the knee with frequent additions of whalebone and horsehair cloth to secure extra stiffness and extension. This garment was followed by still another white starched petticoat, and then two muslin petticoats and finally the outer dress.

Decorated with lace and ribbons, bonnets and caps were worn close to the head.

The invention of the **crinoline** (Figure 1.14), a full, stiff undergarment, became a feature in women's fashions, replacing the layers and layers of fabrics underneath skirts. The width of the skirt signified the wearer's wealth; however, the widening of skirts using a crinoline made it difficult for women to pass through doorways, which resulted in the widening of doorframes to accommodate the dresses. Garments were elaborate and ornate, described as belonging to the style **tapissier** (upholstery style) because the outfits often favored draperies and furniture designed by decorators in the best part of town (Baudot, 1996).

The fashion magazines of the 1850s and 1860s gave insight to the public about the fashions of the times. Figure 1.15 is an illustration of a typical cover of the *Dry Goods Economist*, a trade journal established in 1852. A typical edition contained sections on fabrics, fashions, and notions and included tips on what individual merchants were doing visually to catch the consumers' eye.

One of the most notable people in fashion during this time was fashion designer Charles Frederick Worth (Figure 1.16 is a portrait of Worth). Worth was an Englishman who got his start as a sales clerk at Gagelin, a dry goods store that sold draperies, ready-to-wear clothing, and textiles, in France. Worth married one of the shop girls who also modeled for the store. Worth designed for his wife. Gagelin's customers admired the clothing, and soon, he began designing for these enthusiasts as well. The House of Worth opened in Paris in 1858 (the salon was closed for a year from 1870 to 1871). Defining him as a courtier during this time set him apart from the dressmakers of the era. Worth rid women's wear of much of its lace and frills and replaced it with silver and gold beading and workmanship only attainable by a true couture designer. Worth helped to create the fashion industry in Paris by bringing in house draftsman, cutters, seamstresses, embroiders, clerks, **vendeuses** (saleswomen), and models (Jackie Mullins Personal communication, November 16, 2008). Worth is widely recognized for first establishing the rules of Parisian **haute couture**, a French term meaning fine sewing.

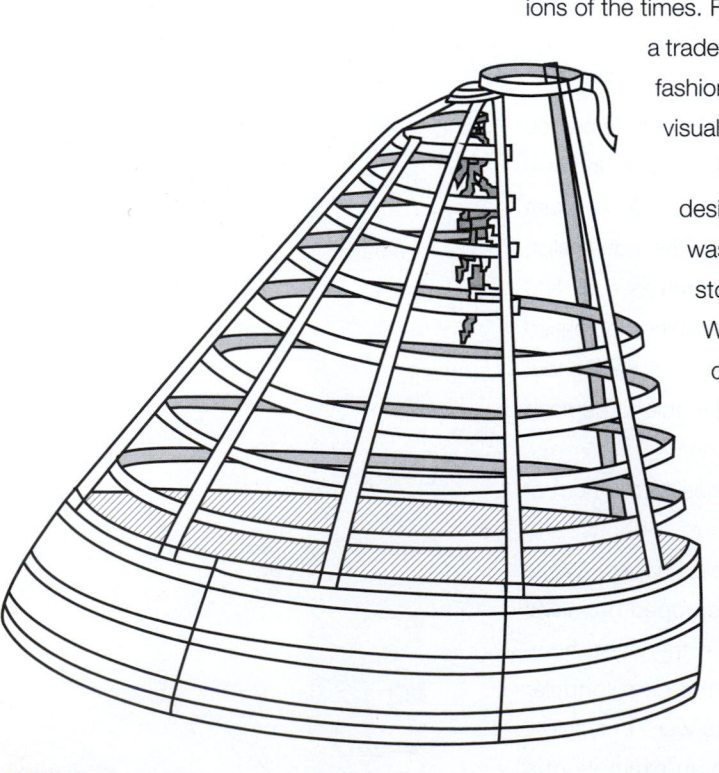

FIGURE 1.14 *A crinoline became a feature in women's fashions, replacing the layers and layers of fabric worn under dresses (Source: Hawa Stwodah).*

DRY GOODS ECONOMIST

31 ST YEAR   NEW YORK, SATURDAY, NOVEMBER 21, 1929   NO. 4297

cotton is going up!

FIGURE 1.15 *Typical cover of the* Dry Goods Economist, *a trade journal for the fabric, fashion, and home industry first published in the mid-1800s (Source: Hawa Stwodah).*

THE LATE M. WORTH.

FIGURE 1.16 *Charles Fredrick Worth, the father of houte couture (Source: Alamy).*

Charles Worth's high fashion designs and his marketing methods for his fashions garnered him the title the "father of haute couture." He used only the finest fabrics and sumptuous trim to create a line of fashions from which he took orders. **Mannequins**, called models today, displayed his work. Worth threw elaborate parties at his home to display his fashions and to connect and network with potential clients. This method of marketing and design proved to be very successful and other fashion designers followed suit. Worth continued to create one-of-a-kind pieces for special clients such as Princess Eugenie and others in the Royal Court, people in the theater, and the wealthy, but his designs were also worn by the middle class. During this time, Worth's designs were found in most fashion magazines around the world. Worth was immensely popular among the wealthy, which was demonstrated by their willingness to travel to Paris to buy their wardrobes.

The Twentieth Century

1900s

The period from 1900 to 1914 is known as **La Belle Époque** (the beautiful age). Paris was still the fashion capital of the world; however, the United States took the lead in Western fashion. World travel was very much in vogue; the wealthy traveled by sea from one continent to another with over 15 trunks of clothing and accessories. More streamlined and fluid garments that departed from the excess of the late nineteenth century characterized the "modern style." Designers now faced the dilemma of producing fresh designs while maintaining their appeal and enticing consumers to continue to buy (Baudot, 1996). Mass productions toward the end of the nineteenth century accelerated the production of garments while making clothing affordable to the public and creating the need for distributing the manufactured garments.

The rise of the department store from the mid 1850s to the end of the nineteenth century was nothing short of a major revolution, not only for business but also for all of society. In fact, what the department store did for the economy and consumers was as dramatic and as far reaching as any other major innovation the world has ever known. (Tamilia, 2002)

See Figure 1.17 for a photograph of the first department store, the Bon Marche in Paris, France. The retail industry excelled at distribution with the setting up of department stores. The department store's supply chain transformed "the store itself, the shopping experience, availability and assortment of goods, credit policies, price awareness, and media and promotional techniques" (Tamilia, 2002). Fashion up to this point was more about the art of the dress and the body rather than making a profit. As production and distribution increased, the ability to profit from fashion was born.

At the beginning of the nineteenth century, a woman stood conscious of her dignity wrapped in the opulent armor of her role. Her figure was pressed into a grotesque S-bend

FIGURE 1.17 *The Bon Marche in Paris, France, was the first department store (Source: Alamy).*

(Figure 1.18) with her breasts pushed outward into a sweeping curve, while an exaggerated curve projected in the opposite direction as a counterweight beneath the tightly corseted waist and flat bottom (Buxbaum, 1999, p. 14). The corset-bound waist divided the body into two parts. From 1870 to 1900, women's fashion saw little change.

During the same period, men wore fitted suits with buttons high on the waist, vests, and high-waisted trousers with cuffs. The wardrobe of a man included "motoring costumes" with dust coats and cap with ear flaps. Particularly interesting was the critical eye given to men's fashion. With the advent and growing acceptance of ready-to-wear, critical discernment of hand-tailored clothing versus ready-to-wear was commonplace.

Paul Poiret, an apprentice of Worth, was one of the more popular fashion designers of the early twentieth century. As seen in modern-day fashion, Poiret's rise to fame was meteoric. Poiret was a visionary; his collections turned fashion upside down with designs that were completely different from everything present before. He traveled around the world to promote his fashions, and like Worth, Poiret displayed his fashions on mannequins at lavish parties.

From 1910 through 1919, the United States became highly industrialized. Mass production of clothing was faster than ever. When the United States entered World War I in 1917, women went back into the workforce and took on jobs traditionally held by men. When women broke out of their traditional roles, they shed their petticoats and the excruciating corset. Women were educated, played golf, entered the workforce, and formed opinions about politics. For the first time in history, women and men dressed for the jobs they were doing. The fashion industry came to a standstill as the majority of resources were directed to help win the war. Comfortable, practical clothing was the order of the day. Women worked in factories wearing overalls, in hospitals wearing

FIGURE 1.18 *A women tightly corseted and pressed into an S-bend (Source: Hawa Stwodah).*

nursing uniforms, and at the post office in postal worker uniforms. Not only were women in the workforce, but children were working as well. People were overworked, underpaid, and, as a result, unhealthy. Mourning was also prevalent and the number of dead from the war increased, requiring clothing of darker colors. Darker colors and monochromatic dressing were strange to many women at that time. Clothing was loose and skirt lengths first rose above the ankle, then to mid-calf. Women's demands for equal rights, including the right to vote, affected the way they behaved and dressed.

During World War I, European designers, feeling the loss of their artistic freedom, closed their shops and quit the fashion business entirely or moved to the United States. Tailors from England, considered the best in the world, fled to the United States with clientele that included both men and women.

1920s

The end of World War I cast light on the major changes taking place in the fashion industry. Life and the way people dressed began to change. The fashions of the 1920s were reflective of easing of tensions following the end of World War I. Americans quickly moved forward in advancing production techniques for ready-to-wear using large-scale production techniques.

FIGURE 1.19 *A woman who dressed in this type of apparel was referred to as a "flapper" during the 1920s (Source: Alamy).*

Faster production met the needs of a new generation of working women and thus an expanding market that no longer had the patience or the money for custom-made apparel.

During the war, European designers had relocated to England and the United States to work. As a result, tailors from Europe saturated the United States. The European designers brought **rayon,** a manufactured, multipurpose fiber similar to cotton, to the United States. Rayon was created by Louis-Marie-Hilaire Bernigaud Comte de Chardonnet in the late 1890s as a substitute for silk, as diseased silkworms had distressed the silk industry.

Women borrowed clothing from the closets of their husbands, creating an androgynous look that Parisian couturiers were slow to adopt; but by 1925 the look was accepted. Women favored the new bustless, waistless silhouette, and the term "**Art Deco**" became synonymous with the look (Baudot, 1996). Hollywood, for the first time, influenced popular fashion. The vigor and exhilaration of the decade came to a screeching halt when the stock market crashed in 1929.

Short skirts, bobbed hair, flamboyant raccoon coats, and people dancing the Charleston defined the decade. The **flapper** (Figure 1.19) was the image of a spirited and carefree woman dancing the Charleston as if she had not a care in the world. Shorter skirts required stockings, thus giving rise to new manufacturing techniques of silk stockings. Important accessories included a natural fox stole (with head, paws, and tail attached), cloche hat, and court shoes. Always present were leather gloves and handbags. Near the end of the 1920s and just before the stock market crash of 1929, skirts lengthened. The sewing machine became an alternative for women who could no longer afford to purchase clothing. The afternoon lounge suit consisting of a double-breasted reefer jacket, straight trousers, and loafers is typical of men's dress during the 1920s. Breast pocket handkerchiefs and two-toned shoes were also popular.

1930s

The Great Depression of the 1930s stood in direct contrast to the fun-loving twenties. In 1929 the depression began in the United States and spread throughout the world. The Great Depression lasted 10 years and its severity and economic devastation are unmatched in the history of the Western World. In the wake of inflation and unemployment, people became frugal. They bought less and did the best they could with what they had. The people of the United States suffered in many ways. President Franklin Delano Roosevelt created social relief programs to assist the suffering population of the United States. Despite these efforts, unemployment and economic stagnation continued.

The 1930s was a time of practical fashion. The thirties also saw the emergence of ready-to-wear clothing for women's sports. Influential European designers included Coco Chanel and Elsa Schiaparelli. Gabrielle "Coco" Chanel was a major influence on women's fashions. Chanel gave the fashion world the little black dress, the jersey dress, and the "Chanel" jacket (Figure 1.20). She relaxed the rules and allowed women to dress down while looking and feeling very feminine. Elsa Schiaparelli's influences included famous artists such as Salvador Dali and Jean Cocteau, and fashion designers Madeleine Vionnet, known for her signature bias cut, and Cristobal Balenciaga, a Spanish designer known for unique modern shapes. Mainbocher was an American designer who firmly established himself in the Paris fashion scene and was a favorite of the Duchess of Windsor (Stone, 2009).

The Hollywood influence on fashion was cemented in the thirties as Americans began going to the movies to escape the everyday pressures. Movie stars Marlene Dietrich, Greta Garbo, Joan Crawford, Katharine Hepburn, and Jean Harlow were the fashion icons of the

FIGURE 1.20 *A Gabrielle "Coco" Chanel tweed Chanel jacket, as seen in 1954, remains a classic (Source: Alamy).*

day. They wore fashions by costume designers Adrian Greenberg and Mariel King. Figure 1.21 portrays one of the fashion icons of the day.

New fabrics appeared in the 1930s. The first nylon stockings were knitted and sold in 1938 and became an overnight success. **Lastex**, a rubberized fabric, forever changed the undergarment industry with its two-way stretch (Stone, 2009). The ability to produce apparel and textile products from manmade fibers increased the demand for clothing. Easily manufactured from wood, rayon was popular because of its versatility.

Higher waistlines, longer skirts, and subdued elegance dominated women's fashion in the thirties. Silhouettes were leaner and hung closer to the body. Sleeves were in the bishop style, full from the shoulder to the wrist, but tight at the wrist. Hats and gloves were important accessories. Leisurewear was more widely available as the American lifestyle afforded more leisure time. American designer Mainbocher popularized the leisurewear category of women's apparel.

Waistlines were higher in menswear as well, just above the natural waist. Jacket lapels were short and wide, and most jackets were double breasted. Shoulders were square and sleeves were narrow. Cuffed pants in houndstooth and herringbone patterns were popular.

1940s

World War II started at the end of 1939 and Paris, the European fashion capital, vanished until the liberation of France in 1944. Some fashion houses closed while others were able to resume working, albeit with German clients. The Nazis, with an intent to take control of the Parisian fashion houses, planned to move French couture to Berlin and Vienna and to operate it under German control. "The real point of all this was to break up a monopoly that threatened the supremacy of the Reich" (Baudot, 1996, p. 108). Lucien Lelong persuaded the Germans that all couture should remain in Paris, excluding Jewish designers such as Madame Gres. Supplying the war effort was the priority, and as shortages of materials and labor occurred, substitute materials were used whenever feasible (Baudot, 1996). Some experts predicted that this was the end of fashion. Dr. Willett Cunningham refused to call clothing fashion. Cunningham contended, "Fashion implies freedom of choice and this is non-existent when costume becomes nationalized and purely functional in character" (Ewing, 2001). However, "backed by a professional sector which demonstrated, as never before, its ability to adapt" Parisian couture survived and remained resilient even after the war ended (Baudot, 1996).

Beleaguered by sameness, menswear in the forties was shoddy and dull. After the war ended, many men went back to wearing the clothes they had worn before the war or they wore a "**demob suit**" (short for demobilization) that was poorly constructed from cheap fabrics. The only bright spot in menswear was the **zoot suit** (see Figure 1.22). An oversized, voluminous jacket with exaggerated shoulders in bright colors, and high-waisted, pleated trousers that tapered sharply, typified the zoot suit and many regarded it as unpatriotic. The wearers of the zoot suit were associated with criminal activity. The zoot suit may be the only known article of clothing to incite riots when an Anglo police officer attacked Hispanic men wearing zoot suits. The officer deemed the men in zoot suits unpatriotic and arrested them (Hymowitz, 2008).

FIGURE 1.21 *Fashion icons of the 1930s such as Joan Crawford greatly influenced fashion (Source: Newscom).*

FIGURE 1.22 *The zoot suit for men was made of inexpensive fabrics and poorly constructed (Source: AP Wideworld).*

In Paris, wartime restrictions included material rationing called The Limitation of Supplies Order that specified the acceptable quantity of material allowed in manufacturing. Acquiring clothing required a coupon and old garments were recycled. In England, The Incorporated Society of London Fashion Designers set forth clothing requirements. Thirty-two prototypes, called Utility Designs, were mass-produced. The guidelines for the Utility Designs included cloth usage and design; the maximum amount of cloth allowed for coats was 13 feet, the limit for cloth for a blouse was three feet (Baudot, 1996), skirts were 19 inches above the knee, there were only three buttons per garment, and there were no cuffs on pants or sleeves. When the United States entered the war in 1941, the same restrictions on materials were in place, which led to a military look with a very slim skirt and tight bodice. Many women wore beautifully printed and colorful headscarves that did not fall prey to rationing since they were not hats. Seen as fashion, a rarity, all classes of women adorned themselves with headscarves. Pants became more common than ever before and were necessary for the work done by women.

By the late 1940s, with the end of World War II and the beginning of industrial revolution, the fashion industry was gaining strength worldwide. European designers were regaining the right to show and display fashion. In 1947, Christian Dior made history by presenting the "New

Look" (Figure 1.23), which brought back femininity to the world. The fashion world recognizes Dior for saving French haute couture. The United States was characteristically carving its own niche in the fashion world as New York City was developing into the fashion capital. Somehow, in spite of war, shortages, and substitutions, fashion did not die (Hymowitz, 2008).

1950s

Until the 1950s, fashion had neglected the consumer of limited means. The fifties gave way to the greatest change in clothing in fashion history. In the spirit of the times, middle-class people had access to clothing like never before. The United States was a democratic, consumer society and American women were ready for a change from the utilitarian clothing of previous decades. Following World War II, the United States entered a time of economic and population growth ("baby boom") that accelerated consumerism. The factories that produced supplies and munitions for the troops got busy manufacturing consumer products. Americans were moving from the cities into the suburbs where they nested, begging for items like toasters, ovens, televisions, and toys to fill their homes. Americans were optimistic and renewed.

The fifties gave the world the term "teenager." During the fifties, teenagers as a group of new consumers became a targeted market of fashion designers. While the fashions of the twenties were youthful, they were "the fashion" and one could take it or leave it. However, the fifties actively sought the youth market. Some of the veterans of World War II used the GI (Government Issued) Bill to further their education, thus earning more income. Parents had more money to spend on their families and the discretionary income of teenagers benefited as a result. Teenagers had the money to spend on clothes that imitated the styles worn by actors and rock-and-roll stars. Seeing stars on television for the first time catapulted them to role model status for the teenager of 1950s. The cinema continued to gain strength as a fashion influence.

Women wore full-skirted and shirtwaist dresses, both emphasizing the waistline. A common wardrobe of the fifties included poodle skirts, twin sets, ballet shoes, and ponytails. For evening apparel, structured silhouettes featured boning and crinolines. The stiletto heel, introduced in the 1950s, was a major departure from the clunky, heavy shoes worn during wartime. A turning point came in the late 1950s with the creation of the trapeze dress, also called the tent dress. The trapeze shape moved the emphasis from the body to the legs. As the sixties approached, the style fell out of fashion when new looks were created, with the continuing emphasis on the legs. Along with full-skirted and trapeze styles, a slimmer silhouette, often worn by film stars like Doris Day and Sophia Loren, became prevalent. Fashion designers experimented with nylon, polyester, and acrylic, all new to the fashion industry. Polyester was especially popular because of its low price and durability.

Men's apparel was the first area of concentration for the fashion industry. Jackets and trousers were more difficult to sew than dresses and blouses. The look for men included broad shoulders, straight-legged pants, floral ties, and shirts in bright colors with long, pointed collars. The gray flannel suit became important. The rebel and Hell's Angels influences were also prevalent and perpetuated by actors Marlon Brando and James Dean (Baudot, 1996). Cuffed jeans, white T-shirts, and black leather jackets characterized the rebellious style.

FIGURE 1.23 *Christian Dior made history by presenting the "New Look," bringing back femininity to the world (Source: Alamy).*

1960s

The 1960s ushered in a period of the generation gap, protests, free love, freethinking, unrest, and violence. For the first time in history, the youth culture developed a style specific to them without regard for the older generation. The "baby boomers" were teenagers with their own opinions, ideas, and styles. "Flower Power" was the motto of the hippy culture and the foray of the Beatles caused a "British Invasion." Chaos ensued after the assassination of America's beloved president, John F. Kennedy. Not long after the president's death, the assassinations of Martin Luther King, Jr., and Robert Kennedy occurred within two months of one another. The United States was embroiled in a violent and costly war in Vietnam, which was broadcast every night on the evening news. Two significant historical events occurred in 1969: Woodstock, a music festival, and man's first walk on the moon.

Early in the sixties, women's styles remained somewhat conservative. Jacqueline Kennedy was the fashion icon and women everywhere sought to replicate her sophisticated style. The epitome of class and elegance, Mrs. Kennedy was famous for her pillbox hat and pearls. As the decade progressed and social unrest increased, fashion evolved. Hemlines grew shorter with the miniskirt becoming popular in 1966. The go-go boot was the perfect accessory for the miniskirt and white was the most popular color. Wild colors, Pucci prints, and Eastern influences were, however, prevalent. Bell-bottoms, bikinis, and babydoll dresses were new and fresh. Figure 1.24 demonstrates the typical "hippie" look of the 1960s.

In menswear, the three-piece suit survived but lighter fabrications were common. Men's shirts were darted and worn in bright colors and loud prints, and trousers were low waisted. Men's fashions also became more fitted and closer to the body than in previous decades, making most men more conscious of their physiques. Long hair, worn down to the collar, and jeans grew in popularity. In the sixties, men became more involved in their appearance; however, they were a long way from their female counterparts.

London was the hot bed of fashion during the sixties. Major British influences were Mary Quant, the Rolling Stones, and the Beatles. Anchored on Carnaby and King Streets, unisex dressing and the teenage culture gripped the fashion scene and behaviors were forever changed. Biba symbolized London style with "romantic decadence" that characterized the hippy culture. Throughout the years, London has retained its iconic appeal to those longing for the sixties (Baudot, 1996).

In Paris, those in the fashion industry gathered twice a year to see the latest styles shown by the Paris designers, and watched as Paris also became younger (Ewing, 2001). The majority of women accepted fashionable pants and miniskirts. Pierre Cardin introduced his Space Age Collection, in conjunction with human's first moonwalk.

Haute couture dominated the world fashion stage, but mass-produced fashion was making inroads in the United States. The United States excelled at mass production, and the prospect of accelerating the process of delivering goods to the public was appealing. Through advances in technology and fabrics, the fashion industry progressed in ways not seen since mass-produced apparel initially appeared during the Industrial Revolution.

FIGURE 1.24 *The "hippie-look" of the 1960s (Source: Alamy).*

1970s

The seventies saw a severe recession and social unrest that continued from the sixties. The war persisted in Vietnam and women and minorities fought for civil rights. The pace of fashion sped along with new inventions and new ideas fueling the change. The biggest change in the Western world was the bond between people and their clothes (Baudot, 1996). Pop culture influenced fashion through the movies, television, and the icons they produced.

The seventies were a time of "anything goes" in fashion. The hippie culture was ongoing, and at the same time, suits for both men and women were fashionable. Also important were ethnic designs, disco, preppy, and punk. Vivienne Westwood became the "mother of punk." Westwood started in the mid-seventies and by the early eighties her designs were highly influential. Jeans took on a life of their own with designers Calvin Klein and Anne Klein whetting the appetites of the consumer with designer denim. Figure 1.25 is an ad featuring Brooke Shields in Calvin Klein jeans. The U. S. fashion industry was thriving but the rest of the world, although interested in U.S. fashion, was not rushing to copy its styles. In 1973, President Richard Nixon opened relations with China, and the Far East soon became a dominant force in the production of fashion apparel and accessories, forever changing the fashion world.

For women, the emphasis moved from the body to the legs. Skirts were longer, but varied from mini to midi to maxi. Women were so confused that many opted to wear trousers. The wrap dress designed by Diane Von Furstenberg quickly became a classic (Figure 1.26). In the April

FIGURE 1.25 *Fashion ad by fashion designer Calvin Klein featured 14-year-old model Brooke Shields (Source: Advertising Archives).*

FIGURE 1.26 *The classic wrap dress was designed by Diane Von Furstenberg in 1977 (Source: Alamy).*

FIGURE 1.27 *John Travolta in the leisure suit made popular by the movie* Saturday Night Fever *(Source: Alamy).*

1977 issue of Vogue, the American television star Farrah Fawcett appeared skateboarding in her favorite sneakers (Buxbaum, 1999). "These were not childish Keds or goofy Converses, but good-looking Nike 'Senorita Cortex' running shoes—and they looked as chic as anything the magazine's readers had ever seen" (Buxbaum, 1999, p. 109). The 1970s brought the fitness craze, exacerbated by movie star Jane Fonda, creating a need in the marketplace for fitness apparel. Thus, a movement from spectator to participant in sports began. New sporty styles evolved for both men and women.

A new type of suit inundated menswear in the seventies, known as the leisure suit. The leisure suit, manufactured in polyester in nontraditional suiting colors, called for printed polyester shirts in coordinating colors. Ties were not required with the open jackets and shirts. No one wore this look better than John Travolta in the movie *Saturday Night Fever* (Figure 1.27). Denim gained status in the seventies especially when the back pocket carried the logo of a famous designer, like Calvin Klein. The foremost fashion trend for men in the seventies was the length of their hair. Many men sported long side burns and hair that reached the middle of the back.

1980s

Ronald Reagan was elected president of the United States in 1980. From 1980 to 1982, the United States faced severe recession caused by inflation, Japanese competition, oil crises of the seventies, and the government bailouts of Chrysler and Lockheed. The U.S. economy rebounded and experienced several years of robust growth making the eighties the decade of excess and a period of **consumerism** and **conspicuous consumption** like never before. "**Reaganomics**" was the term used to describe this era of excess and prosperity. People became active participants in fashion rather than spectators. President Reagan and his wife Nancy brought glamour back to the White House. Nancy Reagan's love of designer suits and ball gowns exemplified the mood of the eighties. However, by 1987, the American savings and loan institutions failed and the stock market crashed, leading the United States into another recession.

For a 10-year period between 1978 and 1988, Parisian fashion boomed. French designers, established and newcomers alike, gained recognition all over the world. Christian Lacroix, Jean-Paul Gaultier, Thierry Mugler, and Karl Lagerfeld produced extravagant fashions and over-the-top fashion shows. In the 1980s, a Japanese explosion occurred. Japanese designers Rei Kawakubo, Yohji Yamamoto, Kenzo Takada, and Issey Miyake came to the West. They introduced designs with different shapes and hidden pockets that were out of step with the prevailing fashion of the time. Makeup-less faces, flat shoes, and modest designs characterized the creations of Kawakubo and Yamamota during an era of heavy makeup and cinched-in waists (Baudot, 1996).

The **Yuppie**, the young urban professional with the discretionary income to spend on fashion, emerged in the eighties and was seen as a status symbol by this baby boomer group. This demographic cohort defined conspicuous consumption. Yuppies were concerned about appearance in every aspect of their everyday lives, from the clothes they wore to the cars they drove to the coffee they drank. They were movers and shakers with the vigor to take the business world by storm (Moore, 2008). Yuppies dressed professionally; "**dress for success**" was the buzz in fashion. "**Power dressing**" described dressing for success.

Women's apparel in the mid-eighties was highly influenced by television, movies, and music in pop culture. *Dynasty*, a popular television show, excelled in the trend of power dressing for women. Power dressing included tailored suits with exaggerated shoulder pads, big hair, and huge jewelry. Slim skirts, dolman sleeves, elegant blouses, and wedge dresses also typified the "power dressing" genre. See Figure 1.28 for a picture of a power couple from the 1980s. Nancy Reagan and Princess Diana were familiar images on television inspiring American women to emulate their fashion sensibilities. Madonna rocked the fashion world with her look of overaccessorized everything from jewelry to clothing embellishments, illustrating the look of excess.

In the eighties, men had a more heightened interest in fashion than ever before. Many men's consumer publications such as *GQ* and *Cosmo Man* started in the eighties, exploring fashion, fitness, grooming, and other topics of relevance to men (Moore, 2008). The television show *Miami Vice* created the menswear trend of the white suit, pastel T-shirt, and loafers sans socks. *Top Gun* and *Risky Business* made flight jackets and Ray-Bans "must have" items. The "**Gekko shirt**," a striped shirt with a white collar and cuffs, was inspired by Gordon Gekko (Figure 1.29), a high-power financier played by Michael Douglas in the film *Wall Street*.

Fashion companies found it inexpensive to produce clothing offshore: primarily because of low labor costs, manufacturing was largely undertaken in China. The effect of **offshore production** was the closing of textile and manufacturing plants in the United States. As the millennium drew closer, fashion designers were creating with a worldview in mind, using ethnic cultures as inspiration. While fashion enjoyed vigorous growth in the eighties, a newly diagnosed disease called acquired immunodeficiency syndrome (AIDS) plagued the industry. In the early days of AIDS, larger cities and urban areas were the most impacted. The disease first affected gay men but eventually spread to heterosexuals as well. AIDS ravaged the fashion community and many talented designers were lost.

1990s

As the millennium approached, the globe shrank, with technology making it possible to see and interact with the world at breakneck speed. Generation X was now in the workplace and much more technologically savvy than previous generations. The stock market experienced a 152 percent gain, an indication that people in the United States were accruing wealth. The nineties also saw the collapse of communism in the Soviet Union, leaving the United States as the world's only superpower (Moore, 2008).

People entered the nineties with a more relaxed fashion frame of mind. Accepted as everyday attire were jeans, T-shirts, and Nike running shoes. In 1991, Alcoa, an aluminum company based in Pittsburgh, Pennsylvania, deemed casual attire as acceptable in the workplace. The laid-back attire caught on and it did not take long before companies all over America were promoting casual dress at least one day a week. Customers replaced their esteem for fine French haute couture with apparel from Casual Corner and Ann Taylor (Agins, 2000).

Hip-hop came into the fashion arena from many different places, but most give credit to the music industry and the street scene of the 1980s. In the 1990s, hip-hop made its way to haute couture. The oversized clothing had a direct relationship to the 1940s zoot suit, "originated in the 1940s at the lower end of the socio-economic ladder, and had been adopted by African American and teenage boys in the early 1940s" (Tortora and

FIGURE 1.28 *President Ronald Reagan and his wife Nancy were considered a power couple of the 1980s (Source: Newscom).*

FIGURE 1.29 *The "Gekko Shirt" inspired by Gordon Gekko, a character in the film* Wall Street *(Source: Alamy).*

FIGURE 1.30 *Eminem is a good example to show clothing worn in the hip-hop culture (Source: AP Wideworld Photos).*

Eubank, 2005, p. 415). In the 1990s, the zoot suit became "power clothing" and reached a vast market. Figure 1.30 is an example of clothing worn in the hip-hop culture.

Hip-hop was an important music trend, as was "alternative music," a trend that began in Seattle, Washington, and took the country by storm. Nirvana, Soundgarden, and Pearl Jam were garage bands that moved the music scene from pop to hard rock. The look of the alternative movement was "grunge," characterized by sloppy plaid shirts, jeans, and long unkempt hair.

Lycra was the new fabric for 1990s. Other fabrics such as cotton and wool were mixed with Lycra to add stretch to the fabric. The stretch contributed to a perfect fit and consumers loved the new fiber blended with old standbys like denim. Like the sixties, fashion in the nineties was produced at a fast pace. Lynn Schnurnberger declared in her 1991 book, *Let There Be Clothes*, "It doesn't take centuries for a style to make a comeback—just the next generation, who obviously admire the fashions of the 60's (Schnurnberger, 1991, p. 413). Innovation and technological movements help to speed the creativity and production of fashion.

In the early nineties, women took a more austere and minimalist approach to fashion. After the excess of the eighties, women were ready for a more streamlined look. Women layered their outfits by wearing a skirt or pant, with a jacket, vest, and a blouse. Clothing was loose and flowing and the slip dress was a trendy silhouette. Activewear gained ground with the advent of many specialized pieces. Yoga, running, aerobics, and other sports had garments particular to the activity. Influenced by a robust economy, refined and playful clothing was important in the late nineties.

Menswear was unstructured and black prevailed as the color of choice. Wearing a white shirt that was buttoned to the neck and without a tie became common. Shoes were clunky, thick Dr. Martens, as Nike and other athletic shoes grew in popularity. Street fashion ruled and had designers scrambling to take its cues (Baudot, 1996).

In the past, fashion was a celebration; however, as the twentieth century ended, fashion was about big business. The weight of a ringing cash register and at times the stress of turning a profit crushed the talent and innovation of new and established designers. The autonomy of the fashion designer was diminishing and bankers studied the perilous and fragile industry (Baudot, 1996).

2000 TO PRESENT DAY

Entering the twenty-first century, the United States had a new president, George W. Bush. In 2001, the terror attack of September 11 left Americans shaken to their cores, insecure, emotional, and grasping for those they held dear. **Cocooning**, or drawing toward home, was the fashion. As more companies became globalized, globalization presented both advantages and challenges. Technology continued to permeate every aspect of society from personal computers to cell phones to the Internet. Social networking through Myspace and Facebook gave everyone the ability to stay in touch electronically.

Fashion has changed through the years from hand sewing, home-based industry to multi-million-dollar conglomerates with production all over the world. Most large fashion companies diversified their portfolios by meeting the needs of multiple demographic segments within the fashion industry. The focus today is on the economics of the global fashion industry, and most of the world is looking to the West for new trends.

Speed to market, fast fashion, and Quick Response refer to strategies that bring products from concept to consumer rapidly. Quick Response is a management system used by retailers to get a concept made as quickly as possible into apparel and make it available to the consumers. Companies use software that enables the Quick Response strategy. Zara, a retailer based in Spain, can turn a trend into apparel in as little as three weeks. Later in the text, we take a more in-depth look at the economics of fast fashion and discuss more examples of retailers and manufacturers.

Proportions in women's apparel have been important in this decade. Short over long and long over slim are two key examples. Tunic tops, babydoll dresses, and skinny jeans have taken hold. Designers are taking inspiration from previous decades like the seventies and eighties, making the dresses fresh and relevant. *Sex and the City* introduced the everyday woman to designer names like Manolo Blanik and Jimmy Choo.

Casual dressing and urban looks remain important in the twenty-first century but a new market segment has emerged, the **metrosexual**. Metrosexuals typically live in metropolitan areas and possess a keen fashion sense (a trait usually associated with homosexuals). Meticulous grooming and European cut suits characterize the metrosexual. Men remain less adventurous about fashion than their female counterparts; however, men are broadening their fashion horizons more than ever before. American and European designers influence mainstream fashion in every walk of life. Furthermore, the plethora of men's magazines and media icons inspire the average man to take an interest in grooming and appearance.

Summary

In this chapter, you have gained insight into the historical perspectives of fashion from the Empire Period to the present. Highlights of the history of fashion include famous designers, such as Charles Worth, and inventions such as the cotton gin. You learned about the industrial revolution's impact on the fashion industry. The most important impact of the industrial revolution is the speed at which fashion is produced today.

Key Terms

Art Deco   16
basquin bodice   11
bouffant   11
cocooning   24
conspicuous consumption   22
consumerism   22
corset   8
cravats   9
crinoline   12
demob suit   17
dress for success   22
Empire Period   6
fashion   4
fast fashion   25

flapper   16
frock coats   9
Gekko shirt   23
gigot   10
globalization   11
haute couture   12
industrial revolution   6
La Belle Époque   13
lastex   17
lycra   24
mannequins   13
metrosexual   25
offshore production   23
pantaloons   9

petersham frock coat   11
pioneers   11
power dressing   22
Quick Response   25
rayon   16
Reaganomics   22
redingote   11
sack coat   11
speed to market   25
surtout   9
tapissier   12
vendeuse   12
Yuppie   22
zoot suit   17

Review Questions

1. Who was Paul Nystrom? What is his famous quote and why is it relevant in today's fashion world?

2. Explain the following periods of history from a fashion and economic perspective: Empire, Romantic, the 1800s, and the 1900s.

3. When did fashion magazines come into being and what is their significance historically and today?

4. Discuss two historical designers who had an influence on fashion in the past.

5. Why did the designers close their shops in Europe during World War II and migrate to the United States?

6. What years showed a rise in the use of polyester and rayon? How did these two fibers contribute to the economy?

Critical Thinking

1. Explain why you think fashion has had an impact on the social, economical, political, and cultural areas (provide an explanation for each) and what have been the economic implications.

2. Some people view fashion as a very glamorous industry; therefore, the perception is that fashion is not a "need"-based product. Fashion is a "want"-based product. Do you agree with this statement or disagree? Support your answer.

Internet Activities

Compare two designers, one from the past and one from the current era, and relate how each has contributed to the fashion industry and the economy. The following site will be helpful in your research:

http://www.thebiographychannel.co.uk/biography.htm

Read the essay "The Devil's Blue Dye: Indigo and Slavery" and answer the following questions.

(available at http://www.slaveryinamerica.org/history/hs_es_indigo.htm)

Where does true indigo comes from?

Why it is an important color to the fashion industry both from a fashion and an economic perspective?

Bibliography

About the great depression. (n.d). Retrieved July 29, 2009, from modern American Poetry: http://www.english.illinois.edu/maps/depression/about.htm

Agins, T. (2000). *The end of fashion: How marketing changed the clothing business forever.* New York: Harper Collins.

Austin, S. S. (2000). Here's looking at you sire. *Christian Science Monitor*, 92: 39, p. 16.

Baudot, F. (1996). *A century of fashion.* New York: Universe Publishing.

Buxbaum, G. (1999). *The icons of fashion.* Verlag, Munich, Berlin, London, New York. Prestel Publishing.

Cassin-Scott, J. (2006). *The illustrated encyclopedia of costume and fashion from 1066 to the present.* London: Cassell Illustrated.

Christopher M., & Miller, S. H. (1993). Toward formalizing fashion theory. *Journal of Marketing Research*, 30: 2, pp. 142–157.

Economicexpert.com. (n.d.). Retrieved August 23, 2009 from http://www.economicexpert.com/a/Late:eighties:recession.htm

Ewing, E. (2001). *History of 20th century fashion.* New York: Costume and Fashion Press.

Foley, C. A. (1893). Fashion. *The Economic Journal*, 3: 11, pp. 458–474.

Hymowitz, E. (2008). The forties. In *The Greenwood encyclopedia of clothing through world history*. Westport, CT: Greenwood Press, p. 148.

Klein, A. I. (1963). Fashion: Its sense of history. Its selling power. *The Business History Review*, 37, pp. 1–2.

Little, F. (1931). *Early American textiles.* New York: Century.

Miller, C., McIntyre, S., & Mantrala, M. (1993). Toward formalizing fashion theory. *Journal of Marketing Research*, *30*, 142–157.

Moore, J. G. (2008). The eighties. In *The greenwood encyclopedia of clothing through world history.* Westport, CT: Greenwood Press, p. 96.

Nystrom, P. (1928). *Economics of fashion.* New York: Ronald Press.

Schnurnberger, L. (1991). *40,000 years of fashion: Let there be clothes.* New York: Workman Publishing.

Sproles, G. G. (1979). *Fashion: Consumer behavior toward dress.* Minneapolis: Burgess.

Stone, E. (2009). *The dynamics of fashion*, 3rd edition. New York: Fairchild Books.

Tamilia, R. D. (2002). *The wonderful world of the department store in historical perspective: A comprehensive international bibliography partially annotated.*

Tortora, P., & K. Eubank. (1994). *Survey of historic costume*, 2nd edition. New York: Fairchild Publications.

Tortora, P., & Eubank, K. (2005). *Survey of historic costume: A history of western dress*, 4th edition. New York: Fairchild Publications, pp. 264–266.

Encyclopedia of the nations. Retrieved August 23, 2009 from http://www.nationsencyclopedia.com/Americas/United

THE LANGUAGE OF FASHION

OBJECTIVES

After reading this chapter, you will be able to:

- Describe the terms of the fashion industry in relation to the people, merchandise, and the business of fashion
- Recognize the four segments of the fashion industry
- Interpret and understand the principles of fashion

What is fashion but a series of trends? Often slow to take hold, they blaze for a while before gradually dying out.

—FRANCOIS BAUDOT, *A Century of Fashion* (1999)

2

*F*ashion has a language of its own and learning to speak the language is imperative to understanding the industry. This chapter will engage the reader with terms and their use in the business of fashion. The vocabulary is the navigational tool that allows one to communicate with others regarding fashion. Some of the terms are well known and are common on the pages of a fashion magazine, while others are more obscure or take on new meaning in the context of fashion. This chapter will begin with a discussion on the language of fashion followed by an exploration of the divisions of the fashion industry and the principles of fashion.

Language of Fashion

As with any language, context and meaning are important to communicating, and the language spoken in the fashion industry is no different. The language of fashion describes the people that work in the field and the apparel manufactured and sold in retail stores. The fashion industry employs thousands of people who work tirelessly to bring to the public apparel they want at prices they demand. The primary roles in the industry are designers, buyers, retailers, wholesalers, and jobbers. To achieve success, each of the groups is dependent on one another.

Designers create garments by working either as **freelance designers**, selling their designs to various fashion companies, or for a manufacturer that caters to the brand image and target market. In some cases, designers are able to work without restrictions and let the organic origination of ideas take place. Other times, the constraints and aesthetics set forth by their employers confine the designer to a certain look or overall idea. The creativity and vision of a designer has the potential to spark new fashion by providing new ideas to manufacturers who in turn sell goods to retail buyers. Designers must design garments that can be manufactured and wholesaled (sold by wholesalers or jobbers) to buyers and retailed in stores for use by the ultimate consumer.

Buyers plan assortments and make merchandising decisions accordingly. Buyers also manage budgets, called **open-to-buy** (more on open-to-buy in Chapter 5). Buyers shop in regional, national, and international markets in search of items that are appealing to the target market of the store. Figure 2.1 is a photo of buyers working at MAGIC in Las Vegas, Nevada. Buyers know that success depends on their ability to stock store shelves with fashions interesting to their consumers. The buyer performs a vital function in bringing the designer's ideas and creativity to the ultimate consumer. Retailers, of all types, employ buyers across the United States and abroad.

Retailers constitute the channel that brings products from the manufacturer to the ultimate consumer. Fashion would not exist without retailers. Retailers purchase goods at wholesale prices and resell the goods at retail prices to the public at large. Retailers have a base of customers that they cater to through merchandising and operational efforts. There are many diverse retail models, such as department stores, specialty stores, discount stores, and warehouse clubs (for more information, refer to Chapter 4).

Buyers often buy goods from **wholesalers**. Wholesalers are intermediaries that buy goods from manufacturers and resell the merchandise to retailers, who in turn sell the merchandise to the ultimate consumer. Manufacturers act as wholesalers by selling their apparel and accessories directly to buyers of retail stores. Retail stores attain most goods through this method of purchasing.

FIGURE 2.1 *Buyers working at the MAGIC trade show in Las Vegas, Nevada.*

Jobbers also sell merchandise to retail buyers. The term "jobber" has dual meanings in the fashion apparel industry. It is often synonymous with wholesalers as described in the previous paragraph. More specifically, a jobber buys goods from manufacturers and sells them to buyers; however, a jobber does not work for the manufacturer as a wholesaler does. For example, if a jobber buys jackets from a manufacturer the jobber takes ownership of the jackets. The jobber liquidates the merchandise by selling it to retail buyers, who then in turn sell the jackets to the consumer. The potential profit for the jobber comes from selling the jackets to the retail buyer and likewise the potential profit for the retail buyer comes from selling the jackets to the consumer. Buying goods from a jobber creates an additional avenue through which goods flow. Jobbers buy goods from manufacturers. Many of the goods purchased by jobbers are private label brands of major retailers, which jobbers resell to stores that are unable to purchase the labels directly from the manufacturer. Jobbers will also acquire odd lots of merchandise and sell them to smaller retailers or retailers that specialize in opportunistic buying tactics. Whether buying from a wholesaler or jobber, buyers seek out fashion appropriate for their customer base.

Fashion is the apparel, accessories, and home fashions deemed desirable and appropriate for the time. Throughout the ages (as demonstrated in Chapter 1), fashion has transformed and then returned to something more familiar. As of the writing of this book, pants are narrow and tops are voluminous (Figure 2.2). As this look runs its course, pants will widen and tops will become shorter, as dictated by fashion. Fashion varies by peer group and the desire to fit in with a particular group influences members of the group to accept what is fashionable for that group.

Design is critical to fashion as the creative process of creating new apparel and accessories. Design differs depending on the type of manufacturer and the consumer the manufacturer is targeting. High fashion design is the apex of avant-garde; whereas, many designs intended for the general public are the adaptations of previously successful styles. Based on diverse ideas of fashion and personal tastes, consumers purchase what they regard as attractive and acceptable.

FIGURE 2.2 *Voluminous tops and skinny pants are an example of a trend in 2011 (Source: Hawa Stwodah).*

FIGURE 2.3 *Men's leisure suits were popular in the 1970s (Source: Alamy).*

"There's no accounting for **taste**" is a widely used quotation that sums up the differences in tastes among people. Taste is highly personal and it is difficult to explain why one considers another to have good taste or bad taste. At any point in time, the appropriateness or attractiveness of fashion is in good taste; however, changes in thought or attitude provoke change in fashion, and with it, the notion of good taste. For example, in the 1970s men's leisure suits (as seen in Figure 2.3) were fashionable and tasteful. In 2010, viewed as a joke or a costume, the leisure suit is no longer a symbol of good taste.

The individual garment is the item most associated with fashion. The garment symbolizes an individual's personality. The **style** describes the distinctive look of a garment that makes it different from other garments. Pants, dresses, and shirts are all types of styles; however, consumer demand dictates the variation of the styles that go in and out of fashion. For example, pants are always in style but the cut of the pants will change. Pant styles can vary by rise, low rise or high waisted; by length, clam-digger, cropped, or full length; or by leg opening, skinny, straight, boot cut, or wide leg. The variation of the pant style depends on the fashion at the time. A **style number** designates the variations of a style. Determined by manufacturers and used by buyers in the placement of orders, style numbers are critical to the ordering process.

Fashion is cyclical and lasts for a finite amount of time. Referred to as the **fashion cycle**, apparel follows the typical bell-curve shape (Figure 2.4). All clothing fashion cycles begin with the introduction stage. This stage represents the launch of a new item and **fashion innovators** begin purchasing. Fashion innovators are the first to experiment and purchase new trends. Innovators are typically young and wealthy. The fashion cycle progresses with the rise stage, which indicates acceptance of the new item by **fashion leaders**. Fashion leaders are the first in their peer groups to accept new trends. The

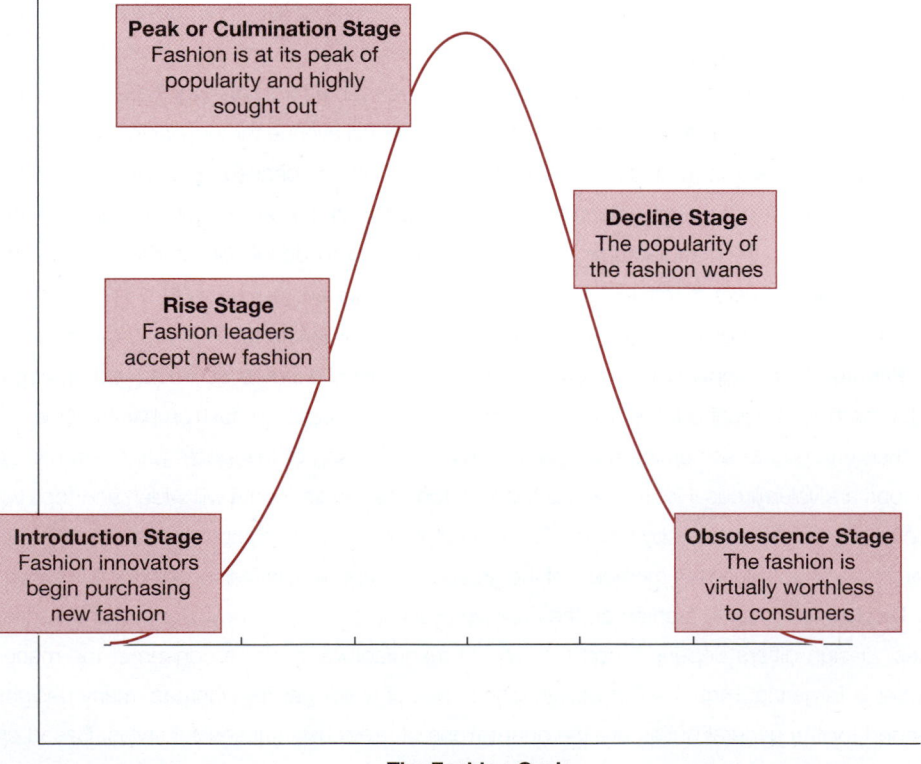

Peak or Culmination Stage
Fashion is at its peak of popularity and highly sought out

Decline Stage
The popularity of the fashion wanes

Rise Stage
Fashion leaders accept new fashion

Introduction Stage
Fashion innovators begin purchasing new fashion

Obsolescence Stage
The fashion is virtually worthless to consumers

The Fashion Cycle

FIGURE 2.4 *The Fashion Cycle.*

rise continues until the item has reached its peak or culmination, meaning that the garment will never be more popular and sought out than it is at this particular point in the fashion cycle. At this stage, the garment has reached mass acceptance, fashion innovators and fashion leaders are no longer purchasing the garment, and instead fashion followers are the primary consumers. After an item peaks, decline will begin, and while some consumers will continue to purchase the garment, its popularity wanes and will continue to do so until reaching obsolescence. At the obsolescence point, the item is virtually worthless to any consumer. The length of a fashion cycle is impossible to predict, varying widely from item to item.

Fad is an oft-used term that defines a short-lived fashion. Fads do not cross over to the next season but fads can become trends through adaptation of the style. The speedy acceptance and decline of a fad makes their identification difficult. In the late sixties, the "granny look" was a most ironic fad. Free love and sexual promiscuity were at an all-time high, yet this fad was decidedly prim and proper. The look consisted of long, frilly, floral-printed dresses and laced-up "granny" shoes. Worn, regardless of need, were "granny" glasses, also known as Ben Franklin glasses, which were half frames that sat on the end of the nose (Figure 2.5). The hairstyle that completed the look was an old-fashioned bun. The look was a fashion statement during a period of time when there was a negative feeling among the youth toward the political system.

A fad becomes a **trend** when the general direction of fashion begins moving in a certain trajectory and more fashion consumers accept the fad. Trends and fads can begin anywhere, but unlike a fad, sustained consumer demand creates a solid foundation that defines a trend and differentiates a trend from a fad. Throughout time, trends emerge, run their course, and disappear as new trends materialize and take their places. Corsets began disappearing from the wardrobes of women in the 1920s. The 1960s ushered in shorter hemlines. In the 1970s, pants became staples for women, and in the 1980s, "power dressing" was the essential attire of executives across the United States.

A fashion **classic** is a fundamental piece of one's wardrobe. Classics are the building blocks of garments with the balance of a wardrobe put together around them. Because classics progress slowly through the fashion cycle, they remain "in style" for a longer time, in some cases lasting many years. The little black dress, denim jeans, and navy blue blazers are garments that exemplify classic clothing. Figure 2.6 is an example of the little black dress.

The **silhouette** is the outline or shape of a garment. Enhanced by details such as pockets, trims, buttons, or zippers, all garment designs start with a basic silhouette. As artists use basic shapes to begin drawings, so fashion designers use basic silhouettes to begin their designs using different variations and details. The three basic silhouettes, each with several adaptations, are the straight, bell, and bustle. Figure 2.7 shows the fundamental silhouettes fashion design students learn when they begin sketching. Designers, manufacturers, and buyers use a garment's silhouette or describe a style.

A **knockoff** is a copy of an original, higher-priced design. It can be a handbag, a dress, a scarf, or any piece of fashion apparel or accessory. The basic look of the design is very similar, if not exactly like the original except that the item is made from inexpensive fabric with inferior construction techniques. Knockoffs are of paramount concern to designers and high-end brands. The impact of knockoffs is millions of dollars annually (see Chapter 11).

Haute couture is a French term meaning "high fashion." In France, the Chambre Syndicale, a fashion governing body, sets standards for the fashion industry and decides which houses belong to the elite category of haute couture. True haute couture designers are members of the Chambre Syndicale. Haute couture garments are hand sewn, made to

FIGURE 2.5 *"Granny" glasses, also known as Ben Franklin glasses, symbolized the iconic "granny look" fad of the 1960s (Source: Hawa Stwodah).*

FIGURE 2.6 *The little black dress is a true classic (Source: Alamy).*

FIGURE 2.7 *Fundamental silhouettes learned by budding fashion designers (Source: Hawa Stwodah).*

measure, and many times are one of a kind. These clothes are of the highest quality and prohibitively expensive for most consumers (more information on haute couture in Chapter 9).

Manufacturers produce four to seven **lines** per year. A line is merchandise offered for sale for a season. In general, the seasons are spring I, spring II, summer, fall I, fall II, holiday, and resort. Merchandise presentations consist of classifications of product appropriate for the season. Children's wear typically presents four lines a year, while women's wear proffers up to 10 lines per year. Likewise, menswear presents seasonal offerings further in advance than junior sportswear that shows merchandise closer to the delivery date. Lines can be comprised of an entirely new product or a combination of new product and revamped previously seen product.

Classifications segment merchandise within a line. Classifications include tops, bottoms, activewear, accessories, dresses, and outerwear. Classifications differ by retailer and manufacturer. For example, in the junior department a retailer may simply have the classifications of tops, bottoms, dresses, and activewear, whereas another retailer in the junior department may be more detailed in classifying merchandise with tops divided by knit tops, woven tops, sweaters, and bottoms segmented as pants, skirts, shorts, and jeans. Classifications provide information that determines what the consumer is purchasing. A retailer may see that tops are selling well, but without the added benefit of knowing that knit tops are outselling woven tops, a buyer may purchase more wovens than knits. Classifications enable both manufacturers and retailers to maximize products that are performing and minimize underperforming goods (more information on classifications in Chapter 8).

The successful selling of merchandise depends on the **price point**, which must be in line with what the consumer is willing to pay for the product. Price point is the retail price of merchandise. Knowing what goods are worth at retail is an integral and critical skill of a buyer. Retailers develop merchandising concepts based on one or more of eight price points. Most stores cross price point lines, but not to an excessive degree. Merchandise in the **discount price point** is low quality, disposable, and sold in large quantities in discount stores, like Walmart. **Budget price points** appeal to a large number of consumers. Sold in stores like Sears, merchandise in this price point is a deviation of goods that have reached the culmination stage of the fashion cycle. **Moderate price points** cover most of the consuming public and include most products sold in stores such as Kohl's including brands like Levi's. Considered by the average consumer to be designer merchandise, goods at **better price points** are found at Macy's and Nordstrom and include brands like Jones NY. Merchandise in the **contemporary price point** is trendier, appealing to a young and stylish consumer at a slightly higher price point than better. **Bridge** is the price point that "bridges" the gap between better and designer price points. Many designer labels, like Donna Karan, also produce bridge lines. The **designer price point** is the ready-to-wear line of many designer labels. Couture designers often create ready-to-wear lines in the designer price point. The ready-to-wear lines pay the bills for the couture lines. Finally, the pinnacle of price points is **couture**. (Table 2.1 illustrates the various price points.)

A practice used in the fashion industry for many years is **licensing**. Designers and celebrities allow manufacturers to produce goods bearing their names for a fee or royalty. The benefit to the designer or celebrity is monetary. The manufacturer profits by gaining the capacity to put goods into the marketplace bearing the name of a well-known personality. The retailer's advantage is the ability to offer products to consumers with well-known names, and in many cases the products are exclusive to the retailer. Licensing offers many advantages, but there are disadvantages as well. The quality of the merchandise can be an issue for the designer or celebrity. The name on the label is the name that consumers associate with the product; therefore, if an item purchased proves to be of poor workmanship, consumers will place responsibility on the name rather than on the manufacturer. Employing designer and celebrity names that have lost favor with consumers can impede profitability and be very costly for both the manufacturer and the retailer. Christian Dior was the first designer to license his name. Today, a plethora of designers and celebrities are on everything from jeans to kitchen appliances. A new trend in licensing has designers and celebrities licensing their names for products and apparel sold exclusively in particular retail outlets. Daisy Fuentes for Kohl's (Figure 2.8) and Tommy Hilfiger for Macy's illustrate this trend.

Private label merchandise describes goods designed and produced exclusively for a particular retailer's target audience. Developing private label lines affords the retailer the opportunity to serve specific customer needs, fill gaps in brand name offerings, and increase profit margins. Price competition on private label goods is virtually impossible because a retailer's competitors are unable to carry the private labels of other stores. Retailers, like

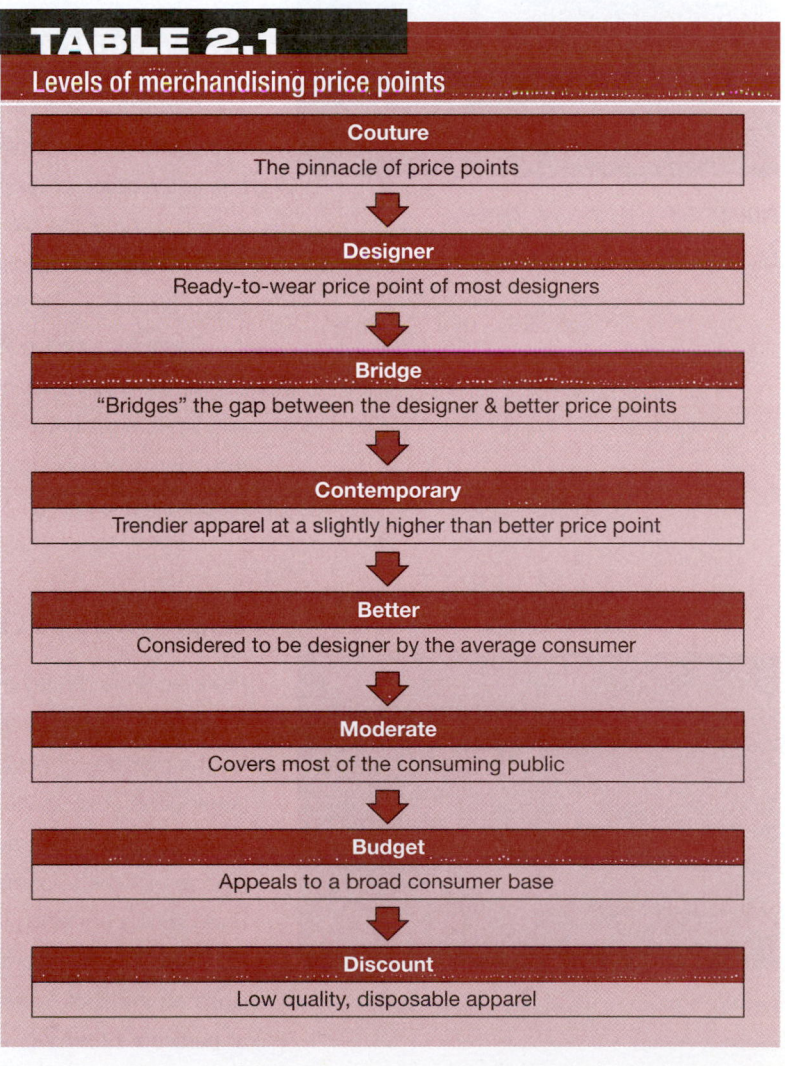

TABLE 2.1
Levels of merchandising price points

Couture
The pinnacle of price points

Designer
Ready-to-wear price point of most designers

Bridge
"Bridges" the gap between the designer & better price points

Contemporary
Trendier apparel at a slightly higher than better price point

Better
Considered to be designer by the average consumer

Moderate
Covers most of the consuming public

Budget
Appeals to a broad consumer base

Discount
Low quality, disposable apparel

FIGURE 2.8 *Daisy Fuentes for Kohl's (Source: Newscom).*

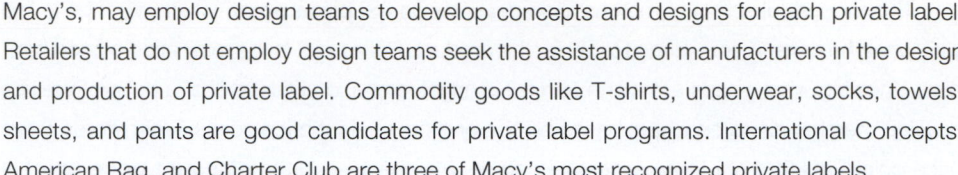

Macy's, may employ design teams to develop concepts and designs for each private label. Retailers that do not employ design teams seek the assistance of manufacturers in the design and production of private label. Commodity goods like T-shirts, underwear, socks, towels, sheets, and pants are good candidates for private label programs. International Concepts, American Rag, and Charter Club are three of Macy's most recognized private labels.

Levi's, Ralph Lauren, and Nautica are examples of **national brands**. Manufactured and marketed nationally and sometimes internationally, each brand evokes an image of lifestyle, quality, and price range based on the consumer the brand targets. For example, Levi's conjures the picture of an American original, hard-working brand. The Levi's image dates back to the beginning of the company when the durability and strength of denim made it the fabric of choice for workwear. Figure 2.9 depicts the iconic Levi's red tab.

Sectors of the Fashion Industry

There are four sectors that contribute to the fashion industry: raw materials, manufacturing, retail, and support. Each sector has a specific purpose that is critical to the fashion business. The sectors operate independently and interdependently with one another. However, the support sector works with the other three simultaneously. Let's look at each sector in greater detail.

Raw Materials Sector

The **raw materials sector** includes fiber production, weaving, spinning and dyeing, printing, and finishing. It is comprised of those who cultivate and produce the materials necessary to create the fabric or textiles used in the production of fashion apparel and accessories. Sheep farmers in Argentina, silkworm farmers in China, or a synthetic fiber manufacturer in the United States all produce materials used to create textiles that become fashion. The global raw materials sector produces over $400 billion in annual sales with steady sales growth each year.

Textile production in the twentieth century changed. As discussed in Chapter 1, the invention of improved machinery during the industrial revolution automated many processes in fiber and fabric production. In recent years, computer technology made sweeping advancements in the creation of fibers and textiles. In addition to apparel, the end use of textile industry products included home fashions, automobile interiors, medical, bioengineering, and industrial products.

Manufacturing Sector

Manufacturers display their fashions to retail buyers at various markets throughout the world. A **market** is a place where buyers and sellers, who share a common interest, come together for the purpose of buying and selling. Fashion markets are located throughout the world in larger cities such as New York City, Los Angeles, Atlanta, Paris, Milan, and London. Buyers of fashion goods will travel to a variety of venues during **market weeks** to view and purchase fashions for the upcoming season. Buyers shop domestic and foreign markets by attending trade shows or visiting a vendor's showroom where they meet with a sales representative to view lines for the upcoming season. Knowing that it is difficult for buyers to make buying decisions on the spot, sales representatives provide them with **line sheets**. Line sheets contain all pertinent information—style numbers, size scales, colors, delivery date, and costs—a buyer

FIGURE 2.9 *Levi's is an iconic national brand (Source: Alamy).*

requires for order writing. Buyers may place their orders during market week or wait until they return to the office; however, manufacturers often have deadlines for orders. Throughout the year, sales representatives travel to stores and buying offices to see buyers. In addition, buyers use the Internet as another avenue for viewing product.

Retail Sector

The **retail sector** is the bridge between the manufacturing sector and the customer. Fashion would not exist without the retail sector. Fashion retailers come in a variety of formats ranging from brick-and-mortar stores to mail-order catalogs to Internet sites to television. Technological advances make shopping convenient as information on countless fashion products is made available at the fingertips of the consumer. Web-based retailers such as bluefly.com, an online retailer of designer apparel, or zappos.com, the largest shoe site in the world, make it easier than ever to shop, and coupled with at-home delivery and free returns, consumers are adapting to the cyberspace way of shopping. Retailers distinguish themselves through business models, merchandise assortments, pricing, unique market strategies, size, and services offered to the consumer.

Each type of brick-and-mortar store is unique and caters to a particular group of consumers. Examples include the department store, specialty store, discounter store, off-price retailer, direct retailer, factory retailer, and category killer. Nonstore retailers include home shopping networks, Internet sites, catalogs, and mail order. An in-depth discussion on retail distribution can be found in Chapter 4.

Support Sectors

The **support sector** provides the fashion industry with services such as resident buying offices, fashion forecasting, and trade journals. The services offered in the support sector include consumer support services and trade support services. Consumer support services include areas such as consumer fashion magazines like *Elle*, *Cosmopolitan*, *Gentlemen's Quarterly*, and *Vogue*. Most magazines also offer Internet sites loaded with fashion trend information and blogs. Fashion is entertainment as seen by the numerous television shows with a fashion theme like *Project Runway* and *America's Next Top Model*. These shows do not sell directly to the consumer, but sell the concept of fashion.

Trade support services include any type of service that supports those working in the fashion industry. The services range from advertising and publicity to store design, visual merchandising, forecasting, and publishing trade journals. **Trade journals** are periodicals published for people in the fashion industry. Through these journals, readers stay apprised of the news in the fashion industry. Trade journals report on fashion trends, business news, stock market information regarding fashion companies, importing and exporting information, up-and-coming designers, and manufacturers. *Women's Wear Daily*, *Footwear News*, *Home Fashion News*, and *Stores* are trade journals written for specific categories of business. For example, published five days a week with each day reporting on a specific classification of the women's business, *Women's Wear Daily* is the "bible" of the fashion industry. Table 2.2 illustrates the four sectors and their relationship to one another.

Trade associations are groups of people working in the fashion industry that share similar interests. They are the voice of those who work in the industry while simultaneously keeping their members abreast of laws, statistics, and industry trends. Trade associations

TABLE 2.2

The four sectors of the fashion industry

Raw Materials Sector
Those that produce the materials necessary to create fiber or textiles used in the production of fashion apparel and accessories.
Supplies raw materials to the manufacturing sector.

Manufacturing Sector
Produce and present apparel and accessories to buyers at market for sale at retail.
Production materials for the goods are supplied by the Raw Materials Sector.

Retail Sector
A bridge between the manufacturing sector and the ultimate consumer.
Apparel and accessories are purchased from the manufacturing sector and presented in retail venues for purchase by the consumer.
The retail sector is vital to the existence of the fashion industry.

Support Sector
Any type of service that supports those working in the fashion industry.
Provides services to the fashion industry such as resident buying offices, fashion forecasting, and trade journals.
Works simultaneously with all sectors of the fashion industry.

present seminars to trade association members regarding a variety of applicable topics such as fashion trends. A few well-known trade associations are Cotton, Inc., American Apparel and Footwear Association, and the Fashion Council of America.

Principles of Fashion

The principles of fashion are the basic concepts about fashion apparel and their relationship with the consumer. Modern examples for the five principles of fashion serve to clarify their meaning and relevancy.

Fashion Mirrors the Times

Fashion is a reflection of culture and its values, which change and evolve over time. Apparel and its use speak volumes about an individual, his or her culture, and the current state of affairs. Apparel—viewed as a symbol of one's religious beliefs, an expression of one's peer group, or as a preference based on where one lives—transforms with the world. For example, short skirts imply consumers feel confident about the world and their individual circumstances. The converse is also true: The more dire consumers' circumstances appear, the more austere and conservative their apparel becomes. In some cases, religious beliefs rather than fashion tastes influence how individuals dress. The abaya, as seen in Figure 2.10, is a Muslim garment that covers the female body from the head to the feet and symbolizes Muslim religious beliefs. Fashion as an industry is a constant state of flux and greatly affected by the times. It is the nature of the industry to react to the needs and demands of the consumer.

Fashion Is Evolutionary Not Revolutionary

Consumers do not buy complete wardrobes every season; items are discarded and replaced with new ones to be worn with those deemed acceptable for the current season. It is this continuous updating and supplementing of wardrobes that drives the fashion industry. Outsiders have the impression that fashion changes rapidly, but that is hardly the case. Designers and manufacturers keep one eye on the past and one eye on the future as they plan their lines for upcoming seasons. Refreshing profitable styles with new colors and fabrics breathes new life into a stale style without introducing an entirely new item. Jeans exemplify changes, expedited by consumer preferences and fashion tastes, by modifying the color of the denim, the width of the leg opening, or the length of the rise. Sometimes jeans are very basic in nature without embellishment or trims. At other times jeans are embroidered, foiled, glittered, or painted and sometimes they are somewhere between basic and adorned. The denim silhouette can remain constant while the treatment of the denim and decorations evolve. Consumers are accustomed to seeing new fabrics, colors, and treatments each season; however, silhouettes generally evolve over a period of two to three years depending upon the fashion cycle.

FIGURE 2.10 *An abaya is a Muslim garment that covers the body from the head to the feet, symbolizing religious beliefs (Source: Hawa Stwodah).*

All Fashions End in Excess

Fashions go to the extreme in style and then the style reverses to the opposite direction. As trends emerge and gain acceptance by consumers, updates continue until the style has reached obsolescence. As this process occurs, the trend will morph until it reaches its limit, at which time the style will swing back to the other end of the scale. For example, in the early 1960s, waistbands on pants began a downward decent. Referred to as hip-hangers and later renamed hip-huggers, the pants stayed on the hips and clung to the thighs (Figure 2.11). As the trend progressed, the waist reached an extreme and could not go any lower. At that time, the waistline began to creep back up until it reached the very high waistline worn in the late seventies.

The Consumer Dictates Fashion

Designers create new styles every season. Merchandisers edit the styles based on the product's prospective salability. Through the process of design and editing, merchandisers and designers generate a line to present at market. Retail buyers make style selections based on the needs and desires of their customers and the selling history of the item and brand. Once the goods are in the stores, the consumer either accepts or rejects the styles. The consumer "votes" on designs by purchasing them from retailers. By purchasing merchandise, customers are dictating fashion. Conversely, merchandise rejected by consumers does not become fashion, at that

FIGURE 2.11 *In the early 1960s, low-rise pants were known as hip-huggers (Source: Alamy).*

time. There are times that retailers put forward new items before the customer is ready to accept them. It is a savvy buyer that knows the item was ahead of its time and deserves another chance sometime in the future. Retailers are in business to sell merchandise, and regardless of the designer or the garment, if merchandise does not sell, it is not fashion. This principle proves that designers do not dictate fashion. It is only with the ringing of the cash register that designs become fashion.

Importance of Fashion in the World Today

The fashion industry employs more people worldwide than any other industry today. Whether it is garment production in Asia, a weaver in Guatemala, a thread supplier in India, or a retailer in Europe, almost every country in the world is involved in some sort of fashion-related activity. The buying, selling, and producing of fashion built careers in the support services sector like fashion journalism, photography, and forecasting.

Since the mid-1970s, the fashion industry has seen a continuous shift of manufacturing from the United States to offshore. Originally, the shift was due to low-cost labor but today it is because of the globalized position of brands and retailers. As more countries became industrialized and their infrastructures became more modern, global partnerships became less complicated. Trade among countries continues to grow with the United States and other countries initiating trade with one another. Currently, there are 14 free trade agreements between the United States and countries around the world with an additional four trade preference programs. The purpose of these agreements and preference programs is to encourage companies to conduct businesses within the global arena. There are incentives such as free tariffs or reduction of tariff rates to conduct business with certain countries. (See Chapter 11 for a detailed examination of trade agreements.)

When retailers find domestic markets saturated, most of them step into the global marketplace. Through catalogs, brick-and-mortar stores, the Internet, or other distribution methods retailers are finding ways to tap into vast, new markets. With the onset of the Internet and other communications such as e-mail, consumers can receive information about a product, purchase the product, receive the product, and use the product all within a short time frame. Thus, consumers save time and money, while retailers gain customers they may not have otherwise acquired without the expense of building new retail stores.

summary

Summary

Fashion is a global industry with a language all its own. Successful navigation within the industry requires a working knowledge of the terms and phrases used. In addition to the vernacular of the fashion industry, the four sectors—raw materials, manufacturing, retail, and support—define each level of fashion. The contributions of each sector are critical to bringing fashion to the ultimate consumer.

In this chapter, you also learned that there are four principles of fashion. Fashion mirrors the times, fashion is evolutionary not revolutionary, all fashion ends in excess, and the consumer dictates fashion. Finally, the section on the importance of fashion in the world today demonstrated that fashion is an important part of domestic and global trade.

Key Terms

Review Questions

1. What is private label merchandise? How does private label merchandise benefit the retailer?

2. Explain the difference between a wholesaler and a jobber.

3. What is the fashion cycle? Describe each stage of the fashion cycle.

4. What price point best describes merchandise found at Macy's? Why?

5. What is the difference between licensing and private label merchandise? Can merchandise be both licensed and private label?

6. Describe the importance of fashion in the world today.

7. What are the four sectors of the fashion industry? What sector is the connection between fashion and the consumer? What sector works with all other sectors simultaneously?

Critical Thinking

1. Visit a men's department in a nationally known department store in your area. Write a report answering the following questions:
   a) Label name
   b) Category of merchandise (sport shirts, jeans, suits, etc.)
   c) Position on the fashion cycle
   d) Price range ($25–50 / better, bridge, moderate, etc.)

2. The text proposes the fashion principle that consumers, rather than designers, dictate fashion. Do you agree or disagree with this statement? Why or why not?

Internet Activities

Find two fashion blogs to follow and compare the two. What is the focus of each blog? Which blog is more on trend? What do you like and dislike about each blog?

FASHION

ECONOMICS

OBJECTIVES

After reading this chapter, you will be able to:

- Understand why you should study fashion from an economic perspective
- Examine and interpret the key principles of economics
- Explore important viewpoints in economics
- Recognize the interaction of supply and demand in the marketplace

A love of fashion makes the economy go round.

—LIZ TILBERIS

3

The fashion industry has captured the attention of the world, not only for its efforts in churning out the latest looks in apparel but also for its economic contributions to the global economy. The fashion industry is vast and plays a major part in domestic and global economies. For that reason, the economic decisions made by fashion companies influence not only the fashion industry but other industries as well, with varied results. The results can be positive or negative, or both. The fashion industry exemplifies the "can't have it all" scenario; therefore, consumers must make decisions about what they will have and what they must give up to get it. The chapter begins with the focus on fashion from an economic perspective while introducing economic theories and concepts relevant to all types of business using current fashion examples in the market.

Economics is the study of how societies and individuals allocate **scarce resources** to satisfy their unlimited wants and needs. Economists use this definition to study the choices made by people. Economics is a social science that studies many topics ranging from how societies manage scarce resources in order to produce and distribute the goods and services to understanding resources and scarcity in the marketplace. Economists form their study based on two perspectives referred to as microeconomics and macroeconomics. Economics focuses on many topics such as consumer behavior; supply and demand; governmental policies; international trade policies; business cycles; causes of inflation and unemployment; financial systems; and economic growth in underdeveloped, developing, and developed countries. Microeconomics describes the depth and breadth of economic behavior and the daily ongoing decision making by consumers and firms. Macroeconomics covers "big picture" topics such as inflation, budget and trade deficits, currency exchange rates, interest rates, taxation, government spending, and employment. This chapter demonstrates the extensive reach of the fashion industry and its impact on other businesses and industries.

Microeconomics and Macroeconomics

Microeconomics

Adam Smith first introduced the theory of microeconomics in *The Wealth of Nations* (1776). In *The Wealth of Nations*, Smith dealt with "how individual prices are set, studied the determination of prices of land, labor, and capital, and inquired into the strengths and weaknesses of the market mechanism" (Lawson and Peck, 2004, p. 30). Modern-day economists define **microeconomics** as the study of the choices based on decision making by individuals, families, businesses, and organizations and how these choices affect the market. Microeconomics is studied from a more personal level than macroeconomics. The decisions made are relative to the price of the product. These individual and collective decisions have a direct effect on markets for goods and services.

Considering both the seller and the buyer on a smaller scale is the study of microeconomics. For example, how will the price of children's clothing affect a family with twin infants? How will the addition of a new Walmart in a town affect other retailers? In 2003, city leaders in Richmond, Virginia, asked the question, "How does a city support two area lifestyle shopping centers, both upscale, within less than ten miles of each other?" These are the types of questions asked by businesses, families, and organizations when making decisions. In summary, the study of microeconomics and the fashion industry specifically examine the behavior of consumers; this in turn affects the subindustries that supply the materials to create the fashion, plus those that sell the fashion.

Macroeconomics

Macroeconomics deals with broad economic questions such as these: Is our economy in a recession? What factors are inhibiting the growth of the economy? What effect will an increase in the minimum wage have on unemployment? Why are nations growing?

The effect of decisions made by consumers, companies, and governments is what intrigues **economists**. Economists use a scientific approach by gathering data from primary and secondary sources and expressing relationships and correlations with graphs and charts. They also use models based on certain assumptions. Using data and models enables economists to make sound economic predictions for the future, including forecasting the rate of inflation in the near future or the price of oil in two months, both of which affect the price of polyester and other manufactured fibers.

This chapter serves as a basic introduction to economic principles, using fashion industry examples upon which economists base their study of economics. The foundation of economic study as it applies to the fashion industry begins here.

The Key Principles of Economics

An **economic principle** is an assertion or a general statement about consumer behavior and business in an economy. Economic principles form the foundation of the study of economic behavior, which is the study of consumers from a psychological perspective as they make economic decisions in the marketplace, and through the continued study prove economic behavior and become an economic law. Generally, the principle is used as a tool by economists to build upon theories of economic behavior. An example of an economic theory would be that the price of a product goes up when demand for the product is high. For example, let's say you are the senior merchandise manager of Nike studying the quantity of Nike shoes sold the past six months based solely on their price. Other factors that influence the quantity sold, such as the price of other athletic shoes, the time of year, and consumer incomes are not considered. The only factor is the price and the number of Nike shoes sold. Next, after examining Nike shoe sales, problems are examined, referred to as the economizing problem, and the appropriate decisions are made.

The Economizing Problem

The **economizing problem** is the need to make choices because the economic wants exceed economic resources, meaning that society has unlimited wants but scarce resources. Because income is finite, everyone makes spending decisions. Some wants are basic in nature, like food, clothing, and shelter, while other wants are more luxurious such as expensive cars, lavish vacations, designer clothing, and the latest Nike shoe. Like the goods purchased, services also satisfy our wants; therefore, choices must be made about the services purchased as well. Since people have limited resources and unlimited desires, it is virtually impossible for most people to have their wants fully satisfied. This is the crux of economizing, choosing goods and services that provide the most utility. As seen in the economizing problem of Nike shoes sold, if you, as the vice-president of Nike, analyze the shoe sales and conclude that sales were sluggish compared to last year at the same time, you must explore why. Investigating consumer behavior is one avenue to explore. From the consumer perspective, it could be that the Nike shoes are too expensive for your income, maybe the design is not fashionable, or perhaps another pair of Nike shoes is not needed this season. The consumer may want a new pair of Nike shoes, but has a limited amount of discretionary income. Hence, Nike must come up with a plan to increase sales and appeal to the consumer from an economic perspective by understanding the consumer's unlimited wants and needs. An examination of the competition, pricing, styles, and other variables is also warranted.

Utility

Utility is the total satisfaction a consumer gets from consuming a good or a service. Utility is related to theories of consumer behavior. Consumer behavior studies why consumers make certain purchase decisions, how they determine what they are going to purchase, and what effect influences such as advertising, role models, and price have in their decision-making process. The bottom line is that consumers purchase goods or services with the expectation of gaining total satisfaction or utility. There are three relevant things to know about utility. (1) Utility and usefulness are not the same: Designer shoes may offer utility to a fashionista but have no useful purpose for another (other than serving the basic need of clothing). (2) Utility is personal: The utility of a product is different for every person. For instance, a prom dress offers utility to someone going to a prom, but no utility to a person going to a barbeque. (3) Utility is difficult to quantify. Take the Nike shoe example; the utility to the consumer could be the satisfaction of wearing the latest pair of Nike shoes to school.

Total Utility and Marginal Utility

Total utility is the total amount of satisfaction a person derives from consuming a particular quantity of a good or service. In the fashion industry, total utility is referred to as the total amount of satisfaction a person derives from wearing a particular garment or accessory. The value of the fashion product to the consumer depends on the consumer. In fashion, total utility might be wearing a garment one time, several times, or many times over the course of years. For example, one consumer buys a Gucci handbag from the spring 2011 collection for $1,790 because she loves the handbag and she plans to take the bag with her on a cruise; another consumer buys the same handbag because it coordinates perfectly with her summer wardrobe; another buys the handbag because she likes it and the price fits within her budget. The Gucci handbag has utility for those consumers whose needs and wants are satisfied by purchasing the handbag, but no utility for others.

    Marginal utility is the additional satisfaction a consumer gets by consuming an extra unit of a product. Marginal utility equals the change in total utility that results from the consumption of one more unit of a product. For example, when the consumer initially bought and wore the Nike shoes, the total utility was high, initially growing until it reached 88 (see Figure 3.1 for a graph displaying total utility and marginal utility, and Table 3.1 for the same information displayed in a table format). As the shoes were worn and eventually went out of style, the marginal Nike shoe utility diminished. The consumer had reached total enjoyment. The next five times the shoes were worn the consumer's utility slowly decreased and total Nike shoe utility decreased as well. The satisfaction of wearing a new pair of Nike shoes was beginning to wear off, but the total marginal utility diminishes after a certain amount of times the shoes are worn. Look at the slope of the curve in the table and you can conclude that as the number of times the Nike shoes are worn the curve continues to slope downward, referred to as a negative slope. After the ninth time wearing the shoes, the marginal utility is in the negative zone meaning that the value of wearing the shoes decreases for the consumer.

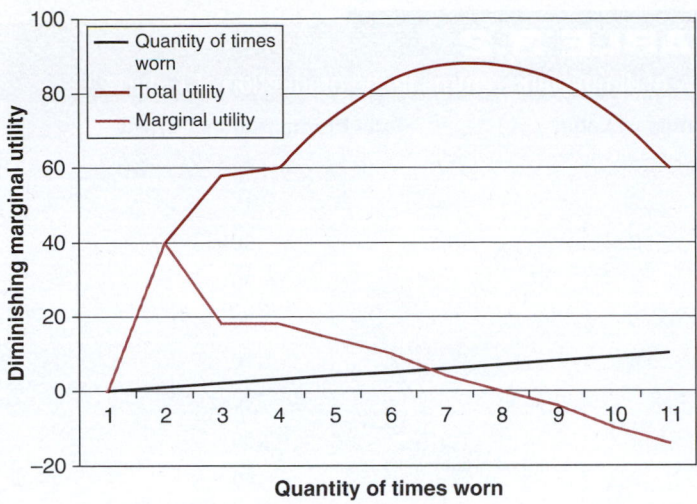

FIGURE 3.1 *Graph displaying total utility and marginal utility.*

The **law of diminishing marginal utility** demonstrates that if consuming successive units yield smaller and smaller amounts of marginal utility, then the consumer will only purchase additional units of a product if the price falls. As less utility is obtained from the product, the consumer will choose not to buy more at the reduced price and spend additional dollars on products that provide utility to him or her.

Diminishing Returns as Related to Production

In the production process, the **law of diminishing returns** is the principle that says as successive increments of a variable resource are added to a fixed resource, the marginal product (the total change in total product associated with each new unit of the variable resource) will eventually decrease, as demonstrated in Table 3.2. As seen in the table, the production of T-shirts decreases after the eighth worker is added due to the amount of equipment and plant production capacity necessary to increase production. If an apparel manufacturer is manufacturing T-shirts, the manufacturing facility is outfitted with a fixed amount of equipment such as

TABLE 3.1
Diminishing marginal utility

Quantity of Times Worn	Total Utility	Marginal Utility
0	0	0
1	40	40
2	58	18
3	60	18
4	74	14
5	84	10
6	88	4
7	88	0
8	84	−4
9	74	−10
10	60	−14

TABLE 3.2
Law of diminishing returns in the production of T-shirts

Quantity of Labor	Total Production of T-Shirts
1	14
2	15
3	30
4	90
5	100
6	110
7	120
8	150
9	140
10	115

dyeing, cutting, and sewing machines. If the manufacturer hired just one or two workers, total output and productivity (output per worker) would be very low. The workers would have to perform many different jobs without realizing the advantages of specialization.

Specialization is the concentration of knowledge on a particular skill or function used to produce a small number of goods and services. Specialization reduces the amount of time that is lost by switching workers from one job to another and allows the procedures within the manufacturing process to be used to their fullest capacity. Therefore, the T-shirt manufacturer could hire more workers and train them on particular tasks that would in turn keep the machinery running and increase productivity, as well as improve the marginal productivity of each worker. However, the increase in productivity could not go on indefinitely. If the manufacturer continues to hire employees, overcrowding would eventually take place, and workers will have to wait in line to use machinery. Thus, the workers would be underutilized and total output would increase at a diminishing rate. Given that the plant is a fixed size, each worker would have less capital equipment at his or her disposal as more labor was hired. The marginal product of the extra workers would decline because labor is more than capital equipment. If the apparel manufacturer continued to hire workers, there would be so much overcrowding that marginal product would be negative and total production would decline (Brue and McConnell, 2008).

The law of diminishing returns assumes that all units of labor are of equal quality. The assumption is that each new worker has the same innate ability, motor coordination, education, training, and work experience. Marginal product diminishes because more workers are used relative to the amount of plant and equipment available, not because successive workers are less skilled (Brue and McConnell, 2008). Refer to Table 3.3 for an illustration of the law of diminishing returns.

Economic Value Added

A fashion company can add utility to a fashion product by adding value in several ways: (1) the way the product is made, whether it is haute couture or ready-to-wear; (2) adding embellishments to the product, such as buttons or trims; (3) using high-quality fabric; (4) distributing the product in a specialty store or high-end department store; (5) having the product in the store at the right time, especially if the item is a high-demand, trendy item; (6) placing the item for

(1) Units of the Variable Resource (labor)	(2) Total Product	Marginal Product (MP), Change in (2)/Change in (1)		Average Product (AP), (2)/(1)
0	0	15	Increasing	-
1	15	23	marginal	15.00
2	38	30	returns	19.00
3	68	21		22.67
4	89	15	Diminishing	22.25
5	104	7	marginal	20.80
6	111	0	returns	18.50
7	111	−7		15.86
8	104	−8	Negative	13.00
9	96	−10	marginal	10.67
10	86		returns	8.60

sale at the appropriate time or even not placing the item in the store and creating scarcity of the item; and (7) advertising the fashion product through the news media, fashion shows, and red carpet events.

The consequences of choice lie in the future. Whatever decisions are made, the result or effect of the decision will be realized at some point after the decision is made. For example, Rock & Republic, a premium denim line, started in 2003 had been very successful because of its edgy, rock-and-roll influence and great fit. In the fall of 2009, Rock & Republic spun off a new line of denim called Plain Wrap. This line targeted a younger consumer segment. Michael Ball, founder and creative directive of Rock & Republic, was quoted in *Women's Wear Daily*, "This is a new initiative with a new perspective for the consumer that wants fashionable basics with staying power." Uniquely the economic value added to the line is the name of the product imprinted on each of the pieces. For example, "HOODIE" was printed across the back of the hoodie, and "STILETTO" was printed on the side of the shoe. This line was launched at a lower price point than the other lines carried by Rock & Republic, enabling the brand to expand its consumer base. Then Rock & Republic filed for bankruptcy in 2010 and later that year was bought by Vanity Fair Corporation. In 2012, it will be sold exclusively by Kohl's department stores.

Purchasing Power

Purchasing power is the real value of money in terms of the quantity of goods and services the money will buy. In other words, it is how much can be purchased with each monetary unit of amount of income earned. The **reality principle** states that the purchasing power of money is more important to people than the face value of money. The amount a dollar will buy varies inversely with the price level, all other things being equal. A give-and-take relationship exists between the general price level and the purchasing power of the dollar, meaning that when the "cost of living" goes up, the value of the dollar goes down, and vice versa. Lower prices increase the value of the dollar because it takes fewer dollars to purchase goods and services. Conversely, higher prices lower the value of the dollar because it takes more dollars to purchase goods and services. In difficult economic climates where consumers' paychecks are not keeping up with increasing prices on food, energy, and other necessities, the Federal Reserve must sustain a tricky balancing act of fighting inflation and encouraging growth at the same time.

The purchasing power of consumers is vital to the fashion industry. Generally speaking, the higher the consumers' income, the more they will spend on apparel; on the other hand, the lower their income, the less they will spend on apparel. *Women's Wear Daily* reported on July 9, 2008, that in 2007, wealthy people said a decline of 10 to 15 percent in their net worth would prompt them to spend less on luxury (Seckler, 2008). Obviously, if wealthy consumers notice a 10 to 15 percent drop in their net worth and change their purchasing habits, the less fortunate will surely feel the effects of the decrease as well and accordingly spend less on the goods in their price range.

Furthermore, while food, clothing, and shelter are necessities that can be purchased using disposable income, it is arguable whether all clothing purchases in the United States today can be classified under "necessities." After spending on acquiring food, clothing, and shelter, the remaining income is discretionary and used for items that are optional. Discretionary income is reduced when the prices of essential items increase. So, if the assumption is that not all clothing purchases are necessary and can be considered elective, then it follows that fashion purchases are impacted as a result of a decrease in discretionary income.

Important Viewpoints in Economics

Understanding the basics of economics leads to a better understanding of the contributions of the fashion industry to the world economy. Many decisions go into making a garment or creating a service for the fashion consumer, but the basic question is this: Will this product or service produce a profit? People making merchandising decisions that affect a company's inventory—the buyers, product developers, fashion designers, and retail store managers—have to determine what the consumers want and need by using economic information, sales history, and current trends. This chapter is concerned with the economic decisions made.

Economic Choices

Economics, as previously discussed, is about choices made with limited resources including the factors of production: land, labor, capital, technology, and entrepreneurship. As resources are scarce, societies must choose after weighing the costs and benefits of each choice and considering the **costs**, including opportunity costs.

Scarcity

Scarcity means that limited resources are unable to provide all the benefits we desire and that these limited resources can be used in different ways. Scarcity limits options and demands choices. For example, most of us face scarcity every day—we want more than we can have, whether it is time, money, a good, a service, or some other resource. In the consumer marketplace, this might simply mean sacrificing money to obtain food or clothing or cable TV. This sacrifice is known as **opportunity cost** (discussed in depth later in this chapter).

In 1979 Brian Smith, a surfer, created boots from sheepskin under the brand name UGG. Initially, the boots were popular with the Californian surfing crowd as well as Australia's circle of surfers. The UGG boot became very trendy in the nineties and sales have continued to grow (Figure 3.2). In 2003, the UGG brand of boot took off due to its popularity among celebrities. During the 2006 and 2007 holiday seasons, it was very difficult for a consumer to find and purchase a pair of UGG boots. There are a couple of factors that could have contributed to the shortage or limited supply of UGG boots in the marketplace. Perhaps the company did not accurately anticipate the demand for the boots and as a consequence underestimated the number of boots that needed to be produced or perhaps a certain raw material, like top-grade sheepskin, which is usually in high demand and seasonally in short supply, was unavailable. Regardless, the price for UGG boots (during the 2007 holiday season) was not inflated, keeping to the usual retail price of $110. Instead, retailers like eBay, an online auction and shopping website considered by some to be the world's largest online marketplace, used the principles of demand and scarcity to drive the retail price of the boots to as high as $400.

Economists believe that, although consumers' needs and wants are never scarce, their resources to satisfy those wants and needs are scarce. All societies face the problem of scarcity and must answer the three basic economic questions: What to produce? How to produce? and For whom to produce?

FIGURE 3.2 *UGG boots are in high demand even today (Source: Alamy).*

Factors of Production

The **factors of production** are land, labor, and capital and the decision about what to produce begins with these factors. Without these factors, production cannot occur. This is the first question that someone starting a business must ask: What factors of production are necessary and available to realize my vision?

Land refers to all natural resources, anything provided by nature. Cotton is an important land-based factor of production for a business that makes T-shirts. Cream is a vital land-based component for an ice-cream manufacturer.

Labor is human production, the physical and mental effort that is necessary to produce something. This is what employees provide, whether it is balancing the books, painting a house, cleaning floors, or writing a legal brief, in exchange for wages (Figure 3.3).

Capital is physical and human capital. **Physical capital** is the manmade items that are used to produce something else. Buildings, manufacturing machines, vehicles, paper, computers, telephones, and desks are all physical capital. **Human capital** is the knowledge and skills people have acquired to build goods and services. Human capital accumulates through training, education, and experience. Every worker has acquired some level of human capital. The knowledge used by a worker, whether it is a designer sketching of a new design or a store manager creating an employee's work schedule, requires intelligence in the form of knowledge and skills.

Fashion companies are required to have **infrastructure** and capital. Infrastructure is the foundation needed by an economy to operate successfully. It is the physical means used by the modes of transportation such as roads, railways, airways, and waterways. Those modes of transportation, necessary to move goods and people, provide the means to move textiles and apparel from one point to another. For example,

FIGURE 3.3 *Bangladeshi garment workers sewing T-shirts at a factory in Dhaka (Source: Newscom).*

after producing a garment in China, the garment must be transported to the final destination for selling or to a warehouse for distribution, which can be located anywhere in the world. The transportation used to reach the destination is often a ship, then a train, and finally a truck.

The societal question of "What should we produce?" refers to goods and services in its society. In 2006, the government of Nigeria supported the Textile Revitalization Fund to help stimulate its textile industry to be more competitive with Asian countries. Nigerians initially asked, "What do we produce in order to place our country in a global competitive situation?" After much research and analysis by the Revitalization Fund Committee, they came to a conclusion to build and promote the cotton industry in Nigeria. The next question asked by the Nigerians was, "How to produce?" The answer by the Nigerian textile industry was to build a stronger infrastructure within the country of Nigeria in order to be more globally competitive in the production of cotton. For the last question asked, "For whom to produce?", the answer was to produce cotton for the domestic textile industry because the production of cotton benefited and added value to the textile industry.

Economic outcomes are important to the fashion industry. Producers and distributors make decisions affecting the fashion industry and consumers founded on actual situations rather than abstract theories. It is important to note that "economists have had notorious difficulties pinning down a term as volatile as fashion" (Gick and Gick, 2007, p. 4). Economic decisions with regard to fashion are being made around the world and these decisions affect economies on a local, national, and global scale. For example, while a textile manufacturer is trying to make the decision to add labor to his factory in China to meet the time demands of delivery, a consumer shopping in New York City is deciding where she should purchase a winter coat: Barney's, Saks Fifth Avenue, or Macy's. Barney's, Saks Fifth Avenue, and Macy's contribute to the global economy in a number of ways. Saks Fifth Avenue and Macy's are publicly traded on the New York Stock exchange. Therefore, there are many individuals sharing ownership, both domestically and internationally. These shareholders have a vested interest in the value and financial stability of these companies, and the money gained or lost from their business endeavors influences the global economy. A fresh and appealing merchandise mix is vital to the success of these retailers. They travel all over the world in search of merchandise that separates their assortments from the competition. Procuring goods both at home and abroad benefits the global economy through the selling of raw materials, production, and distribution.

Opportunity Cost

Within the economic realm, every choice has a cost; the cost is measured in dollars, time spent, or products not chosen. At the heart of economics is the belief that there is no such thing as a free lunch. The lunch may be free from your viewpoint, but someone else had to assume the cost.

The opportunity cost of a decision involves more than the cost in dollars. Rather, it is the sacrifice of the best alternatives. To obtain more of one thing, one forgoes the opportunity of getting the next best thing. Measuring an opportunity cost is not measuring the sum of the alternatives sacrificed; it is a comparison of the best two alternatives. Decision making always involves opportunity costs.

Consider the opportunity cost as seen by the Fashion Center of New York City. The Fashion Center of New York City has seen a decline of space and industry devoted to fashion business activities since the manufacturing of apparel and accessories has moved offshore. New York City has many projects planned for the surrounding area and there is demand for small office and retail spaces for starting companies. However, according to fashioncenter.com, "The existing conditions in the Fashion District—the limits of office use, restrictions on residential development and under-performing retail—are already imposing substantial opportunity costs, both in terms of lost income and City tax revenues." "Without efforts to drive new investment in the area and to attract the dynamic, growing segments of the city's economy, the economic expansion that is poised to occur in the surrounding areas will simply bypass the Fashion District" (The Fashion Center.com). The opportunity costs of lost income and city tax revenue for the businesses of the fashion district are for the most part out of their control.

Another example of opportunity cost is the decision many new fashion designers have to make of whether or not to become an independent designer or work for a company. Some may choose to invest their time and money in a fashion show to show their designs during fashion week in New York City in hopes of being noticed by the press. Other young design-ers may choose to go directly into the workforce and find themselves starting as assistant designers and working their way up the career ladder toward head designer. A new designer may face these alternatives early in his career. If he chooses to show during fashion week, the opportunity cost is the second-best alternative—learning the businesses and gaining experi-ence by working in the field. Gaining recognition in an extremely competitive industry may far outweigh the investment of time and money.

Taking a brand global is an additional example of opportunity cost in the fashion indus-try. The opportunity cost is the next best alternative to going global. For example, instead of going global should money be invested in improving brand image through domestic advertising?

The opportunity cost of increasing the supply of jeans in a store is decreasing the supply of another product to make room for the jeans. Are the other products a more prof-itable choice? Merchants weigh their costs and benefits to make decisions like these on a daily basis: what merchandise to carry, what merchandise to reduce and clear, and what merchandise to reject. Space and financial restraints demand that retailers make these decisions, which are the job of a merchant, but with these choices come the inherent risk of opportunity cost.

American Apparel is a case of opportunity costs faced by a clothing manufacturer and retailer. American Apparel, founded by Don Charney in 1977, employs more than 10,000 people and operates stores worldwide in 19 countries. In 1977 when most apparel manufacturing was moving offshore, American Apparel produced its garments in Los Angeles, California. The deci-sion to produce domestically resulted in the opportunity cost of the less expensive labor offered by offshore production. The benefits, however, outweighed the cost of the cheap labor. By keeping production in the United States, Charney gained the respect of his workers by offering a sweatshop-free environment and a reputation that American Apparel is a great place to work. In addition, in Los Angeles, Charney can keep a watchful eye on the workers, monitor the qual-ity of the garments, and respond quickly to the demands of the consumers. Over 5,000 people work at American Apparel in Los Angeles and the average production worker earns a mini-mum of $12 per hour, plus benefits. In 2006, American Apparel entered into a merger agree-ment with Endeavor Acquisition Corporation. The combined company operates as American Apparel and is the largest garment manufacturer in the United States. Ironically, during a time when many goods sold in the United States are made in China, American Apparel sells goods manufactured in the United States to its Chinese consumers. The future holds many economic decisions involving the opportunity cost of the workers and their working conditions should it become necessary for American Apparel to move or expand its production overseas. For more information on American Apparel, visit American Apparel.net.

One more example of an opportunity cost would be the decision to produce one item rather than another item. A denim bottoms manufacturer produces jeans, capris, and shorts. In any given spring season, a denim manufacturer has to decide the correct proportions of each of these categories to produce. This decision, based largely on fashion trends, trend forecasts, and historical selling information, is often unreliable due to the uncertainty that characterizes the fashion industry. For example, a denim bottoms manufacturer produced 200,000 jeans for the spring season last year. Selling was excellent, earning a healthy profit margin, so the decision is made to keep jeans production equal to last year. However, last spring shorts sales were disappointing, and with a 100,000 unit production, company profits suffered in the classification. Additionally, the capri pant classification performed well last year; 50,000 units were manufactured and while the profit was not as impressive as it was in the jeans category, it was healthy. Therefore, for spring this year, the manufacturer concludes that it would be better to produce an equal amount of jeans but more units in capris than in shorts. This is a risk because production space is limited and the manufacturer is putting production facilities behind capris and giving up the opportunity of manufacturing shorts. The manufacturer must decide on the best, most profitable, and most efficient use of the production facilities available. If fashion trends change and consumers begin to demand more shorts than capris, the cost of producing capris would have been better spent producing shorts. Table 3.4 demonstrates the above-mentioned production dilemma.

Spillover Effect

The benefits or costs associated with producing or consuming fashion goods are not limited to the firm or person producing or consuming them. The **spillover effect** is when decisions affect people who are external to the decision. **Externality** is another word for "spillover." Some goods produce spillover benefits or positive externalities while others produce costs or negative externalities. Positive externality or spillover occurs when the benefits of producing or consuming a good are not restricted to the producer and/or consumer of the good. Negative externality or spillover happens when the costs of producing or consuming the goods are not restricted to the producer and/or consumer of the good. Spillover costs and benefits are an economic problem because producers and consumers make production and consumption decisions based on their own costs or benefits, not total costs or benefits including spillovers. As a result, the amount of certain goods produced or consumed by society may not be optimal. The spillover effect can simultaneously have both positive and negative implications on other entities in any given situation.

TABLE 3.4
Production dilemma

	LY	TY	Difference
Jeans	200,000	200,000	0
Shorts	100,000	80,000	−20,000
Capris	50,000	70,000	20,000
Total	350,000	350,000	0

If the producer manufactures 20,000 more capris than last year and 20,000 fewer shorts than last year and fashion changes, the opportunity of producing additional shorts is lost. Furthermore, profitability is not maximized because the less desirable item was produced.

For example, a company may make the decision to produce in a country like Guatemala, where labor is cheap. The consequence would be a positive externality or spillover for consumers because the consumer of the apparel benefits from a lower-cost garment. However, poor factory conditions or child labor would illustrate negative externality or spillover for the workers in the facility manufacturing the garments.

The spillover effect does not always have to come from the production of apparel and textiles. In this situation, spillover occurs in the transportation part of the supply chain. The American Chemical Society conducted a study and determined that globally thousands of deaths were associated with ship emissions. (See Box 3.1.) American Chemical Society researchers estimate

Environmental News

Death from shipping

Researchers report that international shipping emissions could be responsible for more than 60,000 deaths a year. The new results, published in *ES&T* (pp. 8512–8518) by a team led by James Corbett of the University of Delaware and James Winebrake of the Rochester Institute of Technology, provide some of the first estimates of premature mortality from exposure to particulate matter, nitrogen oxides (NO_x), and sulfate in global ship emissions.

The work "is quite interesting and—in spite of large uncertainties in emission estimates and other information used in the analysis—sends an important policy signal," says Janusz Cofala of the internationally sponsored policy and science research center International Institute for Applied Systems Analysis (Austria). Cofala co-led research for the European Commission that examined sulfate emissions effects in the North Sea. "We used different data sets and different models, [but] our findings seem to be consistent" with those of the new research, he says.

The *ES&T* research was commissioned in part by the environmental groups Clean Air Task Force and Friends of the Earth International, which is a party to International Maritime Organization (IMO) discussions. In November, IMO participants discussed data on ship emissions and whether to require emissions controls or a switch to cleaner fuels. Ships plying international waters tend to burn "dirty" fuels that contain high amounts of sulfur. Under an international agreement adopted by IMO in 2005, sulfate emissions from any ship entering the North Sea must be controlled to prevent acidification of local soils and ocean waters. California is considering similar measures for its ports. Corbett, Winebrake, and colleagues estimated seafaring-ship emissions of $PM_{2.5}$ and other pollutants, including sulfate and NO_x. Using global circulation models combined with a variety of emissions scenarios, they mapped out how emissions would drift over land. After folding in regional demographic data, they could pinpoint areas with a higher likelihood of deaths from cardiopulmonary and lung cancer that are attributable to $PM_{2.5}$ exposure.

Depending on the scenarios and models used, the number of such premature deaths in 2002 ranged from about 19,000 to 64,000. Southeast Asia, India, and Europe bore the brunt of the mortality along coastlines and near ports, but inland France also saw high mortality rates due to atmospheric circulation patterns and population density, the models show. Without emissions controls, the number of premature deaths could increase by 40% in the next 5 years, the authors estimate.

The reported range of deaths "reflects a lot of the uncertainties in the original mortality studies" on particulate matter exposure and its effects, comments Bart Ostro of the California Office of Environmental Health Hazard Assessment. Ostro modeled health effects for the port city of Long Beach with higher-resolution models, the results of which the researchers use for comparison. He says that their assumptions and model results seem "reasonably robust." Ostro also notes that mortality rates hint at the hidden damage from shipping emissions, including asthma and other problems, which contribute to higher costs for health care and the economy.

Observers from within the shipping industry argue that the IMO's current emissions controls are sufficient and that more stringent rules, called for by environmental groups and others, would create heavy cost burdens for shipping companies. Corbett and Winebrake reported further modeling results in a paper coauthored with Chengfeng Wang of the University of Delaware, published in *ES&T* (pp. 8233–8239), in which they argue that measures for controlling sulfur emissions could be more cost-effective than previously assumed. Using emissions data from international oceangoing ships making port in the U.S., they calculate that low-sulfur fuels, onboard scrubbers, and market-based emissions trading programs could save up to $260 million in costs needed to meet control targets.

—NAOMI LUBICK

FIGURE 3.4 *Typical ship that carries cargo such as apparel and accessories (Source: Shutterstock).*

that "shipping-related particulate matter emissions are responsible for about 60,000 cardiopulmonary and lung cancer deaths annually." The majority of deaths are in East and South Asia and along the European coastlines. Figure 3.4 shows a vessel shipping apparel off the shore of Europe. By 2012, a 40 percent growth in emissions is expected (Lubick, 2007).

Marginal Analysis

Economists often weigh the alternatives and determine the best use of resources based on **marginal analysis**. Marginal analysis evaluates how a small increase in a variable affects other variables, such as costs or benefits. It compares marginal benefits with marginal costs. A **variable** is a measurement of a quantity that has the potential to change. A fashion executive usually thinks in terms of either increasing or decreasing a variable in order to increase the profit margin of a company, such as hiring additional staff or adding another sewing machine. The variable may be short term or long term. Figure 3.5 shows how adding workers affects the production of jeans: output increases with each added worker.

If a small increase in a variable adds to benefits more than costs, then increase the value of the variable. If the increase adds more to costs than to benefits, then decrease or leave the value of the variable the same. For instance, if a store plans to increase the inventory of its supply of jeans by adding 1,200 pairs of Levi's jeans to the inventory, and then subtracting 1,200 pairs of Paris Blues corduroys out of the inventory adds $52,800 in benefits and $27,300 in costs, then it is worth adding the additional jeans.

Let's take a look at how graphs are used for analysis purposes to show relationships between marginal costs and profits. For this example, think about the manufacturing sector of fashion where many decisions of how many to produce, when to produce, and what type of product to produce are only some of the questions an owner of a manufacturing plant may ask. For example, a jeans manufacturer is trying to determine whether adding one worker to the production of jeans would be beneficial. In Figure 3.5, the output of jeans is plotted on the *Y* axis and the number of workers (variable) is plotted on the *X* axis.

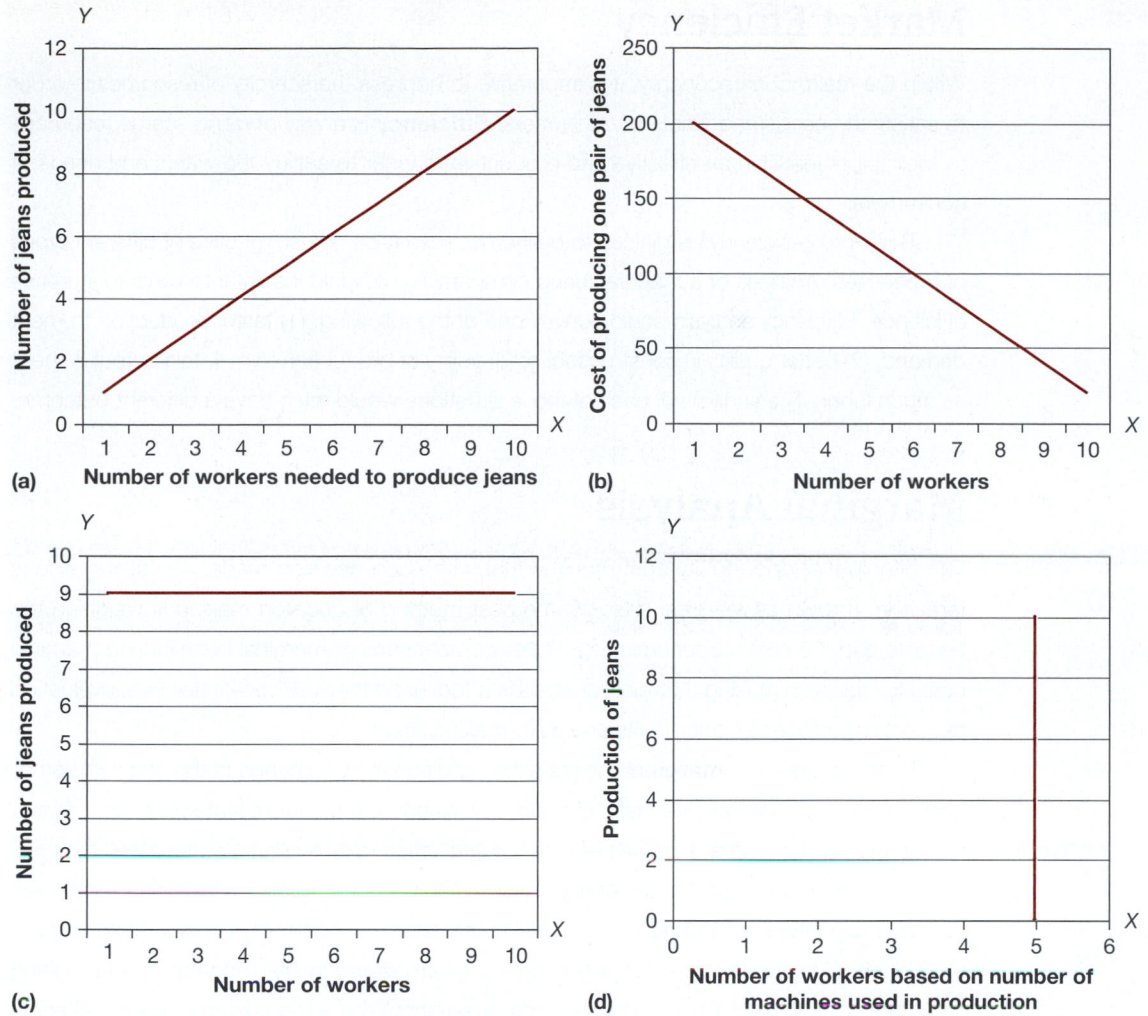

FIGURE 3.5 *(a) X and Y are positively related. (b) X and Y are inversely related. (c) X has no effect on Y. (d) Y does not affect X.*

Figure 3.5a is an example that shows there would be an increase in the production of jeans if one more worker was added (*X*)—then the benefits (*Y*) go up. *X* and *Y* are positively related. The workers are on the *X* axis, causing the production of the jeans.

Figure 3.5b displays *X* and *Y* as inversely related by adding a worker. While *X* could be workers hired, *Y* could be the cost to produce the goods. A reasonable conclusion would be that adding the worker is too costly at this time for the manufacturer. The lesser the number of workers, the higher the cost of producing the jeans. This is an example of a negative relationship between *Y* and *X*.

Figure 3.5c displays that adding the worker does not affect the production at all. The manufacturer could have added the worker and as a result, the other workers slowed down in their production efforts. *X* has no effect on *Y*. The number of jeans produced stays the same if a worker is added due to the fact that there are a limited number of sewing machines, so therefore, production does not increase when a worker is added. Two variables would have to be added in order for production to increase: workers and sewing machines.

Figure 3.5d displays that *Y* does not affect *X*. *X* remains the same regardless of adding workers to the production. The reality may be that adding a worker to increase production will not result in increased output because there are only a set number of machines used in manufacturing the jeans.

Market Efficiency

Within the realm of an economy, it is imperative to address the scarcity of resources in order to satisfy the needs and wants of consumers. **Efficiency** is a way of using scarce resources to their full potential in an effective and productive manner to satisfy the wants and needs of consumers.

The word "efficiency" is difficult to define because it can be suggestive of different types of processes. Analysis of a manufacturing company would yield insight into ways to increase efficiency. Efficiency analysis could convey one of the following: (1) faster production to meet demand, (2) better quality in construction, or (3) ability of production to maintain output without as much labor. The analysis of each of those situations would each have a different outcome.

Marginal Analysis

The principle of opportunity cost requires that with each decision made, something else is foregone. Known as *marginal analysis*, the best method of decision making is weighing the benefits and the costs. Economics spotlights comparisons of marginal benefits and marginal costs for decision making. Marginal analysis is a tool used for cost/benefit analysis, evaluation of economic efficiency, and profits and utility maximization.

To the economist, **marginal** means extra, additional, or a change in the effect of something. Most decisions indicate that a change is imminent to the current state of affairs. Logical, reasonable, and sensible decisions require the evaluation of all available options and the marginal benefits and marginal costs of each. Accordingly when a retailer is weighing the choice between two new lines to add to his or her merchandise assortment, consideration is given to a variety of factors. Let's assume that both lines are similar in style and cache. In weighing the options, a retailer might ask the following questions: Who is the customer we are after? Is this a new or existing customer? What is the sales history of each line? What retailers currently carry each line? Which line has the best price point for the customer the retailer is after? Which line has the best delivery? Which line offers the best shipping and payment terms? Which line has the best sales promotion plan? What will be omitted from the current assortment to garner the space needed for the new product? Once these questions are answered and the benefits and costs for each have been examined, the retailer is able to make the best decision possible given the amount of information available at the time. The retailer may decide to buy one line and not the other, to buy both, or to buy neither. Gap, a global retailer that specializes in casual wear for men, women, and children, made similar choices with its product assortment in 2001 and also added fashion items to its clothing line.

Since its inception in 1969, Gap had been successfully selling basic, classic clothing until it moved into selling trendier, fashionable items, which resulted in financial disaster. In 2001, Gap realized a sales decrease of 4.4 percent with a decline in the stock price followed by the hiring of a new CEO to replace Millard Drexler, who had been with Gap from 1983. The decision to change the product mix with more fashionable product was a miss. It did not increase sales, as the consumer firmly rejected the merchandise, and it resulted in a loss of millions of dollars in profits for Gap.

Benetton has also made its share of controversial decisions based on marginal analysis. Benetton, a fashion company born in 1965, is now an international brand sold in 120 countries. Known for its unique color stories and distinctive sweaters, Benetton has Italian roots. Beginning in the late 1980s and throughout the 1990s, Benetton's advertising campaigns, based on social issues, brought the company negative attention. The decision to use the divisive campaigns proved to be profitable and controversial at the same time. The ads became the image and a leading contributor to the building of the brand.

In a world of scarcity, the decision to obtain the marginal benefits coupled with a certain choice always includes the marginal cost of doing without something else. The decision to change the merchandise assortment at Gap or to run controversial ads at Benetton means foregoing some other product or advertising campaign. It is important to note that decision making always involves opportunity costs.

Economic Analysis

There are two main approaches to economic analysis: positive economics and normative economics.

Positive economics focuses on an analysis of existing facts and cause-and-effect relationships to give a picture of current conditions or to predict future conditions. Positive analysis avoids value judgments: It aims merely to explain the consequences of various alternatives using scientific statements about economic behavior. Scientific analysis is essential to sound policy analysis.

For instance, if a shoe retailer decided to raise the prices of a particular brand of boot, a positive analysis of the facts would determine the effect the price hike would have on sales. Would the quantity of boots sold increase, decrease, or remain the same due to the price increase? What impact would the quantity in units have on total sales volume?

The shoe retailer might examine these additional outcomes as well:

- How will an increase in the state sales tax affect sales?
- How will the move of a large competitor into the neighborhood affect sales?
- How will a rainy weekend affect sales?

It is possible to analyze these questions about reality from an objective perspective.

Normative economics, on the other hand, answers the question, What should be? Normative analysis makes value judgments based on current or future conditions. So, while positive analysis reveals the consequences of various alternative choices, normative analysis weighs the consequences and judges what choice should be made. Normative economics leads to choices in the consumer marketplace and in public policy.

In the case of the shoe retailer, a normative analysis would determine whether prices of the particular brand of boot should be raised, remain the same, or even be reduced to produce the best result for the retailer. Additional considerations for the shoe retailer include the following:

- Should the store add a third salesperson for busy shifts?
- Should the store hold a sale after the holiday season?
- Should the store invest in more upscale product lines?

These are questions about how things might be in the future, not the current situation. Economists sometimes view normative conditions as the way things should be in a moral sense. For example, if we were to answer the first question: Should the store add a third salesperson for busy shifts? Yes, the store should add a third salesperson if the other two salespeople don't get a break or if the burden of selling relies on two salespeople to the point that if one gets sick, there is only one salesperson on the floor and the store loses sales and customers in the long run.

Interaction of Supply and Demand in the Marketplace

As you learned earlier, a market is an environment that allows for the exchange of commodities. In the marketplace, a buyer exchanges money with a seller for a product. This type of arrangement enables people to exchange something they have for something they want.

Markets allow people to live beyond what they produce. For instance, a corn farmer uses the income from sale of the corn that he has produced to purchase other goods. A plumber uses his skills making repairs to earn money, so he can exchange it for goods and other services in the marketplace. Figure 3.6 is a picture of a marketplace, the Mall of Emirates, an international shopping destination in Dubai.

A business sustains itself through these kinds of exchanges. A clothing boutique, for instance, sells dresses so that it can purchase more dresses and can pay its employees, its rent, and its many other bills. It operates—and we operate—in the market to survive. So those operating in the market are motivated by their own self-interest and not by general goodwill. People provide services or goods because they need them to acquire other services and goods.

Not surprisingly, the market's impact is wide-ranging. It determines which products are bought and sold, how much of them are bought and sold, and at what prices they are bought and sold. The market largely determines the prices of goods and services through the interaction of **supply** and **demand**. Supply is the quantity of a product that producers are willing and able to provide at a particular price. Demand is the quantity that buyers are willing and able to purchase at a particular price. Therefore, a product or service will not survive in the market if people do not have sufficient interest in purchasing the product or service.

Similarly, clothing stores typically offer a variety of apparel because few markets would support a store filled with a single style of dress. There would be some consumers willing to pay for the same style of dress, but there would not be enough of them to support a store devoted solely to that style. A store must carry an assortment of inventory appealing to the marketplace. The store relies on the assortment to interest customers enough to purchase merchandise, therefore, generating sales revenue that will pay outstanding debts and create a profit for the store to survive.

In a free market, the law of demand says the higher the price of a product, the lower the quantity people will buy, and the lower the price of a product, the greater the quantity demanded for it. This is evident in the markdowns that retailers take. When an item experiences sluggish sales or sales of a product decrease, a retailer will lower the price, in the form of a **markdown**, in an effort to speed up the rate of sale on that particular item. In Figure 3.7, each point on the graph reflects a direct correlation between price and quantity demanded. When the price of a product increases, it reduces the consumer's purchasing power, and when the price of a product decreases, it increases the consumer's purchasing power. Why is this true? Because although the price of the product changes, the consumer's income remains the same. A price increase means the consumer can buy less with the same income. The **real value** of a consumer's income is its purchasing power.

A shoe retailer with a core group of customers might lose some of those customers if it raised its prices because, by raising prices, it would decrease its customers' purchasing power and make the shoes in the store more difficult for them to buy. Some would be willing

FIGURE 3.6 *The Mall of Emirates, Dubai (Source: Alamy).*

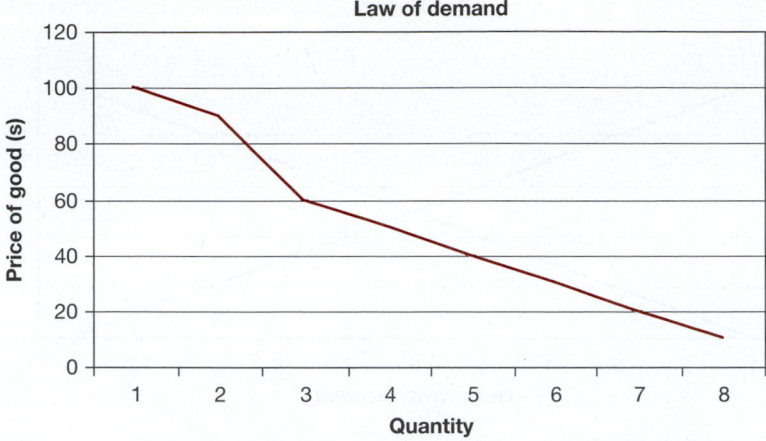

FIGURE 3.7 *Quantity demanded and price correlation.*

to pay higher prices and make a greater sacrifice to purchase shoes from the store, but others would choose not to allocate a greater portion of their income for shoes from that store and would look for cheaper ones.

The **substitution effect** is the effect that a change in price has on the quantity demanded by giving buyers the option to substitute a lower-priced good for goods that are more expensive. For example, the reduction in the price of a particular type of sweater allows the customer to buy more sweaters (the income effect). At the lower price, this style of sweater becomes a more attractive option than a higher-priced sweater, jacket, or shirt (the substitute effect). The combination of the income effect and the substitution effect gives customers the ability and the willingness to buy more goods at a lower price than at a higher price.

Although demand has an inverse relationship to price, supply has a direct relationship to price. In other words, when raising the price on a product, producers will be willing and able to supply more of the product. When the price drops, the quantity supplied will drop. The reason is that sellers are motivated to offer more of a product when the price is high, and more sellers join the market, attracted by the high price. Refer to Figure 3.8, a graph displaying the law of supply. At each point on the supply curve, you can see a direct correlation between price and supply. When the quantity of a product is high, the supply is high; sometimes a surplus may occur, if demand is not high. After the product is sold at a high price, inventory of a product is decreased, price decreases, and demand levels decrease.

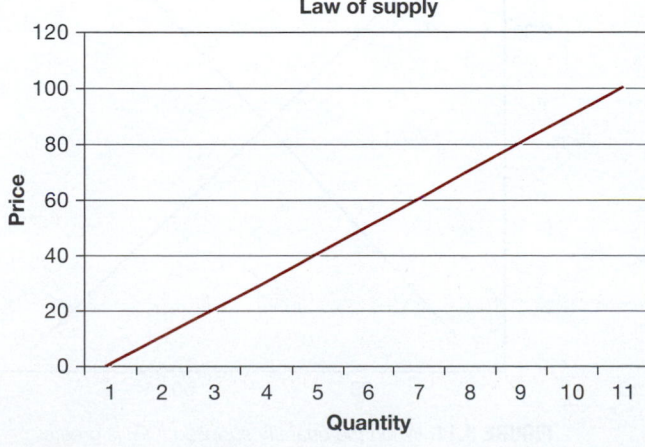

FIGURE 3.8 *Law of supply.*

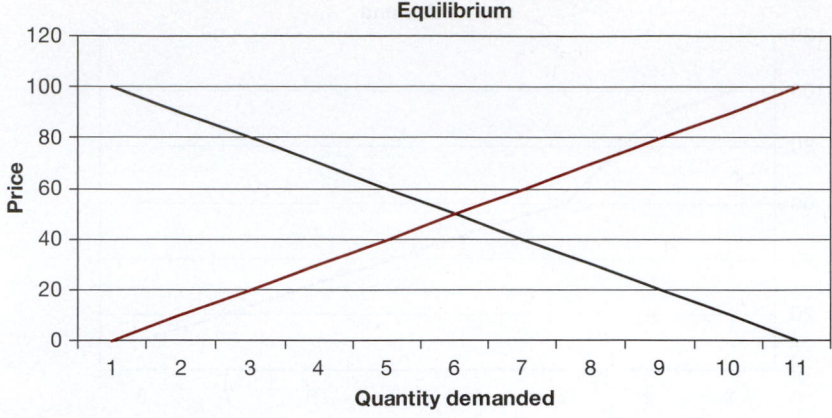

FIGURE 3.9 *Market equilibrium.*

Market equilibrium occurs when the quantity demanded of a product equals the quantity supplied (Figure 3.9). When equilibrium occurs, it is at the intersection of supply and demand, as shown in the figure. Market price is determined at equilibrium point. The market for the product is equal in terms of what is supplied and what is demanded. Economists view equilibrium as showing efficiency in the marketplace. The allocation of resources reflects the value of the product to both buyers and sellers. There is enough demand for the product and enough supplied. When market equilibrium exists, there is no pressure from the market to change the price. However, when there is no market equilibrium—when there is an excess of either quantity supplied or quantity demand—market pressure causes the decrease or increase in the price of a product.

An excess of demand means consumers are willing to purchase more of a product than suppliers are willing to make available. This leads to suppliers raising the price of the product because consumers are willing to pay more. The price increase reduces quantity demand for the product. Some consumers, however, will be willing to pay the higher price. The price continues to rise until there is no shortage (Figure 3.10). As shown in the figure, at the price of 1.00 the consumers are only demanding 60, but the suppliers are only supplying 40; therefore a shortage exists.

An excess of quantity supplied, referred to as surplus, means that suppliers of a product are willing to supply more of it than consumers are willing to buy. Figure 3.11 shows a surplus.

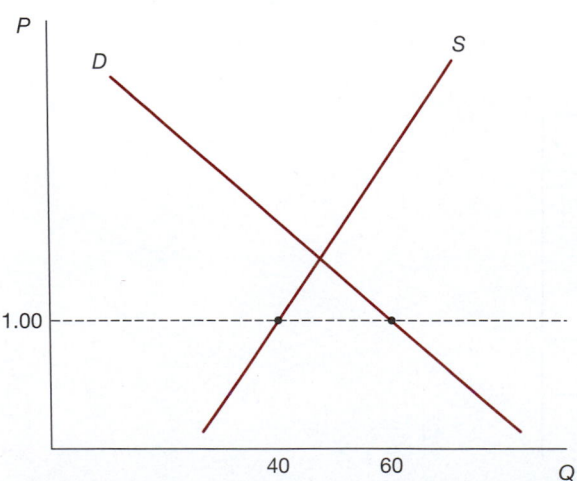

FIGURE 3.10 *When quantity demanded (QD) is greater than quantity supplied (QS), a shortage of product exists.*

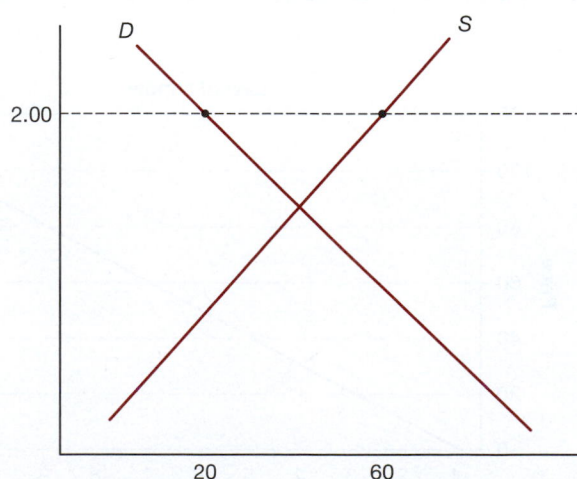

FIGURE 3.11 *When the quantity supplied (QS) is greater than the quantity demanded (QD), there is a surplus.*

In the figure, note that at 20 units demanded there is a supply of 60. This leads to suppliers lowering the price of the product, making it more attractive to consumers by increasing their purchasing power in relation to the product. The price drop increases quantity demand for the product, and price continues to drop until there is no surplus and market equilibrium develops. Put simply, when there is a surplus of a product, its price drops; when there is a shortage, the price rises. Supply and demand react to things besides price change. For example, when pop star Katy Perry endorses a product, people will buy more at every price point, causing the entire demand curve to shift to the right and causing prices to rise.

Zara is a perfect example of utilizing supply and demand and market efficiency. It seeks to discover what the demands of their customers are and reacts to those demands by supplying and pricing their merchandise in the most efficient manner. Zara is a retail chain that is part of the Inditex group division from Spain. In 2012, there were 1,603 Zara stores and 201 Zara kids stores in 78 countries around the world (Inditex.com). According to their website, "Zara's designs are closely linked to their customers." The store managers send daily reports to the Zara corporate office telling them what their customers are requesting. "A non-stop flow of information from stores conveys shoppers' desires and demands, inspiring our 200-person strong creative team" (Intidex.com). This is a perfect example of a fashion business understanding customer needs and then reacting with a rapid turnaround to those needs.

Economic System

Despite the market's influence on an economy, few markets strictly rule the economy. Governments often influence the markets with taxes, regulations, and other practices that can change the availability of certain goods and services, the cost of production, and the prices to acquire them. Economic systems are the systems in place in societies to manage the production, distribution, and consumption of goods and services. Economic systems will be discussed later in the text.

Economic Growth

Economic growth is categorized as supply factors, demand factors, and efficiency factors. There are many factors, such as increases in natural resources, technology developments, modern infrastructures, expansion of well-trained labor, and improved elements of machinery, that aid the expansion of an economy from the supply side. The expansion of the economy from the demand side includes increased output based on economic demand for products and services. The demand for economic growth is rooted in consumers and businesses.

The efficiency factor requires that to reach its production potential, an economy must achieve economic efficiency as well as full employment. As McConnell and Brue state, "the economy must use its resources in the least costly way (productive efficiency) to produce the specific mix of goods and services that maximizes people's well-being (allocative efficiency)." The supply, demand, and efficiency factors all interact, proven when an upset in the balance of any of the components leads to problems with the others.

Summary

In conclusion, this chapter gives you a concrete foundation for the study of fashion from an economic perspective. Microeconomics is the study of looking at consumer behavior through a microscope, analyzing each purchasing decision made by the consumer. Macroeconomics is the study of the big picture of economics such as government regulation, monetary policy, and answering broad economic questions such as, "Is our economy in a recession? What factors inhibit the growth of an economy? Why are nations growing?"

The concepts studied include utility or the total satisfaction a consumer gets from consuming a good or service. Total utility is the total amount of consumer satisfaction and marginal utility is a gain or a loss realized by the consumer when consuming an extra unit or, in the case of fashion, wearing the garment additional times.

You learned that utility encourages a consumer to buy a product and that companies purposefully add value to the product that creates the perception of utility by the consumer.

An extremely important concept is the understanding of economic thought, sometimes referred to as positive and normative economic thought. Positive thinking is an analysis of existing facts and the cause-and-effect relationships currently or in the future for analysis. Normative economic thought answers the question "What should be?", making value judgments based on the current or future conditions of the economy.

Other highlights of the chapter include the understanding and interaction of supply and demand in the marketplace. When supply is high, generally the price of the product decreases; when supply is low and demand is high, the product price is high.

Key Terms

capital   51

cost   50

demand   60

economic growth   63

economic principle   45

economic systems   63

economic value added   48

economics   44

economists   45

economizing problem   45

efficiency   58

externality   54

factors of production   51

human capital   51

infrastructure   51

labor   51

land   51

law of diminishing marginal utility   47

law of diminishing returns   47

macroeconomics   45

marginal   58

marginal analysis   56

marginal utility   46

markdown   60

market equilibrium   62

microeconomics   44

normative economics   59

opportunity cost   50

physical capital   51

positive economics   59

purchasing power   49

reality principle   49

real value   60

scarce resources   44

scarcity   50

specialization   48

spillover effect   54

substitution effect   61

supply   60

total utility   46

utility   46

variable   56

Questions for Review

1. Why is it important for people who work in the fashion industry to study economics?

2. Give a fashion-related example of an opportunity cost.

3. Discuss how an increase in a variable can have an effect on a cost or a benefit.

4. Explain the concept of economic utility from a consumer perspective and from a fashion industry perspective.

5. Discuss the two main approaches to economic analysis.

6. What is the difference between microeconomics and macroeconomics?

7. Explain the "law of demand" and the "law of supply."

8. Define and give a fashion example of the reality principle.

9. Why are fashion companies always giving in to opportunity costs?

10. What is market equilibrium and why is it important?

11. What economic law implies that the consumer will only purchase additional units of a product if the price falls?

12. Explain the phrase, "there is no such thing as a free lunch."

13. List and describe the factors of production.

14. What does the term "marginal" mean to an economist?

15. What would happen in the market for cotton sweaters if the price of cotton increases?

16. Explain the advertising campaign that Benetton used in the late 1980s that brought attention to their company and, as a consequence, increased sales.

17. List and discuss the six components of economic growth.

Critical Thinking

1. Pretend you are the executive vice-president of merchandising for Jam Jeans, a manufacturer of denim jeans for the junior market. Your company created the hot new jean for the "Back to School" season. They are in high demand and your retailers are demanding reorders of the jeans. It is the end of September. If you decide to produce more jeans, you will have to raise the price because the cost of production will increase. Should you increase production? Explain your decision.

   As a fashion executive, you have to make the decision to either produce offshore, where labor costs are lower, knowing that young children are in the labor force contributing to the final product, or produce in the United States, where the cost is higher, but you know that child labor is not involved. What are you going to do and why? What will happen to the end price of your product if it is produced offshore? What if you decide to produce in the United States?

2. Refer back to Figure 3.3 and discuss what type of labor is being used in the picture to produce the fashion garment. Remember to include physical and intellectual labor.

Internet Activities

1. Using the link provided below, complete the online lesson about supply and demand.

   http://www.econedlink.org/lessons/index.cfm?lesson=EM758

2. Read the following online case study about economic growth in India.

   http://www.worldbank.org/depweb/english/modules/economic/gnp/case1.html

   Now, think about the statement "the fashion industry helps economic growth in countries around the world." What is your reaction to the statement? It may be necessary for you to conduct online research to react to the statement.

3. Lava Mind (www.lavamind.com) has many learning tools in the form of simulations that are fun and easy to use. The title of the recommended game to begin your study of economics is "Gazillionaire." Through this game, you "explore new worlds, build a business and make a fortune."

Bibliography

A look back at 25 years of sheepskin. (n.d). Retrieved September, 2008, from UGG Australia, http://www.uggaustralia.com/index.aspx

About the fashion center. (n.d). Retrieved January 2008, from http://www.uggaustrailia.com/experience/history.aspx?p=ex

Bailey, E., Johnson, H., & Punelli. J. (2008). *Conspicuous consumption*. Iowa: Iowa State University.

Brue, S. L., & McConnell, C. R. (2008). *Essentials of economics*. New York: McGraw-Hill.

Gick, E., & Gick, W. (2007). *The devil wears Prada: The fashion formation process in a simultaneous disclosure game between designers and media*, http://www.ces.fas.harvard.edu/publications/docs/pdfs/gick.pdf

Lawson, R., & Peck, H. (2004). Creating agile supply chains in the fashion industry. *International Journal of Retail and Distribution Management*, 32, p. 30.

Lubick, N. (2007). Death from shipping. *Environmental Science Technology*, 41: 24, p. 8206.

Seckler, V. (2008, July 9). Bringing home six figures and few luxuries. *Women's Wear Daily*.

Zara, Inditex. Retrieved 2012, from http://inditex.com/en/press/information/press_kit

FASHION:
BIG
BUSINESS

OBJECTIVES

After reading this chapter, you will be able to:

- Explore the commonalities of fashion retailers
- Gain knowledge of retail models used to sell apparel and accessories
- Examine the types of business ownership
- Identify trends in business ownership

Women usually love what they buy, yet hate two-thirds of what is in their closets.

—MIGNON MCLAUGHLIN, *The Neurotic's Notebook* (1960)

4

Christopher Breward, in his book Fashion, *refers to "an epiphanic moment of engagement between the consumer and fashionable product." The moment of engagement can occur at any time the product is exposed to the fashion consumer. Perhaps it comes while the consumer is reading a magazine, surfing the Internet, watching the latest celebrity on the red carpet, or simply shopping in a store. For the consumer, engagement is an "ah ha" moment during which demand for the product sets in. The consumer's next thoughts are Where am I going to purchase the product? and How much is the product going to cost? If the consumer cannot have the original product, quite possibly he or she will settle for a substitute product. Either way, the selling of the product is important. This chapter is devoted to understanding the big business of fashion, with an emphasis on distributing fashion through various channels of fashion retailing. It covers the understanding of fashion distribution retailers and the monetary contributions made to the overall economy indirectly by the consumer who purchases the fashionable product. You will learn how substantial, propelling, and exciting this particular part of the fashion industry is to the U.S. economy. The discussion includes the commonalities of fashion retailers, types of retailers, forms of fashion retail ownership, and business trends in fashion retailing.*

Introduction

Fashion retailing has evolved from the dry goods merchant store of the mid-1800s. These nineteenth-century merchants offered a one-stop shopping experience more out of necessity than want. They offered a variety of items such as food, farm equipment, cosmetics, textiles, and clothing for consumers to buy. In contrast, today's larger retailer offers three or more types of distribution channels such as brick-and-mortar stores, catalogs, and e-commerce sites. Consequently, customers do not have to travel to a shopping destination such as a mall or store unless they need the product immediately or they want to see the product in person prior to purchase. They can peruse the Internet, catalog, or TV to find their favorite retailer and/or the best product to satisfy their needs and wants 24 hours a day, seven days a week. Technology has changed the way people shop; likewise, product distribution has changed to accommodate consumers.

Through this chapter, you are going to learn about the link between the manufacturer and the customer, the **fashion retailer**. Retailing is the last channel in the fashion supply chain. The entire supply chain typically contributes supplies, services, and materials to the product from the manufacturer of the textile to the retailer that distributes the final product to the ultimate consumer.

The fashion supply chain runs almost parallel to the product development process, about which you learned in Chapter 1. Figure 4.1 provides a comparison of the product development process and the supply chain. Notice how they interact with each other. The focus of this chapter is the retailer, the last stop prior to the consumer owning the product. Since the retailer interacts directly with the consumer, those that work in retail are extremely important to the selling of fashion goods. Whether they are buyers, department store managers, or salespeople, those that work retail can make or break the sale of the product; it is very important that the product sells so that all those involved in making and supplying goods for the final product make a profit.

The chapter begins with an introduction of the commonalities of fashion retailers. Equally important is an examination of the various types of fashion retail businesses or business

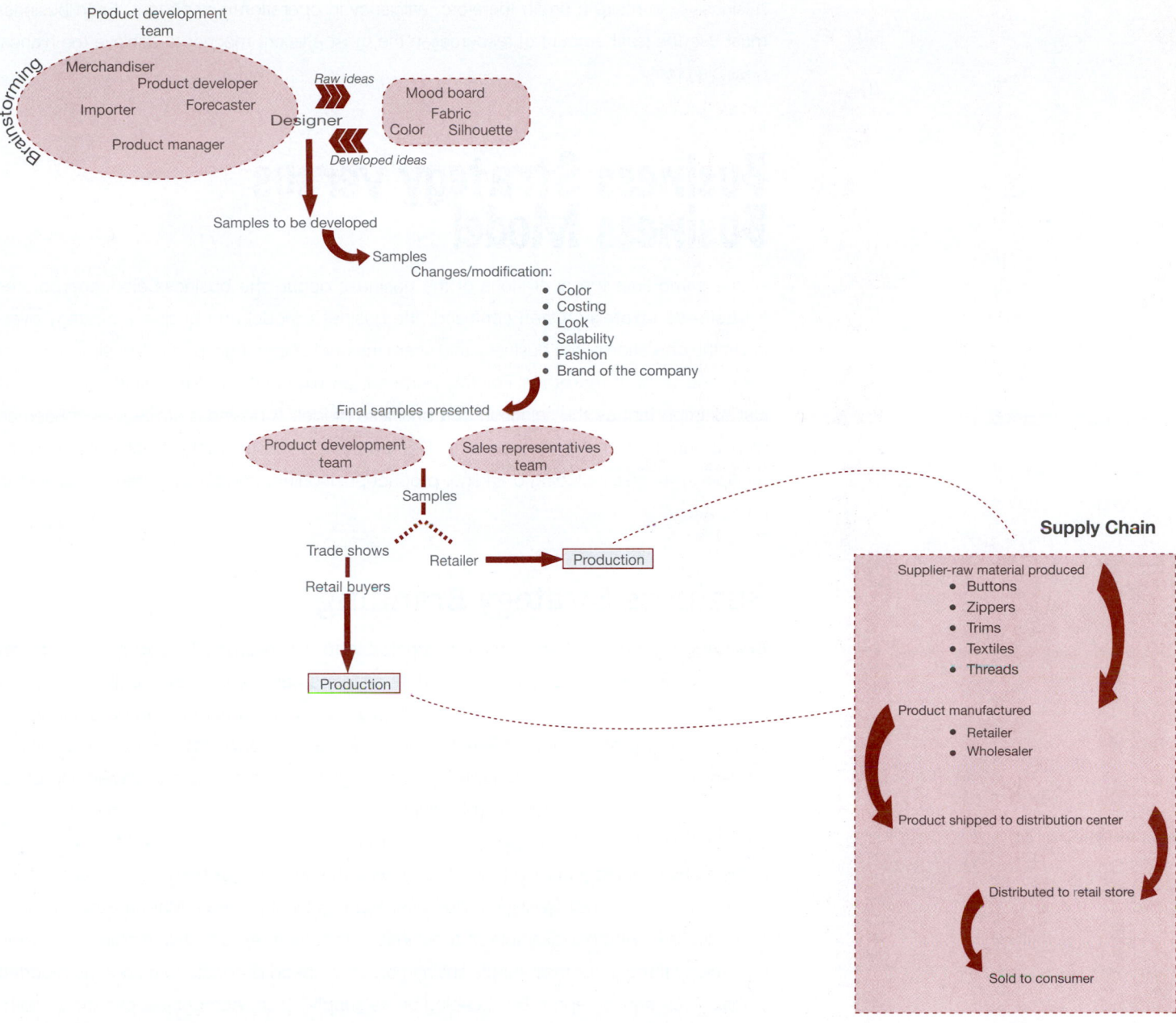

Product Development

Product development team

Brainstorming

Merchandiser
Product developer
Importer   Forecaster
Product manager

Designer

Raw ideas

Developed ideas

Mood board
Fabric
Color   Silhouette

Samples to be developed

Samples
Changes/modification:
- Color
- Costing
- Look
- Salability
- Fashion
- Brand of the company

Final samples presented

Product development team

Sales representatives team

Samples

Trade shows

Retail buyers

Retailer

Production

Production

Supply Chain

Supplier-raw material produced
- Buttons
- Zippers
- Trims
- Textiles
- Threads

Product manufactured
- Retailer
- Wholesaler

Product shipped to distribution center

Distributed to retail store

Sold to consumer

FIGURE 4.1 *Product development and the supply chain compared (Source: Hawa Stwodah).*

models. You will study the large categories of general merchandise stores, **clothing and clothing accessories stores**, miscellaneous store retailers, and non-store retailers as defined by the **North American Industry Classification System**; by doing so, you will understand that without proper distribution channels for the customer to purchase from, the product cannot compete or add value to the economy.

All businesses have a method in which they operate on a daily, monthly, and yearly basis. The purpose of the method is to function in the most efficient way to maximize profit. This is referred to as the **business model**. The business model is simply how a merchant makes money. The business model explains the functions of the business such as the day-to-day operating strategies, expenses of the business, security policies, procedures of the store, and merchandising. "Scholars define a business model as the economic underpinnings of an enterprise's strategy" (Harvard, 2005, p. xv). Keep in mind, it is the goal of all fashion businesses to make a profit; therefore, efficiency in operation is important. Each business must use the least amount of resources in the most efficient manner to achieve the highest possible profit.

Business Strategy versus Business Model

At the same time the operations of the business occur, the business also incorporates a **business strategy**. Often confused, the business model and business strategy overlap in the operation of the business and share the goal of earning a profit. A business cannot have one without the other. For this purpose, an explanation of a business strategy is just as important as the selection of a business model. A business strategy is concerned with competing in the marketplace. Competition takes on many levels and involves multiple strategies including branding, product positioning, and product trendiness, just to name a few.

Business Strategy Branding

Branding a product makes it more recognizable to a consumer. "Use of only one brand name across the entire organization and its offerings can create a powerful image in the mind of the consumer. In time, use of well-established brand names can be stretched to introduce new products into different markets" (Easey, 2009, p. 115). For example, Ralph Lauren began his career in menswear, but through licensing efforts and developing products with his name, the brand Ralph Lauren has become recognizable in other categories such as home fashions, women's wear, children's wear, and accessories. Many who work in the fashion industry believe Ralph Lauren was the first lifestyle brand, followed by many others who turned their labels into lifestyles, such as Donna Karan, Martha Stewart, Reef, and NASCAR. Another example of a business strategy is Aéropostale's plan to invest in technology throughout their supply chain in order to speed products to market as reported in their 2009 annual report. By speeding up its supply chain, Aéropostale can make clothing faster and possibly more efficiently, and be one of the first to distribute the product. Consequently, "while strategy provides differentiation and competitive advantage, the business model explains the economics of how the business works and makes money" (Harvard, 2005, p. xvi).

Fashion Retailer: The Commonalities

It is important to note the four basic commonalities of the fashion retailer as they relate to the business model. As discussed in previous chapters, the first commonality is the customer; second is quick and efficient operations; third is addressing the same business risks; and the fourth is having the right fashionable apparel, footwear, or accessories for sale. These four commonalities working together in a fashion business model create a profit for the fashion merchant. With this in mind, let us examine each of the commonalities.

The Consumer

The consumer is the driving force in the retail business model in the fashion industry. As you learned in Chapter 1, fashion companies used to dictate what was in fashion and what consumers should purchase. However, today's consumer "won't be dictated to. People are more self reliant and cautious and careful for their individuality" (Easey, 2009, p. 23). Consumers, as a result, use much discretion when purchasing; they are required to wear clothing (it is the law), but they are free to choose where to shop and how to spend their money. All consumers are fashion consumers, but their tastes in fashion differ, as do their buying habits. The extent to which someone is fashionable depends upon that person's individual style. For this reason, businesses must establish a profile of their current and future customers.

To profile customers, businesses engage in research activities that assist them in understanding customers' buying preferences and buying habits. An informal method of collecting research is by simply observing the buying and shopping habits of consumers. Coldwater Creek "uses point-of-sale registers to capture sales data, track inventories, monitor traffic and generate EDI." In addition, a company may collect their own data at the point of sale through various means such as an online survey taken by the customer at home or by simply asking for the customer's zip code to determine where most of their customers live. More formal methods, such as subscribing to a professional research firm, can be costly. One of these firms is TRU, a research firm subscribed to by Target, Union Bay, and Victoria's Secret and known as "a global leader in tweens, teens and twenty-something."

If a company desires an aggregate synopsis of how consumers are feeling, they would refer to the economic indicator known as **consumer confidence** (more on consumer confidence in Chapter 7). There are both private and public firms who analyze data and report it as consumer confidence. Also, companies sometimes survey their own customers informally and formally as noted in Kenneth Cole's annual report 2009, which stated, "We listen to tens of thousands of potential and existing customers annually through our market research" (Kenneth Cole, 2009). It is not just about servicing the customer, but also engaging her with employees of the company who can help her make a decision. This facilitates an understanding of the different types of customers that shop for various products associated with fashion. Chapter 9 examines domestic and global consumers.

Quick and Efficient Operations

The second commonality among fashion retailers is timely and efficient operations. These include the daily operations of the business such as transactions with consumers, supply chain management, refunds and returns, and simply general policies and procedures used in the day-to-day running of the business. Some retailers are vertically organized while others use a more traditional means of buying and distributing the product. Figure 4.2 shows how today's retailers are organized.

One important component in any fashion retail model is the quick and efficient way that a fashion business reacts to the demands of their consumers. Part of operations incorporates the quickness of the supply chain, which is very important in reacting to consumers. A slow supply chain (because of a longer manufacturing cycle, for example) potentially leads to lower inventory levels and, depending on the circumstances, means missing the peak of a fashion season, thus retarding the maximization of sales and causing excessive markdowns and discounts. Under Armour's 2009 Annual Report stated, "If we encounter problems with our distribution system, our

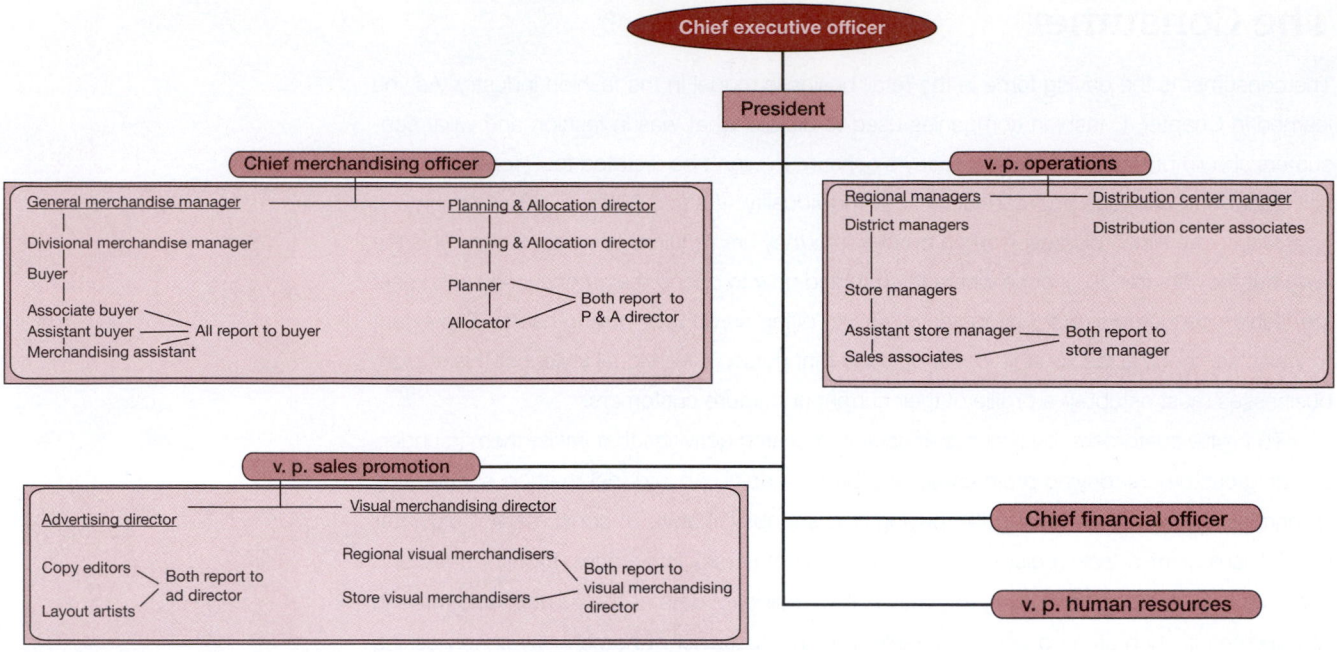

FIGURE 4.2 *Organization of a fashion retailer (Source: Hawa Stwodah).*

ability to deliver our products to the market could be adversely affected." Under Armour operates two distribution centers; should these not run efficiently or if either one is subject to an unforeseen risk such as "software and hardware, power interruptions or other system failures," the efficiency of the distribution channel would be jeopardized and the resulting delay in getting the product to retailers could result in decreased revenue and profit (Under Armour, 2010, p. 17). A quick and efficient supply chain is one in which a store reacts to the demands of the consumer as quickly as possible in order to beat out their competition. Kenneth Cole's 2009 Annual Report stated, "The Company's EDI system also improves the efficiency of responding to customer needs and allows both the customer and the Company to monitor purchases, shipments and invoicing." Keep in mind that meeting the demands of the consumer is the goal and the driver of all fashion retailers.

Risk Factors

Merchants plan and execute objectives of the business every day. In their planning, they must take into account unforeseen conditions, referred to as business risks, which may influence the profit of the business. All fashion retailers face the same three general **risk factors**: unpredictability of the consumer, stability or instability of economic conditions, and efficiency of the supply chain. Although these are not the only risks they share, these three are certainly common among retailers.

Consumers, as discussed earlier, are very unpredictable in what they want and how they spend their money. The economy plays an important role in consumer spending. If there is a slowdown in the macroeconomic environment, as occurred from 2007 to 2009, businesses experience a slowdown in sales because consumer spending, especially discretionary spending, declines. Regardless of the business cycle, businesses must be in constant contact and continually foster relationships with their customers, trying to determine their needs and wants at any given moment. Retailers and other fashion companies spend millions of dollars every year in the never-ending quest of figuring out what the customer wants. For example, Macy's began a localization program intended to better serve the needs of individual communities where Macy's operates stores. "Through My Macy's, we have invested in talent, technology and marketing that allow us to ensure that each and every Macy's store is 'just right' for the customer who shops in that location. We have provided for more local decision-making in every Macy's community. We are tailoring our merchandise assortments, space allocations, service levels, visual merchandising and special events store-by-store" (Macy's, Inc. Annual Report, 2010).

The last common risk is the efficiency of the supply chain. The speed at which the product is produced and distributed to the store has risks associated with it. Time can be a constraint when coordinating production of garments along with receiving trims and other notions that a manufacturer will need to produce a finished product. Once finished, the product must reach the store in a timely manner and be ready for sale at the right time. On the other hand, if the product does not reach the store in a timely manner, the store's inventory will be low, and this will have a negative effect on the profit of the company.

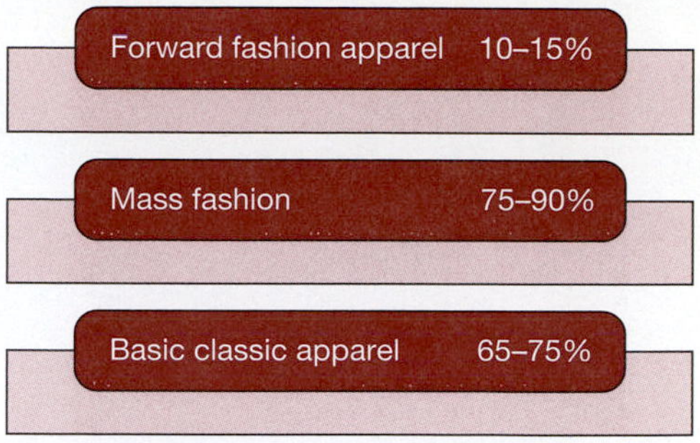

Forward fashion apparel	10–15%
Mass fashion	75–90%
Basic classic apparel	65–75%

FIGURE 4.3 *Percent of floor space devoted to new fashion items.*

The Fashion Product

The fashion product must be present for a retailer to earn a reputation as a fashion retailer. Fashion products range from apparel to cars. Because of licensing, fashion designer names can be seen on an array of things from candy to fabrics. Any commodity that is considered fashionable involves a subjective perspective on the part of the consumer. Just as there are different levels of fashion consumers, there are different levels of fashion products. Not all products in a store's inventory are rooted in fashion; some are classics, some are fads, and other items fulfill basic customer needs.

Typically, the majority of people wear fashion at a given time, while the minority will want to wear something else. It is for this reason that not all of the inventory should be rooted in fashionable items. Retailers largely provide an assortment of clothing in their stores. A certain percentage of clothing must be classic items to appeal to those consumers who are not as fashion forward. These consumers purchase clothing with a utilitarian purpose in mind. It may be winter and they need a new coat. Or perhaps the consumer is a lawyer who needs a conservative wardrobe consisting of navy blue and black suits to maintain her professional image. Figure 4.3 shows the percentage of a typical retail floor space that is devoted to fashion in various types of fashion retailers.

The sales drivers for fashion retailers are the "new look" in fashion. This look can be a fashion trend, a new color, a new design, a shape, or silhouette. Fashion creates emotions in people, and these emotions create desire. If the desire produces a purchase, the emotions of consumers become an economic driver.

Fashion Retailers

North American Industry Classification System

The North American Industry Classification System, or NAICS (pronounced "Nakes"), classifies the types of fashion business models as listed in the U.S. Census Bureau. The U.S. government collects and analyzes all statistical data related to businesses using this classification system. It allows the government to categorize data such as sales, inventories, cost of goods sold, importing, exporting, and other data relative to running a business for two purposes. The first purpose allows NAICS to "facilitate the collection, tabulation, presentation and analysis of data relating to establishments [businesses,]" and the second purpose is to "promote uniformity and comparability in the presentation and analysis of statistical data describing the North American economy" (NAICS). Every business has a classification number for grouping like industries and businesses together. NAICS is used by many companies—such as Dun and Bradstreet, Hoovers, and Standard and Poors— who are in the business of selling data about companies and industries (NAICS). The NAICS classification numbers covered in this chapter range from 448 for Clothing and Clothing Accessories category to 452 for the General Merchandise Stores category. Refer to Figure 4.4 for a better understanding of the listing of the categories explained in the first part of the chapter.

General Merchandise Stores

NAICS 452

According to the U.S. Census Bureau, "Industries in the General Merchandise Stores subsector retail new general merchandise from fixed point-of-sale locations." Establishments in this subsector are unique in that they have the equipment and staff

FIGURE 4.4 *This is an example of category listing for clothing and clothing accessories in a department store.*

2007 NAICS
This is an example of a category listing for clothing and clothing accessories stores. Notice that each type of clothing store starts with 448. As numbers are added to the 448 they are specific to the category.

448	**Clothing and Clothing Accessories Stores**
4481	**Clothing Stores**
44811	Mens Clothing Stores
448110	Mens Clothing Stores
44812	Womens Clothing Stores
448120	Womens Clothing Stores
44813	Childrens and Infants' Clothing Stores
448130	Childrens and Infants' Clothing Stores
44814	Family Clothing Stores
448140	Family Clothing Stores
44815	Clothing Accessories Stores
448150	Clothing Accessories Stores
44819	Other Clothing Stores
448190	Other Clothing Stores
4482	**Shoe Stores**
44821	Shoe Stores
448210	Shoe Stores
4483	**Jewelry, Luggage, and Leather Goods Stores**
44831	Jewelry Stores
448310	Jewelry Stores
44832	Luggage and Leather Goods Stores
448320	Luggage and Leather Goods Stores

capable of retailing a large variety of goods from a single location, "This includes a variety of display equipment and staff trained to provide information on many lines of products" (U.S. Census Bureau, General Merchandise Store). A general merchandise store is a main category or sector of stores that encompasses and crosses over with department and discount department stores. Although these types of stores share some of the same traits, a true general merchandise store can be described as a retail storefront selling a variety of goods without emphasis on a particular product line and having one local point-of-sale area in the store (U.S. Census Bureau). The idea of a general merchandise store can be related to local convenience stores. These stores were the first to grasp the ideas that many big-box stores now fully take advantage of when preparing their retail fronts. Some of these ideas include offering a variety of lines like food, home goods, soft goods, apparel and accessories, and dry goods from a single store location. These stores exhibit other "convenient" qualities, such as employing a staff that is familiar with many different lines of product, rather than focusing on just one department or product category (U.S. Census Bureau).

For all reporting purposes, the general merchandise store encompasses a large category of department stores, discount stores, and warehouse/big-box stores. The following sections will define the different subsectors of the general merchandise store.

Subsector: Department Stores

NAICS 4521

A department store is a subsector of a general merchandise store. In this type of store, the selling floor has numerous departments that sell an assortment of various types of merchandise ranging from clothing to electronics. Soft lines in a department store consist of clothing, home fashions, shoes, accessories, and cosmetics. Hard lines in a department store consist of furniture, electronics, hardware, and bicycles. Not all department stores sell all of these various categories of goods. Figure 4.5 shows the number of different types of department stores based on the products and services they sell. Not all products and services are listed in the table, but the total number of U.S. department stores and sales of those department stores is included. Examples of department stores include Macy's, Dillard's, Neiman Marcus, Saks Fifth Avenue, and Nordstrom. Refer to Figure 4.6 for a picture of a typical department store.

Subsector: Discount Department Stores

NAICS 452112

As defined by the U.S. Census Bureau, "This U.S. industry comprises establishments known as department stores that have central customer checkout areas, generally in the front of the store, and that may have additional cash registers located in one or more individual departments. Department stores in this industry sell a wide range of general merchandise (except fresh, perishable foods)."

A discount department store does not have the ambience of a department store. It is airy and large. Generally, upon entering the discount store, a consumer will get a shopping cart,

FIGURE 4.5 *Business patterns showing department stores that are in the United States with the number of employees they have and the payroll they produce each year. The difference between a firm and an establishment is that a firm is only one free-standing store that conducts business. An establishment may conduct businesses at several places. A department store carries a variety of merchandise such as women's wear, men's wear, children's wear, home fashions, shoes, accessories, cosmetics, and giftware (Source: U.S. Census 2008).*

NAICS number		Employment size	Number of firms	Number of established	Employment	Annual payroll ($1,000)
4521	Department stores	1: Total	138	8,813	1,292,007	24,009,834
4521	Department stores	2: 0-4	84	84	91	6,519
4521	Department stores	3: 5-9	15	15	0	0
4521	Department stores	4: 10-19	4	4	47	1,435
4521	Department stores	5: <20	103	103	0	0
4521	Department stores	6: 20-99	7	7	345	6,124
4521	Department stores	7: 100-499	3	4	317	11,109
4521	Department stores	8: <500	113	114	882	26,230
4521	Department stores	9: 500+	25	8,699	1,291,125	23,983,604
45211	Department stores	1: Total	138	8,813	1,292,007	24,009,834
45211	Department stores	2: 0-4	84	84	91	6,519
45211	Department stores	3: 5-9	15	15	0	0
45211	Department stores	4: 10-19	4	4	47	1,435
45211	Department stores	5: <20	103	103	0	0
45211	Department stores	6: 20-99	7	7	345	6,124
45211	Department stores	7: 100-499	3	4	317	11,109
45211	Department stores	8: <500	113	114	882	26,230
45211	Department stores	9: 500+	25	8,699	1,291,125	23,983,604
452111	Department stores (except discount department stores)	1: Total	65	3,733	550,382	9,934,857
452111	Department stores (except discount department stores)	2: 0-4	32	32	0	2,742
452111	Department stores (except discount department stores)	3: 5-9	7	7	0	0
452111	Department stores (except discount department stores)	4: 10-19	2	2	0	0
452111	Department stores (except discount department stores)	5: <20	41	41	93	4,550
452111	Department stores (except discount department stores)	6: 20-99	4	4	149	2,196
452111	Department stores (except discount department stores)	7: 100-499	1	1	0	0
452111	Department stores (except discount department stores)	8: <500	46	46	314	11,117
452111	Department stores (except discount department stores)	9: 500+	19	3,687	550,068	9,923,740
452112	Discount department stores	1: Total	76	5,080	0	0
452112	Discount department stores	2: 0-4	52	52	0	0
452112	Discount department stores	3: 5-9	8	8	0	0
452112	Discount department stores	4: 10-19	2	2	0	0
452112	Discount department stores	5: <20	62	62	0	0
452112	Discount department stores	6: 20-99	3	3	0	0
452112	Discount department stores	7: 100-499	2	3	0	0
452112	Discount department stores	8: <500	67	68	568	15,113
452112	Discount department stores	9: 500+	9	5,012	0	0

Note: The above chart is taken from the U. S. Census 2008 Business Patterns showing Department stores that are in the United States with the number of employees they have and the payroll they produce each year. The difference between a firm and an establishment is that a firm is only one free-standing store that conducts business. An establishment may conduct business at several places. A department store carries a variety of merchandise such as women's wear, men's wear, children's wear, home fashions, shoes, accessories, cosmetics, and gift ware.

unlike in a department store. The checkout stations are located at the front of the store (Figure 4.7), as opposed to a department store where you find checkout stations in most departments. Also, the merchandise offered for sale has price points below those of a department store. A discount store carries brand names; the brands are more established but may have lost their newness and fashion-forward status, though they still maintain a status of product quality. Discount stores such as Target and Kohl's carry fashion merchandise with designer labels such as Kohl's Simply Very by Vera Wang or Liz Claiborne at JC Penney.

Marketresearch.com (published by First Research, Inc.) reports, "The U.S. discount department store industry includes about 5,000 stores with combined annual revenue of $130 billion" and the "major products sold include apparel (20 percent of sales); personal care products (15 percent); groceries (7 percent); and toys (6 percent)." Figure 4.8 shows sales figures of discount stores.

FIGURE 4.6 *Typical department store (Source: Shutterstock).*

Other General Merchandise Stores: Warehouse Clubs/Supercenters

NAICS 452910

"This industry comprises establishments known as warehouse clubs, superstores or supercenters primarily engaged in retailing a general line of groceries in combination with general lines of new merchandise, such as apparel, furniture, and appliances" according to the U.S. Census Bureau. The terms "warehouse club" and "supercenter" are sometimes used interchangeably. They define those types of stores that make a profit from selling quantities of items as opposed to selling individual items at a high markup price. The store itself is very large and open, with

FIGURE 4.7 *In a discount store, the checkout stations are in the front of the store as opposed to a department store where you find the checkout stations in most departments (Source: Alamy).*

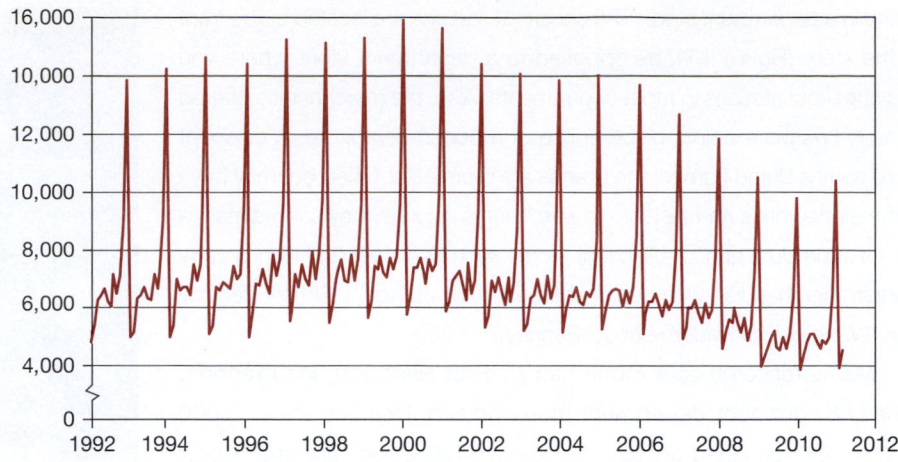

FIGURE 4.8 *Sales figures of various discount stores from 2007 to 2011 (Source: US Census).*

FIGURE 4.9 *Typical big box store (Source: Alamy).*

abundant retail space. The box-like shape of the store gives rise to the term "big box" (Figure 4.9). Typically, these stores contain more than 50,000 square feet (Hoovers). According to Michael Clapman, warehouse clubs average 13,000 square feet.

According to Hoovers, Warehouse Clubs and Superstores has "20 companies with 4,000 stores and combined revenue of about $360 billion." BJ's, Costco, and Sam's Club have sales of $142 billion worldwide. Of this, $1,988,000 was in apparel sales. The warehouse store business model requires customers to pay a membership fee, which is renewable on a yearly basis. Buying in bulk and large volume of merchandise, the assortments are substantial; however, they generally stock "4,000 and 8,000 stock keeping units (SKUs)" (Hoovers). The largest category of business is dry groceries with 11 to 11.5 percent of total sales (excluding candy). Frozen food and tobacco each represent over five percent of sales. Refer to Figure 4.10 for sales of various warehouse clubs from 2005 to 2009. The warehouse store's target customer is not seeking the latest fashion but does recognize established brand names. Most of the apparel and accessories offered for sale are made specifically for the company, which means that it is very rare to find those products in another distribution arena.

Retailing Formats

Not all categories of stores are brick-and-mortar stores. The classification of the retailer through the NAICS system refers to brick-and-mortar distribution. Retailers have other ways in which to distribute products, and the retail survey takes this into account when asking questions relating to sales. Next you will learn about the more contemporary ways in which fashion retailers are reaching their consumers.

All Other General Merchandise Stores

NAICS 45299

This subsector is comprised of establishments primarily engaged in retailing new goods in general merchandise stores (except department stores, warehouse clubs, superstores, and supercenters). "These establishments retail a general line of new merchandise, such

FIGURE 4.10 *Sales of the warehouse/big box stores in a two-year period.*

BJ's	10.63 billion
Sam's	46.10 billion
Costco	306 million

as apparel, automotive parts, dry goods, hardware, groceries, housewares, or home furnishings, and other lines in limited amounts, with none of the lines predominating" (U.S. Census Bureau).

Clothing Stores

NAICS 4481

Under the heading of clothing stores, 12 categories of stores have NAICS codes specific to them (to follow in this chapter) and all begin with the numbers 448. There are four specific subsectors of clothing stores: women's, men's, children's, and family stores, and all are described by the U.S. Census Bureau as "Industries in the Clothing and Clothing Accessories Stores subsector retail new clothing and clothing accessories merchandise from fixed point-of-sale locations. Establishments in this subsector have similar display equipment and staff that is knowledgeable regarding fashion trends and the proper match of styles, colors, and combinations of clothing and accessories to the characteristics and tastes of the customer."

Overall, the specialty store offers specific products of a general nature, similar products, or complementary products. A **specialty store** can offer one brand that might also be the name of the store; for example, Ann Taylor is the name of both a store and the brand sold in that store (Figure 4.11). The same goes for the retailer Gap. Another type of specialty store is the **mom-and-pop store**, which generally carries a small inventory of very specialized merchandise. For example, a women's boutique that targets 18- to 34-year-old women and carries a variety of brand labels is considered a specialty store. Specialty stores can be chain stores or one of a kind, which would be considered a mom-and-pop store. In a specialty store, a customer will receive special attention due to the smaller size of the store and the nature of the products they carry.

In 2010 sales for stores offering apparel and accessories reached just over $219.3 billion (U.S. Census Bureau). In 1999 sales were estimated around $262 billion. See Figure 4.12 for comparisons of sales from 1992 to 2009.

FIGURE 4.11 *Photo of an Ann Taylor store where the store is the brand (Source: Alamy).*

FIGURE 4.12 *Comparison of sales from 1992 to 2009 (Source: US Census).*

NAICS Code	Kind of business	1992	1993	1994	1995	1996	1997	1998	1999	2000	2001	2002	2003	2004	2005	2006	2007	2008	2009
448	Clothing and clothing access. stores	120,346	125,001	129,341	131,593	136,851	140,565	149,433	160,043	167,968	168,858	174,604	180,350	186,096	191,842	197,588	203,335	2,16,087	2,04,866
4481	Clothing stores	85,459	88,222	90,260	90,809	93,820	97,831	104,237	111,792	118,210	117,573	121,518	125,463	129,408	133,352	137,297	141,242	1,58,075	1,52,246
44811	Men's clothing stores	10,185	9,968	10,039	9,322	9,554	10,077	10,204	9,675	9,515	9,632	9,590	9,549	9,508	9,467	9,425	9,384	8,534	7,707
44812	Women's clothing stores	31,840	32,377	30,611	28,723	28,266	27,851	28,363	29,581	31,480	28,633	28,380	28,126	27,873	27,620	27,366	27,113	38,351	35,780
44814	Family clothing stores	33,159	35,311	38,118	40,014	42,275	45,259	50,169	55,333	58,928	60,326	63,534	66,742	69,950	73,158	76,367	79,575	83,001	81,464
44819	Other clothing stores	5,325	5,553	6,026	6,645	7,148	7,359	7,506	8,284	8,852	9,131	9,564	9,997	10,430	10,863	11,296	11,729	11,873	11,406

Men's Clothing Stores

NAICS 448110

The U.S. Census Bureau describes men's clothing stores in the following statement, "This industry comprises establishments primarily engaged in retailing a general line of new men's and boys' clothing. These establishments may provide basic alterations, such as hemming, taking in or letting out seams, or lengthening or shortening sleeves."

Women's Clothing Stores

NAICS 448120

The U.S. Census Bureau explains the women's clothing stores industry as follows: "This industry comprises establishments primarily engaged in retailing a general line of new women's, misses' and juniors' clothing, including maternity wear. These establishments may provide basic alterations, such as hemming, taking in or letting out seams, or lengthening or shortening sleeves." According to IBISWorld.com, women's clothing stores have annual revenue of $48.5 billion with profit of about $1.6 billion. There are 43,505 women's clothing stores in the United States. The four major companies in this industry are Charming Shoppes, Limited Brands, Ann Taylor stores, and Talbots (Figure 4.13), which collectively comprise approximately 18.8 percent of women's clothing stores. Figure 4.14 shows the sales growth and/or decline of the top women's clothing stores over the past/future eight years.

FIGURE 4.13 *Talbots is one of the four major women's clothing companies (Source: Alamy).*

Family Clothing Stores

NAICS 448140

Competitors in the family clothing store sector include department stores like Macy's and JC Penney and specialty retailers like Gap. The NAICS description of the industry is as follows: "This industry comprises establishments primarily engaged in retailing a general line of new clothing for men, women, and children, without specializing in sales for an individual gender or age group.

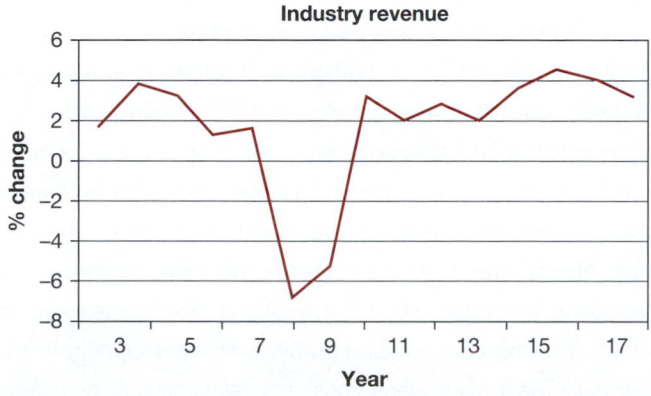

FIGURE 4.14 *Growth and decline of women's clothing stores over the past ten years.*

These establishments may provide basic alterations, such as hemming, taking in or letting out seams, or lengthening or shortening sleeves" (U.S. Census Bureau).

Nonstore Retailers

NAICS 454

Within the nonstores sector, 16 subsectors further define the category. According to the U.S. Census,

Industries in the Nonstore Retailers subsector retail merchandise using methods, such as the broadcasting of infomercials, the broadcasting and publishing of direct-response advertising, the publishing of paper and electronic catalogs, door-to-door solicitation, in-home demonstration, selling from portable stalls and distribution through vending machines. Establishments in this subsector include mail-order houses, vending machine operators, home delivery sales, door-to-door sales, party plan sales, electronic shopping, and sales through portable stalls (e.g., street vendors, except food). Establishments engaged in the direct sale (i.e., nonstore) of products, such as home heating oil dealers and newspaper delivery service providers are included in this subsector.

Electronic Shopping and Mail-Order Houses

NAICS 45411

The U.S. Census Bureau uses NAICS 45411 to identify the electronic shopping and **mail order** industry. "This industry comprises establishments primarily engaged in retailing all types of merchandise using non-store means, such as catalogs, toll-free telephone numbers, or electronic media like computers or interactive television. Included in this industry are establishments primarily engaged in retailing from catalog showrooms of mail-order houses" (U.S. Census Bureau).

Home Shopping

NAICS 454113

Television shopping, also called home shopping, has evolved over the past decades by using hosts along with celebrities, entrepreneurs, and designers/artists to feature and demonstrate the use of a variety of products to consumers. After they are shown the featured product, consumers place orders by calling in and paying most commonly with either credit or debit cards (Harvard, 2005). Figure 4.15 is a photograph of a QVC host and guest. The top two competitors in the television shopping business are QVC (Quality, Value, Convenience) and HSN (Home Shopping Network). While originally home shopping was presumed to sell inexpensive and low-quality goods, today some of the biggest powerhouse brands, such as Yves Saint Laurent, Clinique, and Marc Bouwer, are proudly featured on these shopping channels (Int'l Cosmetic News). The multibillion-dollar home shopping industry seeks to inform and amuse its audience with hosts who have engaging personalities and can relate to the consumer, inevitably resulting in more sales (Kaplan). Home shopping has been seen as a great sales opportunity, as it establishes consumer relationships, provides education and entertainment, and lastly offers an additional form of product distribution (Harvard, 2005).

FIGURE 4.15 *One of the two competitors in the television shopping business is QVC (Source: Alamy).*

Television shopping represents every aspect of the fashion industry, from clothing to home goods, cosmetics, and jewelry; the outlets for consumers are endless.

Although for a while it seemed as though technological innovations were aiding television shopping, companies are now struggling to develop ways in which they can keep sales up. As the younger generation grows, their interest in television shopping shrinks, as seemingly anything can be purchased via the Internet. Both QVC and HSN have established websites to maintain a presence in the market. HSN.com is ranked among the top ten e-commerce websites (Kaplan). In order to continually appeal to their established market, HSN has entered into a partnership with Comcast that will allow viewers to "shop by remote." Ultimately, this will eliminate the need to call in to place an order, as consumers will be able to purchase items seen on TV with their remote control. Top competitors in the cable and home shopping industries have raced to get access to this technology to keep both industries strong (Goetzl). Figure 4.16 shows the top home shopping channels in sales from 2001 to 2010.

FIGURE 4.16 *The top home shopping channels in sales from 2001 to 2010.*

- Home Shopping Retailer TV										
	2001	2002	2003	2004	2005	2006	2007	2008	2009	2010
QVC	3,894	4,362	4,889	5,687	6,501	7,000	7,397	7,285	7,352	7807
HSN	1,830	1,922	2,230	2,248	3,051	3,290	2,908	2,824	2,750	2967
ShopNBC	462	540	591	624	692	767	782	568	528	562
Shop at home	178	196	238	293	359	—	—	—	—	—
Sales reported in $million										
Top Home Shopping Channels Sales from 2001 to 2010 http://files.shareholder.com/downloads/ABEA-4CW8ZW/1538292648x0x466763/6AC82A25-9B40-4A49-9776-E53A5D2DFFD7/LibertyAnnual4-2007.PDF http://files.shareholder.com/downloads/ABEA-4CW8ZW/1538292648x0x491124/BBB72533-6EE7-4451-9924-499D37F4C963/Liberty_Media_Corporation_Annual_Report_2010.pdf http://hoovers.api.edgar-online.com/EFX_dll/EdgarPro.dll?FetchFilingHTML1?SessionID=9VFGFW0T83rDSCF&ID=7747269#D10K_HTM_TX154069_8 http://subscriber.hoovers.com.proxy.library.vcu.edu/H/company360/financialHistory.html?companyId=16246000000000 http://academic.mintel.com.proxy.library.vcu.edu/sinatra/oxygen_academic/my_reports/display/id=226633&anchor=atom/displaytables/id=226633										

Contemporary Channels of Fashion Retailing

Two contemporary channels of fashion retailing include the pop-up store and the kiosk. These are both new methods in the distribution of apparel and accessories. A company might use a pop-up store or kiosk in conjunction with their main store or perhaps as a start-up but will not generally use these as their only channel of fashion retail.

Pop-Up Stores

A pop-up store is a temporary store that opens for a specific period of time. The pop-up store idea is one of the most innovative retailing trends to occur in the past 10 years. In this model, a store opens in a space, garners attention from consumers, captures as much money as it can, and exits. It is advantageous to both the consumer and the business because a pop-up store can serve many purposes. See Figure 4.17 for a picture of the Gucci pop-up sneaker store that opened in New York City in August 2009. Gucci refers to their stores as "Gucci Icon-Temporary" (hypebeast.com) (Edelson). The pop-up does not require a large monetary investment. A temporary store opens in a vacant space and can cost anywhere from $150,000 to $1,000,000 (Sherman). The goals of pop-up stores range from trying to build a particular brand to introducing a new brand or serving as a test store to see if it is viable to open up a permanent store in the location. "The pop-ups may have a museum or art-gallery-like feel, especially when a company is selling a brand, not merely products" (Sherman).

FIGURE 4.17 *"Gucci Icon-Temporary" a pop-up store that is temporary (Source: Alamy).*

Kiosks

A kiosk, often referred to as a mall cart, is a temporary space that is run by a merchant in high-traffic locations such as airports, malls, and sports centers. Kiosks are most often specialty stores and make up a $10 billion industry (Figure 4.18). The phenomenon of the kiosk business has only grown throughout the years, as this type of business allows the **licensee** of the kiosk greater flexibility and less risk (as there is virtually no overhead, low stock, minimal marketing and operating expenses, and the ability to operate on a month-to-month lease). The initial investment in a kiosk or mall cart ranges from $2,000 to $10,000, depending on size and location, and merchants are often able to quickly pay off these fees with their high markups and low expenses (Entrepreneur). Kiosk businesses can encompass every aspect of the fashion industry, from jewelry cleaning to sunglasses, cosmetics, and bed linens, and the uniqueness and flexibility of having a kiosk leaves the licensee with endless possibilities for profit.

Technology has further enabled the idea of the kiosk. Automated retail stores, or ZoomShops, are the most recent offspring of the traditional stationary kiosk. These electronic stations accept only debit or credit cards, have higher price points, and do not require any employees (Morrill, 2008). Retailers such as Macy's, Best Buy, Apple, Elizabeth Arden, and Coty have introduced these "vending machines" in high-traffic areas to sell their electronics and high-end cosmetics and fragrances. This trend began in Japan, where virtually everything

FIGURE 4.18 *A kiosk such as this is a temporary space in a high-traffic location (Source: Hawa Stwodah).*

is sold from an electronic kiosk, and has slowly started to catch on in the United States (Birchall, 2008). Although the trend has not fully penetrated the fashion industry, it seems as though this could be a new movement in retailing.

Types of Business Ownership

Ownership of a business can be organized in different legal arrangements. Sole proprietorships, partnerships, and corporations are the three primary forms of business ownership. The type of ownership a company assumes is characterized by the configuration, size, and domain of the business and the organizational configuration best suited for that business. Each type of ownership is distinguished by the specific legal rights and responsibilities as well as advantages and disadvantages that are unique to each form of ownership (Table 4.1).

Sole Proprietorships

A sole proprietorship is a business that is owned and operated by one person. All legal rules and regulations are the responsibility of the one owner. Owners, or proprietors, typically supervise the operation of the business. It is this type of ownership that shaped

TABLE 4.1

Advantages and disadvantages of the types of business ownerships

Type of business	Advantages	Disadvantages
Sole Proprietorship-A business owned by and operated by one owner.	1. Easy to form 2. Owner makes all decisions 3. Takes all profits 4. Easy to sell and transfer ownership 5. Accounting is very simple compared to a partnership and corporation	1. Unlimited financial responsibility 2. Personal finances and business finances are blended into one 3. Owner has all financial liability 4. Owner has all personal liability 5. Time consuming for one person to operate a business
Partnership-Relationship existing between two or more persons who join to carry on a trade or business.	1. Risks of operating a business are shared 2. Each partner generally complements each other's skill set. 3. Easy to form 4. Few government regulations 5. Life cycle of a partnership generally longer than a sole proprietorship	1. Unlimited financial responsibility 2. Unlimited liability for decisions by each partner 3. Interpersonal conflicts arise 4. Dissolving a partnership is more difficult than a sole proprietorship 5. Profits are shared
Corporation-A legal entity that has the ability to acquire resources, own assets, produce and sell products, incur debt, extend credit, sue and be sued, and perform the functions of any other type of enterprise.	1. It is considered a legal entity under the law with more opportunities for access to capital 2. Attracts many investors 3. Vast management expertise 4. Transferring ownership is simple 5. Addition or subtraction of owners does not disrupt business	1. Increased tax burden 2. Increased level of government intervention 3. Managers direct the day-to-day operations of the company and not every stockholder 4. Dividends paid to stock holders are considered personal income, which can create a tax burden to stockholders 5. Board of Directors oversees the management of the company, which means at times decisions made can benefit their own self-interest and not the whole company

American retailing. Many of today's well-known retailers, such as JC Penney (James Cash Penney), Macy's (Rowland Hussey Macy), and Walmart (Sam Walton), were founded by sole proprietors (Figure 4.19).

Today, over 90 percent of all retailers and 72 percent of all businesses are sole proprietorships (U.S. Census Bureau). However, these sole proprietorships generate only 20 percent of sales. Also known as mom-and-pop stores, these stores are most often comprised of one location and are managed by the owner. Mom-and-pop stores are ordinarily specialty stores due to the larger capital and space requirements of department stores. There are several advantages and disadvantages to the sole proprietorship.

There are many advantages that make the sole proprietorship attractive for an entrepreneur. As a business with one owner, the sole proprietorship is easy to form and easy to dissolve, which accounts for the large number of sole proprietorships in the United States. There are no special legal requirements other than obtaining necessary licenses and permits.

The number-one reason people establish a sole proprietorship is for the control it offers. There is no one to answer to when a sole proprietor makes a decision regarding the business; the owner can make all decisions regarding the business without the counsel of a partner, giving the proprietor the flexibility to move the firm in any direction deemed appropriate. A sole proprietorship provides autonomy and independence, which gives the owner the freedom to live life the way he or she sees fit. A proprietor can take a vacation or a day off without asking permission from the "boss" (assuming they can be away from the business for a period of time). A proprietor can work his or her own hours.

FIGURE 4.19 *Sam Walton, the founder of Walmart (Source: Superstock).*

Another key advantage is that a sole proprietor does not have to share profits. Once the taxes are paid, the remainder belongs to the owner. There is no separation between the individual and the firm, and thus the accounting is very simple in a sole proprietorship. The business is simply an extension of the owner. The earnings of the business are considered the earnings of the owner and become part of his or her personal income. The proprietor pays personal taxes and is not subject to the same taxes as a corporation.

The American government has very few rules and regulations regarding sole proprietorships. There are no special conditions to complete to start a proprietorship. Once the proprietorship is established, government intervention is minimal. Furthermore, it is simple to sell or transfer the business at the discretion of the owner. It is as easy to end as it was to begin. If an owner decides that he or she no longer wants to be in business, the business can be sold or closed. State and local governments must be notified and any unpaid debts must be addressed, and then the sole proprietorship no longer exists.

The primary disadvantage to a sole proprietorship is unlimited financial responsibility. Because the sole proprietorship is an extension of the owner, the owner's personal finances and business finances are melded together as one. Therefore, if the business suffers economic hardship, the owner can expect to suffer economic hardship. All monetary obligations of the business become the personal obligations of the owner and a creditor can legally seek to take not only the owner's business assets but his or her personal assets as well. The example below demonstrates the personal liability of a sole proprietorship.

A fashion merchandising graduate opens a small bridal business on the Internet. The business of huge, lavish expensive weddings increased over the past four years and she orders $200,000 worth of bridal party apparel. After a few months, the recession hit the economy very hard and consequently, the bridal business. The supplier of the wedding gowns is seeking payment as soon as possible. The bridal salon owner cannot pay the supplier, or any other creditor, due to low demand for wedding apparel. The owner is personally liable and responsible for $200,000. The supplier has the right to sue the owner of the bridal salon, which means that any of her personal possessions can be taken from her.

Another major obstacle is a lack of capital. All businesses must have capital (money and other assets) to operate. Without the benefit of an established business and the lack of legitimacy that a corporation offers, raising funds can be difficult. Investors are not likely to invest in a sole proprietorship. Therefore, sole proprietors must rely on personal assets and loans to finance their businesses, severely limiting the amount of money available to start, operate, or invest in the business.

Often, people enter into sole proprietorships with limited management expertise and without the necessary skill sets, knowledge, and experience to handle all aspects of the business. A sole proprietorship is limited to the knowledge that the owner possesses. No one is an expert in everything, and deficiency in critical areas can cause proprietorships to fail.

Another issue that is frequently overlooked with a proprietorship is the amount of time required to run a business. The commitment is enormous and running a business is hard work. More often than not, the owner ends up spending more time working in the business than he or she would working for someone else. Most business owners will agree that this is time well spent; nevertheless, the time requirement is great and must not be discounted.

Lack of continuity is another concern for a sole proprietorship. Because a sole proprietorship is not a separate legal entity, it usually terminates when the owner becomes disabled, retires, or dies. As a result, the sole proprietorship lacks continuity and does not have perpetual existence like other business organizations.

Partnerships

A partnership is the relationship existing between two or more persons who come together to carry on a business. Each person contributes money, property, labor, or skill and expects to share the profits and losses of the business. Partners share the risks, profits, and losses. Partnerships are the natural outgrowth of the sole proprietorship.

Partnerships make up almost 10 percent of the businesses in the United States and are responsible for about 8 percent of the sales volume (U.S. Census Bureau). It is a common misconception that all partnerships are small businesses. In fact some partnerships are rather large. For example, Dolce and Gabbana (Figure 4.20) began their partnership in 1982 and in 2007 reported sales of $1.34 billion. Currently, the firm produces shoes, accessories, menswear, women's wear, and children's clothing. In addition, the company distributes fragrances, eyewear, and footwear through various licensing agreements. Dolce and Gabbana operates 93 stores and 11 factory outlets worldwide and its products are sold in over 80 countries around the world.

Like sole proprietorships, partnerships are easy to form. There is considerably less red tape than when forming a corporation. Once the proper licenses and permits have been obtained, a partnership is in business. It is prudent for the partners to draft a partnership agreement to elucidate their understanding of issues such as profit sharing and the continuity of the business in the event a partner retires or dies. Although a partnership agreement is not required by law, a well-crafted document anticipates future disagreements and helps resolve disputes before they develop.

FIGURE 4.20 *Dolce and Gabbana, long-time business partners (Source: Alamy).*

Another plus for a partnership arrangement is increased management expertise. Partnerships are often formed to take advantage of the partners' complementary skill sets. Combining areas of expertise into a partnership increases the firm's prospects for success. In addition to more expertise, the partnership also has access to more capital. By combining the money, assets, and borrowing capacity of all the partners, the amount of available capital is multiplied. Many partnerships are formed for this reason alone.

One notable advantage of a partnership is that there are few government regulations. Like a sole proprietorship, partnerships are subjected to fewer government directives than a corporation. For example, the partnership is not required to register with the state, which frequently involves a large fee; however, such registration is mandatory to establish a corporation or limited liability company. There is little government interference after a partnership is formed as long as the business follows business regulations and each partner pays personal income taxes.

Also in a partnership, each individual partner, not the partnership, is taxed. The partnership is not legally separate from its owners and does not pay separate income taxes. Each partner pays income taxes on his or her share of the profits, regardless of whether or not the profits are taken out of the business. Unlike a regular corporation, there is no need to file separate tax returns for the corporate entity and its owners.

Partnerships also benefit from greater business continuity. Because more than one person is involved, the life cycle of a partnership is longer than that of a sole proprietorship. If a partner dies or decides to no longer be a part of the business, the partnership comes to an end but the business is ongoing. The people left in the partnership can decide to proceed with one less partner or add another partner to the business.

In a partnership all parties involved are subject to unlimited financial liability. Like the sole proprietorship, there is no separation between the partnership and the owners. A major disadvantage of doing business as a partnership is that all partners are personally liable for business debts and liabilities (e.g., a judgment in a lawsuit). Also problematic is the scenario in which one partner makes a decision that obligates the partnership, and then all partners become accountable even if they knew nothing of the decision.

Profit sharing is another drawback of a partnership. When a partnership is formed, the partners agree to the way in which profits will be split, usually based on the amount of capital each partner invests, the amount of time each partner spends working in the business, and any special proficiency a partner contributes.

Interpersonal conflicts are a reality in a partnership. The way in which these conflicts are handled is vital to the continuation of the business. Disagreements can range from business philosophies to personal habits. Most conflicts can be overcome; however, in some cases they are so severe that the only option is the dissolution of the partnership.

Dissolving a partnership is more difficult than ending a sole proprietorship. Often the dissolution of a partnership is an emotionally overwhelming experience and can have far-reaching consequences. Personal and professional relationships can be irreparably damaged.

Corporations

In an 1819 ruling, Chief Justice John Marshall of the U.S. Supreme Court described a corporation in this way: "A corporation is an artificial being, invisible, intangible, and existing only in contemplation of the law." A corporation has many of the privileges and obligations of a person. It is a legal entity that has the ability to acquire resources, own assets, produce and sell products, incur debt, extend credit, sue and be sued, and perform the functions of any other type of enterprise. Corporations also have moral and social responsibilities. Most large, publicly traded fashion companies, like Macy's, Target, and Guess, are corporations.

Corporations are owned by stockholders, also called shareholders. Stockholders purchase shares of common stock, representing ownership in the company. Stockholders have the right to vote for corporate officers and to share in dividends. Corporations make up about 18 percent of the firms in the United States; however, they produce 72 percent of the sales revenue and control most of the business assets in the United States (U.S. Census Bureau).

As an entity separate from its owners (stockholders), a corporation has limited liability, meaning that the owners have no personal liability in the obligations of the corporation. A stockholder can only lose the amount of money invested in the stock purchased in a firm.

Corporations have more opportunities for access to capital. Since the ownership of the firm is divided among many reasonably low-cost shares of stock, a corporation can attract many investors. It is possible for a corporation to be owned by just one individual, but some corporations have in excess of a million stockholders.

Vast management expertise is a benefit a corporation has that sole proprietorships and partnerships lack. There is formality and structure in the management of a corporation. A board of directors, which ultimately leads the firm, is elected by the stockholders. The board of directors appoints managers to run the company, and these managers then employ people in the organization that possess the knowledge and skills necessary to run the company on a daily basis.

Transferring ownership in a corporation is simple because the company is divided into shares of stock that are relatively low in cost and easy to sell and purchase. No permission is needed for buying and selling stock in a corporation. As legal entities, corporations are immortal. Because the company is "owned" by many people, the addition or subtraction of owners is not disruptive to the business. A complete change of ownership could take place and the business would continue. Corporations have permanence that allows for long-range planning and growth.

The increased tax burden is a chief disadvantage of a corporation. Taxes are a fact of life for all businesses; however, in addition to the property and payroll taxes paid by sole proprietorships and partnerships, corporations are also required to pay federal income taxes. Additionally, in some states they must also pay state and local income taxes on the profits earned. Furthermore, the distribution of a firm's after-tax profits to stockholders in the form of dividends creates a tax burden for the stockholder. Dividends are considered personal income on which personal income taxes must be paid.

Corporations must endure appreciably more government intervention than sole proprietorships or partnerships. A publicly traded corporation must file reports with both federal and state regulatory agencies. In many publically traded corporations, very few stockholders participate in the day-to-day management of the company. The board of directors hires managers to run the company on behalf of the stockholders. The reality is that many times managers direct the company with their own self-interests in mind rather than the best interests of the stockholders. Table 4.2 shows business output in the United States in a one-year period.

TABLE 4.2

Total output for all businesses per year, more commonly referred to as the Gross Domestic Product. Notice the increase through the years. The growth of the GDP is an indicator that the economy is growing (in billions of dollars)

1929	103.6	1946	222.2	1963	617.8	1980	2,788.1	1997	8,332.4
1930	91.2	1947	244.1	1964	663.6	1981	3,126.8	1998	8,793.5
1931	76.5	1948	269.1	1965	719.1	1982	3,253.2	1999	9,353.5
1932	58.7	1949	267.2	1966	787.7	1983	3,534.6	2000	9,951.5
1933	56.4	1950	293.7	1967	832.4	1984	3,930.9	2001	10,286.2
1934	66.0	1951	339.3	1968	909.8	1985	4,217.5	2002	10,642.3
1935	73.3	1952	358.3	1969	984.4	1986	4,460.1	2003	11,142.1
1936	83.8	1953	379.3	1970	1,038.3	1987	4,736.4	2004	11,867.8
1937	91.9	1954	380.4	1971	1,126.8	1988	5,100.4	2005	12,638.4
1938	86.1	1955	414.7	1972	1,237.9	1989	5,482.1	2006	13,398.9
1939	92.2	1956	437.4	1973	1,382.3	1990	5,800.5	2007	14,061.8
1940	101.4	1957	461.1	1974	1,499.5	1991	5,992.1	2008	14,369.1
1941	126.7	1958	467.2	1975	1,637.7	1992	6,342.3	2009	14,119.0
1942	161.9	1959	506.6	1976	1,824.6	1993	6,667.4	2010	14,660.4
1943	198.6	1960	526.4	1977	2,030.1	1994	7,085.2		
1944	219.8	1961	544.8	1978	2,293.8	1995	7,414.7		
1945	223.0	1962	585.7	1979	2,562.2	1996	7,838.5		

Business Ownership Trends in the Fashion Industry

Business ownership in the textile and apparel industry seems to go in cycles. Going back to the beginning of the industrial revolution, businesses were opening at record pace, due to the number of people who wanted their own business and consumers who demanded fashion. From the early 1920s to the late 1970s, major textile mills owned by families were present in the southern part of the United States. Today, textile production occurs mostly offshore at mills owned by foreign businesses. The 1980s saw a surge in merging and acquiring businesses to create more buying power for larger conglomerates. This section explores business ownership trends beginning with mergers and acquisitions.

Mergers and Acquisitions

A merger or acquisition is the sale of one company to another company, with the acquiring company usually acting as the principal force. Mergers and acquisitions create larger corporate organizations, which is desirable for a number of reasons. Larger organizations have more buying power, which is vital to a retail concern. Expansion is another reason for a merger. Obviously, expansion takes place when another company is acquired, but the value of the stock may also increase, which raises capital needed for other types of expansion such as additional stores, technology, and additional products. Increasing sales is a constant goal in business, and mergers are often the only way to meet this objective. The acquisition of Macy's

TABLE 4.3
Examples of famous mergers and acquisitions in the fashion industry

Parent company	Business investment	Date
Dillard's Department store	Tandy's, Leonard's	1974
	Stix, Baer, Fuller	1983
	D. H. Holmes	1989
	J. B. Ivey	1990
Belk	Profitt's	2004
	McRae's	2004
	Parisian's	2004
Federated Department Stores	Macy's	1994
	Broadway Stores	1995
	Stern's Department Store	2001
Mens Wear House	Dimension Clothing Limited	2010
Philips Van Heusen	Tommy Hilfiger	2010
Advent International	Charlotte Russe Holding, Inc	2009
Golden Gate Capital	J. Jill (bought from Talbotts)	2009
Sun Capitals Partners, Inc.	Kellwood	2008
Sun Capitals Partners, Inc.	The Limited Group	2007

by Federated Department Stores increased sales by expanding the Federated market to the Macy's customer. Refer to Table 4.3 for a historical list of mergers and acquisitions.

Before discussing the other business ownership trends, licensing and franchising, let's look at what game theory is and its significance in the economics of the fashion industry.

Game Theory: Licensing and Franchising

The concept of **game theory** is "the study of how people behave in strategic situations." Game theory is an acceptable, fairly conservative way of thinking about economics. It has not replaced other economic theories, but for the purpose of studying and analyzing fashion businesses it is truly a phenomenal, applicable way of thinking and studying. Economists who study game theory are called game theorists. Two well-known economists introduced game theory in a study written by John von Neumann from Princeton. His colleagues included Albert Einstein and John Nash. Nash won a Nobel Prize in 1994 at the age of 63 for the work he did when he was 21. He also created the **Nash Equilibrium**, a strategy used today to study the theory of games. The movie *A Beautiful Mind* portrayed the life and work of John Nash. Game theorists look at games or situations where there are players as in games. Game theory can be applied to all subject areas, for example, military strategies, politics, and business.

When you think of games, the first thing that comes to mind may be football, softball, tennis, Scrabble, Monopoly, chess, video games, or Internet simulations. All games are based on game theory. Trying to determine ahead of time what strategic move your opponent will make is part of the fun of the game. Begin to think of the fashion business in a theoretical sense as a game in which the players consist of two sides—the consumers and the producers. The players interact in the market, which is the game board. The business of fashion contains the common components found in any game: competition, strategy, and entertainment. David K. Levine, an economist and a distinguished professor in the department of economics at Washington University in St. Louis, is quoted as saying:

> The fashion industry is a fascinating industry—perhaps in part because fashions seem to come and go in waves—and because to staid economists and game theorists focused on utilitarian concerns, it is never certain that fashion is a good thing. Game theorists have studied these fashion waves. Wolfgang Pesendorfer, for example, argues that fashions are used in a kind of "dating" game in which partners signal their attractiveness to one another by acquiring top-of-the-line fashions. Game theory has many other applications to fashion including the licensing of designs and the franchising of distribution chains. (D. K. Levine, personal communication, August 17, 2008)

Companies play the game of franchising and licensing to increase sales and grow market share, in turn contributing to the economy. Their licensed and franchised brands have popular fashion names associated with them such as Bill Blass, Christian Dior, and Ralph Lauren. Benjamin Klein was quoted as saying, "When companies 'differentiate' their products with unique brand names and associated advertising and promotional campaigns, they can charge more than others for what these economists claim are 'truly' identical products. Brand names lead consumers to make what these economists consider to be artificial distinctions between different products. Companies with respected brand names, therefore, can increase prices without losing significant brand names." After a brand name is established, the owner of the brand has the opportunity to **license** or **franchise** the name.

The study of licensing and franchising demonstrates how game theory is applied. Strategic interaction on the part of each player is important to foresee. A classic situation used by many economics professors of all subject areas to teach game theory is called "the Prisoner's Dilemma." The following is a description of "the Prisoner's Dilemma" by Michael Shor from gametheory.net:

> A game frequently displayed in television police dramas. Two partners in crime are separated into separate rooms at the police station and given a similar deal. If one implicates the other, he may go free while the other receives a life in prison. If neither implicates the other, both are given moderate sentences, and if both implicate the other, the sentences for both are severe. Each player has a dominant strategy to implicate the other, and thus in equilibrium each receives a harsh punishment, but both would be better off if each remained silent. In a repeated or iterated prisoner's dilemma, cooperation may be sustained through trigger strategies such as tit for tat.

While that game is undesirable and no one wants to "play" in real life, the math and logistics are used to determine what the outcomes will be depending upon the prisoners' decisions to confess or maintain their silence. Two Internet sites with different versions of "the Prisoner's Dilemma" are listed at the end of the chapter; both will facilitate your learning about game theory. This will enable you to think of the fashion business as a game. Each player is aware of what the other player is doing, but encounters difficulty when anticipating the other player's move.

Game theory is applicable to the buying and selling of fashion, but little research has been conducted in this area. Two strategies will be examined that have proven methods, not through the study of economists, but through the experience of those in the industry. Strategies that apply game theory in the economics of fashion include licensing and franchising.

Licensing

Licensing requires two players and one agreement. The licensee is a party that acquires the rights to utilize a property, usually for a retail product but sometimes for promotional use. The **licensor** is the property owner (Raugust, 2001). It is important to understand that licensing is a contract between two parties: the licensor, which is the company that owns the entity, which can be a brand name, a logo, a designer name, or a combination of these; and the licensee, who buys the rights to use the entity on a product. In essence, the licensee contractually leases the right to use the entity for a set period of time.

All parties in the licensing arrangement benefit. The number-one advantage for both sides is monetary. The amount paid to the licensor is called a **royalty fee**, which is usually a percentage of the profits of the product, or it can also be an up-front amount. Most licensing contracts state that a royalty or some amount of money will be paid to the licensor regardless of the sales of the merchandise. The licensor gets a royalty fee and the licensee is able to sell merchandise because of the value added by the brand or designer name attached to the merchandise. For example, Liz Claiborne, Inc., holds the exclusive, long-term license to produce and sell men's and women's collections of DKNY Jeans and DKNY Active in the Western Hemisphere. The company also has the exclusive license to produce jewelry under the Kenneth Cole brand names of Kenneth Cole New York and Reaction (see lizclaiborne.com). The name of a product can be extended and grown under a licensing deal while being managed for distribution within market-specific areas. Figure 4.21a and b depicts the sales of licensed products from 2008 and 2009.

The primary risk involved for the licensors is the possibility of oversaturation of the brand in the marketplace, which can happen should the licensor lose control. For example, Calvin Klein lost control of his name when he entered into a deal with Warnaco to license his name. In 2001, a court battle ensued between Calvin Klein and Warnaco, with Klein accusing Warnaco of distributing Calvin Klein jeans to two large warehouse club retailers, Costco and Sam's Club. The case was settled and the contract continued.

Licensing can also be damaging to the brand name. If consumer demand is met too quickly through the use of multiple licensing agreements, the image of the brand can be marred. The abundance of a brand in the marketplace creates complacency among consumers. They become tired of the brand and lose their sense of urgency to acquire products with the brand name, resulting in declining sales and revenue. For a licensee, financial risks are the most common type of gamble associated with licensing a product.

Another economic consideration is the up-front portion of the guarantee, known as the advance. The advance can be extreme, especially for some entertainment properties (Raugust, 1995). The laws of supply and demand dictate that a hot film or TV property can command a high advance. Additionally, some entertainment licensors look to incoming advance money to help recoup production costs and therefore try to negotiate high up-front amounts (Raugust, 1995).

Fashion licensing is best associated with the economic concept of rent. **Rent** is essentially what a company does when licensing the name of a brand to use on a product for a specific period of time. Firms rent the brand name to increase their market power. The result

FIGURE 4.21 *Sales of licensed products from 2008 to 2009 (Source: Adapted from EPM Communications Inc.).*

**Retail Sales of Licensed Fashion Merchandise
by Property Type, U.S. and Canada, 2009**

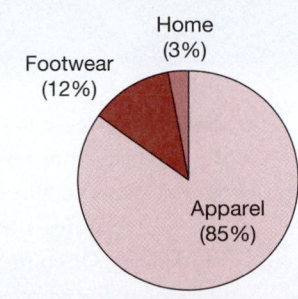

Home
(3%)

Footwear
(12%)

Apparel
(85%)

RETAIL SALES OF FASHION-BASED LICENSED MERCHANDISE, BY PRODUCT CATEGORY, 2009
(dollars in billions)

CATEGORY	2008 RETAIL SALES	2009 RETAIL SALES	% CHANGE 2008–2009	2009 SHARE OF MARKET
Accessories	$8.02	$6.80	−15.2%	37.7%
Eyewear	*$2.33*	*$1.95*	*−16.3%*	*10.8%*
Bags (all)	*$1.14*	*$0.97*	*−14.9%*	*5.4%*
Headwear	*$0.73*	*$0.63*	*−13.7%*	*3.5%*
Hosiery	*$0.30*	*$0.26*	*−13.3%*	*1.4%*
Jewelry & Watches	*$1.97*	*$1.59*	*−19.3%*	*8.8%*
Luggage & Travel	*$0.75*	*$0.65*	*−13.3%*	*3.6%*
Scarves & Ties	*$0.10*	*$0.09*	*−10.0%*	*0.5%*
Other	*$0.70*	*$0.66*	*NA*	*3.7%*
Apparel	$6.22	$5.53	−11.1%	30.7%
Domestics	$0.45	$0.39	−13.3%	2.2%
Footwear	$1.48	$1.27	−14.2%	7.0%
Furniture/Home	$0.96	$0.77	−19.8%	4.3%
Gifts/Novelties	$0.09	$0.08	−11.1%	0.4%
HBA	$2.52	$2.11	−16.3%	11.7%
Fragrance	*$2.05*	*$1.76*	*−14.1%*	*9.8%*
Other	*$0.47*	*$0.35*	*NA*	*1.9%*
Housewares	$0.37	$0.31	−16.2%	1.7%
Infant Products	$0.35	$0.30	−14.3%	1.7%
Publishing	$0.08	$0.07	−12.5%	0.4%
Stationery/Paper	$0.09	$0.08	−11.1%	0.4%
Toys/Games	$0.08	$0.07	−12.5%	0.4%
Other	$0.03	$0.26	NA	1.4%
TOTAL	$20.74	$18.04	−13.0%	100.0%

Note: The 2008 data is restated. Italics=subcategories

can be the creation of a monopoly or an oligopoly, either domestically or abroad. A classic study of rent seeking by economist Richard Posner found that firms in some industries spent up to 30 percent of their total revenue to get monopoly power (Posner, 1975, pp. 807–827).

There are several popular types of licenses: designer, celebrity, art, corporate, entertainment, sports store name, or brand name. All categories of apparel and accessories, including cosmetics, have some form of licensing attached to products. An article by Regina Molaro examines the impact of celebrity licensing (Box 4.1).

STAR POTENTIAL

Celebrities, designers, style icons and musicians are debuting exclusive collections at retail. Industry experts discuss what it takes for a luminary to shine at retail.

In recent years, retailers have been on the move stitching licensing deals with renowned fashion designers, style icons and even musicians. Beyond offering budget-conscious fashionistas super stylish threads at extremely affordable prices, these celebrity-inspired collections also bring retailers some perks—exclusivity and lots of press.

It may seem like these high profile designer collaborations kicked off at Target with the debut of Isaac Mizrahi and Mossimo, but the concept is certainly not revolutionary (think Jaclyn Smith at Kmart and Kathy Ireland).

However, within the last decade or so, designer affiliations certainly seem to be on the rise. Swedish retailer H&M quickly became renowned for its partnerships with topnotch fashion designers and style icons, and over the years, it has stitched many licensing deals with high-end fashion houses such as Marimekko, Stella McCartney, Roberto Cavalli and beyond. Even the Gap and upscale retailers such as Brooks Brothers have debuted exclusive designer partnerships. Overseas, London's Topshop also struck some high profile deals, including collections with model Kate Moss, and more recently, Swedish designer Ann-Sofie Back and Jonathan Saunders.

Beyond stitching agreements with celebrated fashion designers, it seems like there's some star power in style icons and music luminaries as well. Years ago, we saw Madonna launch a collection at H&M, and more recently she debuted a junior collection, "Material Girl" at Macy's in a collaboration with her daughter Lola. Other musical talents have also struck a chord in the fashion industry, including Victoria Beckham (a.k.a Posh Spice), Lady Gaga and even Steven Tyler of Aerosmith and "American Idol" fame.

Some industry experts such as Patricia Pao, CEO of consulting firm, The Pao Principle, believe that this licensing trend still has lots of star power, but others such as Pam Danziger, president of boutique market research firm, Unity Marketing believe that this movement may be losing its luster.

"This trend has been around forever," says Pao. "It started in the mass market with Kathy Ireland and Jaclyn Smith and the 'Olsen Twins' (at Walmart) and then expanded to Paris Hilton, Jessica Simpson and Sweetface (Jennifer Lopez)." Although many of these brands have already lost their luster, Pao believes there's still some potential for celebrity collections. "These brands died because their associated celebrities just put their name on the brand. They weren't actively involved," says Pao.

She cites Mary-Kate and Ashley Olsen's Olsenboye, the debut of Material Girl and Kim Kardashian for Bebe as some success stories. "However, in order to be successful, I believe the celebrity must wear the clothing," says Pao. "L.A.M.B. is so successful because Gwen Stefani actually incorporates pieces from the collection into her wardrobe." Of course, the collection must exude a real sense of style and offer topnotch quality. On target is Olsenboye, which resembles a lower priced version of the Olsen duet's upscale Elizabeth and James fashion collection.

LUMINARY POWER

Of course, luminaries always generate lots of media attention and consumer buzz, and they have enormous fan following but, it takes much more than that to create a retail success story. Some industry experts believe that ideally, the celebrity should be widely recognized as a visionary—a real style setter. "The Olsens are undisputed style makers, and Madonna and her daughter, Lourdes (Lola) are tastemakers as well," concludes Pao.

Negative publicity can certainly make any star fade fast, which can also have an enormous impact at retail as well. Unity Marketing's Danziger predicts that, in time, the celebrity turned designer trend will pass with the tipping point being Kim Kardashian's marriage debacle. "Few celebrities can actually bring a unique and interesting perspective to fashion" says Danziger, an expert on the luxury market. "A few do, such as the Olsen Twins and Jessica Simpson, but most of them don't. Just look at the teaming of Lindsay Lohan and Ungaro.

Danziger, who recently authored a book, *Putting the Luxe Back in Luxury*, believes the union of retailers and topnotch fashion designers such as Vera Wang holds much more promise. "Vera Wang is really doing it right. From a licensing point of view, what's notable is that she expanded from a bridal brand to a lifestyle brand and she's done it in a way that's very strategic," says Danziger. Too much exposure can have a negative impact since part of the allure is that the brand is unique and special. There's a delicate balance to maintain."

Is there a secret to generating retail star power? "It depends on the partnership," says Pao of The Pao Principle. "Kate Moss for Topshop was tremendously successful because the clothes were great and they really reflected Kate Moss' taste and style. Simply Vera, Vera Wang at Kohl's has also been hugely successful because Wang was very actively involved in the partnership."

Danziger believes that among fashion designers, Wang is one of many who have truly mastered the art of reaching various consumers at all price ranges—from affordable luxuries (at Kohl's) to mid-range (David's Bridal), and true luxury collections worn with grace by her elite celebrity clientele.

What sets Vera Wang apart from other licensed brands—most of whom have done limited lower-end collections with single partners—is Wang's determination to create a lifestyle brand similar to the successful brand built by Ralph Lauren. Estimates of the size of Wang's company vary from $700 million, according to *The Wall Street Journal* to $175 million from *Women's Wear Daily*.

Certainly the most noted license, and likely the one generating the most revenue, is Simply Vera, Vera Wang. So far, there's no evidence that Wang's stellar debut in the discount and middle markets has negatively impacted her luxury business. The licensing expansion also provides more capital for future growth.

In addition, Wang dons items from the collection and Kohl's both advertises and promotes the collection. Also personally involved in promoting their collection are material girls Madonna and Lola. "The launch of 'Material Girl' at Macy's was designed to create a frenzy among young style-setters who wanted to be the first to have this bold new fashion brand," says Martine Reardon, executive vice president of marketing, Macy's.

As noted, fashion icons certainly lend lots of credibility to these types of retail partnerships. Just look at the debut of Lady Gaga's Workshop Collection at Barneys New York. The beauty collection includes nail polishes, artificial nails, lipstick, lip gloss and accessories such as false lashes and makeup brushes. Gaga's personal nail artist, Naomi Yasuda, worked directly with Kiss Products to create the chic tip collection.

Before venturing into these types of licensing partnerships, celebrities, style icons and musicians should consider that there are a number of consequences to be considered prior to expansion. "Inferior products or designs can certainly wreak havoc on a brand's reputation," says Unity Marketing's Danziger.

SHIFTING GEARS: STARS REALIGNED

We've watched the rise of celebrities and even musicians, so which luminaries will be the next ones to shine at retail? Roseanne Morrison, fashion director of consulting firm, The Doneger Group believes editors and style icons will represent the next wave of licensing. "If you think of (photographer/blogger, stylist and former model) Haneli Mustaparta, Taylor Tomasi Hill (fashion editor and icon) and (editor and stylist) Giovanna Battaglia—these women are all noticed by the fashion cognoscenti and set style in motion. In addition to designers and celebrities, these women will be the next set of collaborators."

"The biggest change in this licensing movement is the rise of the stylist," agrees Pao of The Pao Principle. Look at the success of Victoria Beckham, whose 2011 earnings on her style savvy collection were expected to soar to $100 million. Beckham's secret to retail success: she creates fashions with her own personal sense of style top of mind.

Beyond Vera Wang, industry experts also count Ivanka Trump, Rachel Zoe, Gwen Stefani's L.A.M.B, Material Girl, Olsenboye, and William Rast among other super success stories.

Pao notes that Rachel Zoe's collection has taken off despite the fact that it's not such a great clothing collection. Zoe managed to land the Rachel Zoe collection at upscale retailers such as Bergdorf Goodman, Bloomingdale's, Neiman Marcus, and Saks Fifth Avenue. "Zoe has a lot of fans through her television show and her history dressing celebrities. Women who buy Rachel Zoe want some of her magic," says Pao.

Based on Rachel Zoe's success, Pao also believes that this area is going to be further saturated. "We're already seeing other stylists such as Kelly Wearstler enter the market too."

Is there potential for authors and other types of luminaries? *The Girl With The Dragon Tattoo*, which debuted in theaters in December 2011, introduced a fashion collection at H&M. According to the designer, the clothing line sold out in 10 minutes in Los Angeles. It will be interesting to watch which other groups will be among the next rising stars.

Source: Regina Molaro.

The business arrangement of designers licensing their names dates back to the 1950s when Christian Dior allowed his name to be used to license hosiery. The hosiery company initially offered $10,000 for the rights to use his name, but he rejected the offer and countered for a percentage of sales. He later went on to license his name on many fashion items such as ties and perfume. Pierre Cardin also licensed his name around the same time.

FIGURE 4.22 *Disney is an example of licensed apparel (Source: Corbis).*

During the 1960s Pierre Cardin was the first fashion designer to license his name on a nonfashion product, a crock-pot. Today Pierre Cardin has well over 800 licenses on various products.

With licensing, names of designers eventually become brand names, like Calvin Klein or Ralph Lauren. Consumers recognize the name and associate the quality of the designers with the name and are more apt to buy the licensed product. Licensing garners a designer recognition by expanding the distribution of the designer's name, but the financial risk falls on the licensee.

Art is a popular license today. There is a global demand for T-shirts, totes, and other simple apparel items with art or picture logos. For the use of a famous painting, the licensing contract is between the museum where the painting is hanging and the licensee, the manufacturer of the apparel or accessories. Lucky Brand Jeans entered a licensing agreement with the Louvre Museum in Paris, France, to produce T-shirts bearing the portrait of Mona Lisa.

Corporate licensing involves using the names or trademarks of large companies who sometimes offer apparel to their employees for purchase or gratis. Companies such as Bank of America, SunTrust, and Coca-Cola all have company logos that are used on apparel products. Corporate licensing is not a large percentage of the market, but if the corporation is well known, it can benefit from the licensing effort.

Entertainment licensing can range from a new movie to a popular celebrity or a cartoon such as *The Simpsons*. Big players in this field are Disney, Warner Brothers, and Marvel. Disney's 2010 sales of licensed merchandise reached $28.6 billion (Wrap Media, 2011). Figure 4.22 is an example of licensed apparel.

Sports licensing is common in areas such as baseball, football, basketball, skating, snowboarding, hockey, and wrestling. The most often licensed sports are Major League Baseball, Collegiate Licensing, and the National Football League (Wrap Media, 2011). Each of these sports has its own governing body, which may act as a mediator for the sport. However, if a sport has team owners, then each owner will negotiate the contract for his or her team's licensing deal.

Franchising

Franchising is beneficial to both manufacturer and retailer. This form of business has been around since the Civil War but has only become popular in the fashion industry within the past 10 to 15 years. A franchise is a legal business relationship in which a firm or an individual buys the exclusive right to conduct a retail business under the franchiser's registered or trademarked name, using specified operating and financial procedures, in a stipulated territory or trading area. The person or company selling the franchise is called the **franchisor** and the person buying the company or name is known as the **franchisee**.

Within all segments of the fashion industry, popular franchises include Nicole Miller, Benetton, and The Body Shop. The franchisor is the legal owner of the business and maintains the authority to grant permission for others to enter into a franchise relationship and to use the business concept. The franchisee agrees to abide by the franchise agreement and has purchased the rights to use the business concept. The "franchise fee" is the amount paid to the franchisor by the franchisee and can range anywhere from several thousand to several million dollars.

Franchising has a number of advantages. The name of the business is already established, eliminating the need for the franchisee to build a brand and a clientele. The franchisor offers assistance at start-up, which continues throughout the life of the business. Advertising, organization, operations, and other services are outlined in the franchise agreement. Also, buying a franchise reduces some of the risk that can be associated with starting a new business.

Franchising is not without its disadvantages. The franchisor usually maintains control over how the franchisee conducts business. A franchisee may find this inhibiting at times when decisions have to be made concerning an owner's particular business. Controls can range from design of the store, merchandise sold in the store, store fixtures, placement of fixtures, and, for a retailer, the location of fitting rooms.

Summary

This chapter has provided a sharper understanding of the commonalities and differences of the various types of fashion retailers. Additionally, the types of fashion retailers and the categories of merchandise carried by these retailers clarified the retail segment of the fashion industry. Furthermore, an explanation and examination of the NAICS system revealed the importance of tracking the retail industry to the U.S. economy. Fashion retailers are the last point in the retailing supply chain supplying products to the ultimate consumer, making retailers the most important facet of the fashion industry. Fashion retailing began in the mid-1800s as dry goods merchants and has developed into large retailers, catalogs, television, and online retailers. The chapter also discussed the fashion supply chain and the parallel to the product development process. Lastly, the chapter reviewed business models. All businesses operate using a business model to maximize sales and optimize profit. The business model explains the functions of the business such as the day-to-day operating strategies, expenses of the business, security policies, procedures of the store, and merchandising.

Key Terms

business model 69
business strategy 70
branding 70
clothing and accessories stores 69
consumer confidence 71
corporation 89
department store 75
discount department store 75
electronic shopping 82
entertainment Licensing 98
fashion Licensing 94
fashion product 73
fashion retailer 68
franchise 93

franchising 92
franchisor 98
franchisee 98
game theory 92
general merchandise 74
home shopping 82
kiosks 84
license 93
licensee 84
licensor 94
mail order 82
men's clothing store 81
mergers 91
mom-and-pop stores 79

Nash Equilibrium 92
nonstore retailer 82
North American Industry Classification System 69
partnership 88
pop-up stores 84
rent 94
retailing formats 78
risk factors 72
royalty fee 94
sole proprietorship 85
specialty store 79
sports licensing 98
warehouse clubs/supercenters 77

Review Questions

1. Discuss the four commonalities of the fashion retailer.

2. What is the difference between a business model and a business strategy? Give an example of each.

3. Explain how the supply chain operates in conjunction with product development.

4. Why is consumer confidence important to the fashion industry? Give an example of how a fashion retailer could measure consumer confidence.

5. What can businesses do to overcome risk factors?

6. What are the advantages and disadvantages of businesses using more than one channel of distribution for a product?

7. Explain the North American Industry Classification System.

8. Define the three types of business ownership. Give an example of each type.

9. Which type of business is the easiest to form? Why?

10. Discuss a business trend. How does it influence the apparel industry?

11. What is game theory?

12. How can game theory be applied to fashion businesses such as licensing and franchising?

13. Which type of business must endure more government intervention?

14. What is the economic value to a designer when he or she licenses his or her name?

15. Discuss the economic concept of rent? How is it associated with fashion licensing?

Critical Thinking

1. You have developed a line of jewelry that is very contemporary. In order to make your line more recognizable, you are going to buy a license to name the jewelry line. You have narrowed your licensing type to a celebrity. Research two celebrities who you think represent your jewelry by adding economic value. Secure five pictures of jewelry by drawing them or have someone draw them (you can also use magazine pictures) that depict your line and then write a brief report. In your report, include the following: (1) description of your line, (2) advantages and disadvantages of each celebrity, (3) whom you think would be the best fit for the license name of the jewelry line, (4) why you are going to distribute your line in a department store, and (5) what other channels you are going to use to sell and why.

An alternative to this report would be to create a mood board using the research information.

Present your findings to the class. You take on the role of owner of the jewelry line. The class takes on the role of jewelry buyers for various types of department stores. After the presentations, each buyer will discuss what three lines of jewelry they selected and why.

2. What do you think the future of fashion retailing will be? Include in your answer how the future fashion cycle will affect the profits of a company, business models of the future, the effect of fashion on the economy of the United States, the capability of new companies to enter the market and make a profit, and the barriers they will face as they enter the market in the future.

Internet Activities

1. Go to the North American Industry Classification System site http://www.census.gov/eos/www/naics/index.html and find the NAICS code for a jewelry business. What does each of the numbers represent?

Bibliography

Big-box store definition. (2010). Big box stores. *BusinessDictionary. com—Online Business Dictionary*. Retrieved from http://www. businessdictionary.com/definition/big-box store.html

Birchall, J. (2008, August 1). Best Buy taps High-end vending kiosks. *Financial Times.* Retrieved from http://search.ft.com/ search?queryText=Best+buy+taps+high-end+vending+kiosks

Breward, Christop C. (2003). *Fashion*. Oxford: Oxford University Press.

Coldwater Creek Annual Report (Rep.). (2010). Retrieved from http://phx.corporate-ir.net/phoenix.zhtml?c=92631&p =irol-reportsannual

Easey, M. (2009). *Fashion marketing*. Oxford: Wiley-Blackwell.

Edelson, S. (2010a). "Sam's club apparel boost: A positive for Wal-Mart." *Women's Wear Daily*.

Edelson, S. (2010b) "Gucci to open flash sneakers shop."

Goetzel, D. (2009). Media Post News. Comcast to expand 'Shop by remote', increase number of ebif-enabled homes. Retrieved from http://mediapost.com/publications/?fa=Articles; http://www.census.gov/compendia/stab/2011/11s0743.pdf

Hoovers.com. (2012). Warehouse clubs and superstores. Austin, TX. Retrieved on January 2012, from http://subscriber.hoovers.com.proxy.library.vcu.edu/H/industry360/overview.html?industryId=1531

Ibis. (2010). Industry at a glace. Retrieved from http://www.ibisworld.com/industryus/ataglance.aspx?indid=1067

Internet Retailer Strategies for Web-Based Retailing. (2010). Retrieved from http://www.verticalwebmedia.com

Harvard Business School. (2005). 'Introduction,' in *Harvard business essentials: Strategy : Create and implement the best strategy for your business.* Boston, MA: Harvard Business School, pp. xv–xvi.

Jewelry retail. (2010, June 25). *M2 Presswire*.

Kaplan, M. (2009, December 5). Shopping networks switched on. *Weekend Australian*, 30.

Kenneth Cole Productions. Annual Report (2009). New York. New York Stock Exchange, p. 20. Retrieved from http://secfilings.nyse.com/files.php?symbol=KCP&fg=24

Morrill, D. (2008, December 31). Vending machines go upscale. *Contra Costa Times*, KRTCC00020081231e4cv00009.

Posner, R. (1975). The social costs of monopoly and regulation. *Journal of Political Economy*, 83, pp. 807–827. Press Room. Retreived October 8, 2008, from http://www.macys.com/

Raugust, K. (1995). *Merchandise licensing television industry*. Newton, MA: Butterworth-Hernemann.

Raugust, K. (2001). *The licensing handbook*. New York EPM Communications, South-Western Thompson Learning.

"Report: Disney raked in $28.6B from licensed merchandise in 2010." *Wrap Media*, May 18, 2011, no page. Web. 24 June 2011. Retrieved from http://www.thewrap.com/media/article/report-disney-made-286b-2010-licensed-merchandise-27526

Sherman, L. (2008). "Pop-up shops: Small stores, big business." *Forbes*.

Signet jewelers Ltd inversor day-final. (2010). *CQ FD Disclosure*.

The US shoe store industry. (2010). *M2 Presswire*.

Top US store chains from costco wholesale to gap, inc. posted. (2010). *Plus News Pakistan*.

"TRU—About TRU." *TRU—Tweens, Teens, and Twenty-Somethings Research.* (26 July 2010). Retrieved from http://www.tru-insight.com/about.cfm?page_id=41.

2009 Under Armour Annual Report. (2010). Baltimore. Retrieved from http://files.shareholder.com/downloads/UARM/972634597x0x360368/01216DBE-7A84-4544-AD04-809BF1EF2C78/UA_2009_Annual_Report.pdf

U.S. Census Bureau. (2007a). 2007 *NAICS definitions, 452, General Merchandise Stores.* Retrieved from http://www.census.gov/cgi-bin/sssd/naics/naicsrch?code=452&search=2007%20NAICS%20Search

U.S. Census Bureau. (2007b). *2007 NAICS definitions, 4521, Department Stores*. Retrieved from http://www.census.gov/cgi-bin/sssd/naics/naicsrch?code=452111&search=2007%20NAICS%20Search

U.S. Census Bureau. (2007c). *2007 NAICS definitions, 452112 Discount Department Stores*. Retrieved from http://www.census.gov/cgi-bin/sssd/naics/naicsrch?code=452111&search=2007%20NAICS%20Search

U.S. Census Bureau. (2007d). *2007 NAICS definitions, 45299, Other General Merchandise Stores*. Retrieved from http://www.census.gov/cgi-bin/sssd/naics/naicsrch?code=452990&search=2007%20NAICS%20Search

U.S. Census Bureau. (2007e). *2007 NAICS definitions, 448, Clothing and Clothing Accessories Store.* Retrieved from http://www.census.gov/cgi-bin/sssd/naics/naicsrch?code=448&search=2007%20NAICS%20Search

U.S. Census Bureau. (2007f). *2007 NAICS definitions, 448110, Men's Clothing Stores.* Retrieved from http://www.census.gov/cgi-bin/sssd/naics/naicsrch?code=448110&search=2007%20NAICS%20Search

U.S. Census Bureau. (2007g). *2007 NAICS definitions,448120 , Women's Clothing Stores.* Retrieved from http://www.census.gov/cgi-bin/sssd/naics/naicsrch?code=448120&search=2007%20NAICS%20Search

U.S. Census Bureau. (2007h). *2007 NAICS definitions, 454, Non-Store Retailers.* Retrieved from http://www.census.gov/cgi-bin/sssd/naics/naicsrch?code=454&search=2007%20NAICS%20Search

U.S. Census Bureau. (2007i). *2007 NAICS definitions, 45411, Electronic Shopping.* Retrieved from http://www.census.gov/cgi-bin/sssd/naics/naicsrch?code=45411&search=2007%20NAICS%20Search

U.S. Census Bureau. (2007j). *2007 NAICS definitions, 453310 Used Merchandise Stores.* Retrieved from http://www.census.gov/cgi-bin/sssd/naics/naicsrch

U.S. Census Bureau. (2007k). *2007 NAICS definitions, Non-store Retailers.* Retrieved from http://www.census.gov/cgi-bin/sssd/naics/naicsrch?code=454&search=2007%20NAICS%20Search

PROFIT =
SUCCESS

OBJECTIVES

After reading this chapter, you will be able to:

- Identify the importance of the consumer in planning product assortments
- Gain knowledge of pricing models used in the apparel and textile industry
- Learn the steps and formulas used in retail planning

We are putting the customer at the center of everything we do.

——TERRY LUNDGREN, president and CEO of Macy's, Macy's Annual Report (2009)

5

*H*ow does a fashion company define success? The "rights of merchandising" guide the retailer by having the right product, in the right place, at the right time, in the right quantities, with the right sales promotion. If any one of the rights is wrong, the products presented to consumers will not meet the projected sales goals. A fashion company must achieve the formula to be successful and realize a profit. Earning planned profits equals a successful business; however, there is a limited amount of time a business can operate without making a profit before it has to close. The title of this chapter, "Profit = Success," is simple but extremely significant to the overall economic well-being of a fashion company.

After reading this chapter, you will gain an appreciation of the importance of meeting the needs and desires of the consumer and the impact planning has on success. Following the study of meeting customer expectations, the examination of the nature of pricing models used in the apparel and textile industry from a retail perspective commences. Lastly, you will acquire knowledge of retail planning through the development of a six-month plan and the examination of markup and markdowns, leading to an understanding of the job of a retail buyer.

The Consumer

The management of businesses, both in the short and long run, is a necessity to meet the needs of the consumer, strengthen a company, and make a profit. The bottom line of any business strategy is to make a profit and continue doing business. Strategies vary; for example, for every pair of shoes purchased by a customer, Tom's Shoes donates a pair of shoes to a child without shoes. Coach, known for fine leather accessories, uses a business model aimed at keeping their consumer emotionally attached to their product. Tom's and Coach understand that the key to making a profit is to satisfy consumer demand. Satisfying consumer demand occurs through identifying the right consumers and matching them to the right product at the right price. There is much more to understanding the fashion business than most consumers realize because from the customer's perspective, "it's all about them." The consumer is unconcerned about whether fashion sells or not; customers simply want their demand and needs to be met through the purchase and use of a product. In the words of Giorgio Armani, "In the end, the customer does not know, or care, if you are small or large as an organization… she or he only focuses on the garment hanging on the rail in the store." Chapter 9 examines the consumer in detail.

Pricing

Customers buying fashionable clothing seek utility and prestige. Utility means the wearer receives a function from the clothing and prestige means that the clothing is desirable and trendy, giving the wearer status. A significant factor in meeting consumer expectations of utility and prestige is providing merchandise at a price the customer deems satisfactory. Buyers and product developers are keenly aware of the customer's demand. For example, stores such as Kohl's and Macy's consider that a function of meeting consumer demand entails selling merchandise at promotional or reduced prices; therefore, planning markups accordingly to accommodate price reductions is important. Markdown merchandise is very common for retailers because customers expect it and like the value markdowns offer. Additionally, since retailers plan the markdowns, the relative cost, relative retail, and relative profit are a part of the pricing decision. As a result, the retailer can estimate gross margin and profit.

Pricing merchandise is a difficult task and different retailers employ different schools of thought. The three types of pricing most often used are **demand-oriented pricing**, **cost-oriented pricing**, and **price discounting**. Demand-oriented pricing is determined when demand for a product is high. A higher demand allows for higher prices. Low demand necessitates lower pricing. Demand for fashion items, and consequently prices for fashion items, follows the fashion cycle (discussed in Chapter 2). From the introductory level to the culmination point, prices are higher because demand is on the rise. However, as merchandise demand peaks and begins its descent into obscurity, prices fall with the demand. In other words, at the beginning of a season prices offered for new seasonal merchandise are much higher than at the end of the season.

Cost-oriented pricing involves the application of a markup percentage to the cost of an item to determine the final selling price of the item. For example, if the markup goal for a particular department is 60 percent, then the buyer would apply a 60 percent markup to the cost of an item to arrive at the retail price. This method takes the guesswork out of pricing; however, seasoned buyers are aware that some items are worth more to consumers, while others are worthless and adjust the retail price accordingly. Meeting the 60 percent markup goal occurs when the aggregate or average markup of the department equates to 60 percent. A thorough discussion of markup occurs later in this chapter.

Retailers know that underestimating the competition gravely affects their success. Competition-oriented pricing is a means of positioning a firm within the marketplace based on price. This type of pricing is dangerous and leads to pricing wars where the only retailer left standing is the one that can afford the continued reduction in prices. Ignoring the competition is unwise but pricing decisions based solely on the actions of the competitor endanger a retailer. Successful retailers offer products that meet the needs and desires of their target markets at prices the market perceives to be of value. Figure 5.1 lays out additional types of pricing in the fashion industry. These are a few pricing strategies used by retailers in the fashion industry today. As you can see, some of the strategies overlap each other.

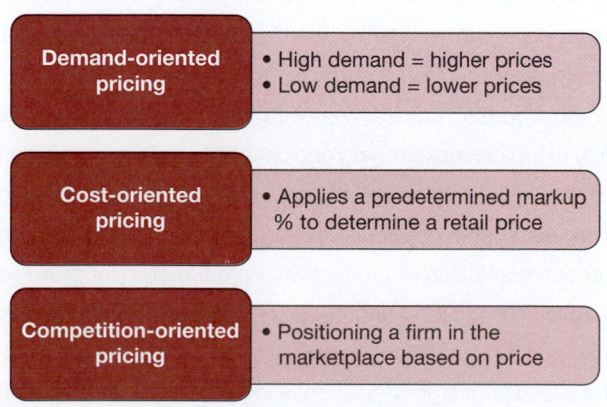

Demand-oriented pricing	• High demand = higher prices • Low demand = lower prices
Cost-oriented pricing	• Applies a predetermined markup % to determine a retail price
Competition-oriented pricing	• Positioning a firm in the marketplace based on price

FIGURE 5.1 *Pricing strategies.*

By now, it is evident how important the consumer is to the retailer and the skills buyers possess in planning assortments and pricing products. The next section investigates planning, buying, and pricing of products from a mathematical perspective.

Retail Buying

Retail buying is an integral component of the fashion industry. Designers create garments that manufacturers produce, but unless a buyer purchases the garments, the ultimate consumer never sees the designer's creation. The **buyer** serves a central and primary role in bringing fashion to the customer and without the buying element, fashion, as we know it, would not exist. Let's take a closer look at the buyer's role.

The Buyer's Role in Retailing

Buyers have expertise in understanding the wants and needs of their customers. Buyers also possess analytical skills used to plan and understand the fashion industry. Taste level is an important factor; however, it is more important for the buyer to temper their taste with that of the customer. The buyer assimilates vast amounts of information and distills it to a point that allows for decision making. The integration and adaptation of information is a difficult job. Buyers work long hours planning, purchasing, and reacting to the ebb and flow of business. The national economy, local economy, gas prices, industry trends, fashion trends, weather, and unexpected events are hurdles that buyers navigate and accommodate along the way. The job of a buyer is complex and riddled with opportunities for success and failure.

Today, most newly graduated fashion students begin their buying careers as **assistant buyers** where the fundamentals are learned and grooming for additional responsibility occurs. The responsibilities of a buyer are vast. It is widely believed that buyers lead glamorous lives jet setting to New York and other sensational locations. While it is true that buyers often visit thrilling and attractive cities, the job is far from glamorous. First, buyers must please their customers. Second, buyers are obligated to achieve plans and goals required by owners, stockholders, and other stakeholders in the company. To please customers and stakeholders, buyers have numerous responsibilities including the tasks of monitoring selling of goods currently on the retail floor, making markdown assessments, and developing strategies that will drive sales and increase profits. The negotiation hat is a major component of driving sales and achieving goals. A buyer negotiates price, payment terms, merchandise deliveries, margin assistance, advertising allowances, exclusivity of product, and vendor returns on a daily basis.

In an average workday, buyers meet with their **divisional merchandise managers** to discuss a variety of topics; make buying choices; write orders for the merchandise; and attend several meetings a day regarding advertising, new stores, or other important company business. Buyers answer scores of phone calls and e-mails daily. Buyers experience stress and frustration, and at times a loss of productivity from the amount of responsibility, the requirement to realize plans and goals, and constant criticism. Given this information, why would anyone choose to be a buyer? Buyers have passion for the industry that drives them; in addition to that, the success of a good season, a love of fashion, the adrenaline rush of constant change, and the dynamics of the industry as a whole keep a buyer motivated. Now that we know what a buyer's job is, let's examine how a buyer does his or her job.

The Buying Process

The buying process begins with planning. Before purchasing the first piece of merchandise, the buyer completes a **six-month plan** that details sales, inventory, markdowns, purchases, turnover, and gross margin. Figure 5.2 depicts a six-month plan. The plan is a six-month plan because it encompasses six-month increments called **seasons**. The **spring season** typically covers February through July, while the **fall season** covers August through January. The goal

FIGURE 5.2 *The six-month plan is a tool used to plan sales, inventory, markdowns, and purchases for the spring and fall seasons.*

Six-Month Plan

Department: _____   Department: _____
Buyer: _____   Season: _____
Date Prepared: _____   Last Revision Date: _____

		LY	Plan TY	Revised	Actual TY		Notes:			
Season's Totals										
Markup %										
Gross Margin %										
Turnover										

		AUGUST	SEPTEMBER	OCTOBER	NOVEMBER	DECEMBER	JANUARY	FEBRUARY	SEASON TOTAL
	Last Year	$ 150.0	200.0	140.0	170.0	260.0	80.0		1,000.0
	Plan TY	168.0	210.0	126.0	178.5	283.5	84.0		1,050.0
	% Inc/Dec TY	12.0	5.0	−10.0	5.0	9.0	5.0		5.0
	% Total TY	16.0	20.0	12.0	17.0	27.0	8.0		100.0
	% Total LY	15.0	20.0	14.0	17.0	26.0	8.0		100.0
	Revised								
	Actual								
STOCK/SALES	Last Year	3.9	3.0	4.1	3.6	2.5	6.3	5.7	
	Plan TY	3.9	3.0	3.9	3.6	2.6	6.2	5.6	
	Revised								
	Actual								
BOM STOCK $	Last Year	$ 585.0	600.0	574.0	612.0	650.0	504.0	580.0	586.4
	Plan TY	655.2	630.0	491.4	642.6	737.1	520.8	570.0	606.7
	Revised								
	Actual								
MARKDOWNS $	Last Year	$ 72.0	40.0	60.0	48.0	120.0	60.0		400.0
	Plan TY	99.2	52.0	56.7	66.2	148.4	50.1		472.5
	% to Sales	59.1	24.8	45.0	37.1	52.3	59.6		45.0
	% by Month	21.0	11.0	12.0	14.0	31.4	10.6		100.0
	% to Sales LY	48.0	20.0	42.9	28.2	46.2	75.0		40.0
	% by Month LY	18.0	10.0	15.0	12.0	30.0	15.0		100.0
	Revised								
	Actual								
PURCHASES $	Last Year	$ 337.0	306.0	333.0	363.5	305.0	278.0		1,922.5
	Plan TY	242.0	123.4	333.9	339.2	215.6	183.3		1,437.3
	Revised								
	Actual								

of the plan is to create an **open-to-buy (OTB)** that will guide the buyer in purchasing merchandise by making certain that sales goals are achievable by stocking the correct amount of inventory and taking the proper markdowns to keep inventory moving through the store. The turnover goal guarantees that the store has planned the correct amount of inventory in relationship to sales.

Planning

Planning Sales

Six-month planning begins with **sales**. Sales are the dollars received for merchandise, calculated by multiplying the number of units sold times the retail price. Sales are the most important and most difficult piece of the plan, not from a mathematical perspective, but from a conceptional one. Because sales are the basis of all other elements of the plan, it is crucial to take a broad and objective view when planning sales. A sales plan that is too aggressive will result in high inventory levels that lead to markdowns and gross margin erosion. Conversely, a sales plan that is too conservative will result in a lack of inventory that will hinder sales and consequently gross margin. There are many considerations when planning sales, and most retailers begin with last year's actual results. In addition to last year, three to five years of history guides them as well. History helps them to repeat success and avoid mistakes. While reviewing history, current and future factors also come into play. Current sales trends, fashion trends, national economic conditions, local economic conditions, gas prices, changes in sales promotion, and weather are a few of the considerations taken into account as a sales plan comes together.

Mathematically, sales are an easy calculation. It is common for upper management to decide what the overall sales increase will be for the company and then disperse the increase throughout the departments within the company. For example, upper management may decide that the company will plan an overall sales increase of 7 percent and make the men's department responsible for a 5 percent increase over last year's sales for the fall season. This simply means that the men's department goal is to sell 5 percent more than it sold last year in the fall season. Hence, if the men's department sold $1,000,000 last fall, the goal this fall would be $1,050,000, calculated as follows:

$1,000,000 (last year's sales) $\times$ 5% (this year's planned % increase)

$\qquad$ = $50,000 (this year's dollar increase) + $1,000,000 (last year's sales)

$\qquad$ = $1,050,000 (this year's sales plan) or more simply

$1,000,000 (last year's sales) $\times$ 105% (5% sales increase)

$\qquad$ = $1,050,000 (this year's sales)

When given last year's actual sales and this year's planned sales, the percentage increase calculation is as follows:

$$\text{Percentage increase calculation} = \frac{\text{this year's sales plan} - \text{last year's actual sales}}{\text{last year's actual sales}}$$

or

$$= \frac{\$1,050,000 \text{ (this year's fall sales plan)} - \$1,000,000 \text{ (last year's actual fall sales)}}{\$1,000,000 \text{ (last year's actual fall sales)}}$$

$$= \frac{\$50{,}000 \text{ (this year's dollar increase in sales)}}{\$1{,}000{,}000 \text{ (last year's actual fall sales)}}$$

= 5% increase in sales this fall over last fall

The total season's sales are broken down by month so that each month of the season has a planned sales goal. Each month is allocated a percent of the total sales plan based on various criteria such as last year's sales, shifts in holidays, and changes in the promotional calendar, to name a few. The calculation for the percent allocation for last year is as follows:

$$\text{Percent allocation for last year} = \frac{\text{the sales for each month}}{\text{the season's total sales}}$$

= % allocation for each month last year

Therefore, if August sales were $150,000 last year and the total sales for the fall season were $1,000,000 the calculation is:

$$= \frac{\$150{,}000 \text{ August sales last year}}{\$1{,}000{,}000 \text{ Fall total sales last year}}$$

= 15% August percent to total fall sales last year

On the other hand, if August percent of sales last year was 15 percent and last year's total sales were $1,000,000, August dollar sales can be calculated as follows:

$1,000,000 (last year's total fall sales) $\times$ 15% (August percent to total last year)

= $150,000 (August dollar sales last year).

The buyer uses the percent allocation of sales last year for each month in the season and the other aforementioned variables to establish appropriate percentage allocation for the current year. After determining the percentage by month, the sales plan for the season multiplied times the percent allocation for each month equals the sales plan for that month. For example, August was 15 percent of the fall sales last year and this year the buyer is planning August to produce 16 percent of the fall business. To calculate August sales this year, total fall season's sales of $1,050,000 is multiplied times the August allocation of 16 percent or

$1,050,000 (sales plan for fall) $\times$ 16% August % of sales = $168,000 August sales

This procedure continues until every month of the season has a calculated sales plan.

Planning Inventory

After sales, inventory planning is the next portion of the six-month plan to complete. The discussion of inventory, also known as stock, takes on two forms, **beginning of month (BOM)**, meaning the amount of inventory available at the beginning of a month, and **end of month (EOM)**, the inventory available at the end of a month. Both are relevant; however, inventory planning focuses on the BOM inventory. Keep in mind that the EOM of one month is the BOM of the following month, so if the August EOM is $609,000 then the BOM for September is $609,000. There are many methods of inventory planning; however, for reasons of simplicity, this text will discuss only the **stock to sales ratio** method of **stock** (inventory) planning. A stock to sales ratio is the relationship of stock (inventory) to sales. It is a way of determining the correct amount of stock (inventory) needed when a certain amount of sales are planned.

As with sales, history plays a role in the assessment of the stock to sales ratio. The calculation of the stock to sales ratio last year is:

$$\text{Last year's stock to sales ratio} = \frac{\text{last year's actual BOM inventory for the month}}{\text{last year's actual sales for the same month}}$$

Therefore, if August sales were $150,000 last year and the inventory was $585,000 the calculation is:

$$\frac{\$585,000 \text{ (last August actual inventory)}}{\$150,000 \text{ (last August actual sales)}} = 3.9 \text{ stock to sales ratio for August}$$

Repeating the calculation will yield a stock to sales ratio for each month. It is important to note that it is possible for every month of the season to have a different stock to sales ratio. Knowing what the stock to sales ratio was for each month of the season last year is important when ascertaining the stock to sales ratio for this year; however, it is highly unusual for the stock to sales ratios to be identical from year to year. After determining the stock to sales ratio for the planning season, the mathematics for calculating inventory is:

$$\text{Planned sales} \times \text{planned stock to sales ratio} = \text{planned BOM inventory}$$

For example, if August planned sales are $168,000 and August planned stock to sales ratio is 3.9, then the inventory plan for August is $655,200, computed as follows:

$$\$168,000 \text{ (August planned sales)} \times 3.9 \text{ (August planned stock to sales ratio)}$$
$$= \$655,200 \text{ August planned inventory}$$

Planning Turnover

In a retail store, goods sell, and once sold, replacement merchandise arrives, which sells, and once sold, replacement merchandise arrives, and so it continues. The velocity at which this happens is **turnover**. Figure 5.3 demonstrates how cash buys goods, then the goods sell and once sold, replacement merchandise arrives, which sells and once sold, replacement

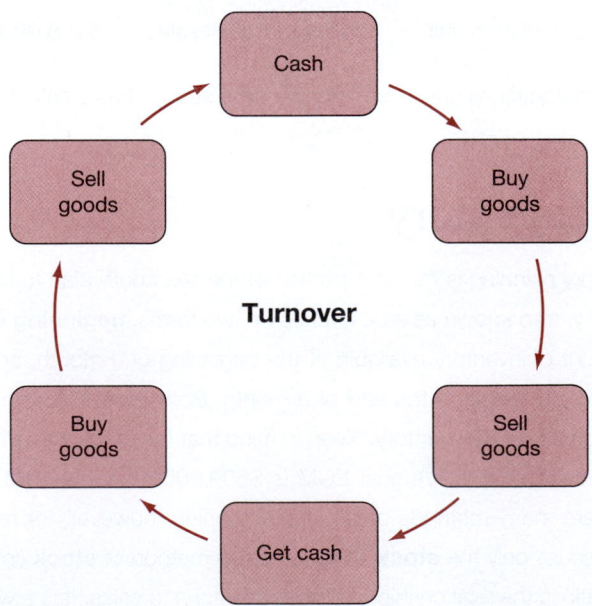

FIGURE 5.3 *Turnover cycle.*

merchandise arrives, and so on. Turnover is the number of times merchandise becomes cash. Vitally important to a retailer, the turnover rate measures the efficiency of the merchandise purchased and how well a buyer controlled and maintained inventory levels. The formula for calculating inventory is:

$$\frac{\text{planned season sales in dollars}}{\text{average inventory in dollars}} = \text{turnover}$$

For example, if planned sales for fall are $1,050,000 and the average inventory for the season is $606,700, the turnover rate for fall is 1.8.

$$\frac{\$1,050,000 \text{ fall planned sales}}{\$606,700 \text{ fall planned average inventory}} = 1.73 \text{ fall planned turnover}$$

Average inventory is the average of the planned BOM inventory for each month plus the BOM for the first month of the following season, divided by seven for an average. In our example, the sum of the BOMs for August, September, October, November, December, January, and February (BOM of spring season) equals $4,247,100 divided by seven, resulting in an average seasonal inventory of $606,700.

Planning Markdowns

Markdown planning follows inventory planning. Markdowns are a reduction in the retail price of merchandise. Markdowns are a necessary component of retailing and, even under the best of circumstances, are unavoidable. Used to accelerate selling, during sales promotions, and to clean up broken assortments, markdowns are valuable and worthwhile but require tight management and control. Because markdowns can erode gross margin, judiciousness is important. Pricing and buying errors create markdowns, necessitating great care when making assortment and pricing decisions. Planning markdowns requires planning in dollars and percents. As discussed earlier with sales and inventory, history is the springboard for planning markdowns as well. Considerations such as sales trends, fashion trends, promotional calendars, and calendar shifts (changes in holidays) impact the markdown plan in the same manner they influence the sales plan.

To begin planning markdowns, it is imperative to calculate last year's percentage of actual markdowns in relationship to sales. To calculate markdowns percentage of sales for the season the formula is:

$$\frac{\text{last year's total season markdowns}}{\text{last year's total season sales}} = \text{markdown \% of sales for the season}$$

For example, if the season's markdowns were $400,000 last year and the total season's sales were $1,000,000 last year, then markdowns percentage to sales was 40 percent. Calculated as follows:

$$\frac{\$400,000 \text{ (last year's total season markdowns)}}{\$1,000,000 \text{ (last year's total season sales)}} = 40\% \text{ markdowns percent of sales}$$

Using the resulting figure as a basis for this year's markdown plans, the planning team will set a markdown goal for the current planning season. For example, the sales plan for the fall season is $1,050,000 and knowing that markdowns were 40 percent of sales last year, it is decided that markdowns will be 45 percent of planned sales this year, meaning that markdowns will be planned at $472,500 for the fall season:

($1,050,000 fall sales plan $\times$ 45% fall markdown plan = $472,500 fall markdown plan)

As with sales, it is necessary to allocate markdowns by month and the process is similar to the allocation of sales by month. The calculation is:

$$\frac{\text{last year's markdown dollars by month}}{\text{last year's total season markdown dollars}} = \% \text{ of markdowns by month}$$

With markdowns last August of $72,000 and total markdowns for the season of $400,000, the August percent to total markdowns or the August allocation of markdowns last year was 18 percent. In other words, 18 percent of the total markdowns taken in the fall season last year occurred in August. The calculation is as follows:

$$\frac{\$72,000 \text{ August markdowns last year}}{\$400,000 \text{ total fall season markdowns last year}} = 18\% \text{ markdowns for August last year}$$

The process continues by calculating the percent for each month of the season. At the conclusion of calculating every month in the season, the sum total percent of all the months will equal 100 percent. Each month's calculated percent is a guide for determining what the markdown percent allocation should be this year and that percent multiplied by the total markdown plan produces the markdown plan by month. In other words, last August the markdown percent to plan or allocation was 18 percent and this year the plan is 21 percent. The planned allocation of 21 percent multiplied times the planned total markdown dollars of $472,500 results in a markdown plan for August of $99,225. The calculation is as follows:

$472,500 (total markdowns planned for the season) $\times$ 21% August % by month
= $99,225 (August markdown plan)

Each month follows the same procedure until all months' markdown dollar plans are calculated.

Markdowns calculations include a percent of sales by month. As previously shown, markdowns are calculated as a percent of total markdowns as a first step in markdown planning. The same calculation produces the markdown percent of sales for each month. Using August markdowns and sales as an example, August markdowns are planned at 59.1 percent of sales computed by dividing August planned markdowns of $99,225 by August planned sales of $150,000, which equals 59.1 percent. Therefore, monthly markdown percent of sales is:

$$\text{Markdown percent of sales for the month} = \frac{\text{monthly planned markdown dollars}}{\text{monthly planned sales dollars}}$$

or

$$= \frac{\$99,225 \text{ (August planned markdowns)}}{\$168,000 \text{ (August planned sales)}}$$

$$= 59.1\% \text{ markdowns percent of August sales}$$

As demonstrated above, markdown planning occurs in dollars for the total season and for each month of the season. In addition, markdowns planning also happens as a percent of total sales and as a percent of sales for each month of the season. Lastly, markdown planning includes markdowns allocated monthly, or as a percent of total markdowns by month.

The detail in markdown planning erroneously leads people to believe that markdowns are the most difficult element of the six-month plan, and mathematically speaking that is arguable. However, it is the sales portion of the plan that is the most difficult to predict and plan largely because sales are the foundation for the entire plan. After sales, inventory, and markdown planning is complete, computation of the purchase plan transpires.

Planning Purchases

With the other elements of the six-month plan complete, planning **purchases** is simple and straightforward. The purchase plan is the result of the planning of sales, inventory, and markdowns. The figures derived from planning sales, inventory, and markdowns lead to a purchase plan for each month of the season. The formula for calculating purchases is:

> (+) monthly sales plan
> (+) inventory plan for the following month (EOM)
> (+) monthly markdown plan
> (=) total merchandise needs
> (−) inventory plan for the beginning of the month (BOM)
> (=) monthly purchase plan

As an example of how the formula works, the previously mentioned August figures will be used and the end-of-month (EOM) number, also the same as the September beginning of the month inventory (BOM), is $630,000. Using the August figures, the purchase plan is determined as follows:

> (+) $168,000 August planned sales
> (+) $630,000 August planned EOM (September planned BOM)
> (+) $99,225 August planned markdowns
> (=)$897,225 total merchandise needs
> (−) $655,200 August planned BOM
> (=) $242,025 *August planned purchases*

The calculation continues for each month in the season. The total of the purchases for each month equals the seasons planned purchases. Purchases by month are like a checkbook. The $242,225 August planned purchases are how much can be spent on new merchandise in the month of August. Buyers keep a running total of money available to spend by subtracting the retail value of each order placed from planned purchases, leaving a balance on which additional goods may be bought; this is called *open-to-buy*. Open-to-buy and the balance in a checkbook are similar in that the amount listed is all you have to spend for that month. When a buyer exceeds the OTB balance, the buyer is overbought. For example, assuming that a buyer placed orders totaling $157,000 (**on order**), the OTB is as follows:

> (+) $168,000 August planned sales
> (+) $630,000 August planned EOM (September planned BOM)
> (+) $99,225 August planned markdowns
> (=) $897,225 total merchandise needs
> (−) $655,200 August planned BOM

(=) $242,025 *August planned purchases*
(−) $157,000 August on order
(=) $85,028 *OTB*

Other Retail Math Concepts

In addition to the six-month plan, several critical retail math concepts round out the information provided by the six-month plan including income statements, gross margin, markup, and pricing of merchandise. Our examination begins with the income statement.

INCOME STATEMENT

The **income statement**, also known as a profit and loss statement, serves a financial function more than a merchandising function, but it clearly illustrates the importance of what a buyer does in terms of net sales, cost of goods sold, and gross margin. The income statement shows income, gross margin, expenses, and profit or loss measured over a specific period. The income statement begins with **net sales**. Retailers sell goods keeping a running total of the sales known as **gross sales**; however, not all goods sold "stay sold," meaning that customers return items and some of the sold merchandise ends up back in the retailer's inventory. Net sales equal the goods that "stay sold." Moreover, at times there are allowances made to customers, like giving a sale price after merchandise has been purchased, that are deducted from gross sales. Buyers have a tremendous responsibility for net sales because the merchandise selected by the buyer is the offering to the customer; if the customer does not respond by buying the merchandise, the buyer is accountable. As a mathematical equation the path to net sales is:

gross sales − customer returns and allowances = net sales

The **cost of goods sold** is the first deduction made from net sales. Cost of goods sold is the billed cost of merchandise purchases plus freight charges and any workroom or alteration costs incurred preparing the merchandise for the selling floor. The cost of the merchandise purchased is 100 percent the responsibility of the buyer. Buyers work with the vendor community, selecting products, and negotiating prices, shipping terms, and other concessions for the benefit of the retailer. Paying too much for goods results in lower profits for the retailer for which the responsibility falls on the buyer.

GROSS MARGIN

The result of subtracting cost of goods sold from net sales is **gross margin**. Gross margin is the primary measurement of how well a buyer is performing his or her duties. The gross margin number is central to the assessment of a buyer because buyers are accountable for sales and cost of goods sold. The income statement begins to shape up as follows:

(+) gross sales
(−) customer returns and allowances
(=) net sales
(−) cost of goods sold
(=) *gross margin*

After the gross margin point of the income statement, the buyer has virtually no accountability. The next portion of the income statement is **operating expenses**. Operating expenses encompass salaries, rent, advertising, supplies, insurance, and the like. Operating expenses are an operational responsibility rather than a merchandising responsibility. That said, it is the buyer's duty to make certain that enough gross margin is realized to cover operating expenses and profit. If the buyer's merchandising efforts fail to produce the gross margin needed to pay for expenses, the company will not earn a profit. The income statement in the skeletal format is as follows:

> (+) net sales
> (−) cost of goods sold
> (=) gross margin
> (−) operating expenses
> (=) profit or loss

or

> (+) $1,050,000 planned net sales for fall
> (−) $609,000 cost of goods sold
> (=) $441,00 gross margin
> (−) $399,000 operating expenses
> (=) $42,000 *net profit*

Viewing the figures on the income statement as a percentage of net sales is more beneficial, at times, than the dollar figures alone. Percentages allow for comparisons between departments, stores, and companies. Net sales, the basis for all the factors, are always 100 percent. Dividing the other components by net sales derives the percentage of net sales for each component. As seen in the example below, cost of goods sold is 58 percent, calculated by dividing the cost of goods sold in dollars by the net sales in dollars:

$$\frac{\$609,000 \text{ cost of goods sold}}{\$1,050,000 \text{ net sales}}$$

$$= 58\% \text{ (cost of goods sold are 58\% of net sales)}$$

The calculation for each factor of the income statement is precisely the same. Below is the previous income statement including the percentage of net sales for each component:

> (+) $1,050,000 100% planned net sales for fall
> (−) $609,000 58% cost of goods sold
> (=) $441,000 42% *gross margin*
> (−) $399,000 38% operating expenses
> (=) $42,000 4% *net profit*

As seen here, the gross margin achieved is 42 percent of sales. The question of whether or not this percentage has achieved the buyer's goal depends on the goal itself. It is clear, however, that the gross margin was high enough to cover expenses and yield a $42,000 or 4 percent net profit.

Markup

Markup is the difference between the billed cost of an item and the retail price of that item. Simply put, if a buyer pays $10 for a sweater and retails the sweater for $24, the markup is $14.

$$(+) \ \$24 \text{ sweater retail}$$
$$(-) \ \$10 \text{ sweater cost}$$
$$(=) \ \$14 \ \textit{sweater markup}$$

Markup in dollars is relevant; however, more germane to the topic of markup is the percentage of markup. The formula below calculates markup as a percentage:

$$\frac{\text{retail of the item} - \text{cost of the item}}{\text{retail of the item}} = \frac{\$ \text{ markup of the item}}{\text{retail of the item}} = \text{markup \% of the item}$$

Therefore, using the example above:

$$\frac{\$24 \text{ sweater retail} - \$10 \text{ sweater cost}}{\$24 \text{ sweater retail}} = \frac{\$14 \text{ markup}}{\$24 \text{ sweater retail}} = 58.33\% \text{ markup}$$

The procedure remains the same regardless of the quantity purchased. If a buyer purchases 144 sweaters for $10 and retails the 144 sweaters for $24, the markup percentage does not change.

$$144 \text{ sweaters} \times \$10 \text{ cost each} = \$1,440 \text{ total cost}$$
$$144 \text{ sweaters} \times \$24 \text{ retail each} = \$3,456 \text{ total retail}$$

$$\frac{\$3,456 \text{ total retail} - \$1,440 \text{ total cost}}{\$3,456 \text{ total retail}}$$

$$= \frac{\$2,016}{\$3,456}$$

$$= 58.33\% \text{ markup}$$

Each department in a retail store has a markup percentage goal. The markup percentage required varies by department and even by classification within a department. The markup percentage plan or goal is an aggregate figure, meaning that some merchandise will achieve a higher-than-planned markup while other merchandise will achieve a lower-than-planned markup. However, the achievement of the overall, or cumulative, markup plan indicates a buyer has priced merchandise with an appropriate markup. If the actual markup is lower than planned, the risk of a lower-than-needed gross margin is increased. If the actual markup is higher than planned, the risk of overpricing items, and therefore losing sales, is increased. It is possible to see a classification performing very well at retail and underperforming on the gross margin line, because of a lower-than-required actual markup. In this situation, it is necessary to reevaluate the pricing structure of the classification. After the financial plans are completed and approved, buyers begin assortment planning.

Pricing

The accountability of buyers for net sales makes the selection and pricing of merchandise critical. Pricing merchandise is one of the most difficult aspects of a buyer's job and the importance of proper merchandise pricing cannot be overemphasized. Buyers buy merchandise for resale in retail stores. The buyer selects merchandise and writes orders to the vendor at the agreed-upon **cost** (the wholesale price the retailer pays the vendor for the goods). Tasked with establishing a retail value for the merchandise, the skill is in retailing the goods at a price the customer is willing to pay and still achieve the markup goal of the department. Buyers work with markup goals to ensure that the retail price placed on the merchandise will yield enough gross margin to cover expenses and profit.

Assortment Planning

Financial plans are vital but they do not determine what to buy; they provide an amount to purchase in dollars, but the buyer decides the correct balance between knit tops and woven tops and the best vendors from which to purchase the merchandise. A buyer's experience, customer knowledge, and taste level drive the assortment plan. **Assortment planning** is the decision-making process that determines what the sales floor will house at any point. Imagine the sales floor of a store: The merchandise found there began with financial plans but came to fruition with an assortment plan. The buyer decided what vendors, merchandise, color story, and sizes the department would carry. Assortment planning begins at the departmental level. Most **department** stores break down the total business of the store by departments (hence the name department store) and then by **classifications**. Men's wear, women's wear, junior's, children's wear, shoes, accessories, intimate apparel, and cosmetics are common departments in a retail store. Within the departments are classifications where planning, buying, and monitoring of merchandise occur in smaller sections. Classifications vary by store but in men's wear it is common to find classifications of shirts (knits and wovens), sweaters, outerwear (jackets and top coats), pants, jeans, accessories (cuff links, ties, small leather goods, etc.), furnishings (underwear, socks, and pajamas), and clothing (suits and suit separates). Each of these classifications represents a portion or a percentage of the overall men's business. The percentage of the classification business, based largely on the prior year, does change slightly year to year. Additionally, fashion trends dictate altering percentages at times. For example, if jeans are more of a fashion item this year than last year, it behooves the buyer to plan to have more jeans, necessitating the reduction of the percentage of another classification. The buyer uses the percentages for each classification to determine the purchases needed for each classification. This process can be manual; however, in larger retail stores, the six-month planning occurs by classification, giving each classification an individual six-month plan.

After planning at the classification level, buyers drill down further to guarantee that customer needs and emerging trends are covered. Assortment planning can take several forms and is retailer or even buyer specific. Planning a classification by vendor is necessary. Knowing the allocation of dollars by vendor ensures that the best-selling and highest gross margin vendors are getting the correct amount of open-to-buy. Sometimes it is essential that a buyer plan a classification by price point. If a junior's shorts buyer is planning for the spring season and knows that there are two primary price points of $24 and $30 for shorts with $24 being the highest volume price point, the buyer can break down the open-to-buy dollars by price point and by vendor. This means the buyer will know how many $24 shorts to buy from each vendor and how many $30 shorts to buy from each vendor. A further breakdown by fabrication is possible as well, if that is a factor in the assortment. Assortment planning aids in the decision making of what to buy. Figure 5.4 is an example of a vendor assortment plan.

A question often asked of buyers is, "How do you know what to buy?" It is a simple question with a complicated answer. There is no magic formula for knowing what will sell, but

FIGURE 5.4 *Vendor assortment plan.*

Buyers   Arrington/Reamy
Season   Fall
Year   2012

Month		August		September		October		November		December		January		Total Season	
$ Purchase Plan		Plan	Actual	Plan	Actual	Plan	Actual	Plan	Actual	Plan	Actual	Plan	Actual	Plan	Actual
Vendor	% total														
	277.6		**215.3**		**261.6**		**307.5**		**253.3**		**200**		**1515**	
Levi s	30%	83.3		64.6		78.5		92.3		76.0		60		455	0
Paris Blues	20%	55.5		43.1		52.3		61.5		50.7		40		303	0
OTB	15%	41.6		32.3		39.2		46.1		38.0		30		227	0
Angels	15%	41.6		32.3		39.2		46.1		38.0		30		227	0
Tracy Evans	10%	27.8		21.5		26.2		30.8		25.3		20		152	0
Joe Benbassett	10%	27.8		21.5		26.2		30.8		25.3		20		152	0
Total	100%	277.6	0	215.3	0	261.6	0	307.5	0	253.3	0	200	0	1515	0

Note: The purchase plan figures from the six-month plan are allocated by vendor by month. Upon placing orders, the actual amount purchased is recorded against the purchase plan.

buyers use the tools available to them to answer this question. History affects the purchasing of an item, and an item that performs well is worth repeating. Fashion trends also influence purchasing decisions. Merchandise touted as "hot" or "must have" is included in the assortment. Buyers want to stay abreast of the newest merchandise and trends. Customers are the final litmus test on whether or not to purchase an item. If the customer in question is unlikely to purchase a product, then the buyer is unwise to include it in the assortment. Knowing the customer and understanding his or her needs, wants, and fashion sense is the best test of what to buy. Answering the question of what to buy leads to how much to buy.

The amount to buy is dependent on the purpose of the merchandise. Merchandise featured in advertisements requires larger quantities to fulfill customer demand. Customer demand and manufacturing minimums necessitate the purchasing of large quantities for programmed and private label goods. **Fixture fill** involves buying enough merchandise to fill a fixture so the size of the fixture dictates the number of units. **Test quantities** are small and fit the bill for new fashion or unproven items the buyer is "testing" before buying larger amounts. The size of the store itself has a bearing on the quantity of merchandise ordered; since stores vary in size, the quantity needed varies as well. Buyers consider all of the aforementioned and many other factors in their decisions regarding quantity. Buying too little of an item results in lost sales, and buying too much of an item results in excessive markdowns and lost gross margin; the goal is to buy as much as can be sold at a profit.

In addition to knowing what to buy and how much to buy, knowing when to buy determines the success or failure of merchandise. The delivery of goods at the wrong point in a season will retard the acceptance and sell-through of the item. For example, a shorts buyer knows that delivering shorts in December is too early. In most regions of the United States, the weather is not conducive to wearing shorts in December. Even if the shorts are the hottest trend in the most desired fabrics at a fabulous price, the timing of the delivery will prevent the shorts from selling.

Markets

Chapter 2 discussed the definition of market and the different types of markets, but why do buyers go to market? The obvious and correct answer is to buy merchandise. However, there is much more to a market trip than buying merchandise. Markets are educational for buyers. It is at market that buyers learn current and future fashion trends, what is happening currently at retail, news about other retailers, and news about manufacturers. Buyers go to market to establish and solidify relationships with the vendor community. It is much easier to work with someone with whom one has established a relationship, particularly where negotiation is a factor, which is crucial in a buyer's job.

An average day for a buyer at market starts at around 8:30 or 9:00 A.M. with appointments for the week made prior to arriving. On the first day, a buyer usually visits a **resident buying office** to meet with the **market specialist** for his or her department. A resident buying office is an organization that offers retailers a variety of services. Resident buying offices forecast vendor, style, fabric, and color trends each season. These offices assist with planning assortments and coordinating private label programs, vendor location, vendor problems and issues, and appointments. The market specialist provides trend information and insight into what is currently going on in the marketplace. The market specialist shows new items, proven basics, and new vendors and also assists with appointments and vendor issues as they arise. Meeting with the resident buying office is strategic to a buyer's understanding of current and future happenings in the industry. After meeting with the resident buying office, the buyer begins seeing vendors.

Appointments with vendors last from 30 minutes to six hours, depending on the vendor and the type of merchandise offered. A junior denim buyer can see a jeans vendor in 30 to 45 minutes. However, a denim collections vendor appointment, where the presentation includes multiple classifications and deliveries, can take six or seven hours. (Figure 5.5 is typical of a buyer's market itinerary.) It is advisable to devise an agenda for each appointment prior to the meeting. The agenda could include items such as vendor performance in the way of selling and gross margin. Discussions also include shipping problems, quality problems, competition,

FIGURE 5.5 *An itinerary for a typical market week in New York.*

Itinerary for Arrington / Reamy
Market   New York March Market
Hotel   Hotel Metro

Time	Monday	Tuesday	Wednesday	Thursday	Friday
8:00					
8:30	Donegar Buying Office 7th Ave 3rd floor Elizabeth & Maureen	Union Bay 485 7th Ave 11th floor Connie 555-1212	At Last 525 7th 15th floor David 555-1212	Wrapper 1407 Broadway 3rd floor Ilene 555-1212	
9:00					
9:30	Levi's 1411 Broadway 11th Floor Christin 555-1212	Southpole 525 7th Ave 17th floor Matt 555-1212	Next Era 1407 Broadway 20th floor Stephen 555-1212	Byer 1407 Broadway 8th floor Rodney 555-1212	
10:00					
10:30					
11:00	Paris Blues 1466 Broadway 11th Floor Jacob 555-1212	Baby Phat 530 7th 15th floor Sara 555-1212	Eyeshadow 1407 Broadway 33rd floor Terri 555-1212	My Michelle 1407 Broadway 2nd floor Rose 555-1212	
11:30					
12:00	OTB 1407 Broadway 20th Floor Marney 555-1212	Tracy Evans 530 7th Ave 19th floor Alison 555-1212	Anxiety 1407 31st floor Laura 555-1212	Depart NYC	
12:30					
1:00	Angels 1407 Broadway 11th Floor Elise 555-1212	Hydraulic 215 W 40th 2nd floor Nadine 555-1212	G.A.S. 1400 27th floor Jeff 555-1212		
1:30					
2:00	US Polo Association 1400 Broadway 15th floor Isaac 555-1212	Currants 1411 Broadway 3rd floor Gail 555-1212	Fashion Ave 1400 Broadway 12th floor Steve 555-1212		
2:30					
3:00			Quizz 1385 Broadway 15th floor Jackie 555-1212	Flight Home	
3:30					
4:00	Zanadi 1385 Broadway 5th floor Marc 555-1212	Golden Touch 1410 Broadway 8th floor Susan 555-1212	Moa Moa 1411 Broadway 29th floor Keith 555-1212		
4:30					
5:00					
5:30					
6:00					

Note: This itinerary is representative of a market week for a junior sportswear buyer. The appointments are made.

and advertising, to name a few. Figure 5.6 is an example of an agenda used for a vendor meeting. Negotiation takes place during these talks. Buyers request that vendors allow for merchandise returns, margin assistance, better prices, and exclusive product offerings, to name a few. Of course, buyers visit vendor showrooms to shop the line, or view what the vendor is offering for the upcoming seasons. Negotiation is important at this stage of the meeting, as buyers begin making selections and prices become the topic of conversation.

Market weeks present a venue for information gathering and gossip. A buyer can learn what is going on with other retailers, manufacturers, and collect countless tidbits of information and what it all means to the industry. Buyers also glean information about best sellers, poor performers, shipping problems, and manufacturers and retailers likely to go out of business.

Buyers connect with other buyers in the marketplace and share a great deal of information with one another. As strange as it may seem, buyers collect pivotal knowledge from other buyers in the marketplace, developing friendships along the way. Buyers see one another in showrooms, often running into one another multiple times a day. There are vendor dinners, cocktail parties, and other vendor-sponsored events where buyers connect.

Most markets in the United States are in major cities like New York or Los Angeles. When visiting large cities, buyers shop local retail establishments for the education and inspiration of

FIGURE 5.6 *An agenda helps a buyer prepare for meetings with vendors at market and ensures that all pertinent topics are discussed and the meeting remains on track.*

Vendor Meeting Agenda

Vendor: _____   Appointment: _____

Attendees: _____   Address: _____

_____

		Sales Plan	% Change from LY	LY Actual	% Change from Previous Year	Vendor Door Count TY	Vendor Door Count LY
Annual Sales							
Purchases	Cost						
	Retail						
GM	Projected $						
	Projected %						
	Plan $						
	Plan %						
	Difference						

Store Issues for Vendor:

_____

_____

_____

Vendor Issues for Store:

_____

_____

_____

Resolutions:

_____

_____

_____

Resolutions:

_____

_____

_____

FIGURE 5.7 *The selling by style reports provide details about individual item selling and recap selling by vendor.*

Style Selling Report

Buyer:	Deidra Arrington		Department: Men's Sportswear													
Style #	176803	Vendor #	7992	Vendor	Levi Strauss			Date:	7/5/2012							
							Item Description		Stripe polo							

Last Rcpt	Total Rcpts	On Order	On Hand	Total Sales	Stock/Sales	% Sold	Sales by week											IMU%	GM%
							1	2	3	4	5	6	7	8	9	10	11		
10-Jun	1200	0	417	783	2.3	65.3%	182	218	77	306	0	0	0	0	0	0	0	56.2	42.48

Note: Style selling reports detail the style #, the vendor, and give a description of the item. Other detailed information includes the number of units received, the number of units sold, the number of units on hand, sales by week, the initial markup %, and the gross margin %. Buyers use this information to determine the performance of an item in decisions such as markdowns, reorders, and advertising.

what is on store floors in major cities. Usually, fashion trends begin on the East Coast or the West Coast and migrate toward the middle of the country. Visiting these cities gives a buyer a heads up about what is trending. Not all fashion trends seen in New York or Los Angeles will survive in Middle America, but knowing that is also important. Besides visiting the retail floors, seeing the street scene in the larger cities provides a vast amount of information and inspiration. Fashion is heavily influenced by the street, and observing street trends is crucial to forecasting the next mainstream fashion explosion. Once the financial and assortment plans are completed and buyers have traveled to markets and purchased goods, the major task of tracking merchandise selling begins.

Merchandise Reporting

Inundated with information, buyers sift through and prioritize the facts needed to make decisions and monitor selling, and markdowns. Automatically generated printed reports provide a great deal of the information. When detailed tasks dictate, additional, more specific information is available through ad hoc or buyer-requested reports, for example, the best-selling color in knit tops from a previous season or perhaps a selling report by size. Some of the most common and widely used reports include selling by style, vendor analysis, and the six-month plan/open-to-buy report.

SELLING BY STYLE REPORT

Invaluable to a buyer, **selling by style reports** provide details about item selling. Figure 5.7 is a sample of a selling by style report. Providing information such as units sold by week, percentage of sell-through by week, total percentage sell-through, gross margin by style, markdowns taken on each item, and future order information, selling by style reports are one of the most useful tools in a buyer's tool box. The percentage sell-through by week is the best indication of sales trends. For most retailers, the week's business ends on Saturday. The selling report prints on Sunday with the previous week's information, making it available for review by the buyer first thing Monday morning. A priority for the buyer, the report serves as the principal instrument for making various decisions.

The primary consideration is sales trends. Selling by style reports show selling trends and whether sales are on the rise or in a decline; buyers tune into these trends and make decisions accordingly. The **percentage sell-through by week** is the best indication of sales trends. Percentage sell-through by week is a simple calculation of dividing the number of units sold by the number of units on hand. For example, if a retailer receipts 672 of a particular dress and 387 units of the dress sell in six weeks, the sell-through on the dress is 57.6 percent, simply calculated by dividing 387 (the units sold) by 672 (the units received). Most important is what is selling well and whether a reorder (if possible) is warranted on the item. Retailers strive to maximize items that perform well at retail to increase sales, gross margin, and ultimately profit, and ensuring that enough best sellers are on the floor is the key to maximizing the item.

Also important are slow-selling items. The selling by style report is critical to making markdown decisions. Slow sellers require price reductions (markdowns) to stimulate interest in the item. Merchandise that does not sell creates many issues for a retailer by tying up inventory in slow-selling goods, therefore, requiring a reduction in price, which ultimately yields lower gross margins and profit. It is also important to find out whether there are additional goods on order for slow-selling items. Buyers work with vendors to negotiate a cancellation on remaining goods on order. Profitability will suffer if stores take in additional quantities of slow sellers because of the likelihood that the merchandise will not sell without price reductions. Profitability is important both from a total point of view as well as by item. In addition to the previously discussed information, the selling by style report provides gross margin by style.

Gross margin by style indicates how profitable a particular item is. This is vital when evaluating and analyzing the season's business in anticipation of the next season. For example, if a junior's buyer purchases a cable knit, hooded sweater for the fall and the sweater is a winner in terms of selling and gross margin, the buyer will want to buy the item again next fall. It is important to analyze the performance of the sweater based on selling and predict what quantity could have been sold had the goods been available to the customer. The determined amount becomes a buying plan for the following fall season. Given the information that 95 percent of all the units purchased sold with a very high gross margin of 49 percent, and that the sweater sold in four colors and in sizes of small, medium, large, and extra large, the buyer can clearly see that the customers responded positively to this item. At this point, the buyer will work to determine the number of units to purchase next fall, the number of times the sweater should arrive on the sales floor, the colors to purchase, and the sizes to purchase. The buyer together with the manufacturer will work out a price for the increased quantity and any desired design changes. Many times when an item is repeated in a large quantity, the design is "tweaked" to give it fresh appeal. The changes include new buttons, a change in the cable stitch, the addition of a cuff, and so on. A **program**, so named because the item is "programmed out," can be part of a private label assortment. A highly profitable item is born, birthed through the purchase of a sweater, and maximized using the information provided by the style selling report. In addition to sales by item, knowing the overall performance of vendors is crucial to the total performance of a department, and this is visible using the vendor analysis report.

VENDOR ANALYSIS

Vendor analysis reports, printed monthly, are the report card of a vendor's performance. See Figure 5.8 for an example of a vendor analysis report. A vendor analysis report provides the vendor name; vendor number; and a comparison of sales, purchases, markdowns, gross margin dollars, and gross margin percent of the current year and the previous year. Vendor analysis reports aid the buyer in deciding what vendors to continue to do business with and which vendors to eliminate from the store's assortment. Some vendors request the vendor analysis report monthly, but certainly, the vendor and buyer meet semiannually or quarterly to discuss the state of the business as detailed on the vendor analysis report. Buyers use the information in the vendor analysis report to seek financial assistance, known as **markdown money**, **margin assistance**, or **vendor assistance**, to improve the financial health of the retailer. The thought process is that vendors and retailers are partners in the retailing of the vendor's products, and as such the vendor has a responsibility to the retailer to aid in profitability. The issue of vendor assistance is rife with controversy and potential contentiousness, but is usually resolved to the satisfaction of both the retailer and the vendor.

SIX-MONTH PLAN/OPEN-TO-BUY REPORTS

The six-month plan, as previously discussed, is the method of planning used by the majority of retailers. Completed for two seasons a year, spring and fall, and revised as needed, the six-month plan is the most important financial report used by merchandisers (buyers, divisional merchandise managers, and general merchandise managers). Actual figures update daily and

FIGURE 5.8 Vendor analysis is the "report card" of each vendor because it recaps the business between the retailer and the vendor.

Buyer: Donna Reamy   Department: Junior Sportswear   Date: 7/29/2012

Vendor Analysis

Vendor #	Vendor	TY Sales STD	LY Sales STD	% Chg	TY Sales YTD	LY Sales YTD	% Chg	TY Purchases @ cost	LY Purchases @ cost	TY Purchases @ retail	LY Purchases @ retail	TY MD$	LY MD$	TY MD %	LY MD %	TY IMU %	LY IMU %	TY GM %	LY GM %	TY GM $	LY GM $
12345	Levi Strauss	532,227	472,085.3	11.3	1,330,568	1,273,353	4.3	1,725,214.5	1,582,319.4	3,991,704.0	3,565,388.4	562,830.1	561,548.7	42.3	44.1	56.8	55.6	38.5	36.0	512,241.1	459,023.7
67891	Currants	497,361	450,111.7	9.5	1,243,403	1,102,898	11.3	937,898.9	838,202.5	2,362,465.7	2,095,506.2	518,498.8	470,937.5	41.7	42.7	60.3	60.0	43.7	42.9	543,927.7	473,363.8
11121	Golden Touch	384,581	362,659.9	5.7	961,453	876,845	8.8	767,239.5	709,718.1	1,826,760.7	1,666,004.9	423,039.1	401,594.9	44.0	45.8	58.0	57.4	39.5	37.9	379,966.0	332,229.4
31415	Union Bay	375,687	325,344.9	13.4	939,218	868,776	7.5	1,028,443.7	1,052,609.2	2,348,045.0	2,258,818.1	394,471.4	365,754.8	42.0	42.1	56.2	53.4	37.8	33.8	355,061.8	293,484.8
16171	US Polo Assn	352,213	313,821.8	10.9	880,533	854,117	3.0	990,181.8	1,033,139.3	2,289,437.8	2,306,114.6	371,584.7	357,020.7	42.2	41.8	56.8	55.2	38.5	36.5	338,991.8	311,527.0
81920	Southpole	350,764	339,188.8	3.3	876,910	835,695	4.7	815,829.3	841,962.9	2,152,584.0	2,089,238.1	380,578.9	372,720.1	43.4	44.6	62.1	59.7	45.7	41.7	400,321.7	348,703.9
21222	Byer	321,154	328,861.7	−2.4	802,885	802,885	0.0	690,481.1	760,412.4	1,605,770.0	1,686,058.5	342,029.0	346,846.3	42.6	43.2	57.0	54.9	38.7	35.4	310,572.0	284,356.2
32425	Zanadi	237,682	237,682.0	0.0	594,205	601,335	−1.2	658,854.5	502,355.6	1,663,774.0	1,202,670.9	244,218.3	244,142.2	41.1	40.6	60.4	58.2	44.1	41.3	262,189.4	248,179.4
26272	Hydraulic	200,687	188,445.1	6.1	501,718	488,171	2.7	497,955.1	362,906.4	1,254,295.0	878,708.0	202,693.9	201,126.5	40.4	41.2	60.3	58.7	44.3	41.7	222,066.2	203,491.2
82930	Baby Phat	187,562	197,690.3	−5.4	468,905	484,379	−3.3	514,623.2	604,504.8	1,172,262.5	1,259,385.0	199,284.6	229,111.2	42.5	47.3	56.1	52.0	37.4	29.3	175,569.8	141,903.6
	Department Total	3,439,918	3,215,891.6	7.0	8,599,795	8,188,454	5.0	8,626,721.7	8,288,130.7	20,667,098.7	19,007,892.8	3,639,228.8	3,550,802.8	42.3	43.4	58.26	56.40	40.6	37.5	3,491,063.8	3,069,712.3

register weekly to the report. The figures show actual performance compared to planned performance in **retail dollars**. The **retail price** is the price on the price tag in a retail store. It is possible to view the report between weekly printings if needed, but it is most accurate with a complete week of business recorded. The report details the plan figures and the actual figures for sales, inventory, markdowns, purchases, on order, gross margin, turnover, and shrinkage. The report also details these same figures for the year prior for comparison purposes. This report is a buyer's report card because the onus is on the buyer to achieve sales plans, maintain inventory at acceptable levels, take markdowns according to the plan, sustain inventory levels, achieve gross margin plans in dollars and percents, realize planned turnover, and monitor shrinkage. Available Monday mornings of each week, the buyer and merchandising management review the report and strategize about necessary changes or ways of improving or maintaining current business. The six-month-plan report is the culmination of all style selling and is a high-level view of the performance of a buyer, department, and/or classification.

Summary

The information in this chapter reiterated the importance of the consumer in assortment planning. Using the "rights of merchandising" as a guide, buyers strive to have the right product, in the right store, at the right time, and in the right quantities. Using the right sales promotion is the tool for informing consumers that the product is available. Retail buying and the buyer's role in retailing explained the process and difficulties faced by buyers. The examination of the methods and mathematical formulas of buyers gave insight into what a buying career entails. Lastly, the discussion of the numerous reports buyers use and their place in the decision-making process demonstrated the need for thorough record keeping and statistics in a buying environment.

Key Terms

assistant buyer   106
assortment planning   117
average inventory   111
beginning of month (BOM)   109
buyer   106
classification   117
cost   117
cost of goods sold   114
cost-oriented pricing   105
demand-oriented pricing   105
department   117
divisional merchandise manager   106
end of month (EOM)   109
fall season   107
fixture fill   119
gross margin   114

gross sales   114
income statement   114
margin assistance   124
markdown money   124
markdowns   111
market specialist   119
markup   116
net sales   114
on order   113
open-to-buy   108
operating expenses   115
percentage sell-through   123
price discounting   105
program   124
purchases   113
resident buying office   119

retail buying   106
retail dollars   126
retail price   126
sales   108
season   107
selling by style report   123
six-month plan   107
spring season   107
stock   109
stock to sales ratio   109
test quantities   119
turnover   110
vendor assistance   124
vendor analysis reports   124

questions

Review Questions

1. Why is it important for today's fashion companies to be consumer oriented rather than product oriented?

2. Retailers work to connect to their customers. Give two examples from the chapter.

3. Explain the difference between the customer and the ultimate consumer. Why is it important for the company to market to the customer and not always the ultimate consumer?

4. What perception does a price have to offer to a customer?

5. What is turnover and why is it important to a retailer?

6. The six-month plan is a planning tool used by the majority of retailers. Why is it a useful tool? Ultimately, what does the six-month plan provide retailers?

7. Name the four main components of the six-month plan. Which is the most important and why?

8. Many factors influence sales and must be taken into consideration when planning. Name any four.

9. Name the two primary reasons gross margin is used to evaluate a buyer's performance.

problems

Problems

1. After careful analysis, A & R department store has projected an increase of 8.2 percent for the fall over last year's sales volume. Sales for last fall were $34,880,000 with 48 percent markdowns.
   a) What is the sales plan for this fall?
   b) If markdowns remain 48 percent this year, what is the dollar markdown plan for A & R department Store?
   c) What is the markdown dollar difference between this year and last year?

2. Fill in the blanks:

	MD% Total	MD $	Sales	MD % of Sales
Aug		2,427,200		82.00%
Sept		2,564,100	3,330,000	
oct		1,424,500	2,590,000	
Nov		2,331,000		70.00%
Dec		3,078,400	4,810,000	
Jan		1,036,000		70.00%
Total			18,500,00	

3. Use the figures below to determine:
   a) December planned purchases at retail
   b) December planned purchases at cost
   c) December turnover
   d) December stock/sales ratio

Planned December sales	$4,884,000
Planned December MD %	63%
Planned December BOM	$18,646,000
Planned January BOM	$13,311,000
Planned markup %	62.71%

4. Using the figures below, calculate:
   a) The OTB @ retail if the on order for August is 58,383
   b) The OTB @ cost for August if the planned markup is 63.0 percent

Planned sales	$356,400
BOM stock August	$1,853,000
BOM stock September	$1,530,000
Planned August markdowns	$49,210

5. In a children's department, planned sales for the six-month period February through July were $550.000. The monthly inventories at retail for this period were:

February 1	$190,000
March 1	187,000
April 1	192,000
May 1	190,000
June 1	184,000
July 1	179,000
August 1	162,000

   a) What is the planned average stock for the period?
   b) What is the planned turnover for the season?
   c) If planned sales in June are $46,000, what is the stock/sales ratio for June?

6. For December, the jewelry department had planned sales of $200,000. For the fall season, the department's planned sales were $1,100,000, with a planned stock turnover of 4.0. Determine the BOM figure for December, using the basic stock method.

7. Management was disappointed with the turnover results for the cosmetics department LY. Cosmetics achieved a turnover of 1.37 against a plan of 1.40. How can A & R department store improve the turnover this year?

8. Calculate the sell-through % for a men's polo shirt in units and dollars:

Total received	4,800 units @ $15.00
Total sold	2,310 units @ $15.00

9. The lingerie department of store "A" produced $113,000 in gross sales, customer returns and allowances were $3,000, cost of goods sold was $52,000, and operating expenses were $51,070. Store "B," also in the lingerie department, produced the following results within the same time frame: Net sales were $220,000, cost of goods sold was $100,000, and operating expenses were $110,000.

a) Comparing the two stores, which was more profitable in dollars?

b) Which store was more efficient? Why?

SIX-MONTH PLAN

Department: Department #

Buyer: Season:

Date Prepared: Last Revision Date:

		LY	Plan TY	Revised	Actual TY	Notes:
Season's Totals						
Markup %						
Gross Margin %						
Turnover						

		AUGUST	SEPTEMBER	OCTOBER	NOVEMBER	DECEMBER	JANUARY	FEBRUARY	SEASON TOTAL
SALES	Last Year	$ 300.0	400.0	280.0	340.0	520.0	160.0	175.4	2,000.0
	Plan TY								
	% Inc/Dec TY								
	% Total TY								
	% Total LY								
	Revised								
	Actual								
STOCK/SALES	Last Year	3.9	3.0	4.1	3.6	2.5	6.3	5.7	
	Plan TY								
	Revised								
	Actual								
BOM STOCK $	Last Year	$ 1,170.0	$ 1,200.0	$ 1,148.0	$ 1,224.0	$ 1,300.0	$ 1,008.0	1,100.0	$ 1,164.3
	Plan TY							1,000.0	
	Revised								
	Actual								
MARKDOWNS $	Last Year	$ 142.6	70.6	99.0	78.5	172.3	97.0		660.0
	Plan TY								
	% to Sales								
	% by Month								
	% to Sales LY								
	% by Month LY								
	Revised								
	Actual								
PURCHASES $	Last Year	$ 475.1	467.0	333.0	363.5	305.0	278.0		2,221.6
	Plan TY								
	Revised								
	Actual								

Critical Thinking

1. Using the information and the form provided below, develop a six-month plan.

   Plan Sales:
   - Plan a 5% increase in sales this year over last year.
   - Calculate the monthly % of total sales last year.
   - Using last year's monthly %, allocate sales by month this year.

   Plan Inventory:
   - Use last year's stock/sales ratios to calculate this year's BOM inventory.

   Plan Markdowns:
   - Plan this year's markdowns at 50% of this year's sales plan.
   - Calculate the monthly % of total markdowns last year.

   - Using last year's monthly %, allocate markdowns by month this year.
   - Calculate this year's markdowns % of sales for each month.

   Plan Purchases:
   - Calculate this year's purchases.

   Plan to:
   - Calculate the average inventory this year.
   - Using the average inventory, calculate the planned turnover.

2. Using the purchase plans from the six-month plan developed in question 1 and the form below, construct a vendor assortment plan.

Vendor Assortment Plan

Buyers																
Season																
Year																
Month		August		September		October		November		December		January		Total Season	
$ Purchase Plan		Plan	Actual	Plan	Actual	Plan	Actual	Plan	Actual	Plan	Actual	Plan	Actual	Plan	Actual
Vendor	% total													0	
		0.0		0.0		0.0		0.0		0.0		0		0	0
		0.0		0.0		0.0		0.0		0.0		0		0	0
		0.0		0.0		0.0		0.0		0.0		0		0	0
		0.0		0.0		0.0		0.0		0.0		0		0	0
		0.0		0.0		0.0		0.0		0.0		0		0	0
		0.0		0.0		0.0		0.0		0.0		0		0	0
Total	0%	0.0	0	0.0	0	0.0	0	0.0	0	0.0	0	0	0	0	0

COMPETITION,
THE STOCK MARKET,
AND FINANCIAL
MEASUREMENT

OBJECTIVES

After reading this chapter, you will be able to:

- Apply the competition model by Mike Porter to the business of fashion
- Recognize how to measure the financial health of the fashion industry and public fashion companies and understand the operations of the stock market
- Gain an understanding of how a company analyzes financial information for the purpose of making important decisions concerning the future of the company

I don't watch the stock price. The stock price is like hemlines. It goes up and it goes down.

—DONNA KAREN, May 1997 (Agins, 1999, p. 200)

Global fashion industry **competition** is growing at a rapid rate due, in part, to the media. During fashion week, a designer has a fashion show to present his or her designs for the coming season. Seated in the audience are people from the press such as journalists, fashion photographers, celebrities, and fashion bloggers. Within minutes of the model sashaying down the runway in the latest style, a photograph is snapped, a journalist writes a few lines about the image, sends it to an editor, while a blogger immediately blogs about it through an iPhone. The consumer can now read and see the latest styles without attending fashion week, thus creating immediate demand for a product. If the designer cannot offer it for sale instantaneously at the right price point, and in the right place, then a second-level producer will create something similar in the form of a substitute product called a **knock-off** and the competition begins. Whatever company is the first to deliver the new look will be the one to satisfy initial consumer demand and create a profit.

Competition is a necessary element of the entire apparel and textile industry. Companies compete for consumer dollars, which in turn means that they are competing to make a profit. The U.S. government regulates competition so that no one company will have a **monopoly** (a situation that occurs when a firm controls the marketplace on a particular product or industry) on a product. In essence, the more profit a company earns, the more successful a company is. Companies that only operate in one country are constantly seeking new consumers and market share. As a brand saturates a market, firms seek to take the product global to increase profits.

Through this chapter, you are going to learn about competition among fashion companies applying the model The Five Competitive Forces by Harvard professor Michael Porter, the workings of the stock market as it applies to public companies, and measuring the financial health of a company.

The Five Competitive Forces

To understand any competitive industry, whether it is the car industry, fashion industry, or the supermarket industry, The **Five Competitive Forces**, developed by Harvard Professor Michael Porter, is an outstanding framework to examine the competitive nature of the fashion industry. Porter states, "As different from one another as industries might appear on the surface, the underlying drivers of profitability are the same." The five competitive forces include the degree of **rivalry**, **barriers to entry**, **buying power**, threat of substitutes, and supplier power.

Rivalry

The center of the framework and a driving force is rivalry, in other words, competition and staying abreast of the competition requires constant observation. Questions that arise about the competition include, What is the competing company's financial position in the marketplace? and How can a company contemplating entering the market gauge the stability and viability of the industry? The U.S. Census Bureau reports industry ratios that enlighten firms about the competition in the marketplace. In the case of the fashion industry, the U.S. Census Bureau collects data and divides it into manufacturing and retail stores organized by the North

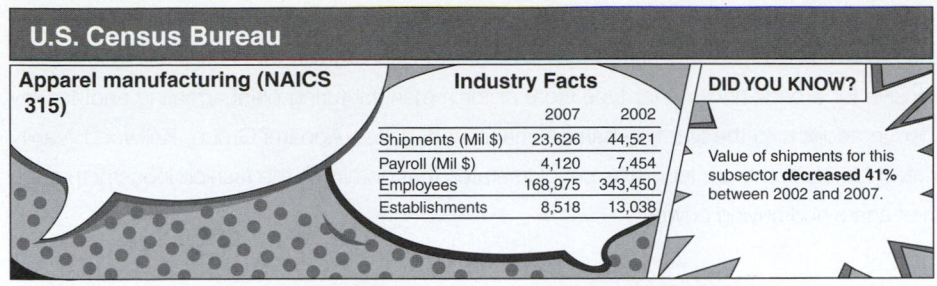

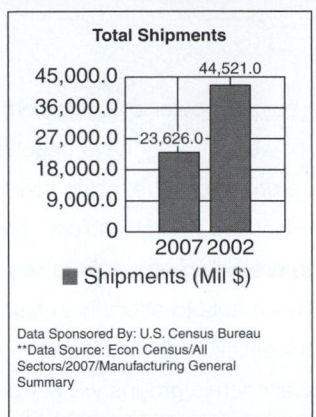

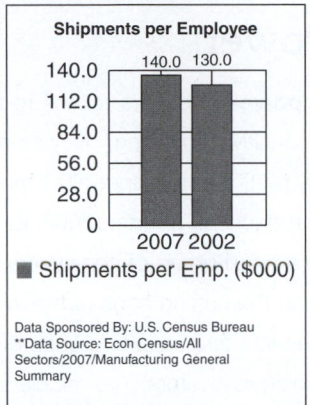

Industry Ratios	2007	2002
Total shipments (Mil $)	23,626	44,521
Shipments per establishment ($000)	2,774	3,415
Shipments per employee ($)	139,821	129,629
Shipments per $ of payroll ($)	5.73	5.97
Annual payroll per employee ($)	24,381	21,704
Employees per establishment	19.8	26.3
Shipments per capita ($)	78.42	154
Establishments per million residents	28.3	45.3

Compare YOUR Business

For more statistics on this industry, see the
Industry Statistics Sampler.

Navigate to a different industry.

FIGURE 6.1 *Manufacturing industry snapshot (Source: Census Bureau).*

American Industry Classification System (NAICS). Industry snapshots are available and can provide information such as dollar amount of shipments, dollar amount of payroll, employees, and establishments. The U.S. Census Bureau also provides comparative statistics based on previous years of the U.S. Census. For example, if a company wanted to compare the clothing and clothing accessories stores in the United States from 1997 to 2007, the data are available. This would allow a prospective retailer to get a view of the competition prior to entry in the market. See Figure 6.1 for a picture of a page from the U.S. Census Bureau on apparel manufacturing.

Barriers to Entry

"New entrants to an industry bring new capacity and a desire to gain market share that puts pressure on prices, costs, and the rate of investment necessary to compete" (Porter, 2008, p. 3). The barriers to entry in the fashion industry make it a difficult industry to enter. One major barrier is that most manufacturing firms only take minimum orders, which can generally be very high and therefore difficult for new entrants to handle. Start-up **capital** for a business is extremely expensive for a brick-and-mortar type store or for a manufacturing plant, creating another key barrier. In addition to the first two barriers mentioned, Jones Apparel Group, Kellwood, Vanity Fair, and Liz Claiborne are four large conglomerates that dominate the fashion industry through market share and buying power.

Buying Power

The **bargaining power** of buyers relates to the buying power of customers. The fashion industry is price sensitive, meaning, "Buyers are powerful if they have negotiating leverage relative to industry participants, especially if they are price sensitive, using their clout primarily to pressure price reductions" (Porter, 2008, p. 7). New and trendy fashions, because of their high prices, have a small group of consumers who are willing and able to pay for the luxury of being on the cutting edge of fashion. Those able to afford high fashion are called fashion leaders and include groups like celebrities, political figures (Figure 6.2), and other fashion innovators. The middle socioeconomic groups will not pay high prices for new and trendy fashion; however, they will purchase knock-offs at various fast fashion retailers. Fast fashion, discussed in Chapter 1, is a concept in which a retailer brings the product to market with a very short lead time. Examples of fashion retailers include Forever 21, Zara, and H&M. The quality of the garment is not an important consideration for this group when purchasing products—it is the speed at which these retailers bring trends to the marketplace.

"Intermediate customers, or customers who purchase the product but are not the end user," such as a wholesaler purchasing from a manufacturer to resell product to the retailer, can be analyzed the same way as other buyers (Porter, 2008, p. 8). Retailers that buy product from wholesalers have bargaining power, that is, the larger volume of merchandise purchased usually equates to a lower price, a disadvantage for a small boutique owner buying brands, like Rebecca Taylor, carried by large retailers. For example, the small retailer purchases 20 pieces at one price compared to Nordstrom's, whose buying power enables them to purchase hundreds of pieces at a lower price; therefore, the line is likely to prove more profitable for Nordstrom's than for the boutique.

FIGURE 6.2 *Cindy McCain in an outfit that cost close to $350,000 (Source: Newscom).*

Threat of Substitutes

The **threat of substitutes** is a force that is relevant and a threat to competitors. "When the threat of substitutes is high, industry profitability suffers. If an industry does not distance itself from substitutes through product performance, marketing or other means, it will suffer in terms of profitability and often growth potential" (Porter, 2008, p. 8). The fashion industry is inundated with substitutes in the form of counterfeit merchandise, knock-offs, and inexpensive fashion sold by typically nonfashion stores such as Walmart and Kmart. Today the majority of the fashion retailers compete on presentations of chic and stylish fashion at desirable price points. In the long run, companies will focus on service, exclusivity of the product, and ecofriendly products to remain competitive.

Supplier Power

Powerful suppliers capture more of the value for themselves by charging higher prices, limiting quality or services, or shifting costs to industry participants (Porter, 2008, p. 6). **Supplier power** is the obligation of the supplier and the producer to build a relationship for using the least amount of resources to produce the product. If suppliers are large within the industry, they have the power to persuade the producer and even the industry to purchase raw materials at a high price. Within the fashion industry, a supplier is only as good as its previous order, which means that if the supplier did not deliver or conduct business in the agreed-upon manner, the wholesaler or the retailer will seek out other suppliers.

"Understanding the competitive forces, and their underlying causes, reveals the roots of an industry's current profitability while providing a framework for anticipating and influencing competition (and profitability) over time" (Porter, 2008, p. 3). As a company analyzes the five forces, they realize how to become better players in the market to create a profit. Understanding the company's position in the marketplace is important to maximizing its profit.

A firm often uses marginal analysis as a tool for cost/benefit analysis, evaluation of efficiency and profits, and utility maximization. Marginal analysis is used by retailers, wholesalers, and service companies. If the marginal revenue is greater than the marginal costs, then the firm should indeed increase its output, but if the marginal revenue is less than the marginal costs, then there is no profit and production can decrease or halt altogether. Profit maximizing output is the most important decision to a firm, and firms must secure the level of output that maximizes profits. Figure 6.3 shows the dollar loss, profit from one pair of jeans, and the profit maximization point.

The marginal approach contends that if the marginal benefit exceeds the marginal cost, then a firm should opt to continue to produce. In economic terms it is considered the **MR = MC** (marginal revenue = marginal cost) rule, when the output of goods is maximizing the profit of a firm. Figure 6.4 shows a short-run profit table for a fashion product. Remember the marginal principle: If marginal cost exceeds the marginal benefit, then stop production, but try to reduce the marginal cost to equal marginal benefit. At start-up, the output of a product is usually low due to quantity demanded and the marginal costs will exceed marginal benefits. If this continues, production of the product should stop. The prices of the inputs determine the price of the output. If the inputs increase in price and cause an overall increase in the final cost of the product, the company will seek a substitute input at a lower cost.

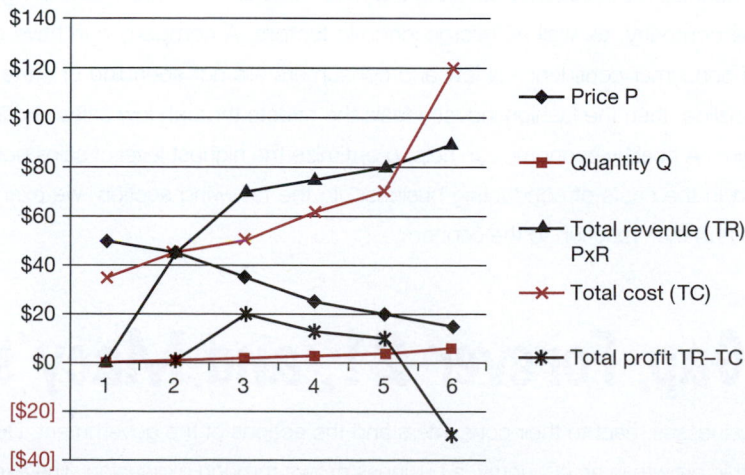

FIGURE 6.3 *Quantity of jeans sold by a simulated fashion company.*

FIGURE 6.4 *Short-run profit table illustrating the marginal cost versus the marginal benefit principle.*

Number of Sewers	Number of Shirts Produced per Hour	Marginal Revenue Price per Shirt	Total Marginal Revenue Q x P = MR	Marginal Cost (MC) per Shirt to Produce	Total Marginal Cost MC x Q	Total Profit TMR – TMC = Profit
1	20	$75	1,500	$30	$600	$900
2	40	$75	3,000	$30	$1,200	$1,800
3	60	$75	4,500	$30	$1,800	$2,700
4	80	$75	6,000	$30	$2,400	$3,600
5	100	$75	7,500	$30	$3,000	$4,500

The long run for increasing economic profit includes, but is not limited to, adding technology to speed production, improving communication, and improving quality and quantity of products produced. Due to the nature of the fashion industry, quick adjustments are necessary in the long run at various times. A producer may have to stockpile fabric to decrease time in the supply chain, or if a plant is running at capacity, another space may be required to open another plant, requiring a long-term lease. The long run and the short run require a business to react quickly and at the same time plan for the future to achieve economic profit. **Economies of scale** is an important factor in achieving economic profit. A company achieves economies of scale by lowering the average cost per unit through increased production since fixed costs are shared over an increased number of goods.

Fashion companies take the state of the economy into consideration when making long-run and short-run decisions. The direction of the economy, whether it is stable or unstable, has a bearing on the direction of fashion at different levels and on various segments. It is business as usual for the luxury market in an unstable economy, but segments that offer moderate price points customary to ready-to-wear, which is inclusive of consumers who seek fashion and value, have to plan accordingly based on what consumers demand and are willing to pay. Since fashion is a cyclical business based on many factors, including the state of the economy, one can only predict what the financial future of the fashion industry and fashion companies will be from season to season. If a silhouette did not sell one season, a company has an opportunity to change the line or silhouette for the next season.

A fashion company's success is based on its net earnings, which are determined from the profits of sales by the company. In the fashion industry, it is difficult to determine what will be selling in a robust economy, but in a down economy, it is even more difficult. As a result, fashion companies are constantly studying the macroeconomic environment along with past sales of the company, as well as microeconomic factors. A company can have everything right, but if consumer confidence is low and consumers are not spending or if the economy is in a downslide, then the fashion industry feels the effects through low sales and in turn low profit margins. A healthy economy can help to optimize the highest level of sales possible and plays a part in the costs of conducting business. In the following section, we examine three companies and their reaction to the economy.

The Gap, Forever 21, and Macy's

Fashion businesses react to their consumers and the actions of the government. During positive economic growth in an economy, a business grows through expansion. The expansion of a business consists of adding new chain stores, adding inventories, and creating new brands.

For example, Gap, Inc., began in 1969 with a concept developed by Doris and Don Fisher to offer a wide range of styles and sizes for everyone. They started the business in San Francisco, California, where the Gap headquarters remains today. Currently, Gap has more than 3,200 stores internationally (Gap Inc., n.d.) and distributes through their website. Until 1983, Gap continued to add stores that carried only one brand with a specific target market; however, in 1983 Gap acquired two Banana Republic stores, which originally sold travel and safari clothing. Later Gap created brands such as Gap Kids and Old Navy, both one-brand-type stores targeting a specific demographic group. Gap has ventured into the Internet with Piperlime, a website devoted to shoe shopping. Piperlime is different from the other concept stores because it carries a wide variety of brands. Gap has changed their marketing campaigns to attract and regain consumers. The new campaigns have not been successful in attracting a new market group. Gap is tasked with reinventing itself as an exclusive brand with exclusive product that is desirable for their target market. It must find its target customers and respond to them. The same formula that worked in the mid-1970s is not applicable today and the onus is on Gap to find the formula that will work today.

The description of Forever 21 on its website boasts that Forever 21 is a "phenomenon in the fashion world" (Forever 21). Don Chang and his wife Jin Sook established Forever 21, initially known as Fashion 21, in 1984. The company now has 481 stores in eight countries and 2011 sales volume was $2.6 billion (Forbes.com). The store sells cheap, fashionable clothing. Highly successful with its original business model, Forever 21's business model has moved from occupying smaller spaces to seeking larger spaces, a few with over 100,000 square feet of space. The increased space has allowed for expansion of product categories and as a result the cheap chic retailer is servicing a broader clientele ("Forever 21 is," 2011). Forever 21 experienced success during the recession that began in 2007. With its trendy apparel and accessories at bargain basement prices, Forever 21 capitalized on shoppers' movement toward less expensive retailers during slow economic times.

As with many successful companies, Forever 21 is plagued with controversy. Numerous allegations charge that Forever 21 knocks off original designs and sells them at a fraction of the cost of the original. Currently, Forever 21 is fighting more than 20 lawsuits by various fashion companies such as Diane von Furstenberg, Anna Sui, Gwen Stefani, bebe, and Anthropology. Most of the complaints filed against Forever 21 have been for copyright infringement. At press time, most of the cases remain on court dockets. With no design copyright laws in place, these cases are tough to fight. However, a recently introduced bill in the U.S. Senate, the **Design Piracy Prohibition Act**, deems this type of business practice illegal. The act gives designers the ability to register designs, extending copyright protection to the designer for three years. Registering every design for copyright may prove to be too cumbersome, but in the introduction phase of new styles and prints it is likely to be an effective deterrent against knock-offs. As a result, consumers will have to pay more for the original designs. While the well-known fashion designers have the resources to pursue the court cases, smaller design houses will not have the funds to go after large companies such as Forever 21.

Macy's is a well-known brand name in the department store business and because of a merger between Federated (Macy's parent company) and May Company, the brand name has become stronger. At the end of the merger, Federated (which later changed its name to Macy's) operated 950 department stores and more than 700 bridal and formal wear stores. There are 65 top-tier retail markets in the United States. When the merger began in 2005, Macy's has operated in 64 of these markets. After the merger, Federated closed some duplicate and underperforming stores. The remainder of the stores, around 400, were renamed Macy's, Inc., officially dropping the Federated name. Its business was sluggish after the merger for a number of reasons: Duplicate stores remained in some markets, the May Company customer had been "trained" to purchase using coupons that Macy's had all but eliminated, and there was resistance by loyal May Company consumers to Macy's. Federated was in a trough point on the business cycle and began to close stores and rename them. Macy's repositioned itself as a major player in department stores. Operating numerous divisions caused Macy's to focus on too many ventures and lose sight of their core department store business. Because of this, they sold the Lord & Taylor division, David's Bridal, Priscilla of Boston, and After Hours Formalwear. The restructuring took two years. The company, listed as Macy's, Inc., on the New York Stock Exchange, includes Bloomingdale's, which is still a part of the Macy's group.

Efficiency

Efficiency from the fashion industry perspective is the most logical, time-sensitive, and cost-saving way to conduct business. Some economists say "efficiency" is an ambiguous word. It is important to clarify the term from a fashion industry perspective. The idea behind efficiency is good business practices. For example, to achieve the highest net profit, a fashion manufacturer may use a method to produce a product at the lowest cost. Because of competition, deflation in fashion prices, increased vertical integration, and shorter fashion cycles, efficiency within the fashion industry is of paramount importance. Fashion has to respond to consumer demand for quality, but also low pricing. Barriers to efficiency in the global market include communication, tradition, lead times, risk of failure, slow adaptation to change, ethical issues associated with production, poor accounting practices, timing of markdowns, and inaccurate pricing. Fashion industry efficiency is rooted in the "rights of fashion"—having the right product, at the right time, in the right place, with the right price, in the right quantities, with the right sales promotion.

Whether a company is a fashion innovator or a fashion follower impacts its measure of efficiency. Innovators such as Prada, Versace, and Gucci are at the top of the trickledown theory, leading fashion with new ideas, styles, and colors. As an innovator, a company has to know when to present new ideas to the marketplace. Once it is determined that the time is right for a new trend, presentation of the garments happens during fashion weeks at various cities around the world. Efficiency makes a company more competitive. Read the article in Box 6.1 titled, "Steps Involved in Making Your Business Competitive" by William King for a summary of how a business can make itself competitive using efficiency. The fashion innovator has to be first to market with a new trend. A company that is a follower of fashion must respond to the fashion of the moment quickly and efficiently, otherwise the moment passes and a new trend will emerge.

At the same time, companies must operate in the most efficient manner possible. The fashion industry utilizes three types of efficiency: **market efficiency**, technological efficiency, and **allocation efficiency**.

Market efficiency has its roots dating back to 1970 when Eugene Fama, an economist, created the concept of an efficient market called Efficient Market Hypothesis (EFH). Fama said, "An efficient market is a market that adjusts rapidly to new information." This concept of efficiency in economics is using an input to its greatest use with a minimum of waste. In other words, efficiency in the stock market is best reflected in the worth of stock at any given time. An efficient market is one in which the resources are used to their full potential while creating

Steps Involved in Making Your Business Competitive

These are the fundamental steps that lead a business to a path of progress and competitiveness enhancing efficiency and effectiveness of the business. There are 7 steps that are discussed below:

1. FINDING THE GAPS

It includes the skills and knowledge your company possesses and is a major determinant of your success. In this step you need to identify your strengths, areas needing further study and areas of concern that could seriously affect your ability to stay competitive. Once you are through with this step, you would have access to practicable online information and other references that will help you bridge any knowledge and skill gaps. Filling these gaps will help in making your organization better prepared and to ascertain benefit from valuable information relating to the various management functions.

2. PRE-PLANNING

Pre-Planning is the process by which the management of an organization foresee its future and develop the necessary measures and operations to achieve future goals. It includes development of the purpose, mission, vision, and value statements of the managing teams; communication of these documents and suggestions for improvement; a culture survey to create a base against which change can be compared; and last but not least celebrating achievements and learning from mistakes. After Pre-Planning the team needs to formulate strategies and clearly identify an action plan on which implementation is to be performed. As part of this phase, you will also need to repeat your mission and restate your company's vision. Although there are many kinds of strategies, in this situation basic strategy should not change much in the short term, whereas sub-strategies can change rapidly in reaction to competitive situations.

3. FINANCING

A financing plan is developed to increase the business competitiveness through an improved knowledge of the techniques and methods of funding available. Equity and debt are two types of financing available to business. Equity is the money that you put into your business and debt is what you borrow from others to invest in your business.

4. INVOLVEMENT OF TECHNOLOGY

Businesses are becoming more dependent on **technology**. By optimizing the use of technology, a business may maintain progress, improve its customer services, and gain a competitive edge over those businesses that are not utilizing their technology. In the modern world, the change of information technology has become a vital part in competition with the real world. Now the question is why do we use technology in business? The answer is simple: It enhances customer service, can decrease cost, can improve communication, can facilitate research, and can increase productivity, efficiency, as well as effectiveness in the business.

5. IMPROVEMENT IN HUMAN RESOURCE

Using this resource to its best advantage is a means to maximize the effectiveness of the other entire systems and procedures already in place. The business or organization having skilled and competitive employees is considered as the most competitive business. Proper human resource management is needed to increase effectiveness in work and to smoothly achieve the goals and accomplish tasks.

6. MARKETING STRATEGY

Marketing and related activities in a business, small or large, ensure that your business gets information from its customers, develops and markets the services to satisfy their needs, and gets feedback on their satisfaction levels. Marketing acts as an interface between the enterprise and its markets. Marketing can be defined as the function that encompasses most activities between the producer of a good or the supplier of a service and the consumers. It is also a set of **business development** activities, which starts with the consumer from whose needs the business gets its service ideas and to whom it will sell its services.

7. PROCESS OF QUALITY ASSURANCE

The Process of Quality Assurance in a business refers to planned, step-by-step activities that determine that testing is being carried out correctly, results are accurate, and mistakes are found and corrected to avoid undesirable outcomes. Quality assurance is a constant set of activities that help the business to ensure that the test results provided are as accurate and reliable as possible. Maintaining quality assurance leads to customer retention, and an image as a competitive business in the minds of clients.

CONCLUSION

Competition in **business** is now found everywhere and in such a competitive world it is difficult for any new business or start-ups to survive and thrive. Implementation of the above steps can definitely help towards effectively competing in any market.

By William King

http://www.sooperarticles.com/business-articles/management-articles/steps-involved-making-your-business-competitive-12778.html

product. This synopsis goes back to the classical theory of demand where supply equals demand and a true equilibrium exists in the market.

It is important to note other types of efficiencies within the study of economics such as wage model efficiency and efficiency of taxes. In this section, the focus will be on allocation and technical efficiency as they relate to macroeconomics in answering the three basic questions: What to produce? How to produce? and For whom to produce? A graph used to illustrate and forecast production and allocation efficiency associated with scarcity is the **production possibility curve (PPC)**. The production possibility curve model is used to create scenarios to determine at what point on the curve to produce with a scarcity of resources. There are three assumptions in the PPC model: (1) Society has a limited quantity of fixed resource inputs, such as labor, capital, and materials, which do not change, and fixed costs such as rent of buildings and utilities expenses; (2) the resources on the whole are being used to their absolute production maximum without changes in production methods; (3) two goods are compared in the PPC. The **Production Possibility Frontier (PPF)** demonstrates what "if" scenarios can be done in terms of production. A curved line represents an economy at full production. Inside the curved line on the chart, the points cannot be achieved and represent inefficient production; points outside of the curve represent something called a new frontier. It could be attainable, but a scarcity of resources or labor exists. If there were new technology or an abundance of resources, then the points outside of the curved line could be within reach.

Refer to Figure 6.5 for an example of a production possibility curve displaying knitted scarves versus sweaters. The figure is a model that demonstrates the production possibility curve of a factory that produces knitwear. The scenario compares producing knitted scarves and sweaters assuming that the factory could be set up to produce both or either of those goods. Curve line C is when the factory is potentially at full production; then we say, "Production is efficient." At point B the factory can produce 800 knitted scarves and 100 sweaters. At point A the factory could produce 600 knitted scarves and 80 sweaters. If we wanted to move from point A to point B for production, then the production of knitted scarves would be scarified. This is called the law of increasing opportunity. At points A and B the factory is not producing

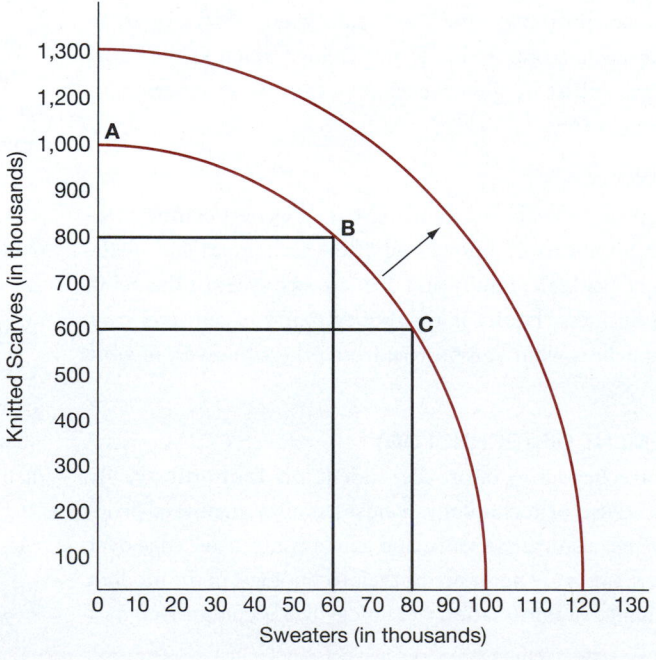

FIGURE 6.5 *Production possibility curve for knitted scarves versus knitted sweaters.*

efficiently. At any point inside the the curve the production is not efficient. For example, look at point D. Production is underutilized, only producing 400 scarves and 40 sweaters. An outward shift of the curve could be due to advancement in technology or an increase in resources. Attaining **technical efficiency** occurs by achieving more output with the same amount of inputs. Utilizing the abundance of technology progress increases the efficiency of fashion companies. Technology connects all levels in the production process and helps those in the supply chain to interact with a quick response. It also helps departments to connect on a global scale (refer to Box 6.2, "Concept-to-Spec Case Study").

Concept-to-Spec Case Study

PLM: Streamlining for Bottom-Line Results

The only way to plan a successful product line is to give all creative players as much visibility into every stage of the development and distribution processes as possible. And while product lifecycle management (PLM) is a core tool to keep all parties abreast of progress, it is the solution's integration to enterprise resource planning (ERP) solutions that will deliver truly streamlined product development.

The key to planning a line is to give direction to everyone in the downstream flow about the design goals that need to be achieved. Too often, however, the process, from sourcing and design all the way up to merchandising, can miss the mark—an issue that can be costly, even when dealing with trendy fast-selling items.

Denim, for example, was one of the hottest items last winter. When one manufacturer decided to exploit the trend, it developed 78 different styles of jeans and 24 different washes. However, one retail partner had a narrow denim assortment and only purchased three styles. Not only did the company over-develop the line by 600 percent, it wasted a significant amount of time and capital.

This scenario is only exacerbated as companies insist on managing the steps and costs related to concept, design, and production using manual processes such as Excel spreadsheets and offline management. Besides being overwhelming, too many people updating information causes redundant information and errors.

By adding a PLM system, these issues can be avoided. These solutions rely on one single data source that is analyzed, and used to manage the entire lifecycle of a product from conception through design and manufacture through distribution. In addition to enlightening internal associates involved in these processes, many companies also give trading partners, including manufacturing factories and fabric mills, access to information to track development.

Industry observers report that retailer and manufacturing partners can experience between 25 and 40 percent efficiency gains, and speed to market can be improved between 25 and 50 percent.

Lines can also be developed within six and nine months using a PLM system. With all parties using the same data, retailers and manufacturers say they are boosting bottom line profits by 10 to 25 percent, and more accurate planning is helping partners reduce markdowns and closeouts.

"It is a single place where the product line exists," said Tim Smith, product development application manager for athletic brand and retailer Under Armour, Baltimore.

Besides allowing all involved associates to monitor and track progress across all areas of product testing, raw materials, styles and sampling, PLM also delivers cost breakdown comparisons and analysis, including price negotiations and profit plans.

"The biggest benefit of the technology is the transparency for accurate information that it provides," said Dale Davidson, vice president and COO for Vesi Inc., a Cincinnati-based manufacturer of collegiate apparel. "Whether internal or external users access the solution, they will all see the same information. They can minimize the need to communicate, or be misinformed, through email. This is especially important when dealing with partners in foreign countries where communications is obviously challenging."

For Under Armour, PLM helps the company quickly and accurately bring product to market. The company is continually expanding product lines and the number of styles it features continues to grow. For example, the company, which launched in 1996, now features apparel, footwear, hard goods and accessories, including a lacrosse line complete with sticks, pads and other equipment.

"We need to manage these faster, and the only way to do that is to reduce the amount of data we were managing, and consolidate our two or three sources of information into a single place," Smith said.

"We continue to throw more associates at design, so we need to be able to bring more merchandise to market without dramatically increasing the number of staff we already have," he said. "That means we needed a single way to communicate, one that used a single source of the truth, and more efficiently brings merchandise to market on a season by season basis."

Since adding the ENOVIA solution from Dassault Systèmes, Under Armour has reduced re-keying data, and now shares development costs with factories, as everyone can monitor development and stay abreast of ongoing updates and changes to the line. "We are saving time by consolidating up to four files of drawing and information into one file everyone can use when producing the line," Smith explained. "We estimate that this consolidation has saved approximately 15 hours per week, per designer."

New York City-based Frazier Clothing Co. understands the issues these retailers are facing considering its role as a private-label manufacturer. "These days retailers need a fast response to consumer demand as well as [the ability to] feature specialty merchandise that sells well at a good price," said Serge Vecher, the company's director of IT.

For Frazier Clothing Co., that process starts with product development management (PDM). A component that fits into PLM, PDM is a systematic tool that focuses on tracking design and production, and analyzes how product is marketed and selling across retail partners. Frazier Clothing relies on the A2000 system from GCS Software, New York City.

"You can have all creative energy involved in design, but at the end of the day we need to answer the business questions: Does it sell, and how successful was the effort," he said. "With visibility into what happens throughout production, retail partners are in a better position to answer these questions."

The solution has eliminated all manual processes, and while the system aggregates data vs. updating files in real-time, the PDM system has still slashed Frazier's analysis time from weeks to hours or less.

Vesi has a similar story, as it creates merchandise for more than 200 collegiate bookstores and multiple department stores. When the company initially launched in 1992, Vesi commissioned agents to be its liaisons with international factories and sourcing, ensuring that accurately ordered product was shipping in a timely manner.

After re-evaluating the additional cost, Vesi brought the process in-house, which it controlled with an Excel spreadsheet. "We developed a time-and-action calendar starting from product development and it tracked product creation from its inception through completion from our internal perspective as well as progress within our factory partners," Davidson explained. "Over time, email communications became cumbersome, we were lacking timely, accurate data and knew it was time to consider PLM."

The company chose the Extended PLM software from NGC Software, Miami. The company was won over on the solution's ability to streamline communications with overseas partners, as well as workflow of transactions between internal and external users. At press time, the solution was going live. Three internal users were accessing the solution, and between 12 and 15 factory partners are connected.

BACK AT THE DRAWING BOARD

While PLM has revolutionized transparency into planning, development, and distribution, there is always room for improvement.

SA VA, Philadelphia, currently relies on a homegrown PLM system that shares files with all production users. While it also has a PDM system, SA VA awaits a time when there will be an integrated system for vertical companies that design, develop, and produce merchandise in their own factory, and sell their own merchandise.

"My turn is so fast that from the time I make a pattern to when it is sold it takes between six and eight weeks, 10 at the most," explained Sarah Van Aken, CEO and founder of parent company, S.V.A. Holdings Corp. "Any information we input into a traditional PLM or PDM would quickly be out of date. I need a customized solution that fits my vertical business model."

Apparel companies are also looking forward to more integrated solutions, especially those linked to ERP systems. Frazier Clothing Co. is already embarking on this concept, as its A2000 PDM software is a module within a base ERP system. Designed specifically for apparel manufacturers, this lays the foundation for all users to access production data in real-time. "As more processes are integrated and automated within one location, we can open many opportunities in terms of visibility," said Vecher.

Vesi is currently underway with its PLM and ERP implementation, and is preparing for an August launch. Once the combination is solidified, all data regarding color, size, style, and availability will be electronically exported to the ERP system, also from NGC, without having to re-enter the information.

Under Armour has already integrated PLM with its ERP system from SAP, Newtown Square, Pa., "giving us a single source of the truth regarding anything we bring to market," said Smith.

The company's next step is to break down the company's four walls and foster more collaboration with vendor partners. "We allow vendors to access samples and get process specifications, but this is still a one-way process," he explained. "We need to achieve two-way collaboration and get more value from our partners' expertise when developing product. This will further benefit us in the areas of cost, yield on materials, and further reduce potential errors."

Taking the concept one step further, some companies eagerly await managing these processes on the go. "We work with and manage partners worldwide, and with everyone relying on mobile technology, the idea that we all can manipulate data throughout the enterprise in real-time is mind-boggling," said Vecher.

"We are not there yet, but the foundation is in place. The next step is to integrate all of these processes and add extended enterprise functionality into the game," he said. "This will allow all approved parties to access data instantly, and ultimately it can enable users to update data in real-time and further speed up the development process."

Deena M. Amato-McCoy is an Apparel contributing writer specializing in retail technology.

If a company is publically traded on a stock market, its in-depth financial information is found at the company's website, at the stock exchange upon which it is listed, and through press releases. For a company to succeed it must show growth and profit. Based on many factors, as discussed earlier in this book, the consequence of a company's growth and profit is seen through the price of its stock. Competition is the compelling challenge that faces companies today as they try to grow and profit in the marketplace.

Many fashion companies sell shares of stock on the stock market, and the pricing trend of the stock is an indicator of the health of the company. The following sections discuss what the stock market is and how it operates, and provides an overview of domestic and foreign stock markets. The forces, or drivers, that keep the stock market moving are analyzed and discussed and capitalization is explained. There are many occasions within the stock market where a clear understanding helps navigate the market, such when reading stock charts and quotes, ascertaining the importance of the annual report, and discerning the meaning behind financial ratios.

The Stock Market

As you learned in Chapter 4, several types of business ownership exist, ranging from a sole proprietorship to corporations. The corporation is the most complicated type of ownership. Corporations, as previously learned, have numerous owners called **stockholders** but how does one buy stock or ownership in a corporation? Investors buy **shares**, smaller pieces of a corporation, on the **stock market**. Owning a share of stock in a company is equal to owning a small portion of a company. Stock markets buy and sell shares of stock and, in the process, set prices for the shares and therefore the value of companies. The selling of previously owned and outstanding securities in the stock market classifies it as a **secondary market**. There are two types of stock, **common** and **preferred**. Issued by most corporations, the majority of a company's equity is held in common stock. Common stock shareholders are usually entitled to vote on corporate governance and may or may not earn dividends. The more stock a shareholder has, the more votes the shareholder has. Preferred stockholders, as the name implies, receive preference over common stock shareholders. For example, when a company pays dividends, preferred stockholders collect dividends before common stockholders. **Dividends** are corporate profits paid to stockholders.

A company that sells stock to the public at large is classified as a **public company**. In the fashion industry, there are many public companies and several of those companies entered the market in the 1990s. During the 1990s, interest rates were low and the stock market was charging along. Beginning in 1992, the fashion meets Wall Street craze began with approximately 40 companies going public with **initial public offerings (IPO)**. An initial public offering (IPO) is when a company sells stock for the first time. Some fashion companies entered via the NYSE while others began issuing stock in the **over-the-counter (OTC) market**. The OTC market is a network of brokers and dealers from around the country linked by technology (more on OTC markets later in this chapter). Between 1995 and 1997 fashion industry leaders Tommy Hilfiger, St. John Knits, Jones Apparel Group, Kenneth Cole, Guess, Gucci, and Ralph Lauren entered the frays of Wall Street (Agins, 1999). Other apparel companies trading on the markets today are Vanity Fair, Liz Claiborne, Kellwood, and Levi Strauss. (The case study at the end of the chapter on Liz Claiborne illustrates the creation of a large fashion corporation.)

A company goes public to raise capital, and typically there are marketing efforts to produce excitement in the marketplace about the company and the initial stock offering. Growth is the primary objective when a company goes public and the influx of capital allows for expansion and an increase in the worth of the company that would not be possible from using debt or the existing stockholder base. Prada has been attempting to go public for a few years.

Types of Stock Markets

The United States has two types of stock markets, **organized exchanges** and over-the-counter markets. Investment markets in the United States began in 1790 with the **American Stock Exchange (AMEX)** when the federal government issued $80 million in **bonds** to repay the Revolutionary War debt. The **New York Stock Exchange (NYSE)**, now operated by **NYSE Euronext**, was born in 1792. In 2008, the American Stock Exchange merged with the NYSE Euronext group. The *New York Stock Exchange (NYSE)* is an organized exchange located at 11 Wall Street, New York, New York. It is the largest stock exchange in the United States with about 2,800 firms trading across the United States and Europe comprising more than 8,000 issues. Investors place orders with brokerage firms that place the order in the exchanges. Originally, brokers purchased seats earning them the right to trade on the NYSE with seat prices ranging from $4,000 in 1878 to as high as $4 million in 2005. However, the NYSE is now a public company, and hence like all public companies, the price of a share is the gauge of the exchange's financial health. Annual licenses permitting traders to conduct business on the exchange replaced seats. Approximately two-thirds of the dollar volume of stock trading takes place on the physical stock exchanges. The Jones Group, Levi Strauss, Liz Claiborne, and Kellwood are fashion apparel companies that trade on the NYSE. Consumer labels from these companies include Jones NY, Nine West, and Anne Klein from the Jones Group; Lucky, Kate Spade, and Juicy Couture from Liz Claiborne; and XOXO, Jolt, and David Meister from Kellwood.

Companies that do not trade their stock on any other exchange use the OTC market. Brokerage firms keep inventory of stocks purchased less frequently and sell the stocks when investors want to purchase them, thus the term "over-the-counter." The OTC market encompasses all parties necessary to conduct securities trades absent from the physical stock exchanges. The structure of the OTC market is similar to other equity security markets in that there are companies, investors, brokers, regulators, and interdealer quotation systems. A self-regulating body known as the **National Association of Securities Dealers (NASD)** governs the OTC. The types of securities and companies traded in the OTC markets are broad. Apparel companies Benetton and Adidas trade their stocks in the OTC market. In the United States, trading of big OTC transpires on the **National Association of Securities Dealers Automated Quotations System (NASDAQ)**. The NASDAQ is the largest OTC market in the United States with approximately 3,100 listings. Other OTC markets include Pink Sheets and the OTC Bulletin Board.

There are stock markets all over the world including Africa, Asia, Europe, the Middle East, North America, and South America. The largest non-U.S. stock markets are London, Euronext, and Tokyo. Globalization and technology make it possible to invest in foreign stocks. There are positives and negatives to trading in foreign markets. Companies all over the world seek the ability to raise capital anywhere they wish, and the globalization of the markets makes it possible to do so. However, there are barriers to investing overseas, as many countries prohibit or severely limit foreign investors in their markets. Furthermore, without the regulations of U.S. markets, investors find getting credible and complete information about companies abroad difficult. **American Depository Receipts (ADRs)** are financial instruments that ease the burden of investing in foreign countries. ADRs are certificates created by banks and other institutions that represent stocks in foreign countries. The certificates are held in trust in a bank in the country where the stocks traded are valued closely to the foreign stocks they represent.

Regulating the Stock Market

To ensure fairness and discourage corruption, the stock market is highly regulated. The fashion industry proved the necessity of regulation in 1993 when legendary fashion house Leslie Fay was rife with scandal. Laced with false entries, Leslie Fay's books overstated the company's sales and income for years. Leslie Fay restated earnings, erasing previously reported income. Leslie Fay stock dropped to below $1 a share, forcing the company off the NYSE. Indictments of several key executives followed and the company's reputation was ruined. The four groups that carefully regulate the stock market include the United States Congress, the **Securities and Exchange Commission (SEC)**, the New York Stock Exchange (NYSE) and other self-regulatory organizations, and individual brokerage firms. The U.S. Congress is the apex of stock market regulation. Congress is responsible for creating and implementing laws that govern the stock market based on market conditions. Congress ensures that the SEC has the power and laws needed to carry out its mission. (See Figure 6.6 for the four bodies of regulators.)

Congress created the Securities and Exchange Commission in 1934 to act as a watchdog for the stock market. SEC regulations exist to ensure that investors receive fair financial disclosure from publically traded companies and to discourage owners, investors, and employees from engaging in fraudulent behavior to manipulate stock prices. The SEC supervises all new companies listed on any exchange and other organizations involved with the SEC. The SEC requires that any company wishing to issue a new stock file a **registration statement** providing financial, legal, and technical information about the company. Generally, companies offer potential investors a **prospectus** that summarizes the information in the registration statement. Additionally, any company listed on an exchange is required to file an **annual report** (more on annual reports later in this chapter). The SEC scrutinizes stock trades made by corporate **insiders** (officers, directors, and major stockholders) who must file periodic reports about the status of their holdings of corporate stock. In addition, the SEC makes recommendations for new laws when warranted. It is important to note that even with the vast amount of required documentation it is up to the investor to determine the value of a security.

The stock exchanges regulate their members by applying their own rules and regulations. For example, the NYSE alone has 1,000 pages of rules, policies, and standards of conduct for its members. *The National Association of Securities Dealers (NASD)* supervises the NASDAQ market. Daily monitoring of trading activity reveals any noteworthy unethical behavior by a stock trader. Exchanges worldwide share suspicious actions with one another.

Individual brokerage firms buy and sell stock for their customers and their employees are highly trained. With strict standards of professional conduct, brokerage firms maintain

United States Congress

SEC
Securities & Exchange
Commission

The NYSE & Other
Self-Regulatory
Organizations

Individual Brokerage
Firms

FIGURE 6.6 *The regulatory structure of the U.S. Securities Market (Source: Hawa Stwodah).*

a high level of integrity and honesty among their peers to ensure transactions are fair for all parties involved. Self-regulation begins here and brokerage firms abide by the three other regulatory groups.

In addition to the buying and selling of stocks, the stock market is in the information business as well. Investors can glean knowledge about a company based on the stability of its stock price. A myriad of factors influence stock prices including annual reports, press releases, new products, lawsuits, recommendations by brokers, and the market.

Drivers of Stock Prices

The price of a stock is rooted in supply and demand: High demand equals a high price and conversely low demand equals a low price. A stock is worth whatever someone is willing to pay for it, meaning that if an investor is willing to pay $20 for a share of stock, the stock will sell for $20. Essentially, buyers and sellers determine the price of stocks. Investors can only buy stocks previously owned by another investor; therefore, sellers must make stocks available to purchasers. How do investors decide when to buy or sell a stock? One of the primary considerations is the financial health of the company. The company's past performance is important, but more significant is its predicted future performance. Determining appropriate stock prices requires knowledge of projected earnings, dividends, interest rates, market share, and risks. If earnings and dividends prospects exceed expected forecasts, a company's stock is more valuable. The opposite is also true: If a company performs poorly, the value of the stock will decrease. Changes in executive management, acquisitions, mergers, introduction of a new line of products, and use of improved technology with expectations of growth in sales and profits create favorable conditions for a company's stock value to increase. For example, in 2005 J. Jill stock rose 21 percent because of the assumption that Urban Outfitters was purchasing the company. The Urban Outfitters acquisition of J. Jill never came to fruition; however, in 2006, Talbot's acquired J. Jill. Figure 6.7 is a list of fashion companies traded on the NYSE. Other circumstances point to an uncertain future like a change in top management, a new competitor in the marketplace, or a major lawsuit causing a reduction in the value of a firm's stock.

The health of an industry is another indicator of the future performance of a company and consequently its stock price. Some industries, like the textile industry, are shrinking, and while a particular company in the textile industry may be doing well, the overall

FIGURE 6.7 *Fashion companies traded on the NYSE (Source: Adapted from NYSE).*

Company listing	Ticker symbol
Carter's, Inc.	CRI
Coach, Inc.	COH
Hanesbrands, Inc.	HBI
The Jones Apparel Group, Inc.	JNY
LVMH	MC
Maidenform Brands, Inc.	MFB
Polo Ralph Lauren Corporation	RL
Quicksilver, Inc	ZQK
Under Armour, Inc.	UA
VF Corporation	VFC

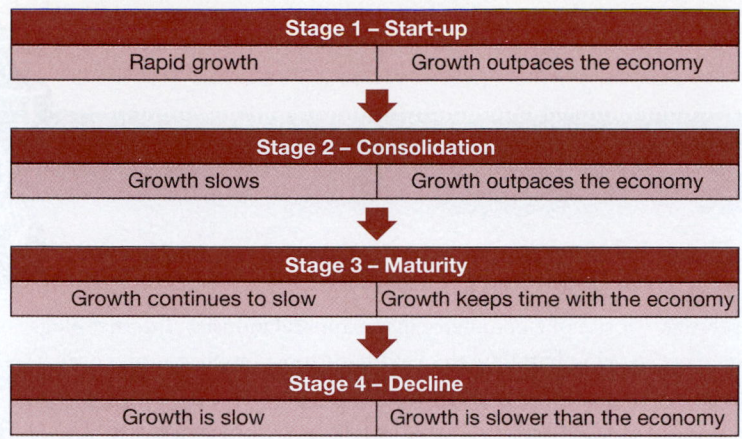

Stage 1 – Start-up	
Rapid growth	Growth outpaces the economy

Stage 2 – Consolidation	
Growth slows	Growth outpaces the economy

Stage 3 – Maturity	
Growth continues to slow	Growth keeps time with the economy

Stage 4 – Decline	
Growth is slow	Growth is slower than the economy

FIGURE 6.8 *The four-stage life cycle of an industry.*

contraction of the industry will cause a drop in the company's shares. Industries have a four-stage life cycle. Stage 1 is the start-up stage where rapid growth occurs. Stage 2 is the consolidation stage where growth slows from the start-up stage but outpaces that of the economy. Stage 3 is the maturity stage where growth keeps time with the general economy. Lastly, stage 4 is a stage of decline where growth is slower than the economy. Figure 6.8 illustrates the four-stage life cycle of an industry. Some industries are cyclical and the price of stock is dependent on whether an industry is in an expansion or contraction cycle.

Economic trends are another important factor when evaluating a stock. Keeping a close eye on economic indicators is a prediction of how well a stock will perform. Economic indicators that point to a healthy economy are a rising gross domestic product (GDP), low inflation, low interest rates, low unemployment rates, a U.S. budget surplus, and the **consumer price index (CPI)**. The CPI gauges the "cost of living" by measuring how much it costs to purchase the goods and services that an average household buys, like food, clothing, and fuel. Low interest rates encourage firms to borrow money and expand or make improvements to their businesses. Low unemployment rates mean that most Americans are working, giving them discretionary income to spend that stimulates the economy. A **bull market** occurs when the indicators point to a growing economy where companies are making money and Americans are working and have more money to invest, resulting in an increase in stock prices. Conversely, if the economy is contracting and unemployment is high and many Americans are looking for work, stock prices fall and a **bear market** occurs. Chapter 7 offers a detailed discussion on economic indicators.

National and world events affect stock prices. When terrorists attacked the United States on September 11, 2001, the financial markets never opened that day. It was on September 17, 2001, that the markets opened following the attack and the Dow Jones Industrial Average dropped 684.71 points, the largest one-day loss in history. September 11 highlighted global ties as William Hummer, principal money manager at Wayne Hummer, Inc., said, "I think there is a greater recognition now that economies and markets are globally tied together." Mr. Hummer went on to say, "There is a better understanding that what happens in China and Europe affects the United States" (Twin, 2006).

Stock prices are driven by celebrity endorsements, runway reports from fashion week, and people associated with politics who wear certain brands of clothing. Michelle Obama's wardrobe is often discussed in the media. Dr. David Yermack conducted research from November 2008 to December 2009 on the effect of clothing worn by Michelle

During the 2008 Presidential campaign, future First Lady Michelle Obama attracted public admiration for her fashion choices. Mrs. Obama sometimes appeared in outfits from avant-garde, prestige designers, but she also favored clothing from mainstream retailers such as Gap or H&M. Sometimes she improvised eye-catching ensembles combining exclusive and mid-market brands.

Mrs. Obama conveyed a message that one could dress elegantly on an ordinary family budget, an idea that made her extremely popular with the public. After the Obamas moved into the White House in 2009, interest in Michelle Obama's wardrobe spread around the world. Her appeal has proved enormously valuable to fashion companies whose garments she wears, especially for major occasions such as international summit meetings or state dinners. Very often, these companies' stock prices rise immediately after Mrs. Obama makes a public appearance wearing their apparel.

The pattern began after an interview on the *Tonight Show* late in the 2008 campaign. Mrs. Obama told the audience that her outfit came from J. Crew and could be bought online, and the company's stock price rose 8% the next day, 25% within a week. A statistical analysis of 189 public appearances by the First Lady showed that fashion company stock prices rose an average of 0.5% just after she wore their brands, with much greater increases on major state occasions. The data indicate that Mrs. Obama's wardrobe added more than $2 billion to the value of certain fashion companies during the Obamas' first year in the White House, an average of about $14 million in shareholder value for every public appearance by the First Lady.

Several factors explain this large value creation, and one of the most important may be the rise of e-commerce in the apparel industry. Internet blogs closely follow the First Lady, posting photos and evaluations of her wardrobe within hours of each appearance. Consumers can immediately purchase the same garments online at retailers' websites. Many of her outfits are sold by middle-class retail chains with hundreds of locations, and these companies might experience nationwide increases in in-store customer traffic. In addition, Mrs. Obama shops from a very wide range of designers, having worn approximately 50 different labels in public during her first year in Washington. Considerable uncertainty surrounds the identity of her outfitters before major events, leading to news coverage, which amounts to valuable advertising for these fashion companies.

If Michelle Obama can create $2 billion in value per year for apparel companies, how much would a designer pay for the professional services of a top fashion model or celebrity endorser? The answer is much less: The highest-paid models in the world make $10 to $20 million per year, while the top product endorsers earn $50 to $100 million. Assuming these people are not being underpaid, the data suggest that most commercial marketing programs are far less valuable to retailers than unsolicited, spontaneous adoption of a company's products by a respected public figure.

Source: David Yermack.

Obama on apparel stock prices. Refer to Box 6.3 for an article written by Dr. Yermack specifically for this textbook discussing his research concerning the public's interest in Mrs. Obama's wardrobe and its impact on the stock market.

The stock market reports fluctuations in prices using various **indexes**. An index is a specific group of stocks and the price reported reflects the combined pricing movements of the stocks in the index. There are several indexes because one does not tell the whole story. The **Dow Jones Industrial Average** (see Figure 6.9 for a graph depicting the Dow Jones Industrial Average), computed since 1896, includes stock prices of 30 **blue chip** companies, or companies considered reliable investments. Because there are only 30 firms in the Dow Jones Industrial Average, changes to the makeup of the average occur on occasion to reflect changes in the economy. The **Standard & Poor's 500 (S & P 500)** tracks stock prices for 500 large U.S. companies, making it a broader overview than the Dow Jones. The **NYSE Composite Index** tracks the prices of all the common stocks listed on the NYSE, making it more broadly based than the S & P 500. The **Wilshire 5000**

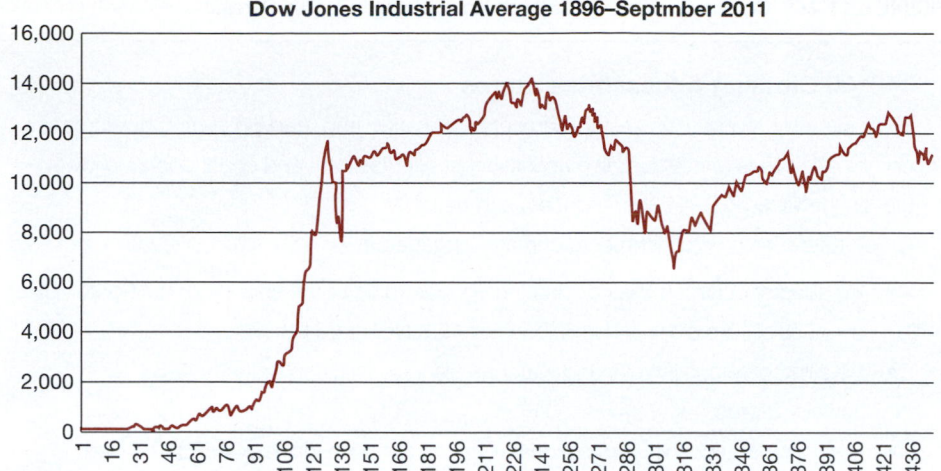

FIGURE 6.9 *The Dow Jones Industrial Average since 1896 (Source: Adapted from NYSE, djia.htm).*

index is the most expansive of all U.S. equity indexes and it computes the value of all NYSE, AMEX, and NASDAQ stocks totaling 6,000 stocks. The **Nikkei Average of Tokyo** and the **Financial Times Index of London** indexes have become part of the daily reporting as well.

Reading a Stock Table

There are various sources for stock activity of a company. Newspapers, trade journals, and other print media print the previous day's trading. Real-time up-to-the-minute stock activity is on various financial sites on the Internet such as Yahoo Financial and the New York Stock Exchange. Understanding how to read the stock table is essential to people who are interested in the financial health of a company. Investors, stockholder, and job seekers look at the financial stability of a company. Figure 6.10 explains how to read a stock table.

Financial Value of a Company

There are two ways to value a company—one is **market capitalization** and the other is the **book value**. Market capitalization is simply the value of a company at a given time. It is the total of all outstanding shares of a company multiplied by the price of the stock. Outstanding

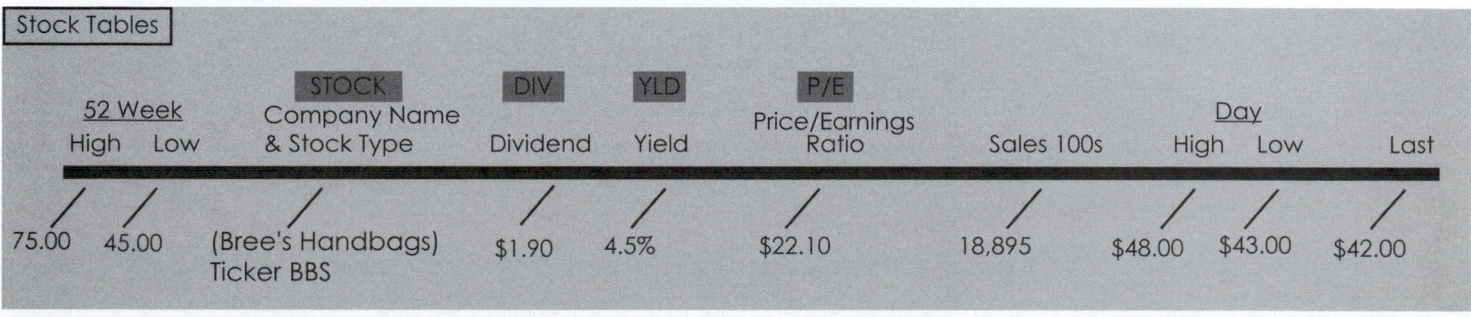

FIGURE 6.10 *How to read a stock table (Source: Hawa Stwodah).*

448150 Clothing Accessories Stores

This industry comprises establishments primarily engaged in retailing single or combination lines of new clothing accessories, such as hats and caps, costume jewelry, gloves, handbags, ties, wigs, toupees, and belts.

Cross-references. Establishments primarily engaged in—

- Retailing specialized lines of clothing via electronic home shopping, mail-order, or direct sale—are classified in Subsector 454, Nonstore Retailers;
- Retailing precious jewelry and watches—are classified in Industry 448310, Jewelry Stores;
- Retailing used clothing accessories—are classified in Industry 453310, Used Merchandise Stores;
- Retailing luggage, briefcases, trunks, or these products in combination with a general line of leather items (except leather apparel), known as luggage and leather goods stores—are classified in Industry 448320, Luggage and Leather Goods Stores; and
- Retailing leather apparel—are classified in Industry 448190, Other Clothing Stores.

2007 NAICS	Corresponding Index Entries
448150	Apparel accessory stores
448150	Clothing accessories stores
448150	Costume jewelry stores
448150	Furnishings stores, men's and boys'
448150	Furnishings stores, women's and girls'
448150	Handbag stores
448150	Hat and cap stores
448150	Jewelry stores, costume
448150	Neckwear stores
448150	Tie shops
448150	Wig and hairpiece stores http://www.census.gov/cgi-bin/sssd/naics/

Privacy Policy 2010 Census Data Tools Information Quality Product Catalog

Contact Us Home

shares of stock are owned by stockholders, including common and preferred stock. If a company stock is worth $25 and there are 500,000 stocks outstanding, the company is worth $12,500,000 ($25 × 50,000 shares). The total of all companies' outstanding shares in a particular industry is **industry market capitalization**. It is difficult to measure the fashion industry as an index because there are many suppliers and various businesses that contribute to the industry. The U.S. Census Bureau measures indexes every five years based on the NAICS codes. Figure 6.11 is an example of the industry index of apparel and accessories stores, NAICS code 452.

"Market caps" is the abbreviated term to market capitalization. Various types of market caps exist based on the value of a company (see Figure 6.12). What the market indicates

Mega $200 Billion & Greater	Big $10 Billion & Greater	Mid $2 Billion to $10 Billion
Small $300 Million to $2 Billion	Micro $50 Million to $300 Million	Nano under $50 Million

FIGURE 6.12 *Market caps (market capitalization) vary based on the value of the company.*

a company is worth through the buying and selling of stock at a given time defines market capitalization. As a result, the market cap of a company can change minute by minute. The book value of a company is based on financial records of the company. The book value is commonly referred to as the net value of a company. The simple formula is assets minus liabilities equal book value. The **balance sheet**, one of many **financial statements** found in a company's annual report, lists the assets and liabilities of a company.

Within the financial statements are various types of ratios used by the company's executives to make decisions concerning the direction of the company. The **statement of cash flows**, **income statement (profit and loss statement)**, and the balance sheet gauge the financial health of a company. These statements are always included in the annual report of a company and are discussed in the next section.

The Annual Report

The macroeconomic environment of the world and a nation can directly impact consumer buying decisions, which in turn affect the direction fashion will take through style, design, color, craftsmanship, and pricing. The direction is visible on the runway with subdued colors and conservative designs, evidence of consumers' state of mind that supports their willingness to purchase fashion in the future. The economic cycles of fashion for the year culminate in the financial state of a company reported to shareholders in the annual report.

A company's annual report will include a mission statement, letter from the president, business initiatives and strategies, industry lists of competitors, inventory status, risk factors, and select financial data. Usually important from an investor perspective and from an economic perspective, the annual report is shared at a stockholders meeting followed by a public viewing of the report on the company website. Annual reports are also found at other sites such as the NYSE. If the economy is stable, where variables such as employment, inflation, and overall business are in perpetual equilibrium, meaning steady and settled, not moving at drastic increases or decreases due to price instability, businesses then attempt to operate as efficiently as possible using limited or scarce resources to maximize a profit. However, when an economy fluctuates or is considered unstable, one in which prices fluctuate due to shocks to the economy by such things as war, attacks of terrorism, natural disasters, and significant increases in prices, businesses are forced to make decisions to operate in an unstable economic situation.

The financial information reported in an annual report is a good perspective of how a company operated the past year. Some financial reports give information in dollar amounts and as a ratio analysis. The advantages of using ratios are that finances appear in a simpler format and it is easy to compare year-to-year performance or one department to another. Most companies use the ratio as a comparison monthly, quarterly, or yearly. Some of the ratios, along with dollar amounts, appear in the annual report. There are many types of ratios used in financial statements. Four important ratios used to analyze the financial health of a fashion company are **operating**, **profitability**, **liquidity**, and **turnover ratios**.

Operating ratios are used for the purpose of measuring efficiency. The formula is:

$$\frac{\text{operation expenses}}{\text{revenue}} = \text{operation ratio.}$$

Profitability analyzes a company's ability to create profit in the future based on its expenses and other costs. This ratio looks at profit reported on the income statement. Calculated as a percentage, there are many types of ratios. Most important to a fashion company is the net profit margin. The formula is:

$$\frac{\text{net income}}{\text{net sales}} = \text{profitability.}$$

Liquidity is important because it measures a business's ability to meet short-term and long-term debts. The ability of a company to liquidate quickly is important. The ratio, called the **current ratio**, shows that a company can function efficiently in the short run. The formula is:

$$\frac{\text{assets}}{\text{liabilities}} = \text{current ratio.}$$

Turnover ratio is important to fashion retailers as it shows the number of times an inventory turns over during a certain period. The formula for turnover ratio is:

$$\frac{\text{net sales}}{\text{average inventory}} = \text{turnover ratio.}$$

Financial Statements

Financial statements are used in accounting practices of a company for reporting purposes. It is essential that a company be focused on making profit, but at the same time concentrate on the cash flow of the business, and fashion companies particularly should also focus on selling and producing apparel and accessories to meet the customer demand. Without cash flow, a company cannot survive. A fashion company can have the best product and the most fashionable line that gets rave reviews from the media, but if poor sales create losses the result is a negative cash flow. The next season, the company must be on target with trends, price points, deliveries, and so on to generate cash flow and profit. The financial statements of a company show how well, or not so well, the company is doing financially. There are many financial statements, but the primary statements are the income statement, balance sheet, and statement of cash flow. The components of the income statement or the profit and loss statement (as seen in Chapter 5) include net sales, cost of goods sold, gross margin, operation expenses, and net profit or loss. The balance sheet states the assets and liabilities of a company. It is a tool to balance the money. Assets on the balance sheet include cash on hand, inventory, fixed assets, and accounts receivables. The liabilities (what the company owes) include long-term debt, stock equity, expenses or accounts payable, and other liabilities. The statement of cash flows is very important because it shows the flow of cash into and out of a company.

Summary

This chapter examined Mike Porter's Five Competitive Forces: model of rivalry, barriers to entry, buying power, threat of substitutes, and supplier power. Through the study of each force, the relevance of the model to the fashion industry was illustrated. A peek into the three fashion competitors gave insight into how a fashion company reacts to a sluggish economy. A discussion of their business models demonstrated that there is more than one method of dealing with an economic slowdown. You learned that companies use financial reports and stock prices as ways of measuring their health and stability. We also explored the tools used to measure the financial health of a company and the operation of various stock markets.

Key Terms

allocation efficiency   138

American Depository Receipts (ADRs)   145

American Stock Exchange (AMEX)   144

annual report   145

balance sheet   151

bargaining power   134

barriers to entry   132

bear market   147

blue chip   148

bonds   144

book value   149

bull market   147

buying power   132

capital   134

common stock   143

competition   132

consumer price index (CPI)   147

current ratio   152

Design Piracy Prohibition Act   137

dividends   143

Dow Jones Industrial Average   148

economies of scale   136

efficiency   138

financial statement   151

Financial Times Index of London   149

Five Competitive Forces   132

income statement   151

index   148

industry market capitalization   150

initial public offering (IPO)   143

insiders   145

knock-off   132

liquidity   152

market capitalization   149

market efficiency   138

monopoly   132

MR = MC   135

National Association of Securities Dealers (NASD)   144

National Association of Securities Dealers Automated Quotations (NASDAQ)   144

New York Stock Exchange (NYSE)   144

Nikkei Average of Tokyo   149

NYSE Composite Index   148

NYSE Euronext   144

operating ratios   152

organized exchanges   144

over-the-counter (OTC) markets   143

preferred stock   143

production possibility curve (PPC)   140

production possibility frontier (PPF)   140

profit and loss statement   151

profitability ratio   152

prospectus   145

public company   143

registration statement   145

rivalry   132

secondary market   143

Securities and Exchange Commission (SEC)   145

shares   143

Standard & Poor's 500 (S & P 500)   148

statement of cash flow   151

stock markets   143

stockholders   143

supplier power   135

technical efficiency   141

turnover ratio   152

threat of substitutes   134

Wilshire 5000   148

Questions for Review

1. Discuss why competition is necessary among fashion companies.

2. Explain the Five Competitive Forces model. Relate each part of the model to the fashion industry.

3. Explain the importance of the MR = MC rule.

4. List at least five things a company can do in the long run to increase its profit.

5. Why do fashion companies analyze their business season by season and not year by year?

6. Discuss the types of efficiency and the importance of efficiency when operating a business.

7. What three assumptions have to be in place to forecast allocation and technical efficiency?

8. Explain the difference between common and preferred stock.

9. List three major companies that entered the stock market between 1995 and 1997.

10. What is the OTC? Give an example.

11. What is the NASDAQ?

12. What four groups regulate the stock market in the United States?

13. How does a company become listed on a stock exchange?

14. What is the purpose of an annual report?

15. Discuss three drivers of stock prices.

16. What is the difference between a bear market and a bull market?

17. Why is market capitalization important to a company?

18. Why do people use ratios as a means of analyzing a business?

19. Why are financial statements printed in an annual report?

20. What is the most important thing a company should focus on; in other words, what is the center of the business?

Critical Thinking

1. You are the CEO of a large fashion company that needs to raise money for the purpose of expanding the company into a new market. The Board of Directors and the stockholders vote to raise money by offering new shares of stock on a stock market exchange. The company needs to raise 10 million dollars. Research and discuss how you would list the stock on a stock exchange, what exchange you would use, and how much is a fair price for the stock. After you decide on a price per stock, how many shares are you going to have to sell to raise $10,000,000?

2. You have $5,000 to invest in a fashion-oriented company stock. Select your stock and follow it for 20 days. Keep a daily log on the price of the stock; for each day list three economic and business factors you think have affected the price. At the end of the 20 days, do the following: (1) create a chart of the stock price; (2) write a synopsis (2 pages) of the causes of the price of the stock over the 20-day period. Each student of the class has to make a one-minute presentation on their stock.

Internet Activities

1) Play a stock market simulation over a period of two months. Below are a few sites that offer free sign-ups. You can play in teams or alone.
a) Investopedia Stock Simulation—http://simulator.investopedia.com/#12911454260152&close
b) Stock Game—http://www.smartstocks.com/

2) Order an annual report for a fashion company from the following website. When you receive your report, answer the following questions:
a) Did the company make a profit or loss? What is the dollar amount? What financial report did you look at to find the information?
b) Who is the competition of the company?
c) What are the risks facing the company?

Bibliography

Agins, T. (1999). *The end of fashion how marketing changed the clothing business forever*. New York: William Morrow.

Besley, S., & Brigham, E. (2005). *Essentials of managerial finance*. Mason, OH: Thompson South-Western.

Bodie, Z., Kane, A., & Marcus, A. (2008). *Essentials of investments*. New York, NY: McGraw-Hill/Irwin.

Forbes.com. (n.d.). Retrieved from http://www.forbes.com/lists/2011/21/private-companies-11_Forever-21_SI70.html

Forever 21 is thinking big. (2011, June 22). *Richmond Times-Dispatch*, p. D3.

Gap Inc. (n.d.). Retrieved from http://www.gapinc.com/content/gapinc/html/investors/realestate.html

Historical data. (n.d.). Retrieved from http://www.nyse.com/pdfs/HistoricalData.pdf

Nasdaq fact sheet 2008. (n.d.). Retrieved from http://www.nasdaq.com/about/2008_Corporate_FS.pdf

Otc 101. (n.d.). Retrieved from http://www.otcmarkets.com/learn/intro

The regulatory pyramid. (n.d.). Retrieved from http://www.nyse.com/pdfs/ts_reg_pyramid.pdf

Stock exchanges worldwide links. (n.d.). Retrieved from http://www.tdd.lt/slnews/Stock_Exchanges/Stock.Exchanges

Tracy, J. (2009). *How to read a financial report*. Hoboken, NJ: John Wiley.

Twin, A. (2006, September 11). *Stocks: 5 years after 9/11*. Retrieved from http://money.cnn.com/2006/09/08/markets/markets_fiveyearslater

What drives stock prices. (n.d.). Retrieved from http://www.nyse.com/pdfs/nyse_chap_04.pdf

Zimmerman, A. (2010). *Zimmerman's research guide*. Retrieved from http://law.lexisnexis.com/infopro/zimmermans/disp.aspx?z=1806

GOVERNMENT
POLICIES
AFFECT
FASHION

OBJECTIVES

After reading this chapter, you will be able to:

- Gain an understanding of the various types of economies in the world
- Discuss the involvement of the U.S. government in the fashion industry
- Examine business growth and competition
- Examine unemployment and inflation and their implications for the fashion industry
- Explore the monetary policy used to control the economy
- Study the economic indicators for the fashion industry

My job is to make women dream.

—JOHN GALLIANO, Christian Dior designer, personal communication with the Associated Press

Of course I'm aware of the credit crunch, but it is not a creative crunch—not at the house of Dior, anyway.

—JOHN GALLIANO, World Culture Pictorial Blog, February 1, 2009

7

The macroeconomics environment of the world and a nation can directly impact consumer buying decisions, which in turn affects the direction fashion will take in a particular season through style, design, color, craftsmanship, and pricing. The direction, viewed beginning with fashion week, occurs twice a year, once in the spring and again in the fall. New York begins each season directly followed by consecutive weeks in London, Milan, and Paris. In an economic downturn the runway is filled with apparel of subdued colors and conservative designs. Subdued colors are an indication of the consumers' mood, which might be a reflection of their conservative willingness to purchase in the future. On the contrary, the sashaying of apparel down the runway made of bright colors, short hemlines, and layers of textiles in fun-loving silhouettes that appeal to most people can be a sign of a positive economic time, a reflection of positive consumer sentiment, and hopefulness that consumers will spend money on fashion in the near future. Fashion weeks are an unofficial **economic indicator** by those who work in the fashion business, a kind of resource used by the fashion industry to gauge the stability of the economy. The current state of the economy is the root of how trends in the fashion industry, including color, silhouette, and textile and apparel design, begin, and sometimes end. This chapter emphasizes the role of government in stabilizing the economy for the sole purpose of conducting business as usual.

In this chapter, we discuss the role of the U.S. government in business, how it works to minimize risks for all businesses through stabilizing prices, creating fair competition, and maintaining employment. Also, the chapter explores the role of the American Apparel and Footwear Associations in lobbying before government on behalf of apparel and footwear companies. "The **American Apparel & Footwear Association (AAFA)** speaks on behalf of the U.S. apparel and footwear industries, and their suppliers, before Congress and a variety of federal and state agencies on issues ranging from trade policy to safety regulations" (AAFA). The growth of a business, the implications of unemployment and inflation to the fashion industry, the importance of understanding monetary policy, and the way in which executives use many types of economic indicators when forecasting growth in the short and long run of a fashion business further connect economics and fashion. The chapter begins with the introduction of understanding the macroeconomic environment followed by understanding the various types of economies operating in the world today. This gives a foundation on which to study government policies affecting the fashion industry today.

Types of Economies

Macroeconomics is concerned with the economy as a whole or its basic subdivisions or aggregates, such as the government, households, and business sectors. When referring to something in aggregate form or units, it is as if they are one, so when an analyst speaks about the overall United States' consumer sentiment, although millions of U.S. consumers are taken into account, they are referred to as one unit. Economists study the current status of a nation's macroeconomy and forecast for the future by using rational and scientific modeling based on aggregates in supply, income, level of government money, interest rates, inflation, and unemployment. Economies today are placed in four broad categories: (1) **traditional economic systems**, (2) **market economies**, (3) **planned/command economies**, and (4) **mixed economic systems**.

A traditional economic system is typical of underdeveloped countries where there is abject poverty and very limited resources. In these countries, traditions pass from one generation to the next. When resources are available, technologies for retrieval do not exist. For example, in Africa, many traditional types of primitive tribes have not moved forward due to their location within the continent, yet somehow they continue to survive. Throughout the years, mainstream fashion ideas have emerged from these economies, in the way of prints and silhouettes through artists or people who have visited various countries and brought back exclusive textiles and jewelry, incorporating them into mass fashion.

The consumer drives the supply and demand of a country in a market economy or capitalist economy. In theory there is very little government intervention; however, many economists find this debatable. In many scholarly writings, economists agree that for a market economy to run efficiently, there has to be government intervention to create a fair competition and a healthy environment for the businesses to run efficiently.

Figure 7.1 is a circular flowchart illustrating how a market economy operates. The market economy works in response to the needs and wants for supply and demand. Within the fashion industry, if there is a change in demand for a particular style, which happens frequently, then there will be a change in supply. Manufacturers produce goods based on consumer demand and strive to manufacture the goods in the most efficient manner possible. By purchasing products, consumers send a message about what they like and desire in the marketplace. Conversely, when consumers do not spend money on a product it is equally clear what they are rejecting in the marketplace.

Many nations are privatizing to balance their own government budget or to build their economies as a market-oriented system. To **privatize**, governments sell government-owned companies to private citizens, thus opening up a market for greater success or failure. For example, China's economy has been in a transition from a centrally planned economy to a market-oriented economy while becoming a major player in the arena of globalization. China has privatized some of its businesses to position it to foreign competitors and to encourage foreign investment. China's retail apparel has experienced increases in recent years and is now a $40 billion industry. Department stores make up approximately 40 percent of the market. This includes domestic retailers as well as foreign retailers like Walmart and brands like Hugo Boss (Chinese Fashion Industry). Sweden, Great Britain, and Australia are examples of countries that have socialist policies, but capitalist characteristics, and more government involvement.

The U.S. economy is based on capitalism and the free enterprise system; however, the government intervenes in the form of law enforcement to protect the consumer, businesses, and the environment and also to guarantee free and fair competition. The government also regulates the markets through its local, state, and federal laws. Therefore, it is a mixed economy. A mixed economy is an economy that integrates the features of a market and command and planned economic system. Most economies of the world are a mixture of command and market.

In a true market economy, there is no government control or influence on decision making. The market will answer the three basic economic questions (as previously seen in Chapter 3): (1) What to produce? The consumers decide what to produce through purchases in the marketplace. (2) How to produce? The businesses in the market economy decide how production will take place. It is very competitive; therefore, most businesses endeavor to produce high quality with low prices. And lastly, (3) For whom to produce? Manufacturers produce goods for consumers who demand the goods and are able to afford the goods. A planned/command economy guarantees workers a job upon completing training for a position. A planned economy is one in which there is very little innovation and no entrepreneurship. Individuals have little say about their futures or production. In a command economy, the government treats all people equally, meaning that no matter the effort, the rewards are the same for all people.

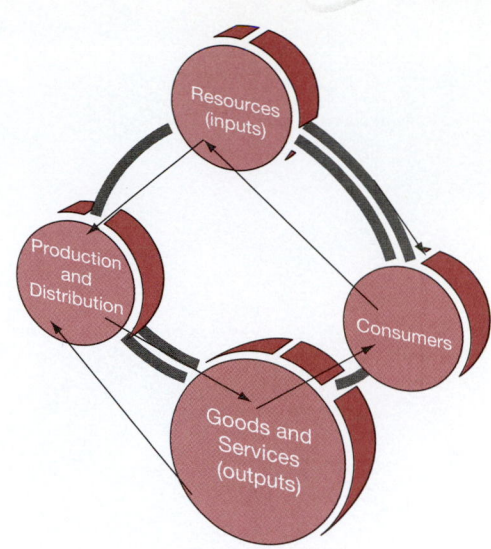

FIGURE 7.1 *Circular flowchart of economics. Resources or inputs go into production (manufacturing) of goods and services, such as apparel items, referred to as outputs. The outputs are sold to consumers who pay for the goods and services, providing jobs in manufacturing, designing, and selling of the goods. These people get paid and buy goods and the cycle continues.*

The advantage of the planned/command economy is that it only produces necessary goods. It can build its economy without relying on outside financial sources such as other nations while utilizing all natural resources, employing those who can work, and maintaining stable prices. The disadvantages are planning for everyone in the economy is difficult; the government dictates economic policies; the value of the type of work performed determines salaries; individual profit motives are discouraged; and the sectors of the economy preferred by the government are given special treatment. The planned/command economy in the short term is very efficient, but in the long run, most command or planned economies fail. There is no fashion industry in a planned economy—only necessary apparel that is need based rather than want based is produced. North Korea and Cuba are two planned economies in existence today.

U.S. Government Involvement in U.S. Fashion Industry

There is U.S. government involvement in the fashion industry from an industry, consumer, and environment perspective. The government protects the industry through trade, commerce, patent, and trademark laws. The government protects the consumer through safety and welfare laws. From an environmental perspective, the government implements environmental laws in manufacturing to protect the environment. For example, you learned in Chapter 4 that a corporation operates as a legal entity under the law, and laws are in place to prevent monopolies from occurring in the United States. Also, there are numerous laws in the United States protecting **intellectual property**. Table 7.1 gives details of laws with examples that govern the fashion industry today.

Competition

Understanding competition and the role it plays in the fashion industry is a foundation for success. Competition, usually studied under microeconomics, is important to the concepts of inflation and unemployment. The discussion of competition here facilitates further understanding of macroeconomics.

A **perfect competition** model includes a large number of buyers and sellers. Buyers know prices, are aware of where they can buy the product, and understand the manufacturing of the product. The firms and the resources are extremely mobile. The firms have control over the price of the product but factors such as the cost of the resources used in production plus additional costs like transportation and labor fluctuate and influence the price. The procurement of the best resources at the best price is the job of the buyer or product developer. Perfect competition does not exist; it is only a model used in economics. It is a benchmark measurement for all other models of competition. Based on want rather than need, the fashion industry is rife with competition. Table 7.2 lists the top 50 largest apparel companies, based on their earnings in 2002–2010. Competitive variables for fashion companies include, but are not limited to, **price**, **design**, **color**, **exclusivity**, **brand name**, **trends**, and **speed to market**. Refer to Figure 7.2 for an example of a garment showing the variables of competition. The next section defines the variables of competition.

Price is critical; goods that are overpriced become stagnant and create excessive markdowns. Goods that are underpriced give the impression that the product is inferior

TABLE 7.1
Laws affecting the fashion industry

Laws Regulating Competition

Antitrust and Unfair Competition Law	Competition laws are also known as "antitrust laws." The main goals of antitrust laws are to protect the interests of consumers and restrict business practices that are considered to be monopolistic and restrain commerce.
Clayton Antitrust Act	This act was put in place to prohibit any mergers or acquisitions between companies that are likely to result in an increase in prices for consumers or a decrease in competition. This act carries only civil penalties.
Federal Trade Commission Act	This act is responsible for forming the Federal Trade Commission (FTC). The act set specific guidelines regarding unfair business practices and authorized the Commission to issue Cease and Desist orders when large businesses are found to be in violation of the guidelines.
Robinson-Patman Act	This act outlawed what were considered to be anticompetitive practices by producers, such as price discrimination. This law was designed to level the playing field between large and small retailers. Violators of this act face criminal penalties.
Sherman Antitrust Act	This act was enacted to outlaw cartels and monopolies.
Cellar-Kefauver	This law outlawed the practice of creating a monopoly through the merger of two or more companies in order to remove competition.

Product and Labeling Laws

Wool Products Labeling Act	This act requires companies to reveal the presence of substitutes or mixtures in their products.
Made in the U.S.A.	In order for companies to market their products as "Made in the USA," they must be able to prove that the product was substantially transformed in the United States.
Fur Products Labeling Act	This act prohibits misbranding, false advertising, and false invoicing.
Flammable Fabrics Act	This act outlaws the manufacturing and sale of flammable apparel and textiles.
Textile Fiber Identification Act	This act bans the false identification of fiber content in textiles.
Fair Packaging and Labeling Act	This act prohibits deceptive labeling and packaging in order to regulate interstate and foreign trade.
Care Labeling of Textile Wearing Apparel Ruling	This ruling requires all clothing to have attached labels to inform the consumers of the proper care for the garment.

Labor Laws

Fair Labor Standards Act	This act requires employers to pay at least minimum wage and overtime pay of one-and-one-half-times an employee's regular wages. Standards are also set regulating the working conditions of minors.
Occupational Safety and Health Act	This act sets health and safety standards for companies and requires employers to provide a workplace without serious recognizable hazards.
Federal Employees Compensation Act	This act provides compensation for the death or disability of federal employees as a result of performing work duties.
Employees Polygraph Protection Act	This act prohibits employers from requiring employees to take lie detector tests, except for certain circumstances.
Consumer Credit Protection Act	This act regulates the garnishment of employee wages.
Family and Medical Leave Act	This act requires companies with fifty or more employees to provide up to twelve weeks of job-protected, unpaid leave to employees for the birth or adoption of a child or for the serious illness of themselves, a spouse, child, or parent.

Trademark, Patent, and Intellectual Property Laws

Trademark Act of 1881	This act was the first to allow for the registration of trademarks. Any trademarks registered under this act were protected for a period of thirty years.
Lanham Act	This act outlines the federal trademark regulations. It prohibits false advertising, trademark infringement, and trademark dilution.
Intellectual Property Rights	The rights given to people or companies over their own creative ideas for a given time period.
United States Patent Law	The patent laws in the United States were established in order to give authors and inventors the sole rights to their writings and inventions. Patents last twenty years after the date they are issued.

Source: Compiled by Danielle Ashe.

TABLE 7.2
Top 50 largest apparel companies

2010 RANK	Last Year's Rank	Company 50	FY	Most Recent FY	Previous FY	% Change Sales	Most Recent FY	Previous FY	% Change Net Income	% Profit Margin, Most Recent FY	% Profit Margin, Previous FY
1	25	Wet Seal	Jan.	$560.9	$593.0	(5.41)	$93.4	$30.2	209.27	16.65	5.09
2	1	True Religion Apparel	Dec.	$311.0	$270.0	15.19	$47.3	$44.4	6.53	15.21	16.44
3	2	The Buckle	Jan.	$898.3	$792.0	13.42	$127.3	$104.4	21.93	14.17	13.18
4	3	lululemon athletica	Feb.	$452.9	$353.5	28.12	$58.3	$39.4	47.97	12.87	11.15
5	5	Guess?	Jan.	$2,128.5	$2,093.4	1.68	$246.3	$215.0	14.56	11.57	10.27
6	4	Urban Outfitters	Jan.	$1,937.8	$1,834.6	5.63	$219.9	$199.4	10.28	11.35	10.87
7	13	Aeropostale	Jan.	$2,230.1	$1,885.5	18.28	$229.5	$149.4	53.61	10.29	7.92
8	7	Gymboree	Jan.	$1,014.9	$1,000.7	1.42	$101.9	$93.5	8.98	10.04	9.34
9	11	Polo Ralph Lauren	Mar.	$4,978.5	$5,018.9	(0.80)	$479.5	$406.0	18.10	9.63	8.09
10	10	JoS. A. Bank	Jan.	$770.3	$695.9	10.69	$71.2	$58.4	21.92	9.24	8.39
11	20	Maidenform Brands	Jan.	$466.3	$413.5	12.77	$37.0	$24.7	49.80	7.93	5.97
12	31	J. Crew	Jan.	$1,578.0	$1,428.0	10.50	$123.4	$54.1	128.10	7.82	3.79
13	17	Gap	Jan.	$14,197.0	$14,526.0	(2.26)	$1,102.0	$967.0	13.96	7.76	6.66
14	6	Nike	May	$19,176.0	$18,627.0	2.95	$1,486.7	$1,883.4	(21.06)	7.75	10.11
15	18	Volcom	Dec.	$280.6	$334.3	(16.06)	$21.7	$21.7	0.00	7.73	6.49
16	21	UniFirst	Aug.	$1,013.4	$1,023.2	(0.96)	$75.9	$61.0	24.43	7.49	5.96
17	27	Carter's	Jan.	$1,589.7	$1,494.5	6.37	$115.6	$77.9	48.40	7.27	5.21
18	32	Phillips-Van Heusen	Jan.	$2,398.7	$2,491.9	(3.74)	$161.9	$91.8	76.36	6.75	3.68
19	14	VF	Jan.	$7,220.3	$7,642.6	(5.53)	$461.3	$602.7	(23.46)	6.39	7.89
20	9	Cintas	May	$3,774.7	$3,937.9	(4.14)	$226.4	$335.4	(32.50)	6.00	8.52
21	19	American Eagle Outfitters	Jan.	$2,990.5	$2,988.9	0.05	$169.0	$179.1	(5.64)	5.65	5.99
22	22	Under Armour	Dec.	$856.4	$725.2	18.09	$46.8	$38.2	22.51	5.46	5.27
23	16	Columbia Sportswear	Dec.	$1,244.0	$1,317.8	(5.60)	$67.0	$95.1	(29.55)	5.39	7.22
24	26	The Children's Place	Jan.	$1,643.6	$1,630.3	0.82	$88.4	$82.4	7.28	5.38	5.05
25	28	Nordstrom	Jan.	$8,258.0	$8,272.0	(0.17)	$441.0	$401.0	9.98	5.34	4.85
26	39	Limited Brands	Jan.	$8,632.0	$9,043.0	(4.54)	$448.0	$220.0	103.64	5.19	2.43
27	30	Cato	Jan.	$884.0	$857.7	3.07	$45.8	$33.6	36.31	5.18	3.92
28	40	The Warnaco Group	Jan.	$2,019.6	$2,062.8	(2.09)	$96.0	$47.3	102.96	4.75	2.29
29	24	Dress Barn	July	$1,494.2	$1,444.2	3.46	$69.7	$74.1	(5.94)	4.66	5.13
30	34	Timberland	Dec.	$1,285.9	$1,364.6	(5.77)	$56.6	$42.9	31.93	4.40	3.14
31	New	rue21	Jan.	$525.6	$391.4	34.29	$22.0	$12.6	74.60	4.19	3.22
32	46	Chico's FAS	Jan.	$1,713.2	$1,582.4	8.27	$69.7	($19.1)	464.92	4.07	(1.21)
33	50	G-III Apparel Group	Jan.	$800.9	$711.1	12.63	$31.7	($14.0)	326.43	3.96	(1.97)
34	23	Levi Strauss	Nov.	$4,105.8	$4,400.9	(6.71)	$151.9	$229.3	(33.75)	3.70	5.21
35	33	Citi Trends	Jan.	$551.9	$488.2	13.05	$19.7	$17.4	13.22	3.57	3.56
36	36	Men's Wearhouse	Jan.	$1,909.6	$1,972.4	(3.18)	$45.5	$58.8	(22.62)	2.38	2.98
37	29	Zumiez	Jan.	$407.6	$408.7	(0.27)	$9.1	$17.2	(47.09)	2.23	4.21
38	8	bebe Stores	July	$603.0	$687.6	(12.30)	$12.6	$63.1	(80.03)	2.09	9.18
39	New	Stage Stores	Jan.	$1,431.9	$1,515.8	(5.54)	$28.7	($65.5)	143.82	2.00	(4.32)
40	42	Superior Uniform Group	Dec.	$102.8	$123.8	(16.96)	$2.0	$2.1	(4.76)	1.95	1.70

2010 RANK	Last Year's Rank	Company 50	FY	Most Recent FY	Previous FY	% Change Sales	Most Recent FY	Previous FY	% Change Net Income	% Profit Margin, Most Recent FY	% Profit Margin, Previous FY
41	New	Stein Mart	Jan.	$1,219.1	$1,326.6	(8.10)	$23.6	($71.3)	133.10	1.94	(5.37)
42	44	Delta Apparel	June	$355.2	$322.0	10.31	$6.5	($0.5)	1400.00	1.83	(0.16)
43	Back	Oxford Industries	Jan.	$800.7	$947.5	(15.49)	$14.6	($271.5)	105.38	1.82	(28.65)
44	47	Perry Ellis International	Jan.	$754.2	$851.3	(11.41)	$13.5	($12.3)	209.76	1.79	(1.44)
45	37	Hot Topic	Jan.	$736.7	$761.1	(3.21)	$11.9	$19.7	(39.59)	1.62	2.59
46	Back	Casual Male	Jan.	$395.2	$444.2	(11.03)	$6.1	($109.3)	105.58	1.54	(24.61)
47	35	Hanesbrands	Jan.	$3,891.3	$4,248.8	(8.41)	$51.3	$127.2	(59.67)	1.32	2.99
48	38	American Apparel	Dec.	$558.8	$545.1	2.51	$1.1	$14.1	(92.20)	0.20	2.59
49	Back	Christopher & Banks	Mar.	$455.4	$530.7	(14.18)	$0.2	($12.8)	101.56	0.04	(2.41)
50	15	Abercrombie & Fitch	Jan.	$2,928.6	$3,484.1	(15.94)	$0.3	$272.3	(99.89)	0.01	7.82

Notes: New = The company is appearing in the Apparel Top 50 for the first time. Back = The company has been ranked in the Apparel Top 50 in previous years but was not ranked last year because of its performance, because it was not publicly traded, etc. Dollar amounts are in millions of U.S. dollars. Levi Strauss & Co. is a privately held company that releases financial data publicly. Apparel does not include department stores in its Top 50 rankings. Nordstrom files with the SEC under "Retail - Family Clothing Stores" (SIC code 5651).

Source: Apparell Magazine, Egell Communications.

in some way. Savvy and thoughtful pricing is the hallmark of an experienced and effective buyer. Pricing is key to a firm realizing planned net sales. Achieving planned net sales is essential to gross margin and the bottom line, profit. With a myriad of goods available for sale, it is expected that prices range from low to high, depending on the product. Consumers equate high prices to quality and workmanship and low prices to low quality.

Design is the style and variation in the silhouette of a garment. A T-shirt is a common silhouette; however, the variations in the T-shirt are the design. T-shirts may be crew neck,

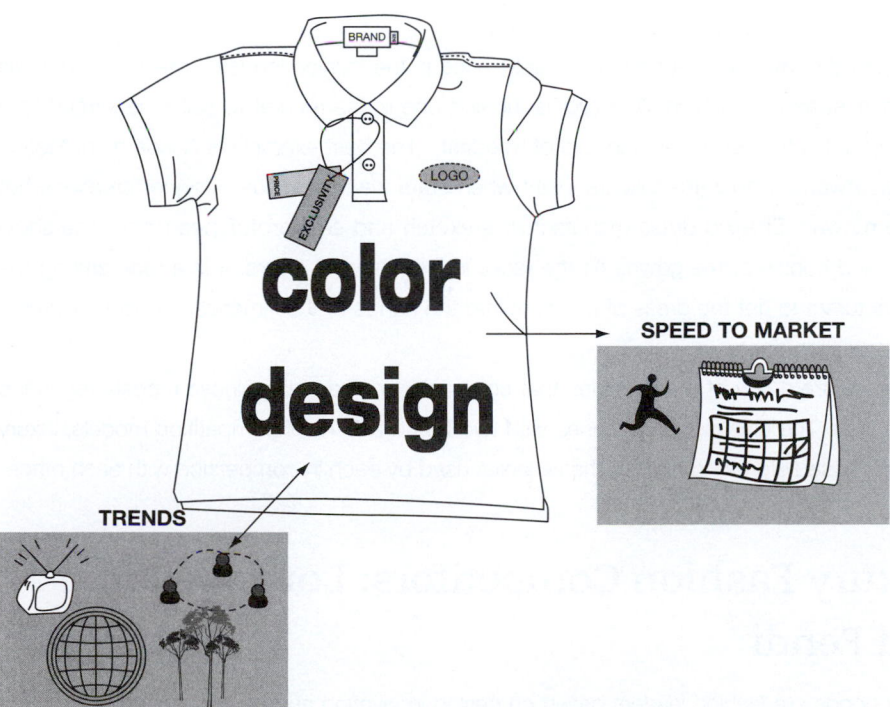

FIGURE 7.2 *An example of a garment showing the variables of competition (Source: Hawa Stwodah).*

v neck, scoop neck, or boat neck. The sleeves may be short, three-quarter, or long. The tee may have trims and embellishment or be decoration free. Each variation of the basic T-shirt silhouette is a design.

Color is the number-one reason a consumer decides to purchase a garment. New and exciting colors entice consumers as do colors that are attractive on the consumer. Color preferences are different in each marketplace. While female customers in the southern United States prefer colors like red, bright pink, yellow, and orange, their counterparts in the northeastern part of the United States prefer muted colors in the black and gray tones. Knowing customer color preferences and planning assortments accordingly are crucial to a retailer's success.

Exclusivity means that a retailer has a product not available by the competition. Exclusivity appears in several forms from private label to brands only found at a particular retailer to product offerings that a retailer may receive weeks before the competition. For example, Charter Club is a Macy's private label and cannot be found in any other retail store. Tommy Hilfiger is a Macy's exclusive because while Tommy Hilfiger is a global brand, Macy's is the only national retailer in the United States selling the Tommy Hilfiger brand. Ralph Lauren is a brand found in many retailers; however, at times Macy's negotiates with Ralph Lauren so that a new collection is shipped to Macy's weeks prior to the same collection being shipped to Macy's competitors, giving Macy's the collection exclusively for a time. All of these scenarios give Macy's a competitive advantage.

Brand names connote quality, dependability, value, and workmanship. Brand names are "the real thing" from which copies originate. Brand names are readily available in department stores. Examples of brand names include Hanes, Nine West, Jones NY, Coach, and Levi's.

Trends indicate the general direction or movement in the marketplace. The fashion industry is dependent on trends and having the right trends in inventory at the right time. Timing is everything for a trend since consumer demand creates trends. A trend that is introduced too early may be unsuccessful because consumers are not ready. Late introduction of a trend inhibits the maximization of sales on the trend.

"Speed to market" is a common phrase used in the fashion industry, meaning the same thing almost as fast fashion. A retailer is the first one in the market to sell a new trend to a consumer. It is the economic principle of "me-first." The best example is Academy of Motion Pictures Awards Show (the Oscars) night when stars wear fabulous designer creations hot off the runway. Shrewd dress manufacturers sketch and sew prototypes before the show is over and copies of the gowns hit the racks in less than 48 hours. It is a race among the manufacturers to get the dress of the night into the hands of the American consumer before the competition does.

Those are a few of the variables that companies include in business models regarding competition. The discussion continues with two brand and retail competition models, luxury and mall-based stores, to explore the variables used by each in competition with each other.

Luxury Fashion Competitors: Louis Vuitton and Fendi

Luxury goods are fashion leaders based on design innovation and quality of the product. For some fashion retailers, competition is not about price but the quality and workmanship of the product, status associated with the brand, and quality service. Louis Vuitton and Fendi compete in a nonprice manner. Figure 7.3 shows an example of a Louis Vuitton handbag. Designers such as Louis Vuitton and Fendi are well known among consumers as both manufacturers and retailers, selling luxury items including handbags and clothing. The brands exemplify a luxury lifestyle that many in the mainstream want to emulate. Their fine workmanship, status signatures, and excellent service (whether acting as a vendor or a retailer) set them apart. Because of competitive factors, both are able to maintain the high price points associated with luxury items.

FIGURE 7.3 *Louis Vuitton is well known among consumers (Source: Newscom).*

Mall-Based Competitors: Aéropostale and Pacific Sunwear

Aeropostle and Pacsun are mall-based fashion retail competitors. Both target specific age groups that overlap. Aeropostle targets 14- to 17-year-olds and Pacsun targets 12- to 14-year-olds. They refer to themselves as having heritage brands reflecting the youthful consumer with a fashionable lifestyle. The apparel prices at both retailers match the value received and the clothing is available exclusively through their stores and websites.

These companies operate on the premise of competition. Competition is a very good thing and makes for a healthy environment in which a business can prosper and grow by forcing companies to become better at what they do. The government supports both types of retailers by encouraging competition, maintaining employment so that people have money to buy goods and services, and maintaining monetary stability in our economy.

Unemployment and the Implications for Fashion

The United States keeps statistics on the unemployment rate to track the stability of the economy. If unemployment is high, there is a slowdown in the economy. If the unemployment continues to rise, then the possibility of recession is imminent. Fashion companies assume that if people are employed, they tend to spend money on fashion. If unemployment is high or rising, companies cannot rely on the same business model to keep their customers. In 2006 unemployment began to rise around the world and department stores struggled to attract new customers, keep their old customers, and make a profit. To combat a sluggish economy, most department stores are focusing on brand names associated with a designer or a private label that gives the store exclusivity. For example, Kohl's has launched exclusive lines by Vera Wang (Simply Vera), Ralph Lauren (Chaps), and Avril Levine (Abbey Dawn). Luxury brands like Prada and Coach have launched their own websites selling products as opposed to their previous websites that were information only.

According to the Department of Labor, as of December 2010, 130,260,000 people in the United States held a job. The number of employed people fell from the beginning of the recession, which technically started at the end of 2007. In December 2008, U.S. employment was at 134,383,000. Because of high unemployment between 2008 and 2010, wholesalers and retailers in the fashion industry adjusted their businesses to accommodate for unemployment. In the industry many people lost their jobs, companies lowered inventories, and retailers and manufacturers lowered sales expectations to lessen the blow of a soft economy.

Inflation and the Impact on Fashion

Inflation is the increase at which the price of goods and services is rising. The cause of inflation is too much available money and too few available goods. Inflation affects the consumer in many ways, but the decreased buying power of the dollar causes a slowdown in spending, causing people to buy necessities like food, shelter, and other basic needs at a high cost. The increased costs of food and gasoline affect the buying power of consumers, leaving them with less discretionary income, thus leading to an atmosphere of spending cautiousness. During times of inflation, the cost of apparel and accessories increase as well. For example, if a shirt normally costs $10, inflation causes the cost of the shirt to rise to $12. The two-dollar increase in price is recouped in the retail prices paid by consumers.

Fashion is not on the list of necessities, so fashion companies have to adjust to economic conditions. During inflationary times, it is harder for fashion companies to plan for the future because an investment in a project costs more during an inflationary period. Furthermore, maintaining the value of their assets and avoiding losses become the priority. Business owners tackle a slow economy by cutting back inventory, laying off workers and therefore causing unemployment rates to rise, and reducing expenses. All of this has a domino effect on the fashion industry. Many examples exist of the effect the 2007–2010 recession had on businesses and consumers. Figure 7.4 demonstrates how inflation affects consumer prices.

Beginning in 2007, because of the home mortgage crises that caused overinflated home values, interest rates fell and the economy started to slow. Known as the housing bubble, the overall economy was affected. People lost their homes and jobs causing the Federal Reserve Bank to step in to stabilize prices and set policies for money. As a result, consumer confidence plummeted, spending decreased, and many employers instituted lay-offs leading to bankruptcies in the global fashion industry. Companies adjusted their inventories, sales to stock ratios, and sales projections. Table 7.3 is a list of companies that went out of business in 2007–2010. Companies unaffected by the recession include Kohl's, Walmart, and Target. These retailers saw sales increases because they sell low-price merchandise.

How does the government control the money supply, inflation, deflation, and recession and create a stable economy? The Federal Reserve Bank plays an important role in the stability of our economy and it is imperative for students of fashion to understand the fiscal and monetary policies of the Federal Reserve Bank. The next section explains those functions.

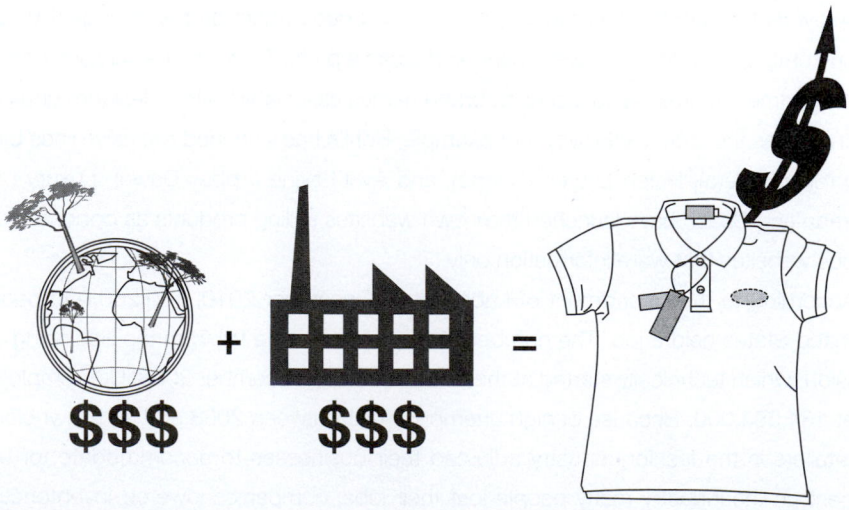

FIGURE 7.4 *Inflation and the consumer (Source: Hawa Stwodah).*

TABLE 7.3

List of fashion companies that went out of business between 2007 and 2010

Fashion Company Closings from 2007 to 2010
Bombay Company
Levitz
Sharper Image
CompUSA
Friedman's Jewelers
Whitehall Jewelers
Boscov's
Goody's Family Clothing
Circuit City
Eddie Bauer
Borders Booksellers
Mervyn's
Linens n Things

Notes: This is a partial list representing the decline of fashion companies; some retailers on this list went out of business, then their names were sold to other companies that may currently operate under those names.

The U.S. Economy Fiscal and Monetary Policies

U.S. fiscal and monetary policies affect the economic decisions made by companies and consumers. Monetary policy influences the performance of the economy reflected in factors such as inflation, unemployment, and economic output.

Fiscal Policy

There is a circular flow of money in the economy for companies to operate effectively. The government affects the operation of companies and the income of consumers through fiscal policy that incorporates taxes and government spending. The variables, controlled by the government, influence aggregate supply and demand; in other words, they influence the macroeconomic environment. The government controls the variables to stabilize the economy, creating a **stabilization policy**. The stabilization policy by the government never stops. It is a daily effort to monitor business, unemployment, and inflation. Monitored by the GDP, the goal of the stabilization policy is to keep the economy stable and avoid unpredictable changes.

Profit (as seen in Chapter 5) is the form of success for companies. Profit is possible by selling products and generating cash that enables a company to grow. The products change over time but companies pursue a business cycle that never ends. Refer to Figure 7.5 for an example of a business cycle that illustrates the highs and lows of a flow of business that is rooted in prices and unemployment. Measurement of business cycles includes economic indicators based on comparisons from previous months, years, or quarters. The exception is that the fashion business does not run in a traditional business cycle and is not dependent

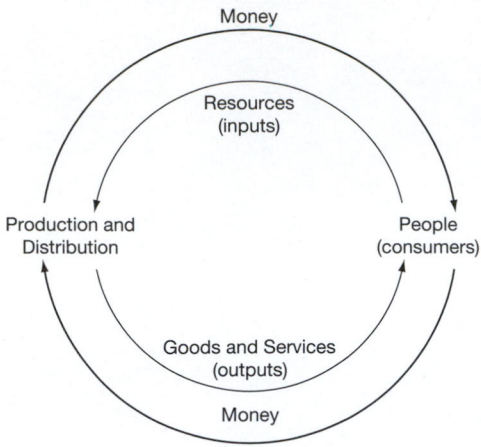

FIGURE 7.5 *An example of a circular flowchart.*

upon the state of an economy to be competitive. Fashion does run in cycles and so does the business of fashion, but the seasonality of fashion accelerates the business cycle. A typical company can analyze a company's growth using the business cycle through a succession of peaks and troughs. The cycle will shift over a period of time, depending on macroeconomic and microeconomic factors. With the success of a trend, a fashion business can profit or not profit depending upon whether a trend is bought by the consumer. For example, the onset of denim in the early 1980s as a premium fabric caused a shift in the fashion business cycle. For those businesses who sell premium denim jeans, they are successful and the business cycle has not declined. On the other hand, in the early 1980s, if the retailer continued to produce bell bottom premium, which was the trend at the end of the seventies, the business cycle would be in a decline. Overall, the fashion business cycle is dependent upon specific results in a short period as opposed to the general business cycle, which can take on a more traditional form of measuring, which includes consumer spending, state of the economy, and growth or decline of the business. Swings or fluctuations in the economy such as a depression or a recession are common to all industrialized nations of the world. Depending upon the state of the economy, fashion companies react to the peaks and troughs. The four phases of a business cycle, as documented by the National Bureau of Economics, are as follows:

- **Contraction** is the time when business begins to slow down. For a nonfashion company this contraction can be a steady decline for many years. For a fashion business, contraction occurs over a period of years or in a shorter period of two months or a slow season.
- **Trough** is the point of contraction; stagnation can turn into a recession. In a trough, the nonfashion business usually experiences sluggish sales because of a recession. A fashion business can survive and thrive based on the product they are selling. The overall fashion industry may be in a trough during a recession, but if consumers are spending, they will select the fashion goods that meet their wants.
- **Expansion** is the growth of an economy or business. Fashion businesses seek to grow and expand when the time is right for each individual firm. They will take advantage of low interest rates and a sluggish economy to plan growth and reposition the company.
- **Peak** is the point in the business cycle at which business activity has reached a temporary maximum. Sales are high and the company is on top of their game.

Figure 7.6 shows two companies representing a business cycle based on recessions. The two companies conducted business through the recession of 2007–2010. You can see that one continued to grow with net sales and one company did not. Both of the net sales figures are taken from the companies' annual report of 2010. As you can see, Pacific SunWear is continuing in the trough of the business cycle.

The fashion business cycle is season-to-season when analyzing for the purpose of making changes or staying on the current road to success. If a silhouette did not sell one season, a company has an opportunity to change the line or silhouette for the next season or discontinue it. While companies do not start from scratch for every season, there is room in the fashion business cycle of a company to change direction quickly. A regular business cycle can be much longer and drawn out. It is not difficult to change directions or quickly create new products in some industries; therefore, the traditional business cycle can be applicable.

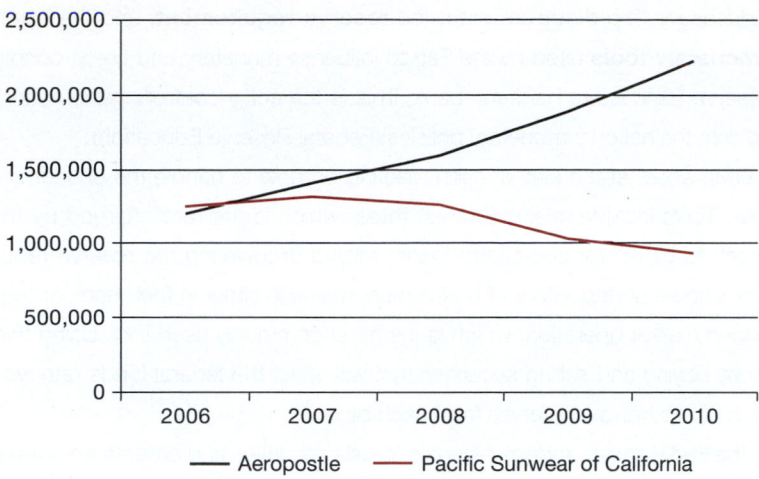

2,500,000
2,000,000
1,500,000
1,000,000
500,000
0

2006   2007   2008   2009   2010

—— Aeropostle   —— Pacific Sunwear of California

FIGURE 7.6 *Comparison of two fashion companies.*

Monetary Policy

The objective of the **Federal Reserve Act**, signed into law by President Woodrow Wilson in 1913, was to develop a decentralized bank, the **Federal Reserve Bank (the Fed)**. There are 12 Federal Reserve Banks throughout the United States, operated by a seven-member Board of Governors appointed by the president of the United States and confirmed by the Senate. They are responsible for analyzing economies both internationally and domestically and setting monetary policy accordingly. Other duties include overseeing the nation's payment systems and the supervision and regulation of various types of banking institutes. The Board also sits on the **Federal Open Market Committee (FMOC)** along with five presidents from the Federal Reserve Bank. The Federal Open Market Committee (FOMC) meets eight times a year to discuss the state of the economy.

The members of the FOMC are briefed prior to the meeting and each receives three books with information about the economy. The **green book** contains information about the forecasts of the economy as predicted by the Federal Reserve staff, the **blue book** gives an analysis of the economy, and the **beige book** gives information about each region's economic standing. After much discussion, the FOMC advises on what, if any, tools of the Fed should be used to create a healthy economy. The beige book is open to the public and is available at http://www.federalreserve.gov/fomc/beigebook/2008/. The following is an excerpt from the beige book about manufacturing as reported by the Richmond, Virginia Federal Reserve Bank, 2008. "District manufacturers reported a modest decline in activity in May as new orders and shipments edged into negative territory. Contacts largely attributed the lower pace to weaker domestic sales. A manufacturer at a North Carolina apparel factory reported a boost in foreign sales, but noted that the advantage had been largely negated by increased raw material costs." This type of statement contributes to the discussion for analyses of the economy. Based on the outcome of the discussion, whether the economy is unstable or stable, or the rate at which it is growing, the tools needed to stabilize the economy will be determined.

TOOLS OF THE FEDERAL RESERVE

The goals of monetary policy include the promotion of sustainable economic growth, full employment, and stable prices. Through monetary policy, the Fed is most able to maintain stable prices; thereby, promoting economic growth and maximum employment (Federal

Reserve Education). The **discount rate**, the **reserve requirement**, and the **open market** are three **monetary tools** used by the Fed to influence monetary and credit conditions. The Federal Reserve Bank is the bankers' bank. This is the entity controlling the nation's money supply and sets the nation's monetary policies (Federal Reserve Education).

The FOMC votes at the end of each meeting on how to handle the economy and what tools to use. Tools include raising interest rates, which is the rate charged by the Federal Reserve Bank to banks for short-term loans; raising or lowering the reserve requirements, which is the amount of deposits that banks must maintain either in their bank or the Fed's; or using the open market operation, which is the most commonly used tool. Using this tool, the Fed trades by buying and selling securities that will affect the federal funds rate, which is the rate at which banks borrow reserves from each other.

When the Fed wants to reduce reserves, it sells securities and collects from the accounts; if it wants to raise reserves, it buys securities and pays for them by making a deposit to the account, maintained by an agent of the Federal Reserve Bank who handles the buying and selling of securities. The third option is to lower discount rates, the rate charged to borrow money from the Fed by banks and other financial institutions.

The decisions the Fed makes can influence the decisions and even the emotions of a consumer or a fashion company. For example, if the Fed lowers the interest rate and a fashion company is considering expanding, the timing would be opportune because the company could borrow money at a lower interest rate for expansion. The consumer would also be more apt to think the Fed's decision to lower interest rates would boost the economy and begin to feel more confident about shopping for apparel and home fashions.

Economic Growth

Economic growth is the sum of all the goods and services produced by an economy in a given timeframe. **Gross domestic product (GDP)** measures economic growth (more on GDP later in this chapter). Economic growth cannot occur without consumer spending. When demand is high, productivity is high to meet the demand and expansion occurs, reflecting the state of the economy. Next, we will examine the historical growth in two fashion businesses. Boxes 7.1 and 7.2 profile two businesses explaining the growth from their beginning to the present. The first discusses how Calvin Klein created much of his business persona collaborating with many famous faces of the 1970s. Refer to the profile of Calvin Klein in Box 7.1. He grew his company based on demand of consumers desiring to dress down. They wanted comfortable clothing with no frills. Kellwood on the other hand grew from Sears suppliers forming a company. It was a planned, organized, systematic organization. Today Kellwood owns many well-known brands and licenses. Refer to the profile of Kellwood in Box 7.2.

Efficiency is very important in the fashion industry as it is the most logical, time-sensitive, and costsaving way to conduct business. Refer to Chapter 6 for an in-depth discussion on efficiency, its types, and its significance in the fashion industry. A graph used to illustrate and also forecast production and **allocation efficiency** associated with scarcity is the production possibility curve (discussed in Chapter 6). Refer to Figure 7.7 for an example of a PPC displaying knitted scarves versus sweaters. The figure is a model that demonstrates the production possibility curve of a factory that produces knitwear. The scenario compares producing knitted

Case Study

Calvin Klein

> *I've met people who didn't even know there was a Calvin Klein; they thought it was just the name of a product.*
>
> —Calvin Klein

ABOUT CALVIN KLEIN

Calvin Klein attended the Fashion Institute of Technology in New York from 1959 to 1962. In 1968 Klein launched his own company, which he simply named Calvin Klein, Inc. At that point he was partnered with Barry Schwartz who invested $10,000 and controlled the business affairs, while Klein designed. This fashion mogul began by focusing on designing women's coats but later branched out, adding a sportswear collection, and by the mid-1970s he had a full women's ready-to-wear line. The seventies gave Calvin Klein a face in the world of fashion and by 1977 the business was already reaping $100 million a year in sales (McKenna, 2007). He is credited with creating the first designer jeans and in doing so revolutionized the world of advertising as well (A&E Television Networks, 2008). In the first week that Calvin Klein jeans went on the market 200,000 pair were sold (McKenna, 2007).

The world of advertising was awakened by his jeans ad featuring Brooke Shields at age 15 saying "Nothing comes between me and my Calvin's" (Media Awareness Network, 2008). He pushed the limits with his use of younger models and the sexual nature of his campaign.

The eighties welcomed Klein's next revolution to the world of fashion. He transformed men's underwear from a functional item to a one that every man wanted to invest time in buying (A&E Television Networks, 2008). His ads were typically in black and white and viewers could feel the steam coming off the page. Klein used Mark Walberg as the face for his underwear campaign and made people think of "tighty-whities" in a whole different way (NY Fashion, 2008). He quickly turned the business of boxers and briefs into a $70 million cash cow (McKenna, 2007). He is an example of selling a product with sex, something that the world of advertising was still getting used to.

By the eighties Klein had also introduced some of his famous fragrances including Eternity and Escape, which are still produced today. Kate Moss was his campaign face for the now famous unisex fragrance cK One and continued his theme of sexuality in his ads with young famous faces (Vogue, 2008). By 1984 he was selling $600 million in branded merchandise in 12,000 stores worldwide (McKenna, 2007).

Klein has received much of his recognition from partnering with famous faces such as Brooke Shields, Mark Walberg, and Kate Moss. Klein has a staple look that is classic with clean lines and no frills. He uses primary colors and is not afraid to show off the figure of males or females who wear his clothing.

Calvin Klein's presence in the denim, underwear, and fragrance markets along with his other business ventures have proven to be successful. Today, his lines gross from $3 to $5 billion each year (NY Fashion, 2008). In 2003 Klein and his partner, Schwartz, sold the company to Phillips-Van Heusen (PVH) Corporation for $700 million. PVH owns brands including Kenneth Cole, Izod, Arrow, Bass, and CHAPS. They lay "claim to one of every three men's dress shirts sold in the United States" and saw buying Calvin Klein as a global opportunity. Critics saw this change in ownership as being a sure death sentence for the company.

PVH bought this company with intentions to take it to a more global level. Tom Murry, Calvin Klein's president, said, "the strong marketing campaign over all those years is what created the demand" (McKenna, 2007). Murry discussed the strategy for globalizing Calvin Klein saying, "It's not American, it's a global image that we're selling" (McKenna, 2007).

A graph, found on Yahoo Finance, shows that sales have been on a steady rise since 2003. Since the acquisition by PVH in 2003 retail sales have risen 60 percent from $2.8 billion to $4.5 billion (McKenna, 2007). This rise in sales has come from the popularity of men's and women's sportswear lines sold in popular department stores (McKenna, 2007).

Calvin Klein spends around $200 million every year selling its brands. About 90 percent of that cost comes from licensees. The company still gets fixed royalties on the sale of all products. They will not, however, disclose what percentage of those sales goes into their pocket but "analysts say fashion industry licensing deals are typically in the 7- to 10- percent range" (McKenna, 2007). This leaves 90 percent to a select group of partners, who create and distribute their products. Calvin Klein makes around 10 percent of PVH's total revenue, but an astounding 40 percent of its profits. Calvin Klein has proved to be nothing but beneficial for PVH's business, with its stocks quadrupling since the takeover in 2003 (McKenna, 2007).

WARNACO CASE

Warnaco Group is a manufacturer of Calvin Klein jeans who, at the end of the nineties, had a major falling out with Calvin Klein, Inc. The issue was that Warnaco had abused the licensing agreement with Calvin Klein by distributing the brand of jeans to unauthorized dealers (Kaufman, 2001). Klein's jeans were

(Continued)

distributed to retailers including Sam's Club, BJ's and Costco. This was not the brand image that Klein was looking for at all and it ended up in a lawsuit taken to federal court in Manhattan. "Klein also alleged that Warnaco was altering its designs and skimping on quality" (CNN Money, 2001). This was detrimental at the time for Warnaco stock. It dropped from around $12 per share to only $1 in early 2001.

The lawsuit from Klein not only aimed to gain millions of dollars in damages, but was also trying to stop the licensing deal, which was not supposed to end for another 44 years. The battle only got fiercer with a counter suit from Warnaco after Klein appeared on Larry King Live. Warnaco accused "Klein of bad dealing and trade libel" (CNN Money, 2001). When the trial finally came the decision came quickly and the terms were not made public. Don Nathan, Klein's spokesman said that the decision in court "settles all issues related to the suit". Since Warnaco's licensing agreement was not terminated, it was safe to believe that both companies agreed on the need for protection and promotion of the company's integrity in the fashion industry (CNN Money, 2001).

GOING GLOBAL

Mr. Murry, the company's president, explains the company's strategy for reaching a more global audience "is to get into every appropriate product category and every appropriate channel of distribution on a global basis" (McKenna, 2007). He goes further to say that they "don't want to get into anything that would damage [their] brand…[they] try to focus on things that will enhance and make their brand stronger" (McKenna, 2007).

Brand building activities include going into the make-up and cosmetics industries. They are partnering with Markwins International, a US-based cosmetic manufacturer, to produce a full cosmetic line (Rozario, 2007). Calvin Klein is also expanding into important economically developing countries such as China. China is of growing importance in the retail market and is forecasted to be the largest luxury market in 2015, exceeding the United States. They have begun to open stores in fashion centers around the world including New York, Milan, and Dubai (The Wall Street Journal, 2006). Expansions like these are reaching potential customers abroad and building brand awareness.

They are also continually introducing new products to keep customers coming. Another example of new product introductions was their move to produce retail travel items (Rozario, 2006). This made their face on leather goods be seen in airports and boutiques around the world. Around half of Klein's licensed sales are coming from places other than North America. The two main moneymakers are Europe and Asia, the latter being the fastest growing market (McKenna, 2007). Partnering with companies on an international level along with being bought by PVH, who had a global vision, has taken Calvin Klein abroad, and its popularity does not look like it is slowing down.

As the international businesses that it is today, Calvin Klein has divisions in Europe, Asia and Japan. Within the empire that has been built on one man's name, there are three lines that are now known globally: The Calvin Klein Collection (Men, women, and home), cK for men and women, and cK jeans for men, women, and children (A&E Television Networks, 2008). One of the keys to Calvin Klein's success is having remained a staple in consumer's closets and not moving with the fashion trends but rather keeping their lines classic. In Klein's own words, "I like simplicity, I like purity, I like anything that's modern. But it has to be exciting, it has to be interesting" (Klein, 2008). He has kept consumers interested through his classic designs and sexuality seen in the ad campaigns since his start and with the move to globalize, Calvin Klein is becoming a household name throughout the world.

REFERENCES

A&E Television Networks. (2008). *Biography*. Retrieved March 31, 2008, from http://www.thebiographychannel.co.uk/biography_story/298:130/1/Calvin_Klein.htm

CNN Money. (January 22, 2001). *Klein, Warnaco settle: Last minute agreement averts high-profile legal battle*. Retrieved April 1, 2008, from http://money.cnn/01/22/companies/warnaco/

Kaufman, L. (January 19, 2001). *Calvin Klein-Warnaco license trial finally set to begin*. Retrieved March 27, 2008, from http://query.nytimes.com/gst/fullpage.html?res E5D7163CF93AA25752C0A9679C8B63

Klein, C. (2008). *Quotes*. Retrieved March 25, 2008, from http://www.thebiographychannel.co.uk/biography_quotes/298:130/Calvin_Klein.htm

McKenna, B. (2007). *Fashion forward*. Retrieved March 25, 2008, from http://www.lexisnexis.com.proxy.lib.odu.edu/us/lnacademic/results/docview/docview.do?risb=21_T3430509573&format=GNBFI&sort=RELEVANCE&startDocNo=1&resultsUrlKey=29_T3430509578&cisb=22_T3430509577&treeMax=true&treeWidth=0&csi=303830&docNo=1

Media Awareness Network. (2008). *Calvin Klein: A casestudy*. Retrieved April 1, 2008, from http://www.mediaawareness.ca/english/resources/educational/handouts/ethics/calvin_klein_case_study.cfmT

NY Fashion. (2008). *Calvin Klein*. Retrieved March 27, 2008, from http://nymag.com/fashion/fashionshows/designers/bios/calvinklein/

Rozario, K. (May 1, 2006). *Calvin Klein reviews focus on leathergoods.* Retrieved March 31, 2008, from http://www.lexisnexis.com/us/lnacademic/results/docview/docview.do?risb=21_T3433728067&format=GNBFI&sort=RELEVANCE&startDocNo=1&resultsUrlKey=29_T3433728070&cisb=22_T3433728069&treeMax=true&treeWidth=0&csi=140610&docNo=1

Rozario, K. (October 15, 2007). Beauty report: ck Calvin Klein beauty. Retrieved March 31, 2008, from http://www.lexisnexis.com.proxy.lib.odufrom,.edu/us/lnacademic /results/docview/docview.do?risb=21_T3430463907&format=GNBFI&sort=RELEVANCE&startDocNo=1&resultsUrlKey=29_T3430463910&cisb=22_T3430463909&treeMax=true&treeWidth=0&csi=140610&docNo=8

The Wall Street Journal. (November 6, 2006). *Calvin Klein plans luxury store in China.* Retrieved March 25, 2008, from http://www.lexisnexis.com.proxy.lib.odu.edu lnacademic/results/docview/docview.do?risb=21_T3430509573&format=GNBFI&sort=RELEVANCE&startDocNo=1&resultsUrlKey=29_T3430509578&cisb=22_T3430509577&treeMax=true&treeWidth=0&csi=303830&docNo=6

Vogue. (2008). *Who's who-Calvin Klein.* Retrieved March 27, 2008, from http://www.vogue.co.uk/whos_who/calvin_klein/default.html

Yahoo Finance. (2008). CALVIN. Retrieved April 2, 2008, from http://finance.yahoo.com/q/bc?s=CALVIN&t=my&l=on&z=l&q=l&c=

Source: Adapted from Media Awareness Network.

Case Study

Kellwood

{ *"Kellwood has always prided itself in the diversification of its sales by channel, by customer and by price point"*

—Robert C. Skinner, Jr., Kellwood's chairman, president, and CEO (Seeking Alpha, 2007, p. 2)

ABOUT KELLWOOD

"The Kellwood Company is a leading marketer of apparel and consumer soft goods" (Kellwood Company, 2008). The company's corporate headquarters is located in St. Louis, Missouri, with an executive office in New York. Their brands are intended to meet and surpass customer's needs and expectations. Kellwood has achieved this by "specializing in branded products" (Kellwood Company, 2008). "They market to all channels of distribution with products and brands tailored to the specific channel" (Kellwood Company, 2008). "Kellwood designs and sells branded and private label products to all types of retailers" (Appleson, 2008).

KELLWOOD'S MISSION

To build on our cornerstones of diversification, fashion and value to enhance our position as a premier marketer of branded soft goods that appeal to a broad spectrum of consumers. (Kellwood Company, 2008).

HISTORICAL PERSPECTIVE

The Kellwood Company is the foremost global "private label and brand label manufacturer, marketer, and merchandiser of apparel, home furnishings, and recreational products"

(Kellwood Company History, 1994, p. 1). Their brands are sold through an array of distribution channels, to try and target all types of consumers. Their apparel products are the heart of its company. According to the *International Directory of Company Histories,* "73 percent of its apparel sales" are accounted for in women's attire, while men's represents "24 percent" and children's represent "3 percent" of sales. Kellwood has many plants located around the world, including Canada, the United States, the Caribbean Basin, and the Far East. The Company has experienced considerable times of development through cautious international and domestic purchases, which has given Kellwood an assortment line of goods (Kellwood Company History, 1994).

In 1961, 15 autonomous suppliers of soft goods to Sears, Roebuck and Co. merged to form the Kellwood Company. The Kellwood name came from two former Sears' executives, Charles H. Kellstadt and Robert E. Wood. This new company brought together different managements and an assorted line of products. The product included a huge variety of apparel, camping equipment, and bedding. The company started with "7,000 employees and 22 plants in 10 states" (Kellwood Company, 2008). At this time, their net sales were "$86.1 million" with their earnings equaling "$1.9 million". This made Kellwood the third largest apparel manufacturer in the United States. Kellwood's first president was Maurice Perlstein, who was the president of McComb Manufacturing Co. The Company was known as a Delaware corporation, with executive offices in Chicago.

(Continued)

Case Study

Kellwood (Continued)

Kellwood had made a five-year plan in 1962. By 1963, the company had exceeded the sales objectives. Since Kellwood was mostly dependent on Sears's revenue, they decided to add more products to their lines to help sales grow. After this move, sales grew to $100 million. The company then expanded to 29 locations in 11 states and for the first time took their company outside the United States' borders. They established a plant in Kingston, Jamaica, which marked the beginning of Kellwood's international involvement that would later label the company's success (Kellwood Company History, 1994).

In 1964, Fred W. Wenzel, who was a former president of one of the original independent 15 companies, was elected chief executive officer and chairman of the board. The logo for the Kellwood Company was created during this time. It was a "K" representing thread through the eye of a needle. By their fifth anniversary, sales had increased "75 percent" since they had started. The company continued to grow, so that by 1966, the company had 36 plants in 13 states and had over 11,000 employees. At this point the headquarters for the company was moved from Chicago to St. Louis and the first data processing center was located in Tennessee, so that the company was able to track inventory and lower administration costs (Kellwood Company History, 1994).

Kellwood passed all the goals established by the company's original founders, and after 10 years in business they became the largest supplier of soft goods to Sears. The development during the past decade caused incomes to fluctuate, but by 1971 the company stood on solid ground. At this point, the company started focusing on purchasing companies that would complete its line of products. Kellwood also began opening factory outlet stores in 1965 and by 1973, there were 29. These outlets were a huge success for Kellwood (Kellwood Company History, 1994).

By the end of 1974, Kellwood had experienced 14 years of rapid growth in both product lines and in plant expansion. The number of employees grew to "18,000 and 62 plants in 17 states" (Kellwood Company History, 1994, p. 1). The earnings had now increased to "8.5 million", thanks to the marketing of Sears. Sears made up 80 percent of Kellwood's sales, which proves that the success of Kellwood is largely because of Sears.

In 1975, Kellwood's success came to an end. A decline in Sears sales, mixed with a recessive economy, caused their earnings to drop just over $400,000 from the previous year. This showed Kellwood the danger of being too close with another company, which caused the management of the company to reassess its relationship with Sears and re-examine the company's future direction. (Kellwood Company History, 1994)

By the next year, the company revamped and earnings jumped back up to $7 million. Kellwood decided to make a new move towards developing a company that was more reliant on brand label business than a private label business.

As the popularity of disco dancing and physical fitness swept the country, the demand for the tight, lightweight dance tops, originated by Danskin, boomed, and Kellwood hoped to gain a foothold in the market share under the Van Raalte label. With Danskin possessing an almost unassailable advantage in the bodywear market, Kellwood aimed for usurping the number-two bodywear manufacturer—Sears. This objective, however, did not indicate an assault on Sears by Kellwood. Sears still purchased 80 percent of Kellwood's volume and owned 22 percent of its soft good supplier (Kellwood Company History, 1994, pp. 1–2).

Most of Kellwood's production attention was spent fulfilling Sear's soft goods orders. The American customers craving for denim products continued to increase, and by 1977 the sales of jeans and pants to Sears surpassed all of Kellwood's other product lines. As consumers headed outdoors more in the late 1970s for exercise and recreation, Kellwood added backpacks to its existing line of tents and sleeping bags (Kellwood Company History, 1994).

Kellwood worked nonstop to enlarge its brand label business in 1978, a year in which sales went over $500 million and earnings reached about $13.5 million, because they had purchased rights to the Fruit of the Loom name for hosiery. Kellwood did this hoping to gain a portion of the $1.39 billion sheer hosiery market from its two largest manufacturers, Hanes Corp. and Kayser-Roth (Kellwood Company History, 1994).

In 1980, Kellwood drastically increased its offshore participation by buying nearly a half interest in Smart Shirts Ltd. of Hong Kong. In 1972, Kellwood formed Kellwood International Ltd. in Hong Kong to assist in import and export activities. With an impressive clientele list, which included Macy's of New York, Inc., Federated Department Stores, The May Company, and J.C. Penney Company, Inc., the purchase of Smart Shirts would ultimately allow Kellwood to decrease its dependence on Sears (Kellwood Company History, 1994).

By the next year, Kellwood had totally redefined its business tactic. Although Sears would maintain as a significant customer

(Continued)

for Kellwood, more stability was preferred. Chairman Wenzel had commented that the philosophy of Kellwood was not to do less business with Sears, but to reduce their percentage by selling more to other customers. To accomplish this, Kellwood's management team decided to radically amplify its involvement in offshore manufacturing and sourcing, sending cut fabric overseas to be sewn and returning the finished product back to the United States. The company concentrated its focus on Central America, the Caribbean, and the Far East. Kellwood discontinued the Van Raalte and Fruit of the Loom labels because of inconsistent earnings (Kellwood Company History, 1994).

Kellwood entered its third decade of business as a company still largely involved in private label business, a result of being more focused. By 1982, earnings had bounced back from an unsatisfactory $216,000 two years earlier to over $8 million. The decisions made a year before began to take shape. The move away from Sears affected Kellwood's sales, but earnings had climbed due to a decline in inventory. A move toward greater international presence was also made in 1982 when Kellwood increased manufacturing facilities in Taiwan and Hong Kong (Kellwood Company History, 1994).

"In July of 1984, Kellwood purchased the remaining shares of its stock held by Sears, thereby ending the investment relationship between the two companies that had spanned nearly a quarter of a century" (Kellwood Company History, 1994, p. 2). By the next year, Kellwood's sales from Sears were equal to sales made to its other customers. This major drop in sales to Sears again affected Kellwood's sales volume, but the 1985 purchase of Cape Cod-Cricket Lane, Inc., helped lift its sales numbers and inflated domestic operations. Kellwood's presence in the Far East was equipped in 1983 by purchasing the remaining percentage of Smart Shirts and by buying a company under Smart Shirts' management in the free-trade area of Sri Lanka. Created in 1984 to aid Kellwood's search for and buying of companies in the Far East, Kellwood Asia Ltd. allowed the company to expand its international operations (Kellwood Company History, 1994).

Near the end of the 1980s, Kellwood increased both domestic and offshore apparel companies by purchasing companies featuring fashion-oriented, branded merchandise. Compared to the lower-priced goods it had supplied to Sears, the higher-priced products required less inventory and offered greater profit potential. The boost in Kellwood's domestic, branded sector was followed by different acquisitions, which helped to balance the continued drop in sales of Sears. By the end of the decade, Sears's portion of Kellwood's sales had fallen to approximately one quarter (Kellwood Company History, 1994).

Kellwood's Far East businesses also grew with the 1989 purchase of Saipan Manufacturers, Inc. located in the Northern Mariana Islands. This company fell under Smart Shirts management. By the end of the decade, Smart Shirts claimed more than 40 percent of Kellwood's operating profits and provided an additional economic boost to replace the losses from Sears (Kellwood Company History, 1994).

"As Kellwood entered the 1990s, its growth over the previous 30 years positioned it as one of the leading apparel manufacturers in the United States" (Kellwood Company History, 1994). Kellwood now had over 250 major retail accounts that included about 25,000 individual stores, and the company's customer foundation had evolved from nearly total dependence on Sears to a wide and diverse clientele (Kellwood Company History, 1994).

On February 11, 2008, Kellwood Company was purchased by Sun Capital Securities for about $767 million (Sun Capital, 2008). Sun Capital had tried to purchase Kellwood twice before, but the bids were too low. This acquisition was due to low shares on Kellwood's part. CEO of Kellwood, Robert C. Skinner, Jr., stated "As a strong, private company, Kellwood will continue to execute on its strategic priority to position the company as a brand-focused marketing enterprise" (Appleson, 2008, p. 1).

KELLWOOD'S BRANDS

The Kellwood Company's main purpose is to provide an even-handed assortment of brands that cater to different lifestyles, to fit an extensive range of consumers around the globe. "From business to evening events to weekend adventures with the family—Kellwood has something for everyone" (Kellwood Company, 2008). The brands of Kellwood are listed (see Table I) as well as their distribution channel and where to buy the brands.

CONCLUSION

With Kellwood's broad line of both brand and private label apparel and its line of recreation and home furnishing products, Kellwood's products will most likely be brands that will continue to fill consumer's closets.

Food for thought:

1. How did a company like Kellwood become such a huge conglomerate?
2. Did Kellwood really need to be purchased by another company to get back on its feet?
3. Should Kellwood have just tried to revamp their strategic plan like they did in 1981 to avoid be purchased?
4. What is the future for Kellwood now that they have been bought? Will they still be one of the fashion industry's top conglomerates?
5. How much did Sun Capital Securities pay for Kellwood?
6. Go to the Kellwood website, www.kellwood.com , find their annual report, and answer the following questions: (a) What were their gross profits for 2006? (b) What were the net profits? (c) What role did the state of the economy have on Kellwood's gross and net profits?

(Continued)

TABLE I
Kellwood brands

Brands	Distribution Channel	Where to Buy
Baby Phat	Online, department stores, specialty stores	Soho NYC, babyphat.com, Macy's, macys.com, Dillards, Carson Pirie Scott, D.E.M.O., Man Alive
Briggs New York	Chain stores, department stores	Macy's, Carson Pirie Scott, Bon-ton, JCPenney, Kohl's, Goody's
Calvin Klein*	Better department stores, specialty stores	Macy's, Bloomingdale's, Lord & Taylor, Gottschalk's, Hudson Bay, A. S. Cooper
CK Calvin Klein*	Fine department stores, specialty stores	Neiman Marcus and select specialty stores
David Meister*	Department stores, specialty stores, catalogs	Neiman Marcus, Saks Fifth Avenue, Nordstrom Bloomingdale's, Lord & Taylor
DBY	Chain stores, specialty stores	JCPenney, Charming Shoppes
Democracy	Upscale department and specialty stores	Macy's, Belk, Loehmann's, Marshall's
Dorby	Chain stores, department stores	JCPenney, Belk, Sears, Goody's, Stage Stores
Gerber Beginnings "the best place to start"	Department stores	Select Sears, Beall's and Peebles
Gerber Everyday Essentials	Mass merchants, specialty stores, food and drug stores	Walmart, Target, Kmart, Toys R Us, Babies R Us, Burlington Coat Factory, Fred Meyer, Meijer, BJ's Wholesale club, Shopko, AAFES
Hanna Andersson	Online, catalog, retail and outlet stores	Visit Hanna Andersson online to find store locations or purchase online
Hollywould	Department stores, specialty stores, online	Hollywould Boutiques, hollywould.com, Bergdorf Goodman, Nordstrom, Neiman Marcus, zappos.com, piperlime.com
Jolt Girls Sportswear	Department stores, specialty stores	Nordstrom, Macy's, macys.com, Dillards, Belk, Parisians, SSI
Jolt Junior Sportswear	Department stores, specialty stores	Nordstrom, Macy's, macys.com, Dillards, Belk, Parisians, SSI
Kelty	Outdoor specialty and national chain stores, sporting good stores, online	Visit the Kelty website to find the nearest location
Koret	Department stores, specialty stores, catalogs, chain stores, mail order, online	Sportswear: Gottschalk's, Stage, Peebles, shopkoret.com, Koret Retail and Outlet Stores
My Michelle	Department stores, specialty stores, chain stores	JCPenney, Dillard's, Belk, Macy's, SSI Kohl's, Nordstroms, Parisians
Napa Valley	Department stores	Exclusively at Dillard's
Onesies	Mass merchants, department stores, specialty stores, food and drug stores	Walmart, Target, Kmart, Sears, Toys 'R Us, Babies 'R Us, Burlington Coat Factory, Fred Meyer, Meijer, BJ's Wholesale Club, Shopko, and AAFES
Pantology	Department stores	Macy's
Phat Farm	Online, department stores, and specialty stores	SohoNYC , www.phatfarm.com, Macy's, macys.com, Dillard's, D.E.M.O., and Man Alive
Plaza South	Department stores, national chains, specialty stores, mail order	Belk, Dillard's, Macy's, Parisians, and Stage Stores
Prophecy	Department stores, specialty stores	Coming soon
Rewind Girls Sportswear	Mid-tier department stores	Kohl's, JCPenney, and Mervyns
Rewind Junior Sportswear	Mid-tier department stores	Kohl's, JCPenney, and Mervyns
Royal Robbins	Outdoor specialty stores, sporting good stores, outdoor national chain stores, online, and boutiques	Visit the Royal Robbins website to find a store near you or purchase online

Brands	Distribution Channel	Where to Buy
Sag Harbor	Department stores, specialty stores, catalogs, and online	Beall's, Belk, Boscov's, Colony Shops, Fred Meyer, Goody's, JCPenney, Kohl's, McRae's, Meijer, Mervyns, Military Exchanges (Nexcom, Airforce, Marines), Moore's, Palais Royal, Peebles, Proffitt's, Stage, www.sag-harbor.com, Sag Harbor outlet stores, and Sag Harbor retail stores
Sangria	Department stores, specialty stores, national chains, mass merchants, and catalogs	Federated, Dillard's, Belk, Bon-Ton, and Boscov's
Sierra Designs	Independent specialty stores, sporting goods stores, and outdoor national chain stores	Visit the Sierra Designs website to find a store near you
Slumberjack	Sporting goods stores, outdoor national chain stores, independent specialty retailers, and catalog retailers	Visit the Slumberjack website to find a store near you
Vince	Luxury specialty and department stores throughout the United States, Canada, Europe, and Asia	Barneys, Bergdorf Goodman, Neiman Marcus, Saks Fifth Avenue, Nordstrom, and Bloomingdale's
Wenger*	Sporting goods stores, outdoor national chain stores, and Internet retailers	Visit the Wenger website to find a store near you
Wenzel	Mass merchant retailers, warehouse clubs, sporting goods stores, outdoor national chain stores, and Internet retailers	Visit the Wenzel website to find a store near you
XOXO*	Department stores, specialty stores, chain stores, and online	Macy's, macys.com, Parisians, Carson Pirie Scott, Boscov's, Belk, Bon-Ton, Dillard's, SSI, and XOXO.com

Note: *Indicates a licensed trademark
Source: www.Kellwood.com "Brands" 2008.

REFERENCES

Appleson, G. (2008). Kellwood agrees to Sun Capital offer. *St. Louis Post-Dispatch*, 1–2. Retrieved April 1, 2008, from http://www.stltoday.com/stltoday/business/stories.nsf/yourmoney/story/9C947D4ED95E163D862573ED000F542B?OpenDocument

Kellwood Company History. (1994). *International Directory of Company Histories*, Vol. 8. St. James Press. Retrieved April 1, 2008, from http://www.fundinguniverse.com/company-histories/Kellwood-Company-Company-History.html

Kellwood Company. (2008). Retrieved April 1, 2008, from http://www.kellwood.com

Seeking Alpha. (2007). Kellwood Company: A Share Price in Tatters, 1–4. Retrieved April 1, 2008, from http://seekingalpha.com/article/46103-kellwood-company-a-share-price-in-tatters

Sun Capital Partners, Inc. (2006–2008). Retrieved April 1, 2008, from http://www.suncappart.com

Source: Adapted from Kellwood Brands.

scarves and sweaters assuming that the factory could be set up to produce both of those goods. Curve line C the factory potentially at full production; then we say, "Production is efficient." At point B the factory can produce 800 knitted scarves and 100 sweaters. At point A the factory could produce 600 knitted scarves and 80 sweaters. If we wanted to move from point A to point B for production, then, the production of knitted scarves would be sacrificed. This is called the law of increasing opportunity. At Points A and B the factory is not producing efficiently. At any point inside the curve the production is not efficient. For example, look at point D. Production is underutilized, producing only 400 scarves and 40 sweaters. An outward shift of the curve could be due to advancement in technology or an increase in resources.

The last section of the chapter will discuss economic indicators. All types of businesses use economic indicators to make decisions concerning their businesses on a daily basis. The decisions made are not generally at the level of a buyer or general merchandise manager, but

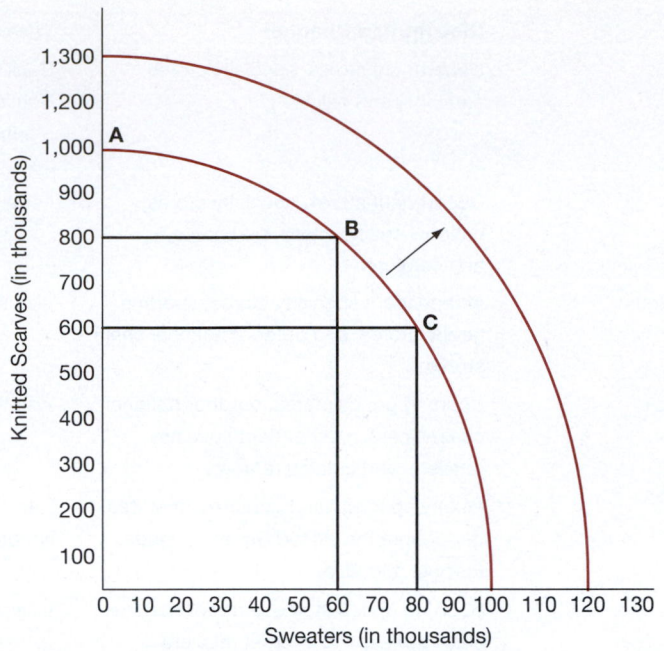

FIGURE 7.7 *Production possibility curve.*

at a much higher level such as a chief executive officer (CEO) or chief financial officer (CFO) of a company, at the Board of Directors meeting. Keep in mind as you learn that the indicators show what is currently happening in the economy, what happened in the economy, and what will happen in the future in the economy. It is a statistical way to look at the economy.

Leading Economic Indicators for the Fashion Industry

Resources used by fashion companies include the U.S. Census Bureau, the Department of Commerce, and the Forrester Research International Council of Shopping Centers. The U.S. Census Bureau conducts several surveys of businesses and consumers to measure America's people, income, and places. The statistical information contained on the Census Bureau's New American Fact Finder website paints a picture of American cities and counties and the people living there. For a fashion company, the information provided by the American Fact Finder helps the business make a decision on where to set up its stores, manufacturing facilities, and distribution centers. A company can easily see the potential labor pool through the demographic information like age and gender. The income levels indicate if a demographic location can support a store in the marketplace. The ethnicity of a marketplace is significant to retailers for a number of reasons, including the target market and assortment planning.

According to the U.S. Department of Commerce website, "The U.S. Department of Commerce has a broad mandate to advance economic growth and jobs and opportunities for the American people." The U.S. Department of Commerce is composed of 12 divisions including the Census Bureau, the Economic Development Administration, and the International Trade Administration. Box 7.3 provides a complete list of the divisions within the Department of Commerce. "The Commerce Department's mission is to help make American businesses more innovative at home and more competitive abroad" (U.S. Department of Commerce, n.d.). Economic activity such as output of production by manufacturing plants and sales per square foot of small retail stores are samplings of information reported to the government by companies either monthly or quarterly. The appropriate divisions like the Department of Commerce or the Census Bureau publish the information in the form of different economic indicators.

An economic indicator is an inclusive statistical measurement of current business conditions based on anything from retail trade to unemployment rates. The Department of Commerce Bureau of Economics and Statistics Administration publish the economic indicators. Independent companies that watch the economy publish the indicators on their private websites. Professional economists perform their jobs measuring and analyzing the economy for the purpose of writing about and reporting on the economy. Those in the retail, wholesale, and service sectors of the fashion industry take advantage of their reporting and use the information to make decisions concerning growth, downsizing, inventory, and investments.

There are three categories of economic indicators: (1) **Leading indicators** have a tendency to move in the same direction as the economy. Examples of those indicators are changes in business inventories, contracts for orders for plant and equipment, and new orders for consumer goods and materials; (2) **coincident indicators** generally run parallel with business cycles. Examples include GDP, manufacturing and trade volume, and industrial production; and (3) **lagging indicators** trail the business cycle. They include short-term interest rates, manufacturing and trade inventories, change in labor cost per output, and manufacturing. It is not necessary for a fashion executive to use all indicators to make decisions. There are nine indicators discussed in this chapter that are pertinent to the fashion industry including the **employment situation**; **personal income and spending**; **advance monthly sales for retail and food services**; **e-commerce retail sales**; **weekly chain-store sales**; **consumer confidence index**; gross domestic product; **manufacturer's shipments, inventories, and orders report**; and the **monthly and annual wholesale trade report**. Keep in mind that these indicators are tools used to analyze and predict the economy. Businesses do not rely solely on indicators for decision making but combine them with other types of information such as sales history, current sales trends, inventories (historical and current), availability of goods in the marketplace, fashion trends, and promotional activities. The study of economic indicators begins with the employment situation.

Department of Commerce Bureaus

Bureau of Economic Analysis (BEA)

Bureau of Industry and Security (BIS)

U.S. Census Bureau

Economic Development Administration (EDA)

Economic and Statistics Administration (ESA)

International Trade Administration (ITA)

Minority Business Development Agency (MBDA)

National Oceanic and Atmospheric Administration (NOAA)

National Telecommunications and Information Administration (NTIA)

National Institute of Standards and Technology (NIST)

National Technical Information Service (NTIS)

U.S. Patent and Trademark Office (USPTO)

Source: Department of Commerce.

The Employment Situation

The first Friday of each month, the Bureau of Labor Statistics publishes and posts on the employment situation report (also known as the **Labor Report**). The report, found at http://stats.bls.gov/news.release/empsit.nr0.htm, covers the results of the previous month. For current statistics on the employment situation in the United States, refer to the Bureau of Labor Statistics at www.bls.gov "This is the big one! No single economic indicator can jolt the stock and bond markets as much as the jobs report," says Bernard Baumbohl. Forecasts about the job market, household earnings, and future stock market result from the information contained in the report. If the report surprises Wall Street, the effect is dramatic. Two surveys measure the employment situation: the household survey and the **establishment survey**. The household survey is very popular because it measures the unemployment rate and provides measures for demographic units. The Department of Labor sends surveys to 60,000 households in the United States with approximately 57,000 responding. The **establishment** survey is a tally of payrolls gathering information from businesses on the current state of employment, in other words, the job market. The **household survey** and establishment survey produce sample-based estimates of employment.

The employment situation survey involves about 40 percent of small businesses with fewer than 20 employees and gathers information about the employed and unemployed. The survey divided by sex, age, and ethnicity segments the information by class of worker, status of worker, part-time or full-time, occupation, hours worked, and aggregate payroll of production and nonsupervisory workers. Every month the employment situation contains two sets of tables. Table A represents measurements of household data taken from the Household Survey and Table B represents the measurements taken from the Establishment Situation survey. A disadvantage of the employment situation report comes from the distortion of the results because of a lack of seasonal adjustments.

The bottom line is that the higher the unemployment statistic, the bleaker the outlook for the economy. Unemployed people have fewer dollars to spend and the consequence is fewer consumer dollars in the marketplace, causing business declines. Apparel is particularly vulnerable to business declines due to unemployment as most apparel purchases are "want" rather than "need" based. Furthermore, wages and salaries are the largest contributors to household income and household spending accounts for more than two-thirds of the economy's total output. It is easy to understand the considerable impact the employment situation report has on the economy.

Personal Income and Spending

Spend it or save it—those are the only two choices for Americans when it comes to personal income. The analysis of how much Americans are spending or saving comes from the **Personal Income and Outlays Report** published by the Bureau of Economic Analysis (BEA) on a monthly basis. Personal income and personal outlays or expenditure comprises the Personal Income and Outlays Report (sometimes called the Personal Consumption Report). Jointly they examine consumer behavior and total economic consumption by recording what Americans receive before taxes, how much they spend, and how much they save.

Personal income is the total or gross income received from wages and salaries, dividends and interest, rental income, and all other income for everyone in the United States before taxes. Profits from the sale of stocks, bonds, and real estate are not included in personal income. Wages and salaries comprise the majority of all income.

TABLE 7.4
Real personal income calculation

(A) U.S. Personal Income September 2011	(B) U.S. Population*	(A)/(B) U.S. Income per Capita
13,022,100,000	312,882	41,619.8

*Population is the total population of the United States, including the Armed Forces overseas and the institutionalized population. The monthly estimate is the average of estimates for the first of the month and the first of the following month; the annual and quarterly estimates are averages of the monthly estimates.

Source: Bureau of Economic Analyses, U.S. Department of Commerce, News Release, http://www.bea.gov/iTable/iTable.cfm?ReqID=5&step=1

Personal consumption on goods and services is the largest component of personal outlays. Included in personal consumption expenditures are purchases of **durable consumer goods** like washing machines, cars, and furniture. Durable goods are those with a life span of three years or more. These goods make up 12–14 percent of the total consumer expenditures because of their longevity and high-ticket prices (Baumbohl, 2008). Americans likewise consume **nondurable goods** like groceries, printer paper, and clothing. Nondurable goods have a lifespan of less than three years or used up after one use. These goods are less expensive and include clothing, cosmetics, gasoline, and office supplies. This category encompasses 30 percent of total consumer expenditures (Baumbohl, 2008). **Services** include manicures, medical treatment, lawn care, and dry cleaning. This is the fastest growing category of the three, making up 60 percent of the total consumer expenditures (Baumbohl, 2008). Of the three categories, services are the category with the greatest outlay of money, followed by nondurable goods and durable goods, respectively.

The Personal Income and Outlays Report provides information necessary for the computation of **real personal income**, **disposable personal income (DPI)**, and **personal savings rate**. Real personal income or personal income per capita is the calculation of dividing personal income by the number of people in the population and adjusting for inflation. The calculation appears in Table 7.4. Disposable personal income (DPI) is personal income minus taxes, which is roughly equivalent to take-home pay. Table 7.5 demonstrates the 2010 personal savings rate figure. Subtracting personal outlays from DPI is the calculation for the personal savings rate: the personal savings rate figure as a percentage of DPI and expressing that figure as a percentage of DPI.

Personal consumption expenditures (PCE) survey examines how much people are spending. In *The Secrets of Economic Indicators*, Bernard Baumbohl indicates, "Traditionally, the average household spends about 95 cents of every dollar received and this high level of consumption fuels two-thirds of all economic activity." PCE is the most inclusive evaluation of consumer spending but it is also the largest factor of GDP. Because of this, significant changes in PCE can be the forerunner for major changes in the business cycle. PCE assesses consumer spending on retail items as well as how much people are spending on credit card

TABLE 7.5
Personal savings rate

(A) Disposable Personal Income	(B) Personal Outlays	(A)−(B) = Personal Savings Rate
11,608,500,000	11,135,700,000	472,800,000

Source: http://www.bea.gov/iTable/iTable.cfm?ReqID=5&step=1

interest payments. Each release will show results for each month in the year-to-date, as well as annually for the previous three years. Dollars paid out by consumers on social security withholding taxes and pension payments made by the self-employed are deducted from PCE. PCE looks at expenditures in three categories to determine what people are buying: durable goods, nondurable goods, and services.

What are people saving? The amount left over after spending on goods, service, loans, interest, and credit cards is what people are saving. It is simply disposable income minus outlays. Currently, there is an alarming trend among Americans where they spend more than they earn. Economists believe that the trend will reverse due primarily to increased interest rates. The escalating cost of credit stalls spending. Likewise, higher interest rates will promote saving as consumers become able to receive a higher return on their investments.

Advance Monthly Sales for Retail and Food Services

The *advance monthly sales for retail and food services* is the first report of the month on consumer spending. Released by the Bureau of the Census, Department of Commerce, revisions can be enormous from month to month. Each report contains revisions of the two previous months to reflect information that is more complete. Annual reports released in March each year can go back three years or more.

This is an important report. As Bernard Baumbohl states in *The Secrets of Economic Indicators*:

> Remove three legs from a table and, well, it isn't much of a table after that. If you imagine the U.S. economy being the table and consumer spending accounting for three of the four legs, you'll understand why the investment community is so super-attentive to any indicator that provides insight into the mood and behavior of shoppers. Consumer spending makes up 70% of all economic activity—and retail sales account for a hefty one-third of that. If consumers can keep cash registers ringing, it is a sign of overall economic growth and prosperity.

According to the U.S. Department of Commerce website, the U.S. Census Bureau conducts the advance monthly sales for retail trade survey. The survey, titled the Advance Monthly Retail Trade and Food Services Survey (MARTS), provides early estimates of monthly sales by category of business for retail and food service firms located in the United States. Approximately 5,000 employers, selected from the larger Monthly Retail Trade Survey (MRTS), receive monthly questionnaires. Because of this, economists regard the retail sales report as one of the top gauges of change in consumer spending. Firms participating in MARTS account for approximately 65 percent of the total national sales estimate. The change in sales from the previous month is estimated using only units that have reported data for both the current and previous months.

E-Commerce Retail Sales

According to the U.S Census Bureau, the e-commerce retail sales "are sales of goods and services where an order is placed by the buyer or price and terms of the sale are negotiated over the Internet, an extranet, **Electronic Data Interchange (EDI)** network, or other online system." This indicator, released on a quarterly basis, presents data gathered from a survey of the U.S. Census Bureau called Monthly Retail Trade Survey, which "provides current estimates of sales at retail and food services stores and inventories held by retail stores." The gross domestic product calculation includes information from the survey in conjunction with other surveys administered by the U.S. Census Bureau, Department of Labor, and other agencies of the federal government.

The report lists the sales in e-commerce and retail trade. According to the U.S. Census Bureau, good use is made of the information "throughout government, academic and business communities." Table 7.6 displays in chart form the **retail e-commerce sales** from the U.S. Census Bureau. It is important to note that the U.S. Census Bureau recognizes the importance of collecting information about e-commerce and has a site called E-Stats—Measuring the Electronic Economy. As more consumers continue to buy online, the statistics will become more valuable to the fashion industry. For example, the luxury industry resisted selling merchandise via websites, using them for the purpose of disseminating information to the consumer. Since 2007, luxury goods brands such as Gucci and Prada have created their own websites to sell their products. "Nearly all **nonstore retail** e-sales occurred in the electronic shopping and mail-order houses industry group. This group includes catalog and mail order operations, many of which sell through multiple channels; 'pure plays' (retail businesses selling solely over the Internet); and e-commerce units of the traditional brick-and-mortar retailers." Monthly reports on retail e-sales contain estimated sales and account for seasonal adjustments. The report compares e-sales from quarter to quarter and with retail sales of the same year and with that of the previous year. "The Census Bureau of the Department of Commerce announced today that the estimate of U.S. retail e-commerce sales for the third quarter of 2010 adjusted for seasonal variation, but not for price." This is valuable information when a fashion retailer is considering whether to continue online sales, create a website for retailing merchandise, or even close brick-and-mortar stores because it identifies trends in e-sales.

TABLE 7.6
Retail e-commerce

U.S. Shipments, Sales, Revenues, and E-commerce: 2009 and 2008

[Shipments, sales and revenues are in billions of dollars.]

Description	Value of Shipments, Sales, or Revenue				Year to Year Percent Change		% Distribution of E-commerce	
	2009		2008					
	Total	E-commerce	Total	E-commerce	Total	E-commerce	2009	2008
Total *	20,014	3,371	22,470	3,774	−10.9	−10.7	100.0	100.0
B-to-B*	9,602	3,073	11,630	3,482	−17.4	−11.8	91.2	92.3
Manufacturing	4,436	1,862	5,468	2,171	−18.9	−14.2	55.2	57.5
Merchant Wholesale	5,166	1,211	6,162	1,311	−16.2	−7.6	35.9	34.7
Excluding MSBOs[1]	3,707	729	4,435	739	−16.4	−1.4	21.6	19.6
MSBOs	1,459	483	1,727	572	−15.5	−15.7	14.3	15.2
B-to-C*	10,412	298	10,840	292	−3.9	2.1	8.8	7.7
Retail	3,638	145	3,953	142	−8.0	2.1	4.3	3.7
Selected Services	6,774	153	6,887	150	−1.6	2.2	4.5	4.0

* We estimate business-to-business (B-to-B) and business-to-consumer (B-to-C) e-commerce by making several simplifying assumptions: manufacturing and wholesale e-commerce is entirely B-to-B, and retail and service e-commerce is entirely B-to-C. We also ignore definitional differences among shipments, sales, and revenues. The resulting B-to-B and B-to-C estimates, while not directly measured, show that almost all the dollar volume of e-commerce activity involves transactions between businesses. See the "Note to reader" for cautions relating to the interpretation of the "Total" shown here.

[1] Manufacturers' Sales Branches and Offices.

Source: U.S. Census Bureau.

It is a good thermometer for checking the progress of business conducted online and for realizing the importance of the Internet as a retail outlet.

Weekly Chain-Store Sales

The weekly chain-store sales report, released by the International Council of Shopping Centers every Tuesday at 9 A.M., is an important indicator to those in decision-making and planning position for retail chain stores. Based on a comparison of sales of a range of chain stores, not limited to the fashion industry, its popularity is evident around the holiday season and back-to-school time.

Consumer Confidence Index

The consumer confidence index, a report released on the last Tuesday of the month by the Conference Board, surveys 5,000 households and looks at how consumers feel about the economy, labor conditions, and spending. It measures the confidence of the average consumer. In addition to the Conference Board, the University of Michigan and *ABC News/ Washington Post* conduct surveys of consumer confidence. The University of Michigan's Consumer Sentiment Survey questions 500 adults monthly, and the *ABC News/Washington Post*'s weekly Consumer Comfort Index interviews 250 people weekly. Refer to Box 7.4 for the monthly report available online from the Conference Board. The attitude of the U.S. consumer is vital to the economy and especially to the fashion industry. When consumers perceive both their personal situation and the national economy to be healthy and robust, they tend to spend more money. They shop, travel, and invest, thus benefiting the economy. The perception of a gloomy economy and a weak job market causes people to stop spending. The reduction in spending by consumers disrupts the U.S. economy. Because the public's discernment is critical to the economy, any sign that consumer confidence is waning gets the attention of Wall Street and Washington.

Gross Domestic Product

Gross domestic product (GDP) is a monetary measure. *The Secrets of Economic Indicators*, by Bernard Baumbohl, describes GDP in the following statement: "it is the total price tag in dollars of all goods and services made in the U.S. It's the sum of all hammers, cars, new homes, baby cribs, video games, medical fees, books, toothpaste, hot dogs, haircuts, eyeglasses, yachts, kites, and computers—you get the idea—sold in the U.S. or exported during a specific period." GDP is the principal gauge of America's economic health. GDP measures an economy's yearly output of goods and services or how fast or slow the economy is growing. It is a predictor of the direction of the economy. Also known as aggregate demand, it is the total market value of all final goods and services produced in a country in a given year. GDP includes all goods and services generated by citizen-supplied or foreign-supplied resources employed within the country. Figure 7.8 illustrates the GDP from 1980 to 2010 and Figure 7.9 illustrates the textile and apparel contribution to GDP from 2004 to 2010. As you can see, the domestic textile and apparel industry output is on a total decline because of offshore manufacturing.

The Conference Board Consumer Confidence Index® Increases Slightly

26 JULY 2011

The Conference Board *Consumer Confidence Index®*, which had declined in June, improved slightly in July. The Index now stands at 59.5 (1985=100), up from 57.6 in June. The Present Situation Index decreased to 35.7 from 36.6. The Expectations Index rose to 75.4 from 71.6 last month.

The monthly *Consumer Confidence Survey®*, based on a probability-design random sample, is conducted for The Conference Board by The Nielsen Company, a leading global provider of information and analytics around what consumers buy and watch. The cutoff date for July's preliminary results was July 14, 2011.

Says Lynn Franco, Director of The Conference Board Consumer Research Center: "Consumer confidence posted a modest gain in July, the result of an improvement in consumers' shortterm outlook. Consumers' appraisal of current business and employment conditions, however, was less favorable as concerns about the labor market continue to weigh on consumers' attitudes. Overall, consumers remain apprehensive about the future, but some of the concern expressed last month has abated."

Consumers' assessment of current day conditions weakened further in July. Those stating business conditions are "good" decreased to 13.4 percent from 13.7 percent, while those claiming business conditions are "bad" increased to 39.0 percent from 38.4 percent. Consumers' appraisal of the job market was also less favorable. Those claiming jobs are "hard to get" increased to 44.1 percent from 43.2 percent, while those stating jobs are "plentiful" remained unchanged at 5.1 percent.

Consumers' short-term outlook improved moderately in July. The proportion of consumers expecting business conditions to improve over the next six months increased to 17.7 percent from 16.5 percent. However, those anticipating business conditions will worsen also increased, to 15.2 percent from 14.9 percent.

Consumers were also mixed about the outlook for the labor market over the next six months. Those anticipating more jobs in the months ahead increased to 16.7 percent from 13.8 percent. However, those expecting fewer jobs also increased to 21.8 percent from 20.7 percent. The proportion of consumers anticipating an increase in their incomes rose to 15.7 percent from 14.1 percent.

Source: Reproduced with permission from The Conference Board, Inc. The Conference Board Consumer Confidence Index™ ©1967–2011, The Conference Board, Inc.

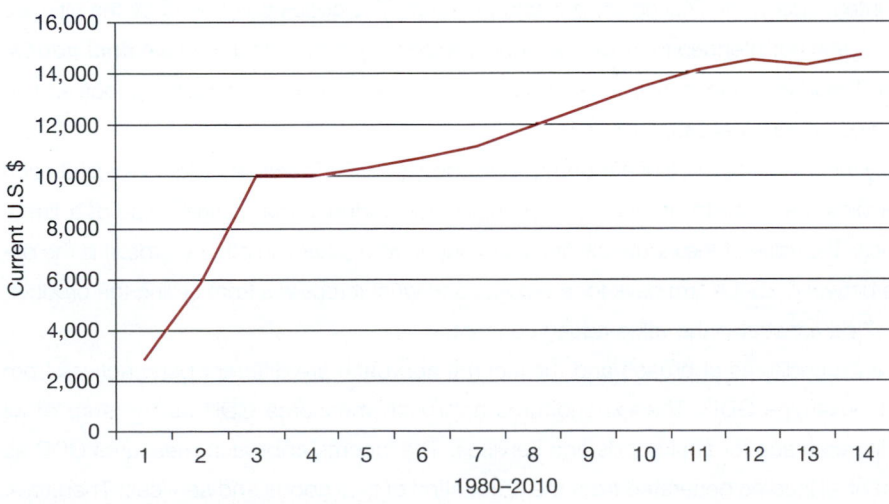

FIGURE 7.8

Gross domestic product in the United States from 1980 to 2010 (Source: Adapted from the Bureau of Economic Analysis).

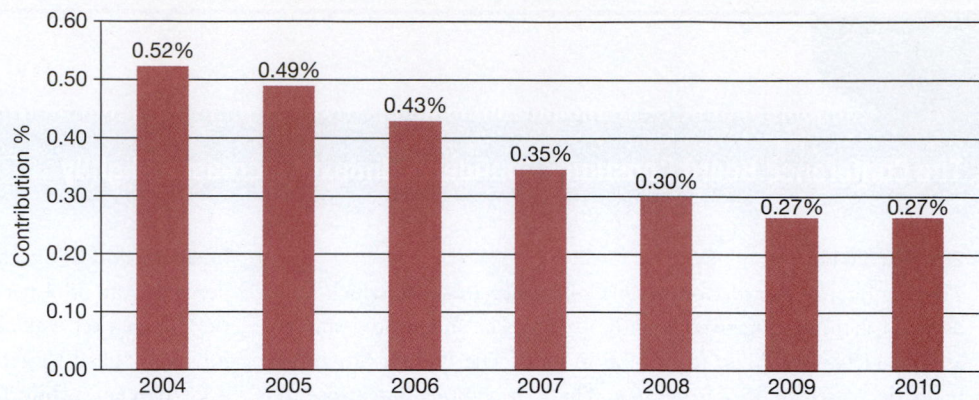

FIGURE 7.9 *Apparel and textiles contribution to GDP 2004–2010 (Source: http://www.bea.gov/iTable/iTable.cfm?ReqID=5&step=1).*

The GDP, reported quarterly by the Bureau of Economic Analysis (BEA), is an indicator of the economic health of a country, as well as a gauge of a country's standard of living measured by GDP per capita. According to the book *The Secrets of Economic Indicators*, GDP is the most important reported statistic in any given quarter. Accurately assessing annual GDP is contingent on counting the output once and only once. To measure output, a designation of how the public assesses the proportional worth of each product in the comparison is dependent on the prices of the products involved. The value of output reflects goods stocked in inventory or sold to customers. During the manufacturing process of goods, the buying and selling of some of their parts occurs many times. To avoid counting those parts each time they are bought and sold, GDP includes only the market value of the final goods and avoids the intermediate goods altogether. Using this method, all of the intermediary goods and services involved in the production are included in the final price of the goods.

Intermediate goods are goods and services purchased for resale or for further processing or manufacturing. For example, a T-shirt manufacturer produces a basic, short sleeve, crew neck T-shirt in 10 colors. These T-shirts, known as "blanks," are sold to another manufacturer who continues to process the "blanks" by adding screen prints, flocking, stone washing, or tie dying. Once the "blank" has gone through all the production stages by the second or intermediary, the final goods are sold to stores. The goods purchased by the ultimate consumer and not intended for resale or further processing or manufacturing are **final goods**. As in the T-shirt example above, stores sell the goods, and consumers wear the goods and no further processing is necessary or desired.

Only the final sales price of a product is included in GDP. Therefore, adding value at each stage avoids the problem of multiple counting. Value added is the market value of a firm's output less the value of the inputs the firm has bought from others. In other words, it is the difference between what a firm pays for a product and what it receives from selling the product. Table 7.7 demonstrates the value-added concept.

The expenditures approach and the income approach are different perspectives from which to examine GDP. The expenditures approach measures GDP as the sum of all expenditures made for final goods and services. The income approach measures GDP as the sum of all income generated from the production of final goods and services. Therefore, GDP can be determined for a particular year by adding all expenditures to buy total output or by adding all revenue gained from its production. Buying and selling are two facets of the same transaction. On the expenditures side of GDP, all final goods generated by

TABLE 7.7

Value added in the production process

Point in Production	Sales Value	Value Added	
	$0		
Cotton Grower	30	$30	(=$30−0)
Cotton Processor	45	$15	(=$45−30)
Jean Manufacturer	55	$10	(=$55−45)
Jean Wholesaler	75	$20	(=$75−55)
Retailer	**180**	$105	(=$180−105)
Total Sales Value	$385		
Value Added		**$180**	

Source: Adapted from Campbell R. McConnell and Stanley L. Brue (2008). *Economic Principles, Problems, and Policies*, Table 6.2, p. 107.

the economy are bought either by households, businesses, or government (known as the domestic sector) or by foreign buyers. On the income side, the total proceeds obtained from the sale of that total output are distributed to the suppliers of resources as wage, rent, interest, and profit.

It is important to distinguish between statistics expressed in "real" versus "nominal" terms. Suppose a dress factory reported sales of $5 million this year, a 15 percent increase over last year. The $5 million represents nominal company sales. However, what do these figures mean? Did the dress factory produce 15 percent more dresses? Did a price increase lead to the 15 percent increase in sales? If the dress manufacturer saw a 15 percent increase in business because the price of the dresses increased by 15 percent over last year, then in real dollars, the true volume of dresses was equal to last year. It is important for a company to know if the growth was due to an increase in prices or an increase in production. For the nation to experience an actual increase in GDP there must be a real increase in output. An increase in real GDP indicates an increase in the standard of living in America. Conversely, GDP growth due to inflation eats away at the standard of living in America because people have to pay more for the same amount as before.

Manufacturer's Shipments, Inventories, and Orders Report

The manufacturer's shipments, inventories, and orders report, also known as **Factory Orders**, captures the quantity of manufacturing sales and orders taken from the **Inventories and Orders (M3) survey**. There are 89 industry categories in the survey based on 473 manufacturing industries. The voluntary survey queries businesses that have a minimum of $500 million in shipments per year. The shipments piece of the survey or **value of shipments** data in the M3 survey represents net selling values, meaning goods shipped from the plant to customer after deducting discounts and allowances and excluding freight charges and excise taxes. The value of products made elsewhere under contract from materials owned by the plant is also included in the shipments. Included in the shipments calculation are receipts for contract work performed for others, reselling of products, miscellaneous activities such as sale of scrap and refuse, and installation and repair work performed by employees of the plant.

Inventories in the M3 survey gather inventory based on the value of end-of-month stocks. Inventory is valued in cost dollars at all stages of production, meaning that raw materials, goods in production, and finished goods are included. The inventories' number concerns those inventories in the manufacturing process. Nonmanufacturing inventories do not affect the overall calculation.

The **New Orders Received and Unfilled Orders** report provides information contained in the Durable Goods Report; but with nondurable items being more important to the fashion industry, information on nondurable items, including apparel, is also included in the report. The New Orders Received and Unfilled Orders report is the net of order cancellations, orders received and filled during the month, as well as orders for future delivery. Based on supply and demand indicators, like retail sales, the report is a reflection of consumer demand. Factory orders are important because they are a sign of a manufacturer's future production and upcoming economic output levels. Factories are most cost effective when operating at full capacity, and without orders factories will not be able to operate at full capacity, and this could lead to the demise of the firm and may indicate a slowdown in the economy. Table 7.8 displays the measurement of new orders from month to month. Orders are defined to include those supported by binding legal documents such as signed contracts, letters of award, or letters

TABLE 7.8
New orders for manufactured durable goods in March 2011

Table 1. Durable Goods Manufacturer's Shipments and New Orders
[Estimates are shown in millions of dollars and are based on data from the Manufacturer's Shipments, Inventories, and Orders Survey.]

Item	Seasonally Adjusted						Not Seasonally Adjusted					
	Monthly			Percent Change			Monthly			Year to Date		
	Jun 2011[2]	May 2011[r]	Apr 2011	May– Jun[2]	Apr– May[r]	Mar– Apr	Jun 2011[2]	May 2011[r]	Jun 2010	2011	2010	Change 11/10
DURABLE GOODS												
Total:												
Shipments............................	196,000	195,049	194,103	0.5	0.5	−1.4	212,357	196,034	197,621	1,162,143	1,080,280	7.6
New Orders[4]	191,983	196,011	192,350	−2.1	1.9	−2.5	205,182	194,906	191,049	1,160,026	1,060,322	9.4
Excluding transportation:												
Shipments............................	150,177	149,075	147,839	0.7	0.8	−0.7	161,289	150,570	148,512	885,163	814,635	8.7
New Orders[4]	146,554	146,382	145,432	0.1	0.7	−0.1	156,058	147,607	146,026	874,874	801,469	9.2
Excluding defense:												
Shipments............................	185,980	184,984	183,930	0.5	0.6	−1.2	201,292	186,150	185,097	1,101,383	1,006,090	9.5
New Orders[4]	181,051	184,316	181,571	−1.8	1.5	−2.7	193,301	185,155	179,189	1,091,360	985,452	10.7
Manufacturing with unfilled orders:												
Shipments............................	141,867	140,785	139,538	0.8	0.9	−2.0	154,828	142,325	145,035	838,395	778,842	7.6
New Orders............................	143,974	148,221	144,500	−2.9	2.6	−2.6	152,630	146,873	141,839	873,981	791,766	10.4
Primary metals:												
Shipments............................	23,800	23,151	22,569	2.8	2.6	0.2	25,704	24,475	19,827	138,896	109,249	27.1
New Orders............................	23,023	22,792	22,637	1.0	0.7	1.5	24,346	24,109	18,710	139,526	113,209	23.2
Fabricated metal products:												
Shipments............................	24,947	24,753	24,616	0.8	0.6	−1.4	26,592	25,438	25,201	146,812	139,167	5.5
New Orders............................	25,640	25,104	24,662	2.1	1.8	−1.9	26,533	25,969	24,277	152,154	142,123	7.1
Machinery:												
Shipments............................	29,054	28,329	27,700	2.6	2.3	−5.2	31,504	29,091	29,119	171,558	155,560	10.3
New Orders............................	31,202	31,932	31,665	−2.3	0.8	0.9	32,620	32,285	31,558	188,613	163,681	15.2

| | Seasonally Adjusted | | | | | | Not Seasonally Adjusted | | | | | |
| | Monthly | | | Percent Change | | | Monthly | | | Year to Date | | |
Item	Jun 2011[2]	May 2011[r]	Apr 2011	May–Jun[2]	Apr–May[r]	Mar–Apr	Jun 2011[2]	May 2011[r]	Jun 2010	2011	2010	Change 11/10
Computers and electronic products[4]:												
Shipments............................	30,268	30,823	31,094	−1.8	−0.9	4.4	31,835	28,650	30,340	178,745	172,310	3.7
New Orders...........................	24,413	24,374	24,299	0.2	0.3	2.0	26,903	21,841	27,000	141,550	139,357	1.6
Computers and related products:												
Shipments............................	5,583	5,594	5,726	−0.2	−2.3	1.7	6,540	4,856	6,045	31,848	28,013	13.7
New Orders...........................	5,713	5,759	5,659	−0.8	1.8	−1.0	6,670	5,021	6,235	31,837	28,190	12.9
Communications equipment:												
Shipments............................	3,092	3,120	3,243	−0.9	−3.8	3.5	3,536	2,978	4,393	18,573	21,997	−15.6
New Orders...........................	3,454	2,998	2,757	15.2	8.7	−2.3	3,700	2,372	3,872	17,374	20,856	−16.7
Electrical equipment, appliances, and components:												
Shipments............................	10,214	10,155	9,985	0.6	1.7	−2.5	11,037	10,182	10,413	59,918	55,826	7.3
New Orders...........................	10,476	10,431	10,114	0.4	3.1	−5.2	11,198	10,467	10,964	62,601	58,914	6.3
Transportation equipment:												
Shipments............................	45,823	45,974	46,264	−0.3	−0.6	−3.7	51,068	45,464	49,109	276,980	265,645	4.3
New Orders...........................	45,429	49,629	46,918	−8.5	5.8	−9.3	49,124	47,299	45,023	285,152	258,853	10.2
Motor vehicles and parts:												
Shipments............................	28,522	28,945	28,898	−1.5	0.2	−5.3	30,964	28,914	29,075	174,631	157,714	10.7
New Orders...........................	28,548	28,944	28,864	−1.4	0.3	−5.3	30,718	28,747	28,678	174,229	156,819	11.1
Nondefense aircraft and parts:												
Shipments............................	6,963	6,719	6,820	3.6	−1.5	−2.0	8,481	6,398	7,701	40,584	37,593	8.0
New Orders...........................	6,832	9,610	7,314	−28.9	31.4	−29.0	7,198	8,794	5,636	46,070	35,942	28.2
Defense aircraft and parts:												
Shipments............................	4,241	4,241	4,195	0.0	1.1	−4.9	4,968	3,956	5,484	24,996	30,408	−17.8
New Orders...........................	4,092	5,145	4,539	−20.5	13.4	0.9	4,745	4,421	5,598	27,750	31,149	−10.9
All other durable goods:												
Shipments............................	31,894	31,864	31,875	0.1	0.0	−0.6	34,617	32,734	33,612	189,234	182,523	3.7
New Orders...........................	31,800	31,749	32,055	0.2	−1.0	−0.7	34,458	32,936	33,517	190,430	184,185	3.4
Capital goods[3]:												
Shipments............................	75,457	74,846	74,095	0.8	1.0	−1.9	82,619	73,944	79,222	442,750	422,811	4.7
New Orders...........................	78,416	81,740	77,510	−4.1	5.5	−5.1	83,488	78,455	79,235	470,909	429,283	9.7
Nondefense capital goods:												
Shipments............................	67,706	66,968	66,135	1.1	1.3	−1.4	74,360	66,084	69,370	394,951	362,457	9.0
New Orders...........................	69,767	72,743	69,144	−4.1	5.2	−5.3	74,345	70,900	69,947	415,692	368,848	12.7
Excluding aircraft:												
Shipments............................	63,862	63,236	62,206	1.0	1.7	−1.5	69,583	62,424	64,693	372,373	340,492	9.4
New Orders...........................	66,140	66,427	65,319	−0.4	1.7	−0.4	70,631	65,036	66,877	388,763	347,835	11.8
Defense capital goods:												
Shipments............................	7,751	7,878	7,960	−1.6	−1.0	−6.0	8,259	7,860	9,852	47,799	60,354	−20.8
New Orders...........................	8,649	8,997	8,366	−3.9	7.5	−3.6	9,143	7,555	9,288	55,217	60,435	−8.6

(Continued)

Survey Description

This report is compiled from results of the U.S. Census Bureau's Manufacturers' Shipments, Inventories, and Orders (M3) survey. This survey provides statistics on manufacturers' value of shipments, new orders (net of cancellations), end-of-month order backlog (unfilled orders), end-of-month total inventory (at current cost or market value), and inventories by stage of fabrication (materials and supplies, work-inprocess, and finished goods). The M3 includes approximately 4,300 reporting units. Units may be divisions of diversified large companies, large homogenous companies, or single-unit manufacturers in 89 industry categories. Due to the small monthly sample, these 89 categories have been combined into 65 publication levels. The survey methodology assumes that the month-to-month changes of the total operations of those companies in the monthly survey effectively represent the month-to-month movements of all establishments that make up the category. The current coverage levels in the survey show that reported data in the monthly survey represent approximately 60 percent of the shipments estimates at the total manufacturing level. Data published represent manufacturing in a calendar month. The data collection is based on a voluntary survey authorized by Title 13 of the United States Code.

The data presented in this release are based on data obtained from a panel of 4,300 reporting units and provide an indication of the activity within the manufacturing sector. The results differ from what would be obtained from a complete enumeration of all manufacturing companies. In addition, a different panel of 4,300 companies would yield different results. The M3 panel is comprised of companies with $500 million or more in shipments and a limited number of smaller companies. From a statistical perspective, the panel is not a probability sample; therefore, the sampling errors that are normally provided with sample surveys cannot be measured. Nonsampling errors are attributable to many sources. The use of company or divisional reports to estimate the monthly change for establishments is one source of nonsampling error. The use of primarily large companies to represent the month-to-month movement of all companies is another potential source. Any corrections will be published in the full report. Corrections received after the full report will be released in the next month's advance report. Any revisions made later than two months will be reflected in the annual benchmark publication.

Additional survey documentation can be found on our website: http://www.census.gov/m3.

U.S. Census Bureau News
U.S. Department of Commerce • Washington, D.C. 20233
FOR IMMEDIATE RELEASE
WEDNESDAY, JULY 27, 2011, AT 8:30 A.M. EDT

Chris Savage or Adriana Stoica
Manufacturing and Construction Division
(301) 763-4832

M3-1 (11)-06
CB11-129

Advance Report on Durable Goods Manufacturers' Shipments, Inventories and Orders
June 2011

New Orders

New orders for manufactured durable goods in June decreased $4.0 billion or 2.1 percent to $192.0 billion, the U.S. Census Bureau announced today. This decrease, down two of the last three months, followed a 1.9 percent May increase. Excluding transportation, new orders increased 0.1 percent. Excluding defense, new orders decreased 1.8 percent.

Transportation equipment, also down two of the last three months, had the largest decrease, $4.2 billion or 8.5 percent to $45.4 billion. This was due to nondefense aircraft and parts which decreased $2.8 billion.

Shipments

Shipments of manufactured durable goods in June, up six of the last seven months, increased $1.0 billion or 0.5 percent to $196.0 billion. This followed a 0.5 percent May increase.

Machinery, up four of the last five months, had the largest increase, $0.7 billion or 2.6 percent to $29.1 billion.

Inventories

Inventories of manufactured durable goods in June, up eighteen consecutive months, increased $1.6 billion or 0.4 percent to $357.2 billion. This was at the highest level since the series was first published on a NAICS basis and followed a 1.2 percent May increase.

Transportation equipment, also up eighteen consecutive months, had the largest increase, $1.2 billion or 1.1 percent to $109.1 billion. This was also at the highest level since the series was first published on a NAICS basis and followed a 1.7 percent May increase.

Capital Goods

Nondefense new orders for capital goods in June decreased $3.0 billion or 4.1 percent to $69.8 billion. Shipments increased $0.7 billion or 1.1 percent to $67.7 billion. Unfilled orders increased $2.1 billion or 0.4 percent to $504.7 billion. Inventories increased $2.1 billion or 1.3 percent to $162.7 billion.

Defense new orders for capital goods in June decreased $0.3 billion or 3.9 percent to $8.6 billion. Shipments decreased $0.1 billion or 1.6 percent to $7.8 billion. Unfilled orders increased $0.9 billion or 0.6 percent to $150.3 billion. Inventories decreased $0.5 billion or 2.3 percent to $20.3 billion.

Unfilled Orders

Unfilled orders for manufactured durable goods in June, up fourteen of the last fifteen months, increased $2.1 billion or 0.2 percent to $862.7 billion. This followed a 0.9 percent May increase.

Machinery, up seventeen consecutive months, had the largest increase, $2.1 billion or 2.0 percent to $111.2 billion. This was at the highest level since the series was first published on a NAICS basis in 1992 and followed a 3.4 percent May increase.

Revised May Data

Revised seasonally adjusted May figures for all manufacturing industries were: new orders, $444.9 billion (revised from $445.3 billion); shipments, $443.9 billion (unchanged); unfilled orders, $860.6 billion (revised from $860.9 billion); and total inventories, $592.5 billion (revised from $593.0 billion).

Figures in text are adjusted for seasonality but not for inflation. Figures on new and unfilled orders exclude data for semiconductor manufacturing. For data, call (301) 763-4673 or go to http://www.census.gov/m3.

Revised and more detailed estimates, plus nondurable goods data, will be published on August 3, 2011, at 10:00 a.m. EDT. The advance report on durable goods for July is scheduled for release on August 24, 2011, at 8:30 a.m. EDT. See back page for survey description.

Table 2. Durable Goods Manufacturer's Unfilled Orders and Total Inventories
[Estimates are shown in millions of dollars and are based on data from the Manufacturer's Shipments, Inventories, and Orders Survey.]

Item	Seasonally Adjusted						Not Seasonally Adjusted			
	Monthly			Percent Change			Monthly			Percent
	Jun 2011[2]	May 2011[r]	Apr 2011	May–Jun[2]	Apr–May[r]	Mar–Apr	Jun 2011[2]	May 2011[r]	Jun 2010	2011/ 2010
DURABLE GOODS										
Total:										
Unfilled Orders[4]	862,707	860,600	853,164	0.2	0.9	0.6	865,044	867,242	811,597	6.6
Total Inventories	357,177	355,584	351,488	0.4	1.2	1.2	356,195	359,840	317,157	12.3
Excluding transportation:										
Unfilled Orders[4]	365,669	363,168	359,387	0.7	1.1	1.2	367,612	367,866	324,475	13.3
Total Inventories	248,116	247,752	245,507	0.1	0.9	1.4	247,441	250,492	224,783	10.1
Excluding defense:										
Unfilled Orders[4]	693,246	692,051	686,245	0.2	0.8	0.6	693,734	696,748	646,954	7.2
Total Inventories	331,400	329,435	325,772	0.6	1.1	1.4	330,469	333,659	292,098	13.1
Manufacturing with unfilled orders:										
Unfilled Orders	862,707	860,600	853,164	0.2	0.9	0.6	865,044	867,242	811,597	6.6
Total Inventories	293,454	291,514	287,738	0.7	1.3	1.4	292,705	295,014	257,804	13.5
Primary metals:										
Unfilled Orders	32,034	32,811	33,170	−2.4	−1.1	0.2	32,291	33,649	27,661	16.7
Total Inventories	33,862	33,733	33,333	0.4	1.2	2.3	34,282	34,441	29,346	16.8
Fabricated metal products:										
Unfilled Orders	63,732	63,039	62,688	1.1	0.6	0.1	64,630	64,689	61,611	4.9
Total Inventories	44,886	44,767	44,160	0.3	1.4	1.7	44,977	45,138	40,769	10.3
Machinery:										
Unfilled Orders	111,214	109,066	105,463	2.0	3.4	3.9	111,333	110,217	84,403	31.9
Total Inventories	57,585	57,239	56,358	0.6	1.6	1.4	57,241	57,923	50,108	14.2
Computers and electronic products[4]:										
Unfilled Orders	124,336	124,067	124,042	0.2	0.0	−0.1	124,379	124,334	120,570	3.2
Total Inventories	48,083	48,110	47,968	−0.1	0.3	1.4	47,327	48,576	44,341	6.7
Computers and related products:										
Unfilled Orders	3,643	3,513	3,348	3.7	4.9	−2.0	3,643	3,513	3,721	−2.1
Total Inventories	5,633	5,711	5,816	−1.4	−1.8	7.2	5,509	5,969	5,972	−7.8
Communications equipment:										
Unfilled Orders	28,642	28,280	28,402	1.3	−0.4	−1.7	28,392	28,228	28,430	−0.1
Total Inventories	9,947	9,739	9,637	2.1	1.1	0.6	9,655	9,752	8,698	11.0

(Continued)

Item	Seasonally Adjusted						Not Seasonally Adjusted			
	Monthly			Percent Change			Monthly			Percent
	Jun 2011[2]	May 2011[r]	Apr 2011	May–Jun[2]	Apr–May[r]	Mar–Apr	Jun 2011[2]	May 2011[r]	Jun 2010	2011/2010
Electrical equipment, appliances, and components:										
Unfilled Orders..................	25,794	25,532	25,256	1.0	1.1	0.5	25,935	25,774	21,719	19.4
Total Inventories..................	15,408	15,476	15,400	−0.4	0.5	1.0	15,415	15,699	14,293	7.8
Transportation equipment:										
Unfilled Orders..................	497,038	497,432	493,777	−0.1	0.7	0.1	497,432	499,376	487,122	2.1
Total Inventories..................	109,061	107,832	105,981	1.1	1.7	0.8	108,754	109,348	92,374	17.7
Motor vehicles and parts:										
Unfilled Orders..................	13,534	13,508	13,509	0.2	0.0	−0.3	13,394	13,640	13,005	3.0
Total Inventories..................	24,993	24,899	24,601	0.4	1.2	0.7	24,670	25,340	22,035	12.0
Nondefense Aircraft and parts:										
Unfilled Orders..................	343,757	343,888	340,997	0.0	0.8	0.1	342,902	344,185	329,428	4.1
Total Inventories..................	59,219	57,839	56,600	2.4	2.2	2.1	59,336	58,866	45,519	30.4
Defense Aircraft and parts:										
Unfilled Orders..................	54,327	54,476	53,572	−0.3	1.7	0.6	54,859	55,082	51,812	5.9
Total Inventories..................	14,253	14,599	14,259	−2.4	2.4	−0.8	14,305	14,639	13,974	2.4
All other durable goods:										
Unfilled Orders..................	8,559	8,653	8,768	−1.1	−1.3	2.1	9,044	9,203	8,511	6.3
Total Inventories..................	48,292	48,427	48,288	−0.3	0.3	0.5	48,199	48,715	45,926	4.9
Capital goods[3]:										
Unfilled Orders..................	655,053	652,094	645,200	0.5	1.1	0.5	656,371	655,502	616,673	6.4
Total Inventories..................	183,033	181,457	178,739	0.9	1.5	1.5	182,322	183,772	158,057	15.4
Nondefense capital goods:										
Unfilled Orders..................	504,709	502,648	496,873	0.4	1.2	0.6	504,281	504,296	469,231	7.5
Total Inventories..................	162,720	160,667	158,368	1.3	1.5	1.8	162,112	162,990	138,041	17.4
Excluding aircraft:										
Unfilled Orders..................	202,068	199,790	196,599	1.1	1.6	1.6	202,484	201,436	176,964	14.4
Total Inventories..................	111,782	111,030	109,894	0.7	1.0	1.5	110,957	112,446	100,288	10.6
Defense capital goods:										
Unfilled Orders..................	150,344	149,446	148,327	0.6	0.8	0.3	152,090	151,206	147,442	3.2
Total Inventories..................	20,313	20,790	20,371	−2.3	2.1	−1.2	20,210	20,782	20,016	1.0

[r] Revised data due to late receipts and concurrent seasonal adjustment.

[1] Estimates of shipments and new orders are for the duration of the period, while estimates of unfilled orders and total inventories are for the end of the period. Not seasonally adjusted estimates of shipments and new orders include adjusted data for non-calendar reporters. Seasonally adjusted estimates include concurrent adjustments for holiday and trading-day differences, where appropriate, as well as seasonal variation, based on the results of the latest annual review of the model parameters. Estimates are not adjusted for price changes.

[2] Based on advance sample. Estimates of manufacturers' shipments, inventories, and orders are subject to survey error and revision. One major component of survey error is nonsampling error, which includes errors of coverage, response and nonreporting. Since the survey panel is not a probability sample, estimates of sampling error cannot be calculated. For further details on survey design, methodology, and data limitations, see http://www.census.gov/manufacturing/m3.

[3] The Capital Goods Industries include Nondefense : small arms and ordnance; farm machinery and equipment; construction machinery; mining, oil, and gas field machinery; industrial machinery; vending, laundry, and other machinery; photographic equipment; metalworking machinery; turbines and generators; other power transmission equipment; pumps and compressors; material handling equipment; all other machinery; electronic computers; computer storage devices; other computer peripheral equipment; communications equipment; search and navigation equipment; electromedical, measuring, and control instruments; electrical equipment; other electrical equipment, appliances, and components; heavy duty trucks; aircraft; railroad rolling stock; ships and boats; office and institutional furniture; and medical equipment and supplies. Defense Capital Goods include: small arms and ordnance, communications equipment, aircraft; missiles, space vehicles, and parts, ships and boats, and search and navigation equipment.

[4] Estimates of shipments for the semiconductor industry are no longer shown separately. Estimates and percent changes of shipments and inventories for the semiconductor industry are included in computers and electronic products, and all other applicable aggregate totals. Estimates and percent changes for new orders and unfilled orders exclude semiconductor industry data.

(*Source:* U.S. Census Bureau, http://www.census.gov/manufacturing/m3/adv/pdf/durgd.pdf)

of intent, although for some industries this definition may not be strictly applicable. Table 7.9 displays the value of the manufacturers' new orders for industry groups including the fashion industry. The previously released information contained in the report lessens its influence on the markets. However, the report is important as a predictor of future economic output and in the calculation of GDP.

TABLE 7.9

Manufacturer's New Orders by Month[1]

Table 2. Value of Manufacturer's New Orders for Industry Groups[1]
[Estimates are shown in millions of dollars and are based on data from the Manufacturer's Shipments, Inventories, and Orders Survey.]

Industry	Seasonally Adjusted						Not Seasonally Adjusted						
	Monthly			Percent Change			Monthly				Year to Date		Percent
	Mar. 2011P	Feb. 2011r	Jan. 2011	Feb.–Mar.	Jan.–Feb.	Dec.–Jan.	Mar. 2011P	Feb. 2011r	Jan. 2011	Mar. 2010	2011P	2010	2011/ 2010
All manufacturing industries[2]	462,914	449,387	446,417	3.0	0.7	3.3	494,762	413,236	412,703	436,921	1,320,701	1,184,405	11.5
Excluding transportation[2]	408,048	397,739	395,225	2.6	0.6	0.7	430,715	365,970	367,047	387,310	1,163,732	1,041,346	11.8
Excluding defense[2]	451,628	438,669	433,222	3.0	1.3	3.0	479,683	402,675	399,489	419,941	1,281,847	1,140,052	12.4
With unfilled orders[2]	159,260	154,602	153,776	3.0	0.5	4.7	178,412	143,403	143,394	156,869	465,209	419,560	10.9
Durable goods industries[2]	209,530	203,651	202,018	2.9	0.8	3.7	233,659	188,731	185,820	206,719	608,210	553,370	9.9
Primary metals	24,598	23,602	23,375	4.2	1.0	2.9	26,818	22,256	23,286	21,324	72,360	58,338	24.0
Iron and steel mills	11,535	10,898	11,358	5.8	−4.1	3.2	12,547	9,986	11,767	9,928	34,300	28,053	22.3
Aluminum and nonferrous metals	11,594	11,252	10,596	3.0	6.2	2.6	12,704	10,891	10,137	10,082	33,732	26,808	25.8
Ferrous metal foundries	1,469	1,452	1,421	1.2	2.2	3.3	1,567	1,379	1,382	1,314	4,328	3,477	24.5
Fabricated metal products	28,807	29,169	28,387	−1.2	2.8	1.3	31,370	27,481	26,106	29,778	84,957	79,339	7.1
Machinery	29,136	27,906	27,772	4.4	0.5	−12.8	33,238	26,215	27,411	29,470	86,864	73,080	18.9
Construction machinery	3,422	3,505	3,562	−2.4	−1.6	−1.4	3,743	3,454	3,551	2,856	10,748	6,110	75.9
Mining, oil field, and gas field machinery	1,795	1,926	1,562	−6.8	23.3	11.2	1,948	1,839	1,467	1,758	5,254	4,459	17.8
Industrial machinery	3,664	3,230	2,234	13.4	44.6	−43.4	4,121	2,645	2,779	3,324	9,545	8,536	11.8
Photographic equipment	765	766	764	−0.1	0.3	41.5	818	698	730	810	2,246	2,159	4.0
Ventilation, heating, air-conditioning, and refrigeration equipment	2,608	2,828	3,338	−7.8	−15.3	−7.3	3,340	1,847	3,361	3,761	8,548	8,357	2.3
Metalworking machinery	1,839	2,258	1,946	−18.6	16.0	−8.8	1,975	2,206	1,897	1,886	6,078	5,068	19.9
Turbines, generators, and other power transmission equipment	4,364	3,050	3,527	43.1	−13.5	−37.4	4,666	3,006	3,454	3,444	11,126	7,810	42.5
Material handling equipment	1,881	1,640	1,955	14.7	−16.1	−4.5	2,232	1,700	1,902	1,959	5,834	5,107	14.2
Computers and electronic products[2]	26,962	27,191	27,154	−0.8	0.1	−5.2	30,413	24,604	23,665	31,151	78,682	77,149	2.0
Computers	4,477	4,004	4,070	11.8	−1.6	−3.6	4,442	3,243	3,902	4,683	11,587	11,063	4.7
Nondefense communications equipment	2,601	2,651	2,664	−1.9	−0.5	−19.6	2,581	2,461	1,988	3,091	7,030	8,346	−15.8

Industry	Seasonally Adjusted						Not Seasonally Adjusted						
	Monthly			Percent Change			Monthly				Year to Date		
	Mar. 2011P	Feb. 2011r	Jan. 2011	Feb–Mar.	Jan–Feb.	Dec–Jan.	Mar. 2011P	Feb. 2011r	Jan. 2011	Mar. 2010	2011P	2010	Percent 2011/2010
Defense communications equipment...	321	375	536	−14.4	−30.0	−16.6	566	364	547	977	1,477	2,064	−28.4
Electronic components...	3,849	3,743	3,777	2.8	−0.9	−4.1	4,078	3,544	3,508	4,218	11,130	11,736	−5.2
Nondefense search and navigation equipment...	885	1,180	1,161	−25.0	1.6	16.8	1,071	1,254	1,098	1,303	3,423	3,154	8.5
Defense search and navigation equipment...	2,503	3,142	2,757	−20.3	14.0	−24.3	3,165	3,417	2,227	3,824	8,809	8,878	−0.8
Electromedical, measuring, and control instruments...	9,539	9,430	9,525	1.2	−1.0	5.1	11,221	8,323	8,373	10,005	27,917	24,970	11.8
Electrical equipment, appliances, and components...	10,756	10,391	10,190	3.5	2.0	−5.1	11,501	10,057	9,744	10,858	31,302	28,703	9.1
Electric lighting equipment...	1,159	1,113	1,268	4.1	−12.2	4.3	1,223	1,114	1,213	1,337	3,550	3,381	5.0
Household appliances...	1,772	1,743	1,521	1.7	14.6	−13.2	1,940	1,631	1,353	1,857	4,924	4,826	2.0
Electrical equipment...	3,721	3,443	3,626	8.1	−5.0	−6.9	4,066	3,394	3,542	3,572	11,002	9,554	15.2
Transportation equipment...	54,866	51,648	51,192	6.2	0.9	29.7	64,047	47,266	45,656	49,611	156,969	143,059	9.7
Motor vehicle bodies, parts, and trailers...	18,561	17,839	17,448	4.0	2.2	1.2	20,121	17,271	16,268	17,123	53,660	48,270	11.2
Nondefense aircraft and parts...	10,876	10,780	7,978	0.9	35.1	5,558.2	13,325	8,080	4,979	4,609	26,384	18,271	44.4
Defense aircraft and parts...	4,758	4,476	5,334	6.3	−16.1	18.9	6,005	4,170	5,471	6,444	15,646	18,178	−13.9
Ships and boats...	2,774	1,061	3,707	161.5	−71.4	136.0	3,251	1,236	4,113	2,262	8,600	7,233	18.9
Furniture and related products...	6,150	5,867	5,778	4.8	1.5	1.2	6,738	5,808	5,334	5,949	17,880	16,652	7.4
Nondurable goods industries...	253,384	245,736	244,399	3.1	0.5	3.0	261,103	224,505	226,883	230,202	712,491	631,035	12.9

P Preliminary. r Revised data due to late receipts and concurrent seasonal adjustment.

1 Estimates of shipments and new orders are for the duration of the period, while estimates of unfilled orders and total inventories are for the end of the period. Not seasonally adjusted estimates of shipments and new orders include adjusted data for non-calendar reporters. Seasonally adjusted estimates include concurrent adjustments for holiday and trading-day differences, where appropriate, as well as seasonal variation, based on the results of the latest annual review of the model parameters. Estimates are not adjusted for price changes.

2 Data on new orders are not available for the semiconductor industry. Estimates and percent changes for new orders exclude semiconductor industry data.

Notes: Estimates of manufacturers' shipments, inventories and orders are subject to survey error and revision. One major component of survey error is nonsampling error, which includes errors of coverage, response, and nonreporting. Since the survey panel is not a probability sample, estimates of sampling error cannot be calculated. For further details on survey design, methodology, and data limitations see http://www.census.gov/manufacturing/m3/.

Source: U.S. Census Bureau, http://www.census.gov/manufacturing/m3/adv/pdf/durgd.pdf

Monthly and Annual Wholesale Trade Report

The monthly and annual wholesale trade report provides three important statistics: monthly sales, monthly inventories, and the inventory to sales ratio. It evaluates 4,500 U.S. wholesalers using the Monthly Wholesale Trade Survey (MWTS) and the Annual Wholesale Trade Survey (AWTS). Most of the wholesale companies surveyed do not sell directly to the ultimate consumer but to retailers selling to the ultimate consumer.

Wholesale sales and inventory data give insight into what is happening in a company and an industry. The ratio of inventories to sales indicates the velocity of production growth in future months. For example, manufacturers must adjust production to keep up with sales or else product shortages will occur. Conversely, if sales fall short of projections, curtailing manufacturing is necessary to avoid excess inventory. There is a delicate balance between having adequate amounts of inventory in stock and having excessive amounts of inventory in stock. The Wholesale Sales and Inventory report provides data beneficial for monitoring economic prospects.

Summary

In this chapter, we studied the macroeconomic environment's effect on fashion direction and trends, including silhouette, color, and pricing. The industry's first look at a season's fashion direction begins with fashion weeks, which take place biannually. The chapter explains that the fashion season begins in New York followed by London, Milan, and Paris and that the runway is like an unofficial economic indicator, indicating the mood in the economy. For example, when the economic outlook is bleak, the runway is filled with conservative apparel. Conversely, bright colors and short hemlines signify a promising economic period. Furthermore, this chapter emphasizes the role of government in steadying the economy through stabilizing prices, creating fair competition, and maintaining employment. Also, the chapter explored the role of the American Apparel and Footwear Association in lobbying Congress on behalf of apparel and footwear companies on a variety of issues from trade policies to safety regulations. Finally, the chapter explored business growth and how unemployment, inflation, monetary policy, and economic indicators connect economics with fashion.

Key Terms

advance monthly sales for retail and food services 179

American Apparel & Footwear Association (AAFA) 158

beige book 169

blue book 169

brand name 160

coincident indicators 179

color 160

command economy 158

competition 160

consumer confidence index 179

contraction 168

design 160

discount rate 170

disposable personal income (DPI) 181

durable consumer goods 181

e-commerce retail sales report 179

economic indicator 158

efficiency 170

Electronic Data Interchange (EDI) 182

employment situation 179

establishment 180

establishment survey 180

exclusivity 160

expansion 168

factory orders 187

Federal Open Market Committee (FMOC) 169

Federal Reserve Act 169

Federal Reserve Bank 169

final goods 186

green book 169

gross domestic product 170

household survey 180

inflation 166

intellectual property 160

intermediate goods 186

inventories 188

Inventories and Orders (M3) survey 187

labor report 180

lagging indicators 179

leading indicators 179

manufacturer's shipments, inventories, and orders reports 179

market economy 158

monetary policy 169

monetary tools 170

mixed economy 158

monthly and annual wholesale trade 179

New Orders Received and Unfilled Orders 188

nondurable goods 181

Review Questions

1. Explain the importance of analyzing the economy from a fashion industry perspective.

2. Why does the macroeconomic environment directly impact consumer buying decisions?

3. Fashion weeks are an unofficial economic indicator. Do you agree or disagree with this statement? Why?

4. Why is competition so important to the success of the fashion industry?

5. List and discuss five variables of competition?

6. Compare luxury competition versus mall competition.

7. What is the implication of unemployment for the fashion industry?

8. What is the implication of inflation for the fashion industry?

9. Explain how monetary policy works? What are the three tools of monetary policy?

10. Discuss the four phases of a business cycle?

11. Why is economic growth important to an economy?

12. Efficiency has always been important, but even more so the past 10 years, why has RFID become one of the important ways a business can improve technological efficiency? List and explain other types of efficiency.

13. Where can you find information on economic indicators?

14. How is each segment of the fashion industry measured?

15. Why does the employment situation impact the stock and bond market?

16. What elements are used to determine personal income? Personal consumption?

17. What is the first report of the month on consumer spending? Why is this report important?

18. What do you call the selling of goods and services or the negotiations of terms of sale of goods and services via the Internet? How is this relative to the fashion industry?

19. Compare and contrast the manufacturer's shipments, inventories, and orders reports. What do they have in common?

20. Name the nongovernmental association that reports its own economic indicator.

21. Why would the Factory Orders Indicator be relevant to forecasting the future economy?

22. After looking at Figure 7.2 and reading the definition of the variables, do you think there are other things that make the company competitive that are not on the garment? What are they?

Critical Thinking

1. Working as a fashion executive in the luxury market, you have noticed that your segment has been successful regardless of what some of the economic indicators are revealing. Predicting the behavior of the consumer in the luxury goods segment is complex and challenging. As an executive of a luxury goods retailer, what type of economic indicator would you invent and what tools would you use to measure the economic indicator? It may be necessary for you to visit the following site to help you contemplate the new indicator: http://www.economicindicators.gov/. Present your indicator to the class.

2. Break the class into four groups. Each group is assigned a specific economy. Based on the type of economy, explain how the fashion industry would operate under the type of government. Give examples of the types of fashions your group thinks that the industry would produce in a five-year period. Present your discussion to the class.

Internet Activities

1. Sustainability is an important issue in today's world and the fashion industry. Based on the site below, discuss at least two of their suggested sustainability indicators. Why do you think this is an important issue? Do you agree with their selection and approach to measuring sustainability?

   http://www.rprogress.org/sustainability_indicators/about_sustainability_indicators.htm

2. Go to the American Apparel and Footwear Association's website www.americanapparelandfootwear.org to learn more about what they are working on concerning governmental issues. You can follow AAFA on twitter, or through their website. As a class, keep a log for one month to see what changes have occurred during that period. At the end of the period discuss what has occurred. Your instructor will tell you the best way for your class to approach this assignment.

Bibliography

Baumbohl, B. (2008). The secrets of economic indicators: Hidden clues to future economic trends and investment opportunities, 2nd ed. Upper Saddle River, NJ: Pearson Education Inc.

U.S. Department of Commerce. (n.d.). Retrieved from www.commerce.gov

DOMINATING
SEGMENTS OF THE
FASHION
INDUSTRY

OBJECTIVES

After reading this chapter, you will be able to:

- Gain knowledge about the components of the segments of the fashion industry
- Discuss the women's wear, menswear, children's wear, intimate apparel, cosmetics, accessories, and home fashion segments of the fashion industry
- Examine the fashion industry segments growing abroad

The only thing that separates us from the animals is our ability to accessorize.

—ROBERT HARLING, STEEL MAGNOLIAS

Fashion industry growth began in the 1900s after World War I, and demand for apparel exceeded the capacity of factories to produce. The exception was in 1921 during the Great Depression when the demand for clothing decreased and production slowed down, causing a decline in the prices of clothing. In the 1920s retail specialty stores and department stores gained popularity. Around this same time, retail specialty stores and department stores organized and streamlined their businesses by categorizing clothing, which made shopping easier for customers and simplified the buying and merchandising process for the stores. The categorization of areas within the store has resulted in the evolution of the major segments of the industry (Nystrom, 1928, pp. 397–425).

The chapter explores the dominating segments of the fashion industry including **women's wear**, **menswear**, **children's wear**, **intimate apparel**, **accessories**, **cosmetics**, and **home fashions**. An examination of the basics of manufacturing for women's wear, menswear, children's wear, and intimate apparel reveals similar processes, but the outcomes vary depending on the target market. The cosmetics industry is laden with regulations that guide the manufacturing methods and the U.S. government regulates the cosmetics industry. The accessories industry follows the fashion trends in the apparel industry. Used to enhance or complete an outfit, accessories as a segment operate as a separate entity and profit center, as subsidiaries to apparel companies, or as companies in their own right. Lastly, insight into the world of home fashions completes the fashion segment study.

Basic Components of the Segments of the Fashion Industry

The four basic components of the fashion industry include manufacturing, wholesaling, retailing (discussed in Chapter 4), and the consumer (discussed in Chapter 9). Manufacturers sell products to retailers. Known as **wholesale**, the selling of these goods is one of the predecessors of mass production. In addition, retailers plan and design lines of private label merchandise and those goods are mass-produced for retail distribution, like the products presented by manufacturers.

Each **segment** of the fashion industry is defined by characteristics unique to that segment. For example, the apparel and soft goods in home fashions segments of the fashion industry include textile manufacturing. The cosmetic or personal-care products manufacturing includes research and development and a long list of governmental regulations. The North American Industry Classification System, introduced in Chapter 4, is applicable to the areas of manufacturing and wholesaling in the dominating segments of the fashion industry. While the processes are different for each product, each dominating segment is grouped together in NAICS, which allows the U.S. government to keep statistical information concerning the economy and inventory levels plus other indicators of how the economy is measured at a given time. This chapter begins with manufacturing and wholesaling, the two commonalties of all the segments of the fashion industry.

Manufacturing of Textiles and Apparel

The U.S. manufacturing industry is highly computerized, and although some sewing by hand and machine still exists, automation is growing. Most of the U.S. apparel and textile manufacturing has moved offshore to countries like China, India, and Bangladesh because of lower labor costs in those countries. In the United States, textile manufacturing is concentrated in California, Georgia, and North Carolina where the processing of fibers creates the yarns that are woven or knitted into fabric (textile). Textile product mills use the raw materials to make household goods such as "carpets and rugs, towels, curtains and sheets, cord and twine, furniture and automotive upholstery, and industrial belts" (Textile). "This U.S. industry comprises establishments primarily engaged in the weaving or braiding narrow fabrics in their final form or initially made in wider widths that are specially constructed for narrower widths and/or making fabric-covered elastic yarn and thread" (Textile). The processing of fibers into yarn takes several forms and there are manufacturers that weave, others weave and finish, and others weave, finish, and continue to fabricate textile into products (Textiles). In the same way that retailers are classified through the North American Industry Classification System, manufacturing too is classified using the NAICS system. The discussion of each industry segment includes a reference to the NAICS number. NAICS defines the clothing wholesale industry as:

> Industries in the Apparel Manufacturing subsector group establishments with two distinct manufacturing processes: (1) cut and sew (i.e., purchasing fabric and cutting and sewing to make a garment), and (2) the manufacture of garments in establishments that first knit fabric and then cut and sew the fabric into a garment. The Apparel Manufacturing subsector includes a diverse range of establishments manufacturing full lines of ready-to-wear apparel and custom apparel: apparel contractors, performing cutting or sewing operations on materials owned by others; jobbers performing entrepreneurial functions involved in apparel manufacture; and tailors, manufacturing custom garments for individual clients are all included. Knitting, when done alone, is classified in the Textiles Mills subsector, but when knitting is combined with the production of complete garments, the activity is classified in Apparel Manufacturing.

The wholesale component of the fashion industry precedes manufacturing at times; while at other times it follows manufacturing. Some manufacturers show samples to buyers of retail stores and collect orders before beginning the manufacturing process. Other manufacturers decide the styles and quantities to manufacture and sell goods from a beginning inventory until all the manufactured quantities are sold. It is possible for a manufacturer to operate under both scenarios. Throughout the text, the examination of the segments includes perspectives from a wholesale or a wholesale/retail brand, depending on the segment. The overview of the segments provides information that highlights the diversity that exists in each segment following the manufacturing process.

Dominating Segments of the Fashion Industry

The fashion industry is a large industry and many of the segments overlap. The main apparel segments include women's wear, menswear, and children's wear. Retailers and wholesalers use classifications to divide each segment for conducting business. A classification identifies a specific type of clothing in the segment. Furthermore, classifications are divided into **subclassifications** to further organize the main segments. For example, a classification in women's

wear is dresses; a subclassification is day dresses. There is no standardization of the classifications used by manufacturers and retailers, but rather a combination of general classifications that have been developed over time that vary by retailer and manufacturer. For example, in Figure 8.1 the young woman and man are typical junior customers. The retailer and the manufacturer realize that they have to satisfy their needs on a continuous basis because their tastes change often.

Most of the classifications today evolved through consumer demand, making the collecting of statistical information by classification and subclassification valuable.

Classifications organize and facilitate the fashion business by systematizing it into smaller and easier-to-manage parts. For example, prior to the 1970s, a separate classification for denim or jeans was nonexistent. At that time, the classification of work clothes, a subclassification of pants or trousers, housed jeans. The classifications carry over into the organization of markets and trade shows as well. Today, a buyer visiting trade shows finds many classifications of products, including denim. The trade show organizers put "like" merchandise together, which is particularly helpful to a time-strapped buyer shopping the show. Wholesalers decide how to classify the product within their line and retailers classify it according to their company policies.

Women's Wear

Women's wear is the largest segment of fashion apparel today but it was not until the industrial revolution that women's apparel became available to purchase for the majority of women. Prior to this time, only the wealthy could afford to buy clothing, while others sewed their clothing at home. The women's wear industry consists of retailers, wholesalers, and manufacturers that produce and sell **misses**, **petites**, **women's**, and **juniors**. The misses portion of women's wear aims for a consumer aged 25 and up with different manufacturers targeting age groups within the misses group. Petites describes female consumers that are five feet, four inches, or shorter, in height; but more than height, petites is focused on the correct proportion. Women's sizes are designed for heavier-set women, and juniors are a younger consumer group, from about 11 to 19 years old.

Regardless of whether a female consumer is a misses, petites, women's, or juniors, shopping is enjoyed by the majority of the segment. According to a report by Mintel published in December 2010, "nearly nine out of ten women surveyed for this report said they have shopped for clothing themselves in the past year (2009) and eight out of ten have made a purchase." Fashion attitudes, an interest in fashion, and a desire to present oneself in the best light are the forces behind the demand in the women's wear industry. The women's wear segment on the whole enjoys shopping; however, there are differences in the factions of the group. The differences (shown in the text below) between the women's wear size ranges of misses, petites, women's, and juniors are apparent in the classifications, the sizes of the clothing, the target market, and the fashion leaders. Figures 8.4, 8.9, and 8.12 designate the classification for women's, men's, and children's

315212 Womens, Girls', and Infants' Cut and Sew Apparel Contractors

This U.S. industry comprises establishments commonly referred to as contractors primarily engaged in (1) cutting materials owned by others for womens, girls', and infants' apparel and accessories and/or (2) sewing materials owned by others for women's, girls', and infants' apparel and accessories.

Cross-References. Establishments primarily engaged in—

- Manufacturing womens and girls' apparel from purchased fabric—are classified in Industry 31523, Womens and Girls' Cut and Sew Apparel Manufacturing;
- Manufacturing infants apparel from purchased fabric—are classified in U.S. Industry 315291, Infants Cut and Sew Apparel Manufacturing;
- Manufacturing womens, girls', and infants' apparel accessories from purchased fabric—are classified in Industry 31599, Apparel Accessories and Other Apparel Manufacturing; and
- Embroidering womens, girls', and infants' apparel on a contract or fee basis for the trade—are classified in Industry 314999, All Other Miscellaneous Textile Product Mills.

consecutively. Figure 8.2 shows how the NAICS is set up for firms involved in manufacturing women's apparel. The next section of the text discusses the fashion leaders in the women's wear industry.

FASHION LEADERS

Fashion is influenced by pop culture and the people that are trendy at the time. There are few that stand the test of time, and as fashion is a fickle business, so go the influence of people in the constant glare of flashbulbs and the fodder of gossip and fashion blogs. Misses, the portion of women's wear that caters to a more mature consumer, is influenced by celebrities like Halle Berry and Jennifer Lopez, supermodels Christy Brinkley and Cindy Crawford, musical icons like Cher and Faith Hill, and even politicians like Hillary Clinton and Sarah Palin. Young celebrities like Kristin Stewart and Blake Lively, musical sensations Lady Gaga and Beyoncé, and reality television stars like Audrina Patridge inspire younger, trendier consumers found in juniors. Junior fashions follow the trends of the moment portrayed in fashion forward and hip styles.

SIZES AND BODY TYPES

Figure 8.3 is an illustration showing the different body types of misses, petites, women's, and juniors apparel. Misses sizes start at size two and increase in even increments to size 16 (sizes 2–16). Petites begin at size two petite and increase in even sizes to size 14 petite (sizes 2P–14P). Women's sizes begin at size 14 and range upward to size 26 and beyond (sizes 14–26W). Juniors start at size zero and increase in odd sizes to size 13 and sometimes sizes

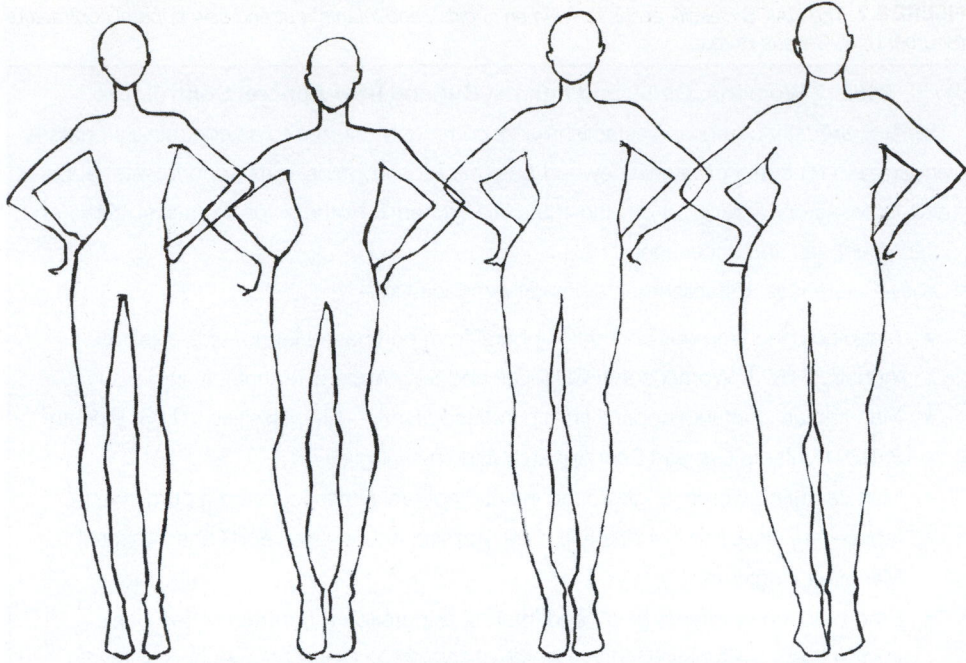

FIGURE 8.3 *Women who are different sizes (Source: Hawa Stwodah).*

15 and 17 (sizes 0–17). The sizes that a store carries or a manufacturer produces vary by company and are dependent on the target customer (Figure 8.4).

INFLUENTIAL COMPETITORS

The influential competitors in the women's wear industry include Vanity Fair, Kellwood, and The Gap. First, Vanity Fair is a conglomerate, worth in excess of seven billion dollars, that owns many brands for men and women. (See Figure 8.5 for a list of brands owned by Vanity Fair Corporation.) Sold globally in 150 countries, Vanity Fair is a growing and sustainable dynamo in women's apparel. The most recent acquisition, and missing from the list, is Rock and Republic jeans.

The second influential competitor in women's wear is the Kellwood Corporation. Kellwood is a conglomerate that owns, designs, manufactures, sells, and licenses many brands. Some of the brands in their portfolio include Rebecca Taylor, Sag Harbor, and XOXO. Kellwood is "an affiliated portfolio of Sun Capital Partners" (Kellwood). Because Kellwood is a private company, financial information is unavailable, but Mike Kramer, an executive with Kellwood, was quoted as saying that Kellwood had sales of one billion dollars in 2010 and that the company will probably go public, as it once was, in 2014. Currently, Kellwood is trying to acquire brands that will boost them from "the racks of Macy's to the likes of Neiman Marcus," as quoted by Mike Kramer in an article from the associated Press (Kumar).

The third most influential company in women's wear is The Gap, with $14,664 million in gross sales in 2010. The Gap is a retailer that manufactures its own brand and has carried basics for women, men, and children since 1969. The Gap has several brands with separate channels of distribution including Gap, Banana Republic, and Athleta, in addition to brands for children discussed later in the chapter. Piperlime is The Gap's online website specializing in footwear and offering brands, other than Gap, to the consumer.

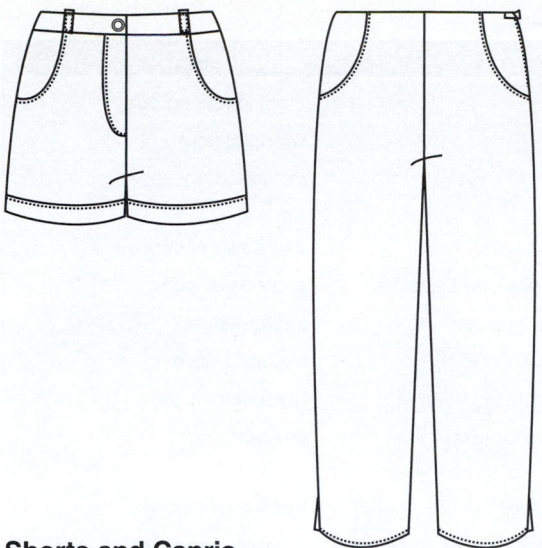

Shorts and Capris

The garment begins around the waist and wraps each leg ending anywhere on the leg above the knee for shorts and below the knee for capris.

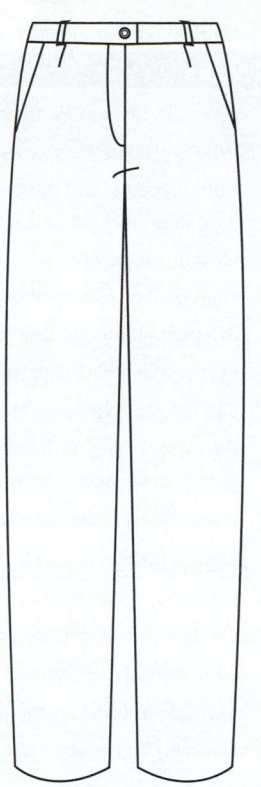

Pants

The garment begins generally around the waist and extends to the ankle, wrapping each leg.

Dresses

The garment contains a skirt and a bodice.

Sweaters

A garment that is knitted either by hand or machine.

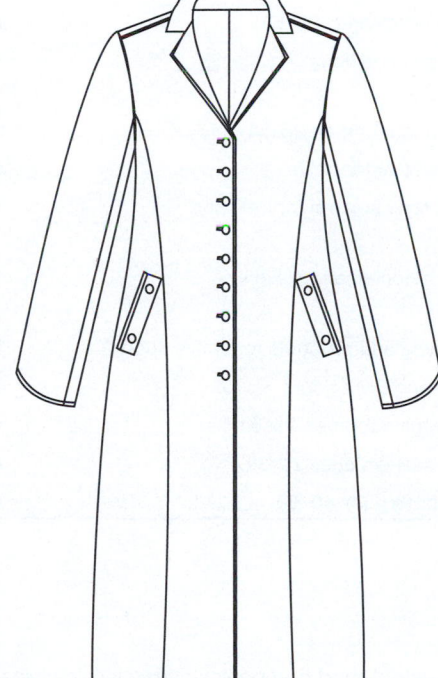

Coats

Considered outerwear and worn over an outfit. Designed for warmth and style.

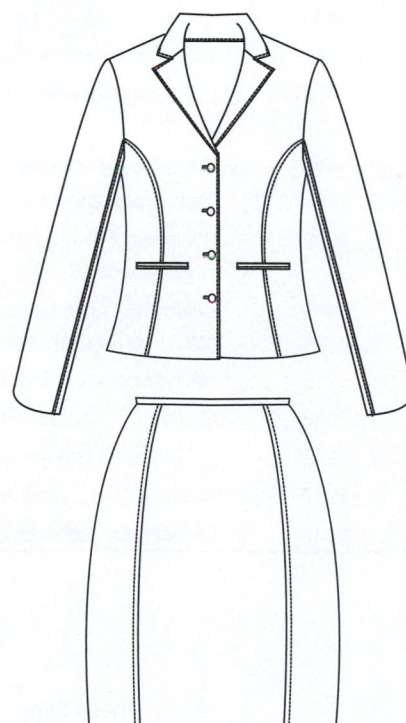

Suits

Two-piece matching ensemble, usually a jacket and pants or skirt.

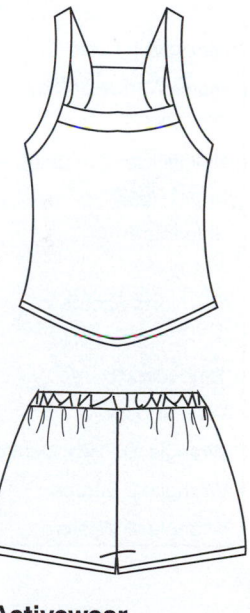

Activewear

Clothing designed to wear for sports.

FIGURE 8.4 *Women's wear: shorts and capris, pants, dresses, sweaters, coats, suits, and activewear (Source: Hawa Stwodah).*

FIGURE 8.5 *These are in the portfolio of brands of Vanity Fair (Source: Adapted from Vanity Fair Corporation).*

Brand	Founded	Ages	Website
7 for All Mankind®	2000	Premium fashion for trendy consumers	7forallmankind.com
Aura by Wrangler®	2005	Wrangler's line for women for customized jeans	wrangler.com
Bulwark	1991	Safe, durable, and dependable clothing for industrial workers	bulwark.com
Chef Designs	2006	Culinary apparel	chefdesigns.com
Eagle Creek	1975	High quality with reliable performance clothing for world travelers	eaglecreek.com
EASTPAK	1960	American manufacturer of packs, bags, luggage, and clothing	eastpak.com
Ella Moss®	2001	Fun and feminine clothing for women ages 18–39.	ellamoss.com
Harace Small	1937	Clothing for public safety officers	haracesmall.com
JanSport®	1967	Sporting, hiking, and business bags including backpacks, laptop case, and functional luggage	jansport.com
John Varvatos®	2000	Luxurious and casual clothing for creative men ages 18–55	johnvarvatos.com
Kipling®	1987	Trendy, fashionable, practical, and informal base for outdoor consumers	kippling-usa.com
Lee® Europe	1889	Clothing for contemporary urbanites from all walks of life	eu.lee.com
Lee® North America	1889	Clothing for women and men ages 25–50	lee.com
Lee® South America	1889	Clothing for self-assured men and women ages 25–35	eu.lee.com
Lucy®	1999	Lifestyle apparel for the active woman	lucy.com
Majestic®	1976	Clothing for baseball enthusiasts	majesticathletic.com
Napapijri	2000	Technical backpacks, bags, and apparel for travelers	napapijri.com
Nautica®	1983	Refined, casual classics that are crisp, clean, and distinct for men and women ages 25–44	nautica.com
Red Kap®	1923	Clothing for industrial and service workers	redkap.com
Reef®	1984	Brand for both men and women ages 16–24	reef.com
Rider's® by Lee	1949	Clothing for female traditionalists ages 25–55	ridersjeans.com
Riggs Workwear® by Wrangler®	2003	Premium workwear for tough conditions.	riggsworkwearbywrangler.com
Rustler®	1965	Pants and shorts that are tough for men 25–54	rustler.wrangler.com
SmartWool®	199	Technical apparel for an active outdoor life	smartwool.com
Splendid®	2002	Stylish and comfortable lifestyle apparel for men and women ages 20–50	splendid.com
The North Face®	1966	Wilderness chic, climbers, mountaineers, skiers, snowboarders, and hikers	thenorthface.com
Timberland®	1918	Hiking boots, outdoor clothing and products for active sports	timberland.com
Vans Shoes®	1966	Clothing for skateboarders and BMX riders	Vans.com
Wrangler® - Real Comfort Jeans	1947	Comfortable and stylish clothing for men 25–54	wrangler.com
Wrangler® Europe	1947	Clothing for sociable style-seekers ages 21–35	eu.wrangler.com
Wrangler® Western	1947	Clothing for authentic cowboys ages 40–60	wranglerwestern.com

These three well-established companies carry classic styles that appeal to the majority of the women in the United States. Price points for the brands owned by Vanity Fair, Kellwood, and Gap are mostly moderate with a few in the better-price zone. Previously discussed, but worth another mention, are competitive forces in the retail arena including Walmart, Kohl's, and Target. Each of these retailers produces their own brands and private labels and carries national brands as well.

TABLE 8.1

Season	Ordering by Retailer/ Buyer	Production	Delivery to Retailer	Bought by the Consumer
Spring	September and October	November	January–March	February–May
Summer	November and January	January–February	April–May	May–July
Fall I/Back-to-School	February and March	May–June	June–August	August–October
Fall II/Winter	April and May	June–July	September–November	October–December
Holiday	June	July–August	October	October–December
Resort	August	September–October	November–December	December–January

SEASONS

In the women's wear industry there are typically six seasons a year for which manufacturers produce lines, which are then delivered to the retailer, and subsequently sold to the consumer. The delivery of merchandise in a timely manner, close to the time of customer need, ensures that the retailer continually receives fresh merchandise, which increases inventory turnover (refer to Chapter 5), a key to retailer profit. Due to the fast pace of changes in fashion and the variables involved in buying and deliveries, seasons are becoming very blurry, especially since a consumer can easily purchase a garment out of season. Table 8.1 shows traditional seasons with an approximate time for delivery of merchandise to a brick-and-mortar store.

Menswear

The menswear segment is comprised of those companies that are involved in the production of manufacturing, wholesaling, and retailing for the male consumer. See Figure 8.6 for the NAICS reference. Menswear has seen drastic changes since the 1960s, when only three categories of menswear existed: clothing worn for sporting events, clothing for

FIGURE 8.6 *NAICS men's classifications (Source: U. S. Census Bureau).*

315211 Mens and Boys' Cut and Sew Apparel Contractors

This U.S. industry comprises establishments commonly referred to as contractors primarily engaged in (1) cutting materials owned by others for mens and boys' apparel and/or (2) sewing materials owned by others for men's and boys' apparel.

Cross-references. Establishments primarily engaged in—

- Manufacturing mens and boys' apparel from purchased fabric—are classified in Industry 31522, Mens and Boys' Cut and Sew Apparel Manufacturing;
- Manufacturing infants apparel from purchased fabric—are classified in U.S. Industry 315291, Infants Cut and Sew Apparel Manufacturing;
- Manufacturing mens and boys' apparel accessories from purchased fabric—are classified in Industry 31599, Apparel Accessories and Other Apparel Manufacturing; and
- Embroidering mens and boys' apparel on a contract or fee basis for the trade—are classified in Industry 314999, All Other Miscellaneous Textile Product Mills.

FIGURE 8.7 *Young man in fashionable attire (Source: Taylor Francis).*

FIGURE 8.8 *Matt Lauer is always fashionably dressed (Source: Alamy).*

work, and clothing for leisure or home. Today menswear encompasses several classifications such as denim, suits and suit separates (clothing), furnishings (underwear, socks, ties), activewear, tops (casual shirts, dress shirts, knit shirts, and T-shirts), pant (casual and dress), and accessories. Traditional and conservative colors defined menswear in the early days. Contemporary menswear uses vibrant color. (See Figure 8.7 for a modern look at men's fashion.)

INFLUENTIAL COMPETITORS

One of the most influential competitors in menswear is Philips Van Heusen (PVH), a corporation that has been in business for over 130 years and owns six brands including Calvin Klein, Tommy Hilfiger, Izod, Arrow, Van Heusen, and Bass. Philips Van Heusen holds licenses to the brands Geoffrey Beene, Donald J. Trump, Michael Kors Collection, and Timberland, to name a few, making it one of the largest global fashion companies. Control of multiple brands at a variety of price points enables Phillips Van Heusen to experience consistent growth. Philips Van Heusen brands are distributed through department stores, company stores, and the PVH website.

Ralph Lauren is a major competitor with over $4.98 billion in sales in 2010; however, not all the sales are in the menswear. Ralph Lauren began 40 years ago with a line of ties that spawned a lifestyle brand aspired to by many, but rivaled by no one. Ralph Lauren's brands include Polo, Black Label, Purple Label, and RLX. Ralph Lauren in collaboration with JC Penney has launched the American Living brand. Distribution of Ralph Lauren brands is carried at department stores such as Macy's and Dillard's, company stores, and websites.

Joseph A. Bank is an impressive competitor with a rich history that goes back over 106 years. In 2010, their net sales were $85.8 million, an increase of 20.6 percent from the prior year. With 500 stores in the United States they attribute their success to "a heritage of quality and workmanship, an extensive selection of beautifully made, classically styled tailored and casual clothing, and prices typically 20–30 percent below our competitors." Joseph A. Bank's merchandise is available in their company stores and online.

FASHION LEADERS

Just like women look to celebrities and well-dressed women as fashion role models, men look to other men for fashion clues. Celebrities who dress well include Ryan Seacrest, George Clooney, and Robert Pattison. Politicians like president of the United States Barack Obama and governor of Massachusetts Mitt Romney are role models for fashion as well. Newscasters Brian Williams, Anderson Cooper, and Matt Lauer (Figure 8.8) are lauded for their fashion sensibilities and admired by men and women alike. Personal styles of fashion designers, like Giorgio Armani and Karl Lagerfeld, often serve as inspiration (Figure 8.9). The music industry is a bevy of fashion inspiration from artists like Justin Beiber, Justin Timberlake, Chris Brown, Sean Combs, Eminem, and Russell Simmons.

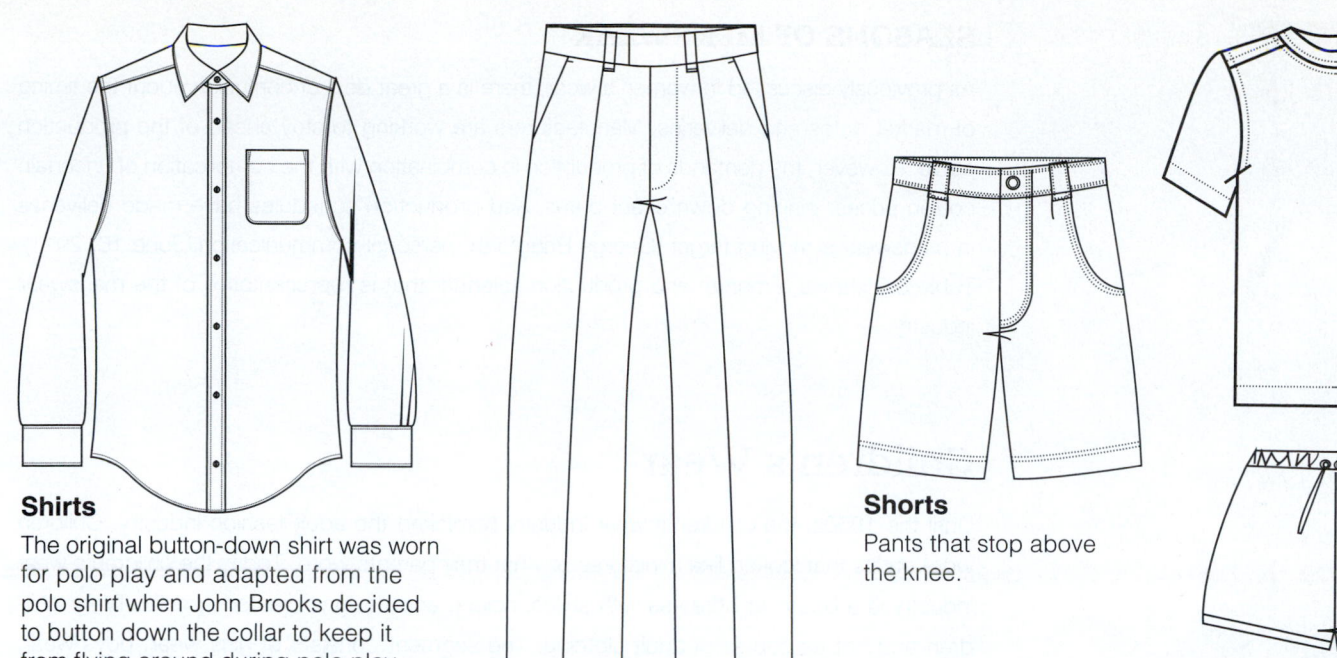

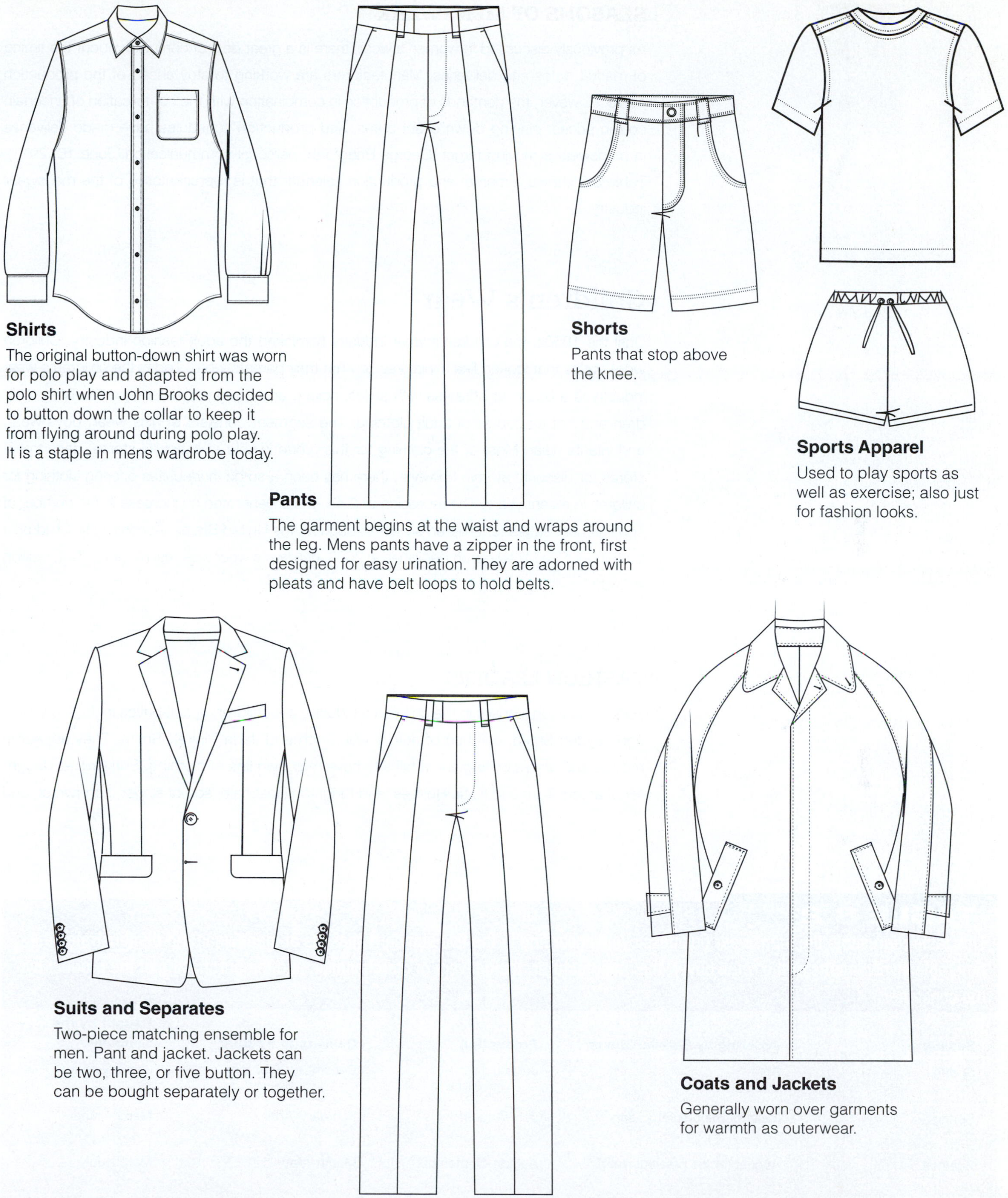

Shirts

The original button-down shirt was worn for polo play and adapted from the polo shirt when John Brooks decided to button down the collar to keep it from flying around during polo play. It is a staple in mens wardrobe today.

Pants

The garment begins at the waist and wraps around the leg. Mens pants have a zipper in the front, first designed for easy urination. They are adorned with pleats and have belt loops to hold belts.

Shorts

Pants that stop above the knee.

Sports Apparel

Used to play sports as well as exercise; also just for fashion looks.

Suits and Separates

Two-piece matching ensemble for men. Pant and jacket. Jackets can be two, three, or five button. They can be bought separately or together.

Coats and Jackets

Generally worn over garments for warmth as outerwear.

FIGURE 8.9 *Menswear: shirts, pants, shorts, suits and separates, coats and jackets, and sports apparel (Source: Hawa Stwodah).*

SEASONS OF MENSWEAR

As previously discussed in women's wear, there is a great deal of confusion about the timing of market dates and deliveries. Manufacturers are working to stay ahead of the production curve. However, the demands of production in combination with the complication of uncertain cotton prices, pinning down exact dates, and production schedules have made deliveries in menswear a moving target (George Bridgforth, personal communication, June 16, 2011). Table 8.2 shows a market and production calendar that is representative of the menswear industry.

Children's Wear

Until the 1950s, the children's wear industry mimicked the adult fashion industry. Children wore outfits that looked like miniatures of what their parents wore. Today the children's wear industry is a booming business with styles, colors, and designs created specifically for children and not as copies of adult clothing. The segment consists of girls wear, boys wear, and infants wear. Most of the clothing for this group is sold at specialty stores, department stores, or discount stores; however, there has been a surge in websites offering clothing for children in recent years. The recession of 2007–2009 generated an increase in the number of consignment stores for children's wear throughout the United States. According to Children's Clothing–US, a Mintel report published in 2009, children's wear was "estimated at $44.1 billion in 2009."

FASHION LEADERS

Today's fashion leaders in the children's industry are children of celebrities including Willow and Jayden Smith, children of actors Will Smith and Jada Pinkett Smith. They appear in movies and at this writing are in talks to have their own line of clothing. Suri Cruise, daughter of actors Tom and Katie Holmes, and Kingston Rossdale, son of singer, songwriter, and

TABLE 8.2

This table represents the menswear business cycle according to the five standard seasons of menswear and demonstrates the timetable involvements of the retail buyer, the manufacturer, the delivery of merchandise, and the purchasing of the product by the consumer.

Season	Ordering by Retailer/Buyer	Production	Delivery to Retailer	Bought by the Consumer
Spring I	April	June–July	December–February	January–May
Spring II	June (of the previous year)	July–August	February–April	March–June
Summer	August (of the previous year)	August–September	March–May	March–July
Fall I/Back-to School	October (of the previous year)	November	June–August	July–November
Fall II/Winter	January	February–March	September–November	September–December

fashion designer Gwen Stefani and grunge artist Gavin Rossdale, are frequently seen in the press for what they wear and even the amount of money spent on their wardrobes. An article appearing on Comcast.net on June 13, 2011, by Audrey Morrison reports that Suri Cruise's shoe collection is worth almost $150,000 and includes a pair of custom-made Louboutins and her wardrobe is estimated at $3.2 million. Fashionable children appear in every American city as seen in Figure 8.10, depicting a young girl in Dirty Richmond, a popular fashion blog in Richmond, Virginia. Figure 8.11 features a couple of young fashionistas wearing popular children's wear fashions. Figure 8.12 shows various children's wear fashions. Like menswear and women's wear, the children's wear industry has several major competitors.

INFLUENTIAL COMPETITORS

The three top competitors in children's wear include The Children's Place, Inc., the Gymboree Corporation, and The Gap. These retailers design, develop, and produce their own brands. With stores located primarily in malls, these three retailers have online presence, operate outlet stores, and produce seasonal catalogs.

The Children's Place Retail Stores, Inc., is a specialty retailer of children's clothing for newborns, infants, toddlers, boys, and girls clothing up to age 10. Their assortments include clothing, accessories, and shoes. With over 995 stores

FIGURE 8.10 *Young lady about 8 years old as she appeared in Dirty Richmond, a blog about fashionable people in Richmond, Virginia (Source: Dirty Richmond Blog, Outfit designed by Fashion Designer Kristin Caskey).*

FIGURE 8.11 *Fashionably dressed tweens (Source: Holly Alford).*

Note that the categories are listed; the definitions are the same as the women's and men's wear, just smaller in size; and style is according to demand of the fashion.

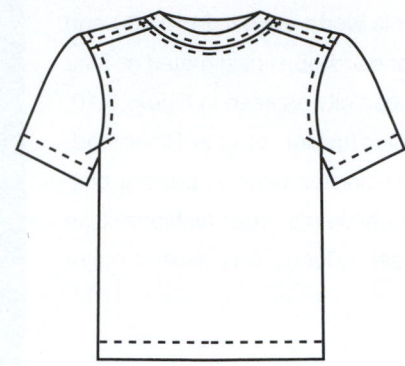

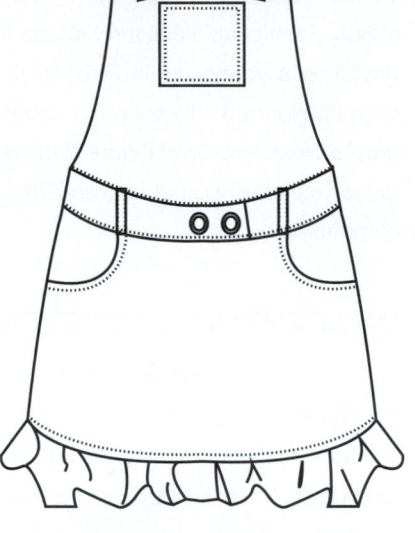

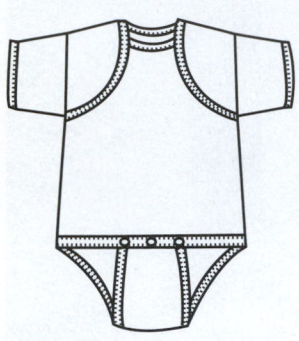

Babies

Includes baby sets, layette sets, body suits, blankets, coveralls, and booties.

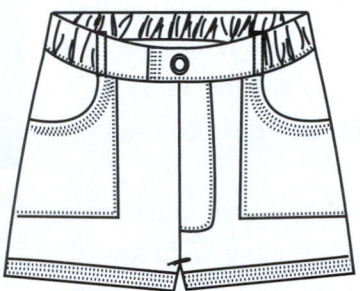

Girls Clothes

Includes dresses, jeans, pants, sweaters, hoodies, and jeans.

Boys Clothes

Includes pants, outerwear, shorts, shirts, sweaters, and dresswear.

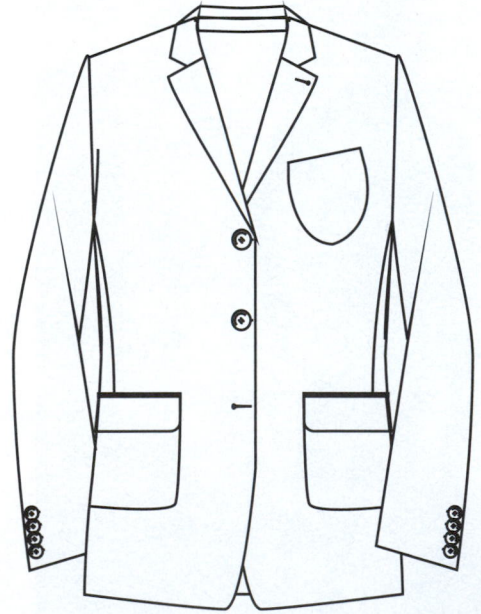

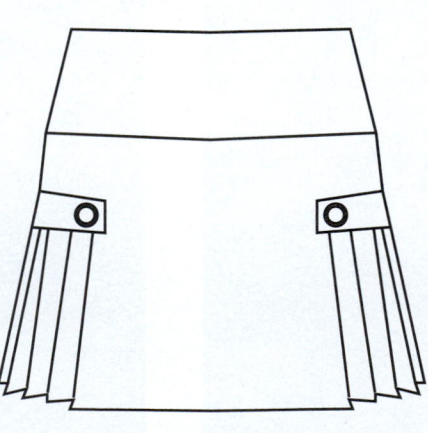

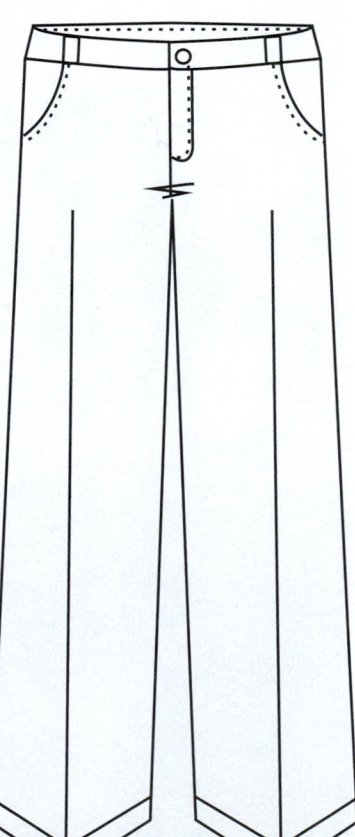

School Uniforms

Includes pants, sweaters, socks, skirts, and khakis.

FIGURE 8.12 *Children's wear: babies, boys clothes, girls clothes, and school uniforms (Source: Hawa Stwodah).*

in North America and a successful website, The Children's Place reached sales of $1.67 billion in 2009.

The Gymboree Corporation—the umbrella corporation for Gymboree, Gymboree Outlet, Janie and Jack, and Crazy 8 brands—designs, manufactures, and retails clothing. In addition, the Gymboree Corporation's division, Gymboree Play and Music, is "a unique, curriculum-based developmental play program today offering play, music and arts classes." In 2010, The Gymboree Corporation posted sales of 1.10 billion (Gymboree).

Lastly, The Gap's children's brands include Gap Kids and baby Gap. These specialty retailers manufacture and sell clothing and accessories for newborns through young teenagers. As stated earlier, Gap's sales were $14.66 billion in 2010.

Intimate Apparel

According to a report published by ReportLinker.com, a professional search engine comprised of manufacturers, wholesalers, and retail companies targeted to women, misses, and girls, the lingerie segment generated sales over nine billion dollars in 2007. The intimate apparel industry was severely affected by the 2007 recession because it contains categories of merchandise that are not seen by others, leaving the wearer to purchase apparel other than intimates; however, "in the past 20 years, lingerie has blossomed from a commodity into a huge money making segment" (ReportLinker.com). Women update their intimate apparel wardrobes annually, a fact validated by an article by Simon Warburton, "a woman…will buy two bras and five pairs of briefs per year, while her wardrobe will contain between five and eight bras" (Global). Intimate apparel is an industry growing at a fast pace due to consumer demand. Figure 8.13 is a contemporary look at the lingerie market today. Intimate apparel is vastly different from the way it appeared in the 1950s, as many modern garments suffice as clothing meant to be seen, rather than hidden under clothes. The primary considerations for intimate apparel (Figure 8.14) are fit and comfort.

FIGURE 8.13 *This model is wearing clothing from the lingerie segment that could be worn as outerwear (Source: Dreamstime).*

INFLUENTIAL INTIMATE APPAREL COMPANIES

Arguably the most influential company in intimate apparel is Victoria's Secret, owned by the Limited Company, which also includes the brand Pink. Fiscal year 2010 posted sales totaling $9,613,000 (sales are for total of all brands by the Limited company). Victoria's Secret sells lingerie, cosmetics, and fragrances. Pink targets a younger intimate apparel consumer. Victoria's Secret is a global brand with 1,000 international locations, a website, and a catalog but its most famous marketing tool is its annual televised fashion show.

Maidenform is another power player in the intimate apparel industry. In 2009, Maidenform's chairman wrote in a letter published in the annual report that Maidenform "outperformed the U.S. intimate apparel market" achieving net sales of $556,709,000. Maidenform began producing and selling bras in 1922. Today the company is comprised of brands including Sweet Nothings, inspirations, luleh, Control it, Maidenform, bodymate, self expressions, and two licensed brands, DKNY and Donna Karan intimates.

Sara Lee is a name that one might not expect in the world of intimate apparel. Known for food products, Sara Lee entered the apparel business in 1968 by acquiring Gant shirts. Since then, Sara Lee continued to diversify by acquiring apparel brands as well as food brands. Sara Lee owns well-known labels like Playtex, Bali, Hanes, Champion, and Wonderbra. Sales for the Sara Lee Corporation for fiscal year 2010 reached $10,793 million.

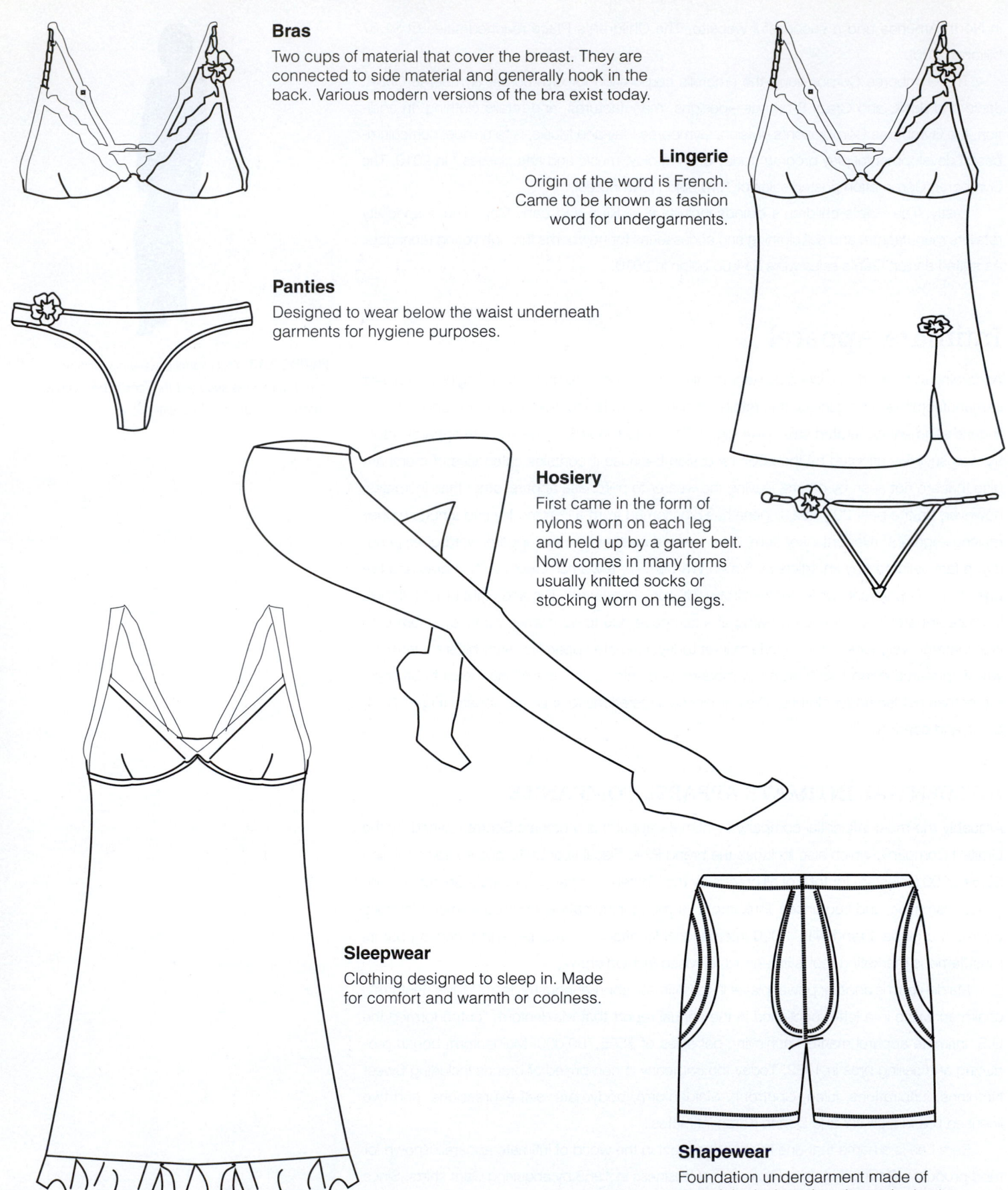

Bras

Two cups of material that cover the breast. They are connected to side material and generally hook in the back. Various modern versions of the bra exist today.

Lingerie

Origin of the word is French. Came to be known as fashion word for undergarments.

Panties

Designed to wear below the waist underneath garments for hygiene purposes.

Hosiery

First came in the form of nylons worn on each leg and held up by a garter belt. Now comes in many forms usually knitted socks or stocking worn on the legs.

Sleepwear

Clothing designed to sleep in. Made for comfort and warmth or coolness.

Shapewear

Foundation undergarment made of materials designed to shape the body.

FIGURE 8.14 *Lingerie: bras, panties, shapewear, lingerie, sleepwear, and hosiery (Source: Hawa Stwodah).*

Cosmetics

The cosmetics segment is comprised of companies involved in the manufacturing, whole-saling, and retailing products used to improve and enhance the appearance and scent of women, men, and most recently, the tween consumer (consumers between or "tween" the stage of childhood and the teen years). Classifications in cosmetics include skin care (antiag-ing products, moisturizers, toners, and cleaners), makeup (foundation, blush, powder, eye shadow, eyeliner, mascara, lipstick, and lip gloss), hair care (shampoo, conditioners, styling products), and bath and body (fragrances, soap, shower gel, lotions). The cosmetics and personal-care industry is highly regulated by the **Federal Drug Administration** through the **U.S. Food, Drug, and Cosmetic Act (F D & C Act)** that requires that "every cosmetic and personal care product and its ingredients be substantiated for safety before going to market, and that they contain no prohibited ingredients." The Federal Drug Administration oversees the over 1.1 billion personal-care items sold in the United States each year (CosmeticInfo.org).

An important part of the cosmetics regulation is **labeling**, also regulated by the Food, Drug, and Cosmetic Act and the **Fair Packaging and Labeling Act**. Compared to other countries, the United States has stricter labeling and safety requirements that have resulted in a low number of safety issues reported to the FDA each year. Figure 8.15 is the NAICS classifications for cosmetics. See Figure 8.16 for various cosmetics.

The cosmetics industry continually conducts research and development in the quest for the fountain of youth. One of the more interesting discoveries is the use of textile fibers in skin treatment products. *New Beauty* magazine reported in its spring 2011 issue that fibers popular in apparel are being used in skin care and antiaging products. For example, cotton is used for its oil absorption and skin-brightening properties. Cashmere conditions and moistur-izes the skin and spandex boosts circulation and increases cell turnover. Silk and linen also have properties shown to improve the condition and healing properties of skin. This ground-breaking research is indicative of the cosmetics industry's research and development ("Skin care with," 2011).

INFLUENTIAL COMPETITORS

L'Oreal is the largest cosmetics manufacturer in the industry with brands including Maybelline, Ralph Lauren, Garnier, Diesel, L'Oreal Paris, Kiel's, Lancôme, and The Body Shop. Net sales for L'Oreal for 2010 were at $19.496 million.

Proctor and Gamble has products in three categories: household, beauty and groom-ing, and health and well-being. Beauty and grooming brands include Braun, Clairol, Cover

---

FIGURE 8.15 *The NAICS classifications for cosmetics (Source: U. S. Census Bureau).*

44612 NAICS Code—Cosmetics

Definition Companies that manufacture and/or market cosmetics, makeup, and skincare products.

Associated NAICS Industry codes

NAICS Codes

325620: Toilet Preparation Manufacturing

446120: Cosmetics, Beauty Supplies, and Perfume Stores

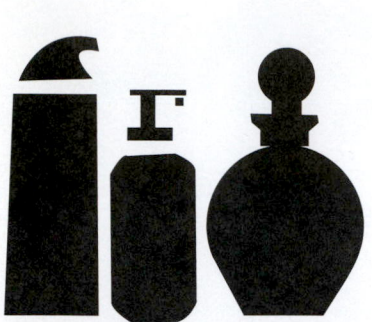

Bath Products

Bath oil, tablets, and salts are designed to use when bathing for cleaning and refreshing purposes.

Baby Products

Baby lotions, oils, powders, and creams are products intended to be used to moisturize and soften the skin of infants and children under the age of three.

Hair Care, Hair Dye, Nail Product, Oral Care, Skin Care Products, and Sunscreen and Suntan Products

These products are produced by many manufacturers. Hair, nail, and oral products are each used to help maintain particular parts of the body. The products vary in what they can do. Sun products help to product the skin from the sun and come in a variety of protection strengths.

Eye Makeup

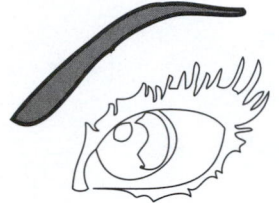

Eyebrow Pencil

Products that apply color to the eyebrows.

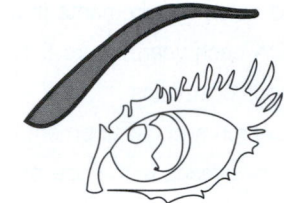

Eye Liner

Products that apply color to the area around the eyes to accent and highlight appearance of the eyes.

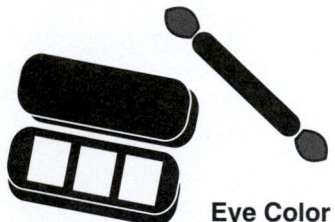

Eye Color

Eye Makeup Remover

Products intended to help easily remove makeup that has been applied.

Mascara

Products intended to enhance the appearance of the eyes by thickening, lengthening, and usually darkening the eyelashes.

Facial Makeup

Cheek Color

Add color to cheeks.

Face Powder

Change the appearance of skin.

Foundation

Creams, lotions, or powders.

Lip Color

Add color, texture, or shine to lips.

Fragrance

Cologne

Colognes are scented liquid products typically made of alcohol and various fragrant oils.

Perfume

Perfume is a product that imparts and diffuses a fragrant odor.

Fragrant Mist

Note: See CosmeticInfo.org for a complete list of cosmetics categories

FIGURE 8.16 *Various cosmetics (Source: Hawa Stwodah).*

Girl, Frédéric Fekkai & Co., Fusion, Gillette, Head & Shoulders, Herbal Essences, I-Iman, Ivory, Max Factor, Nice & Easy, Olay, Old Spice, Pantene, Safeguard, Secret, Ultresse, and Wella. In 2010, sales for the beauty segment of Proctor and Gamble were $19,491 million and in grooming they were $7,631 million. Olay is the number-one beauty brand worldwide.

Estee Lauder, known for cosmetics and skincare products, began in 1946 when Estee Lauder concocted her beauty potions in her kitchen and went to department stores in New York City selling her wears. Estee Lauder invented the concept of a gift with purchase, which allowed women to sample products before purchasing them. Today, 77 percent of the company is still owned by the Lauder family with brands including Estee Lauder, Clinique, Bobbi Brown, and Tom Ford. Net sales in 2010 were $77,795.8 million.

Accessories

According to WeConnectFashion.com, the accessories segment is a $25 billion industry comprised of manufacturers, wholesalers, and retailers. The accessories industry targets women, men, and children, with decorative articles such as belts, scarves, gloves, shoes, ties, or jewelry. Accessories complement the garments worn and follow the trends of the fashion season in apparel and home fashions. Trends appear in colors, textiles, prints, or décor. Mega trends, like the Heritage trend in 2011, influence the accessories worn and seen in home décor. Accessories are generally small and are sold by salespeople to enhance an outfit. For example, if a salesperson sells a suit, then a tie, shirt, socks, cufflinks, and a pocket-handkerchief are accessories to add to the sale. Because accessories are often an impulse purchase, they are positioned in stores at the point of sale, next to the cash register or near clothing. Figure 8.17 explains the NAICS system of reporting accessories and the government's perspective on the classification.

FIGURE 8.17 *NAICS system for reporting accessories (Source: U. S. Census Bureau).*

31599 Apparel Accessories and Other Apparel Manufacturing

This industry comprises establishments primarily engaged in manufacturing apparel and accessories (except apparel knitting mills, cut and sew apparel contractors, mens and boys' cut and sew apparel, women's and girls' cut and sew apparel, and other cut and sew apparel). Jobbers, who perform entrepreneurial functions involved in apparel accessories manufacture, including buying raw materials, designing and preparing samples, arranging for apparel accessories to be made from their materials, and marketing finished apparel accessories, are included. Examples of products made by these establishments are belts, caps, gloves (except medical, sporting, safety), hats, and neckties.

Cross-references: Establishments primarily engaged in—

- Cutting and/or sewing materials owned by others for apparel accessories—are classified in Industry 31521, Cut and Sew Apparel Contractors;
- Manufacturing paper hats and caps—are classified in Industry 32229, Other Converted Paper Product Manufacturing;
- Manufacturing plastics or rubber hats and caps (except bathing caps)—are classified in Subsector 326, Plastics and Rubber Products Manufacturing;
- Manufacturing athletic gloves, such as boxing gloves, baseball gloves, golf gloves, batting gloves, and racquetball gloves—are classified in Industry 33992, Sporting and Athletic Goods Manufacturing;
- Manufacturing metal fabric, metal mesh, or rubber gloves—are classified in Industry 33911, Medical Equipment and Supplies Manufacturing;
- Knitting apparel: mittens, gloves, hats, and caps or knitting fabric and manufacturing apparel: mittens, gloves, hats, and caps—are classified in Industry Group 3151, Apparel Knitting Mills;
- Cutting and/or sewing materials owned by others for apparel—are classified in Industry 31521, Cut and Sew Apparel Contractors.

INFLUENTIAL COMPETITORS

It is difficult to pinpoint leaders in the accessory category (Figure 8.18) because so many companies carry accessories. Retail formats like department stores, women's specialty stores, menswear stores, and general merchandise stores carry accessories. Some of these stores carry the same brands, while others stock their own private brands and still other stores have a market for designer brands. According to research firm IBIS World, Coach Incorporated had net sales of $3.23 billion in 2009. Handbags accounted for 62 percent of the sales with accessories generating 29 percent of the sales. Coach, founded in 1941, manufactures and sells "leather goods, belts, handbags, footwear, jewelry, gloves, hats, scarves and business cases" (IBIS World).

The second competitor is the Limited Group, which was discussed earlier but needs to be mentioned here as a retailer "of women's intimate and other apparel, beauty and personal care products and accessories under various trade names." In 2009, net sales for Limited Brands reached $8.6 billion.

The third competitor is Louis Vuitton, owned by LVMH Group, a conglomerate that owns wines and spirits, luxury leather goods, fine fragrances, watches, and retail venues. Luxury leather goods accounted for 37 percent of the LVMH revenue in 2010. The signature Louis Vuitton logo on canvas is arguably the most counterfeited logo in the world.

Claire's, operated by Apollo Management VI. L.P. since May 29, 2007, is a company that maximizes trends at the culmination phase of the fashion cycle by manufacturing and selling fashion accessories. According to Claire's website, Claire's is a perfect example of a trendy store catering to "tweens, teens, and young adults." Tiffany's, another name plate for the company, carries fine jewelry, sunglasses, scarves, and writing instruments. The target market for Claire's is girls between the ages of 7 and 17, and price points ranging from $2 to $20. Offering most classifications of accessories including handbags, small leather goods, costume jewelry, as well as ear piercing, Claire's operates retail stores, e-sites, and catalogs generating net sales of $1,342,389 million in 2010 (Claire, 2010, p. 24).

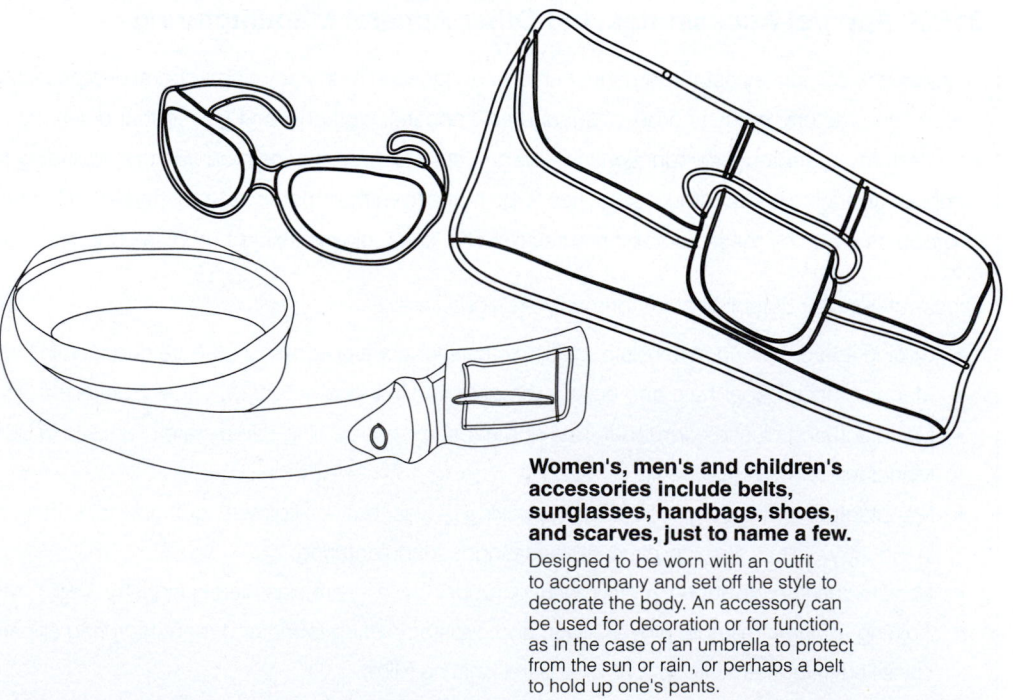

Women's, men's and children's accessories include belts, sunglasses, handbags, shoes, and scarves, just to name a few.

Designed to be worn with an outfit to accompany and set off the style to decorate the body. An accessory can be used for decoration or for function, as in the case of an umbrella to protect from the sun or rain, or perhaps a belt to hold up one's pants.

FIGURE 8.18 *Various accessories (Source: Hawa Stwodah).*

Home Fashions

The home fashions industry consists of those businesses that are involved in the manufacturing, wholesaling, and retailing of products for the home that can be used in either a decorative and/ or functional manner. Figure 8.19 describes the categories of home fashions, more generally

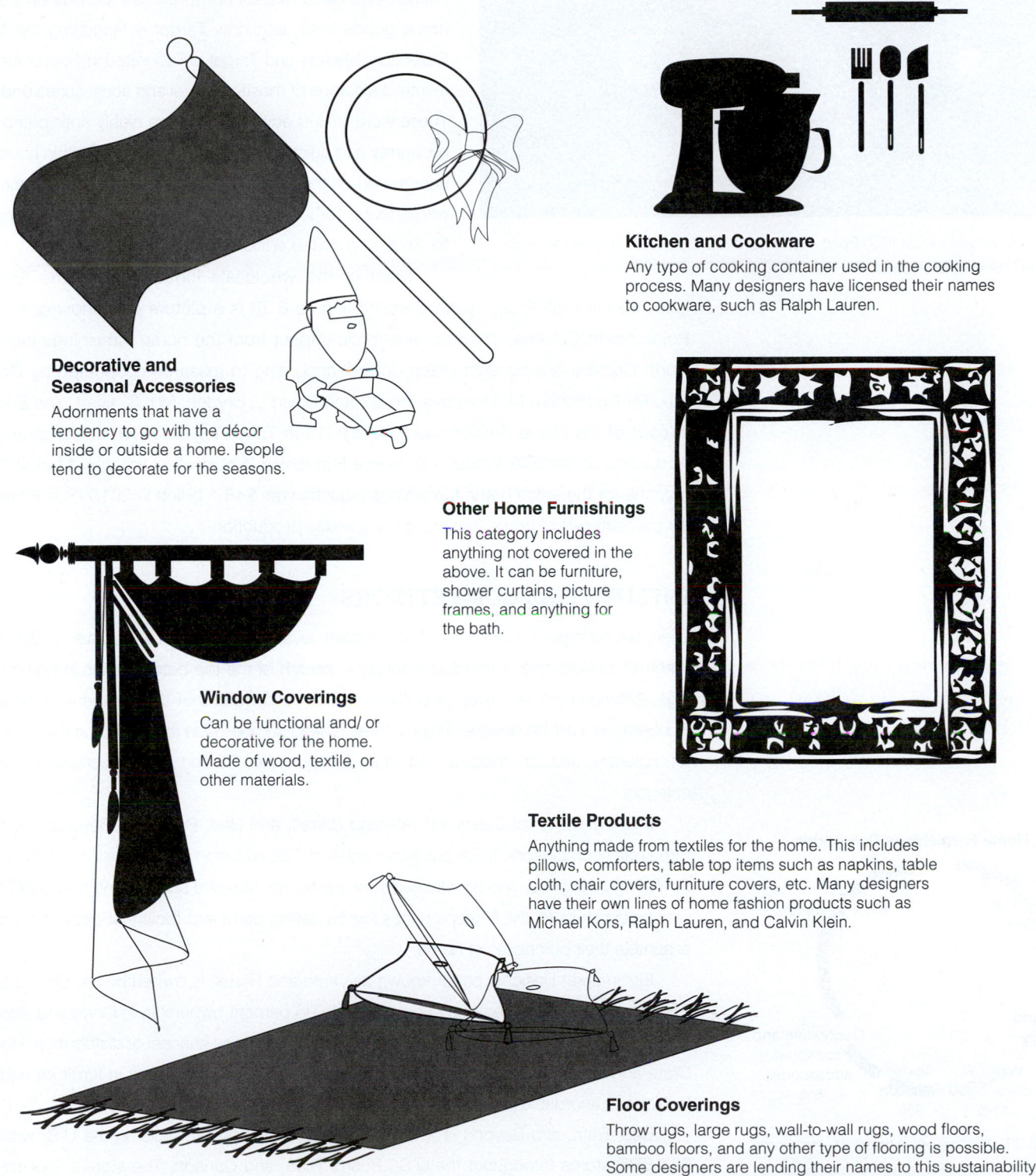

Kitchen and Cookware

Any type of cooking container used in the cooking process. Many designers have licensed their names to cookware, such as Ralph Lauren.

Decorative and Seasonal Accessories

Adornments that have a tendency to go with the décor inside or outside a home. People tend to decorate for the seasons.

Other Home Furnishings

This category includes anything not covered in the above. It can be furniture, shower curtains, picture frames, and anything for the bath.

Window Coverings

Can be functional and/ or decorative for the home. Made of wood, textile, or other materials.

Textile Products

Anything made from textiles for the home. This includes pillows, comforters, table top items such as napkins, table cloth, chair covers, furniture covers, etc. Many designers have their own lines of home fashion products such as Michael Kors, Ralph Lauren, and Calvin Klein.

Floor Coverings

Throw rugs, large rugs, wall-to-wall rugs, wood floors, bamboo floors, and any other type of flooring is possible. Some designers are lending their names to this sustainability but at this writing it is not out in the marketplace yet.

FIGURE 8.19 *Examples of items represent various categories in the home fashions segment of the fashion industry, which has gained popularity in the last twenty years (Source: Hawa Stwodah).*

FIGURE 8.20 *Showroom at High Point, North Carolina, the center of home fashions (Source: AP Wideworld Photos).*

referred to as **home furnishings**. *Home fashions* is quite lucrative, attracting many fashion designers seen entering the market in droves. Designers create their own lines of home fashions or license their names to manufacturers who produce products bearing the designer's name. Ralph Lauren, Vera Wang, Tommy Hilfiger, and Isaac Mizrahi are a few fashion brands that have home goods lines, and now Target is launching the Missoni Collection. Missoni and Target collaborated in September 2011 to introduce a line of mostly apparel and accessories under $40. These were limited editions that were highly anticipated by the consumer and quickly sold out in most stores within hours. Also, unprepared on the technology end, the Target website crashed within hours. Target and Missoni also collaborated on a patio set for $600 and limited edition bicycles (Clifford).

Most of the wholesale industry for home furnishing is located in High Point, North Carolina. Figure 8.20 is a picture of a showroom in High Point, North Carolina. The total economic impact from the home furnishings industry to North Carolina is over eight billion dollars, according to research conducted by Gerald T. Fox, Ph.D., Richard M. Hargrove, Ph.D., and David L. Bryden, M.L.S. titled, *The Economic Impact of the Home Furnishings Industry in the Triad Region of North Carolina* (2007). According to the IBIS World U.S. Home Furnishing Wholesaling Industry Market Report, revenue for the entire home furnishings industry was $48.1 billion in 2010. See Figure 8.21 for percentages of home furnishings wholesale production.

INFLUENTIAL COMPETITORS

There are no large competitors on the wholesale level in home fashions; however, in 2009 *Home Furnishings Magazine* conducted a survey in search of the top brand names in home furnishings. American women, averaging 49 years old, responded that the number-one brand was Rubbermaid. Fashion designer Ralph Lauren ranked number 12 in the textile, furniture, and tabletop category, and Liz Claiborne and Laura Ashley ranked 25 and 29, respectively, in the textile category.

IKEA, Euromarket Designs (Crate and Barrel), and Bed, Bath, and Beyond, are the top three retail competitors. IKEA produced sales of $32.48 billion in 2009 selling furniture, home furnishings, kitchens, and novelty items for the home. Massive showrooms house IKEA's private label products. IKEA keeps prices low by selling parts and tools that allow customers to assemble their purchases at home.

Euromarket Designs, better known as Crate and Barrel, is owned by the Otto Group, an international retail and services company. With 96 percent ownership in Crate and Barrel, the Otto Group does not disclose sales by company, but only by channel of distribution. However, Crate and Barrel have a reputation for fashionable and trendy designs in furniture and home fashions at affordable prices.

Bed, Bath, and Beyond is "the #1 superstore domestics retailer in the U.S. with about 965 BBB stores throughout the U.S., Puerto Rico, and Canada. The store's floor-to-ceiling shelves stock better-quality (brand-name and private-label) goods in domestics (bed linens, bathroom and kitchen items) and home furnishings (cookware and cutlery, small household appliances, picture frames, and more)" (www.hoovers.com).

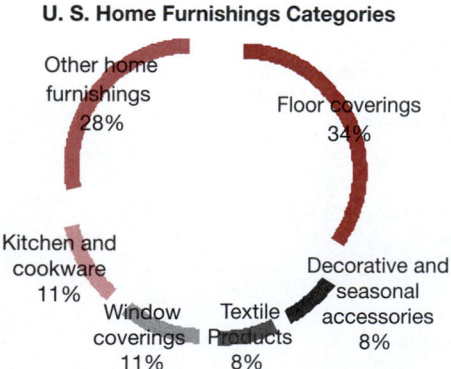

FIGURE 8.21 *The graph represents the home furnishings wholesale industry. Companies in this industry produce products to sell to retailers who in turn sell to the consumer (Source: Adapted from IBIS Home Furnishings Wholesaling, U.S. report).*

Fashion Industry Segments Growing Abroad

Companies go global because the market in which they conduct business is saturated to the point that further growth is impossible and there is a demand for their product in another market. Globalization is discussed in detail in Chapter 11. As countries such as China and India build their economy, the consumers have discretionary income to spend and as previously established, much discretionary income is spent on fashion. Demand dictates supply, which leads companies into new markets abroad. Companies moving into foreign countries face global issues, such as the currency exchange, language

FIGURE 8.22 *Luxury retailers in Asia (Source: Alamy).*

barriers, trade barriers, and duty rates. Resolving these concerns allows the brand to enter the market, establish a customer base, and gain recognition in the global marketplace. Selling Western brands throughout the world is commonplace, as Jason Chow writes about the massmarket retailers like Abercrombie and Fitch Co, The Gap, Inc., and Forever 21 heading to Hong Kong in an article titled, "Mass-Market Retailers Head to Hong Kong" in the *Wall Street Journal*. Prior to the mass retailers, luxury brands such as Prada and Gucci, conducted business in Hong Kong. Figure 8.22 is a picture of luxury retailers in Asia. A new trend that is emerging is the invasion of mass fashion and fast fashion retail brands from other parts of the world in the United States. Zara from Spain, Mango from Spain, H & M from Sweden, and Uniglo from Japan entered the U.S. market with great success.

In conclusion, the segments of all of the fashion industry are growing throughout the world in countries with developed economies and with consumers with discretionary income. Consumers in those economies spend their discretionary income on apparel and accessories. The markets for growing fashion consumers include Eastern Europe, Africa, South America, New Zealand, India, and China.

Summary

This chapter describes the growth of the fashion industry that began in the 1900s after World War I. Growth continued until the Great Depression when the demand for clothing decreased. The chapter explains that in the twenties, retail specialty stores and department stores gained popularity and retailers began organizing by grouping clothing into categories, simplifying purchasing for consumers, and buying for the retailer. The process of categorizing areas of the store evolved into the segments of the industry studied in this chapter, including women's wear, menswear, children's wear, intimate apparel, accessories, cosmetics, and home fashions.

Key Terms

accessories 200
children's wear 200
cosmetics 200

Fair Packaging and Labeling Act 215
Federal Drug Administration 215
home fashions 200

home furnishings 220
intimate apparel 200
juniors 202

Review Questions

1. Why does the fashion industry structure into dominating segments based on types of apparel and accessories?

2. What are the two general commonalities of the segments of the fashion industry according to this chapter?

3. Why is the North American Industry Classification System so important to the U.S. government from a fashion industry perspective?

4. What are the three main apparel segments?

5. What is a subclassification? Why are subclassifications important? Give an example?

6. What is the difference between women's, misses, and juniors?

7. For each segment, give one example of a company that is a major competitor.

8. Who are some of the fashion leaders in the menswear industry? women's wear? children's wear?

9. When does a retail buyer normally buy menswear for spring/summer?

10. When is women's wear produced for fall/winter?

11. Who is the number-one competitor in the lingerie industry today?

12. Who regulates the cosmetic industry in the United States today?

13. Why is labeling cosmetics required by law?

14. Where is most of the home furnishing wholesale industry located in the United States?

15. Who are the top three competitors in the home fashions industry?

Critical Thinking

1. You are a department store manager and you are considering splitting the women's wear and misses wear into two departments because of high-volume sales in both the areas. The vice-president does not want to split the departments. He wants them to remain in one area. Give advantages (at least 5–6) to having the department in two different areas of the store. You may have to visit department stores to support your answer.

2. The cosmetic industry is not only about women but also about the male consumer, and it is a growing fact that the cosmetic industry is turning into a personal wellness industry. Support both of these assumptions based on research. As the vice-president of an international cosmetic company, how would you address and change the marketing to consumers to target both women and men and to make the statement about personal wellness as opposed to cosmetics.

Internet Activities

1. Find three annual reports from three different segments of the fashion industry and discuss the following for all three annual reports:
   a. What are the risks for the company?
   b. What are the plans for the future growth?
   c. What were the net sales?
   d. Explain the product(s).
   e. Who is the target market?
   f. What are the price points?
   g. Compared to the past two years, did the company see an increase or decrease?

2. For each segment discussed in this chapter, find an association that supports the segment and describe the association: women's wear, menswear, children's wear, lingerie, cosmetics, accessories, and home fashions.

Bibliography

Bed, Bath and Beyond. (2011). *2010 Annual report*. Retrieved from http://phx.corporate-ir.net/phoenix.zhtml?c=97860&p=irol-reportsannual

Bureau of Labor Statistics, U.S. Department of Labor, Career Guide to Industries, 2010–11 Edition, Textile, Textile Product, and Apparel Manufacturing, Retrieved from http://www.bls.gov/oco/cg/cgs015.htm (accessed May 14, 2011).

Children's Place. (2011). *2010 Annual report.* Retrieved from http://phx.corporate-ir.net/phoenix.zhtml?c=120577&p=irol-irhome

Claire's. (2010). *2009 Annual report*. Retrieved from http://www.clairestores.com/phoenix.zhtml?c=68915&p=irol-reportsannual

Clifford, Stephanie. "Demand for Target Fashion line crashes web site." *New York Times* [New York], September 13, 2011, no page, Web, Retrieved from March 18, 2012, http://www.nytimes.com/2011/09/14/business/demand-at-target-for-fashion-line-crashes-web-site.html?_r=1

CosmeticsInfo.org. (n.d.). The Personal Care Products Council, cosmetic definitions, Web, April 13, 2010. Retrieved from http://www.cosmeticsinfo.org

Driscoll, Marie. (2011). "Apparel & footwear, retailers and brands." *Standard and Poor Industry Survey*, March 10.

Estee Lauder. (2011). *2010 Annual report*. Retrieved from http://phx.corporate-ir.net/phoenix.zhtml?c=109458&p=irol-reportsannual

Gap. (2011). *2009 Annual report*. Retrieved from http://www.gapinc.com/content/gapinc/html/investors.html

Gerald T. Fox, Richard M. Hargrove, David L. Bryden. (2007). *The economic impact of the home furnishings industry in the triad region of North Carolina*. Retrieved from http://www.highpointchamber.org/regional/images/HPUStudy.pdf

Gymboree. (2011). *2009 Annual report*. Retrieved from http://ir.gymboree.com/secfiling.cfm?filingID=1193125-10-71089

IBIS, Nikoleta Panteva. (2010, December). *Leather Good & Luggage Manufacturing in the US 31619*. Retrieved from http://www.ibisworld.com.proxy.library.vcu.edu/industryus/default.aspx?indid=374

IBIS World, Janet Shim. (2011, April). Home Furnishing Wholesaling in the US 42122.

IKEA. (2011). (2010) Welcome inside yearly summary. Press release. Retrieved from sales. http://www.ikea.com/ms/en_CN/about_ikea/press/press_releases/Welcome_inside_2010.pdf

Kellwood tries on luxury brands. *St. Louis Post-Dispatch*, 6 March 2011.

L'Oreal. (2011). *2010 Annual report*. Retrieved from http://www.loreal.com/_en/_ww/l-Oreal-Finance.aspx

Louis Vuitton. (2011a). LVMH at a glance. Retrieved from http://www.lvmh.com/comfi/pg_enbref.asp?rub=7&srub=0

Louis Vuitton. (2011b). *2010 Annual report*. Retrieved from http://www.lvmh.com/comfi/pg_rapports.asp.

Maidenform. (2011). *2010 Annual report*. Retrieved from http://ir.maidenform.com/phoenix.zhtml?c=190009&p=irol-IRHome

Mintel. (2009, August). *Children's clothing—US*. Retrieved from http://academic.mintel.com.proxy.library.vcu.edu/sinatra/oxygen_academic/search_results/show&/display/id=395070

Mintel. (2010, December). *Women's attitudes toward clothes shopping—US*. Retrieved from http://academic.mintel.com.proxy.library.vcu.edu/sinatra/oxygen_academic/search_results/show&/display/id=483004

Nystrom, Paul. (1928). *Economics of Fashion*, 1st ed. New York: The Ronald Press Company, pp. 397–425.

Otto Group. (2011). *Crate and Barrel*. Retrieved from http://www.ottogroup.com/crate_and_barrel1.html?&L=0

Phillips Van Heusen. (2011). *2010 Annual report*. Retrieved from http://www.pvh.com/investor_relations.aspx

Polo Ralph Lauren. (2011). *2010 Annual report*. Retrieved from http://investor.ralphlauren.com/

Proctor and Gamble. (2010). *2009 Annual report*. Retrieved from http://www.pg.com/en_US/investors/financial_reporting/index.shtml

ReportLinker. (2008). *Report Summary for U.S. Market for Women's Intimate Apparel (Lingerie)*, Retrieved from http://www.saralee.com/InvestorRelations/~/media/SaraLeeCorp/Corporate/Files/PDF/InvestorRelations/2010_AR.ashx

Skin care with fabrics. (2011, Spring/Summer). *New Beauty*, 7(2), 72–76.

The Limited. (2011). *2011 Annual report and proxy*. Retrieved from http://www.limitedbrands.com/investors/default.aspx

U.S. Census Bureau. (2007a). *2007 NAICS definitions, 31599, Apparel Accessories and Other Apparel Manufacturing*. Retrieved from http://www.census.gov/cgi-bin/sssd/naics/naicsrch

U.S. Census Bureau. (2007b). *2007 NAICS definitions, 44612, Companies that manufacture Cosmetics and other Cosmetic type of Manufacturing*. Retrieved from http://www.census.gov/cgi-bin/sssd/naics/naicsrch

U.S. Census Bureau. (2007c). *2007 NAICS definitions, 315212, Companies that manufacture Women's, Girls', and Infants' Cut and Sew Apparel Contractors*. Retrieved from http://www.census.gov/cgi-bin/sssd/naics/naicsrch

U.S. Census Bureau. (2007d). 2007 *NAICS definitions, 315211, Companies that manufacture Men's and Boys' Cut and Sew Apparel Contractors*. Retrieved from http://www.census.gov/cgi-bin/sssd/naics/naicsrch

DOMESTIC
AND INTERNATIONAL
FASHION
CONSUMERS

OBJECTIVES

After reading this chapter, you will be able to:

- Gain an understanding of the domestic consumer by using demographics and market research information
- Understand international consumers and their importance to domestic and global fashion industries
- Gain knowledge of buyer behavior and decision making
- Explore consumer segmentation

Every generation laughs at the old fashions but religiously follows the new.

—HENRY DAVID THOREAU

Worldwide, it is the consumption of apparel, accessories, and fashion-related goods that drive the fashion industry. As previously discussed in this text, understanding consumers and their preferences, behaviors, and motivations is vital to the success of manufacturers and retailers of fashion products. This chapter identifies domestic and international consumers and their demographics and psychographics that lead to consumer decisions. The chapter begins with a look at the domestic (U.S.) consumer.

The Domestic Consumer

Americans consume goods and services like no other single nation. Second only to Europe, Americans indulge in fashion and fashion-related products with gusto. The types of products and the proportion of those products purchased are related to the ethnic and racial background of the purchaser. Age, income, education, and psychology factor into the buying equation too. The psychological reasons for the product choices made by people are examined later in this chapter.

Americans view apparel as more than a necessity: It is viewed as a form of self-expression, as clothes show the world a snippet about the wearer. "Clothing has more functions than just keeping the wearer warm: for example, it also acts as a signifier of socio-economic class and a way of displaying individual identity" (Datamonitor, 2009). In the data below, it is clear that regardless of ethnicity or race, American men and women love fashion and accessories.

Industry

The American fashion industry is changing. In 2010 the fashion industry showed signs of recovery with consistent growth throughout the year. The recovery and growth indicate that Americans are shopping again and when people shop, production increases and the industry benefits on the supply, as well as the consumer side. The industry is also undergoing production changes for good. Offshore production had been the norm for years because of low labor costs; but in 2010, manufacturers began to produce in the United States itself as costs for labor and raw materials, like cotton, increased abroad. Also, many U.S. apparel manufacturers find that the benefits of products being "made in America" outweigh the savings of overseas production. The increase in raw materials prices, especially cotton, hits hard impacting margins by about 1 percent (Ellis, 2011b). Apparel retailing is experiencing changes as well. In 2010, online sales experienced 10 percent growth (Independent retailer. com, 2011), demonstrating that the consumer has choices other than the traditional brick-and-mortar store.

In 2010, U.S. apparel sales increased about 2 percent, with most of the increase coming from adult apparel. Men's and women's apparel gained about 3 percent each. Children's wear decreased in dollars but increased in units (Independent retailer.com). According to Datamonitor, U.S. apparel sales in 2009 reached $305.0 billion, accounting for 30 percent of the global volume. Figure 9.1 shows the compounded annual growth from 2005 through 2009. Fifty-three percent of U.S. sales are in women's wear segment at $162 million. Menswear accounts for 31 percent with sales of approximately $96 million and children's wear rounds out the industry at about 16 percent of the industry's value. Figure 9.2 depicts the classification sales of the U.S. apparel industry.

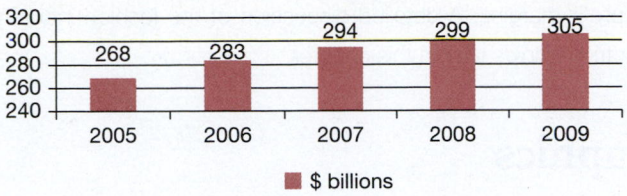

FIGURE 9.1 *Dollar value of the U.S. apparel industry from 2005 to 2009.*

While the U.S. apparel industry is growing, it faces major global competition, especially from emerging markets. According to Seth Pinsky, President, the New York City Economic Development Corporation, "We have to make sure the next generation is at the forefront of these trends and will connect our up-and-coming stable of companies with new markets such as South Asia, India and China. The key to the future of this industry is to make it more agile and flexible" (Feitelbeg, 2010).

Economy

The U.S. economy is the largest in the world; however, the International Monetary Fund predicts that by 2016 China's economy will be the largest in the world. The recession of 2007 hit Americans hard and as a result, the U.S. economy has suffered a setback. Bankruptcy filings jumped 14 percent in 2010 from 2009, according to the Administrative Office of the U.S. courts. In 2011, bankruptcies continued to rise as unemployment approached 10 percent. High unemployment, uncertainty about the future, and a tight credit market had consumers shifting to lower-priced retail outlets to satisfy their clothing wants and needs. Mass merchandisers, outlet malls, and off-price retailers saw an influx of new customers trying to get more for their money. Although the U.S. economy is recovering from the financial crisis that began in 2007, its slow growth is not enough for the United States to retain its status as the largest economy in the world (*Economy watch*, n.d.).

The same issues facing consumers also impacted the manufacturing and retail sectors. As few companies expanded in the United States, foreign expansion became more lucrative with lower exchange rates, making products (especially luxury products) more manageable for overseas buyers. A few luxury companies saw expansion during the recession but very little occurred in the United States. Most luxury companies expanded in China, India, and Russia. China, the longstanding "go to" country for cheap labor and raw materials, started to see rising costs in labor, shipping, and cotton. The increased costs out of China eroded U.S.

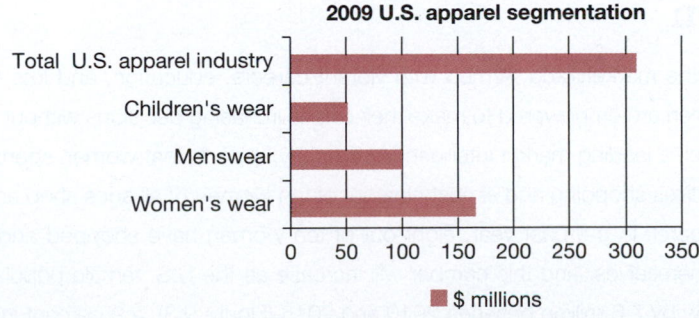

FIGURE 9.2 *The classifications of the U.S. apparel industry percent to total business.*

manufacturer's profit margins. A detailed discussion of the fashion industry in Europe and Asia-Pacific countries follows later in this chapter.

Demographics

Demographics sorts the population by race/ethnicity, income, gender, and age, to name a few. Demographics personifies a population; it gives details and information that make it easier to understand a population. Demographics contribute to predicting the behavior of a group, making it an important resource for fashion companies seeking to meet the needs of a target market. Understanding what a population is, and what it is predicted to be, allows fashion manufacturers and retailers to build a business model that fits consumer demand. Future plans are based on the growth, shrinkage, and changing demographics of a market.

The U.S. population is growing. The largest increases in forecasted growth are in the minorities, in large part due to immigration. According to the United Nations, 2 million people per year will leave poor countries for more developed ones and over half of those immigrants will move to the United States (Kotkin, 2010). The fastest growth is expected in Hispanic and Asian ethnicities. The African American population will grow, but slower than Hispanics and Asians, outpacing the national growth rate. The number of Hispanic and Asian females is rising faster than White or African American women, a significant statistic considering that women do the majority of the purchasing. According to 2010 census data, 9 million people reported belonging to more than one racial group (about 3 percent of the population), of which White and African American was the largest multiple-race combination ("State and county," 2010). More details on demographics by race follow in this chapter.

Age and education impact purchasing decisions as well. The United States has an aging population called "**baby boomers**." Baby boomers are adults born between 1942 and 1964. There are about 72 million Americans in this age group with an enormous amount of purchasing power. However, as the baby boomers age, the population of working and young people increases as well. The 18–34 age group is important to marketers because they buy goods, more so than the baby boomer group, even though they have less buying power. Education impacts the types of goods purchased and the manner in which they are purchased. The more educated the consumer, the more likely he/she is to use the Internet for shopping.

According to Mintel, a leading market intelligence company, the recession affected the lower-middle class more than other socioeconomic groups. However, for households earning more than $25,000 annually, household income has little effect on shopping behavior. As people earn more, they spend more, and higher incomes equate to more clothing purchases. Furthermore, those with higher household incomes are more loyal to brands than lower-income cohorts.

Women

Women rule the marketplace. Armed with vibrant careers, education, and lots of shopping choices, women are empowered to make their own purchasing decisions without advice from anyone. Mintel, a leading market intelligence company, reports that women spend over three years of their lives shopping and almost nine out of ten women of all ages shop and purchase women's apparel. In the past year, eight out of ten women have shopped and purchased clothing for themselves, and this number will increase as the U.S. female population is estimated to grow by 7.6 million between 2010 and 2015 (Figure 9.3), a 9 percent increase from 2005. Women between the ages of 18 and 34 shop more than women in other age groups.

FIGURE 9.3 *U.S. female population by race 2005–2015 (Source: Mintel).*

	2005		2010		2015		% change
	000	%	000	%	000	%	2005–2015
Race							
Asian	6,447	4.3	7,569	4.8	8,728	5.3	35.4
African American	19,759	13.2	20,851	13.2	21,973	13.3	11.2
White	119,806	79.8	124,395	79.0	129,110	78.2	7.8
Other	4,084	2.7	4,664	3.0	5,306	3.2	29.9
Hispanic origin							
Hispanic	20,578	13.7	24,391	15.5	28,421	17.2	38.1
Non-Hispanic	129,518	86.3	133,088	84.5	136,696	82.8	5.5
Total	150,096	100.0	157,479	100.0	165,117	100.0	10.0

Women 65 years old and older are the least likely to shop. The greatest growth in the female population is in the 55-to-74 age group, which is also the group least likely to shop. "Women drive the purchases of 91% of new homes, 66% of computers, 92% of vacations, 65% of new cars, 89% of bank accounts and 93% of food" ("The new consumer," 2011).

Caucasian Consumers

DEMOGRAPHICS

Currently there is little consumer research conducted on the Caucasian segment of the market. Caucasians have the lowest growth rate of all demographic groups in the United States, hence most research is conducted on the growing segments of the population, mainly Hispanics and Asians. As a result of slow growth, the population of Caucasians is aging.

SHOPPING HABITS

Caucasians like shopping in department stores, though they rarely pay full price for clothing. Additionally, because of the large population of baby boomers, there is demand for more stores that cater to women over the age of 25. Most Caucasians concede that they have a hard time finding clothes they think flatter them, making shopping for clothes a chore rather than fun. Whites purchase more pants than other demographic groups due to their significant presence in the corporate world. Whites also prefer easy-care fabrics and classic styles (Mintel).

African American Consumers

FASHION ATTITUDE

Mintel, a leading market intelligence company, reports that fashion is a form of self-expression used by African Americans to influence the way the world sees them; telling the world who they are as an individual without seeking approval or acceptance of others. African Americans,

regardless of age, believe appearance is important. Appearance is a way of fighting negative stereotypes and fostering self-esteem. As a result, brands are not a primary motivator
for a purchase, although African American consumers are influenced by music videos and
celebrity blogs. Likewise, durability takes a backseat to looking good for African American
consumers. Many of the attitudes regarding appearance and fashion stem from the parents
of African American baby boomers. Raised by parents that suffered through segregation and
racism, African American boomers (the largest age group of the African American population by 2015) learned that African American people gain respect, and project an image of
success, by the way they dress. Younger African Americans do not necessarily share this
attitude and dress to suit their own attitudes and ideas regarding fashion.

DEMOGRAPHICS

Mintel reports that the growth rate for African Americans is anticipated to be about 12 percent from 2005 to 2015, a rate that is faster than Whites but lower than Hispanics and
Asians. As a race, African American have lower household incomes than other races in the
United States, with 39 percent of African American households earning less than $25,000
annually. Additionally, African American have the highest unemployment of any U.S. ethnic
group, a factor negatively impacting their income levels. African Americans are nearly six
years younger than all consumers and almost half are between 18 and 49 years old, a key
marketing group (Wasserman and O'Leary, 2010).

Whereas African Americans earn less, their buying power has increased 187 percent
from 1990 to 2008, because of their higher educational levels and the higher-paying jobs
that resulted from education. It is predicted that their buying power will reach $1.1 trillion
by 2014 and by 2013, 9 cents out of every dollar will be purchased by African Americans.
Figure 9.4 illustrates the buying power of the ethnic groups in the United States. As a result
of the recession, African American over the age of 45 reduced discretionary spending over
the last 12 months and African American over the age of 55 cut back on clothing purchases.

One retailer that is recognizing the potential in the African American market is Home
Depot. They understand that treating the African American consumer as a unique group, striv-
ing to meet their demands, opens a new and virtually untapped category of business. Part of
Home Depot's strategy is its new partnerships with Steve Harvey and Tom Joyner.

WOMEN

African American women enjoy shopping and purchasing new clothing and accessories.
A 2010 survey found that nine out of ten women have shopped, eight out of ten African American
women shopped for apparel, and working women between the ages of 35 and 54 purchased

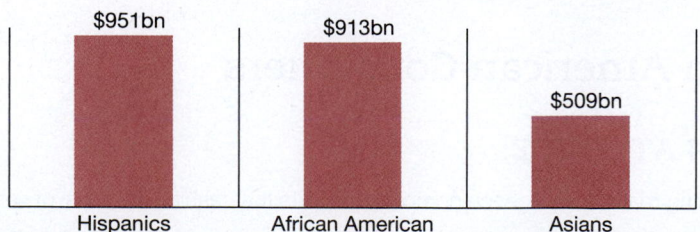

FIGURE 9.4 *Purchasing power by race/ethnicity in 2008.*

clothing from 2009 to 2010. Furthermore, two-thirds of African American women over the age of 55 have purchased apparel in the last year (Mintel).

Although it is a fact that African American women not only shop, but they also purchase, they wait for sales. African American women are not inclined to pay regular price for fashion and shop in stores that offer the best brands and labels for the best prices. Outlet malls and off-price stores appeal to African American women for this reason. Young African American women enjoy shopping in stores like Old Navy and H&M because they are fashion forward at affordable prices. Also important to African American women is feminine attire and clothing for formal events. Many occasions in the African American community, such as church services and funerals, require a dressier wardrobe (Mintel).

MEN

Mintel reports that the recession affected African American men more than any other demographic group. However, African American men, regardless of income, rarely change their spending habits. African American men over the age of 16 spend less than other African American age groups, as most of them in this age group are unemployed, work in jobs requiring uniforms, or do construction work where wardrobes are unnecessary. Interestingly, African American men between the ages of 18 and 34 are primary influencers of fashion trends but they buy less than African American men over the age of 35.

African American men convey their unique styles by dressing to express their "cool" (Mintel). "The word cool...describes anybody who marches to the beat of a different drummer...sexy, alone, mysterious, hip, self-assured, different, quiet, confident, rebellious...Cool is not just a term, it is a lifestyle" (Connor, 1995). The styles worn by African American men are emulated by the general population of young men of all races. Fashion is particularly influenced by young rap stars, not just the clothes, but also by the attitude and the swagger. Pepper Miller, author of *What's Black about It?,* states "Symbols of cool may begin with clothes, but definitely end with attitude" (Miller, 2005).

SHOPPING HABITS

African Americans like fashion and purchase more apparel and footwear per year than any other race or ethnic group. African Americans set trends, but they do not follow them. African American are early adopters, more accepting of new brands and labels, purchasing these before other groups do. For example, African Americans adopted hip-hop in the 1980s, long before the look became mainstream. The hip-hop trend symbolizes language, fashion, and culture demonstrated through rapping, deejaying, breakdancing, and hip-hop fashion. Hip-hop epitomizes the trend-setting power of the African American consumer, apparent in the twenty-first century in the urban market where fashion trends begin driving style and brand loyalty. The world has welcomed and adopted African American culture, icons, music, and fashion, and manufacturers and brands know that acceptance from African Americans means sell-through to other markets. Neil Nelson, founder of BrokenCurve, an urban technology solutions provider, put it best when he said there's a difference between "being cool" and "creating cool" (Mintel).

According to Mintel, African Americans spend a higher percentage of their income on apparel than other racial groups; however, because of the recession, many African American changed their apparel spending habits. From 2002 to 2010, African American consumer expenditures on apparel increased 15.3 percent compared to 9.7 percent by non-African American consumers. During the same time frame, average annual expenditures by African American consumers increased 30.6 percent, while non-African American increased 36 percent. This demonstrates that African American expenditures decreased, except in the area of apparel where spending increased. In hard economic times, rather than deferring purchases, African American consumers look for ways to get more for their money. Apparel purchases reach beyond the parents to the children in the family. African American parents meet the fashion needs and desires of their children before purchasing new clothing for themselves, particularly those parents earning more than $50,000 per year.

African Americans love fashion and consume fashion for fashion's sake by shopping to stay on trend and not to replace clothing. Outfits are planned for each event, and African American women purchase more dresses than Whites or Asians since dressing for church and social occasions is important. African Americans purchase apparel and accessories bearing visible designer logos and more than a third of African American women purchase men's clothing and accessories. African Americans purchase more sneakers, viewed as a fashion accessory rather than a functional item, than their White or Asian counterparts. Nike is the most popular sneaker brand. Regardless of income, stores with liberal return policies, like mid-tier department stores, discount retailers, and mass merchandisers, are preferred by African American consumers. Additionally, African American consumers enjoy shopping in outlet malls.

Hispanic Consumers

DEMOGRAPHICS

Mintel reports that Hispanics are the largest minority segment in the United States. As reported in the 2010 U.S. Census, 50 million people are of Hispanic origin, which calculates to 16.3 percent of the entire U.S. population. By 2050, the estimated number of Hispanics is 102 million, or 25 percent of the U.S. population. Between 2005 and 2010, the number of Hispanic women will grow by 38.1 percent. Most Hispanics are of Mexican heritage; however, a portion of the U.S. Hispanic population hails from Puerto Rico and Cuba. Sixty percent of Hispanics living in the United States are natives. The chart in Figure 9.5 details the demographics of the U.S. Hispanic population. In 2006, 2.47 people lived in non-Hispanic households compared with 3.34 people living in Hispanics households. Family is a valued and treasured part of Hispanic culture and it is common for family members, other than the nuclear family, to live in the same house. Furthermore, Hispanics have many children under the age of 14.

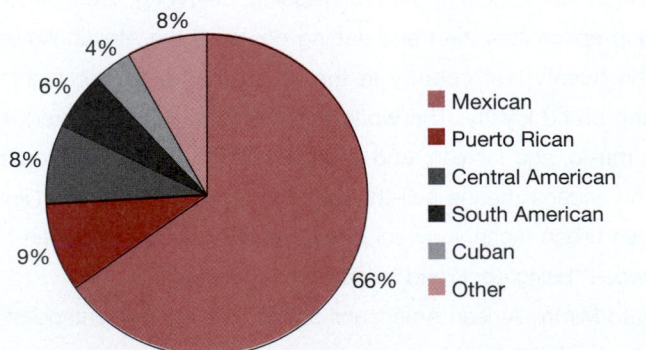

FIGURE 9.5 *Native origin of the U.S. Hispanic population.*

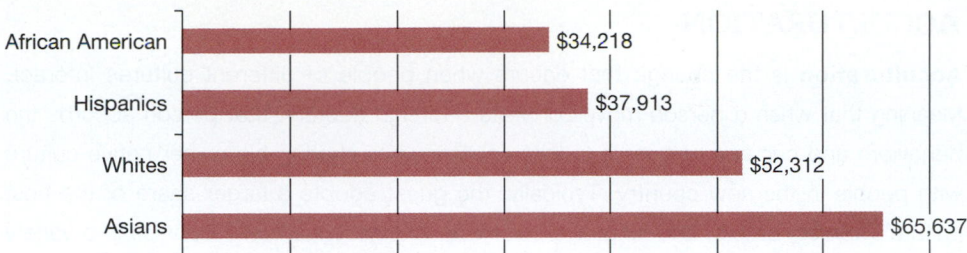

FIGURE 9.6 *Household income in 2006 by race.*

The Hispanic population is growing but household incomes for Hispanics remain lower than for other races and ethnic groups, except African Americans. Figure 9.6 depicts household income by ethnicity. The majority of Hispanic households earn less than $50,000, with the average household income in the neighborhood being $38,000 per year. About 32 percent of Hispanic households earn less than $25,000. Lack of education and jobs in unskilled or semi-skilled labor positions contribute to lower Hispanic income levels. That said, in recent years, income levels before taxes increased 10 percent due to increased immigration and education (Mintel). Furthermore, the projected buying power for Hispanics is forecasted to increase from $1 trillion this year to $1.5 trillion in 2015 (Lockwood, 2011).

The increased buying power and population growth of Hispanics has caught the attention of retailers and national brands such as Macy's, Walmart, Dillard's, J.C. Penney, Kohl's, Kmart, Sears, and L'Oreal. Fashion assortments tailored for the Hispanic customer, combined with advertising campaigns, demonstrate this demographic group's growing strength in the fashion industry. The photograph in Figure 9.7 illustrates Walmart's efforts to appeal to their Hispanic customer base. In 2009, Penney's spent $50 million and Walmart spent $66.1 million toward advertising directed at the Hispanic market (Lockwood, 2011). Jennifer Lopez and Marc Anthony, in partnership with Kohl's, are developing a lifestyle brand aimed at Hispanics. Marc Seichert, chief marketing officer at L'Oreal, commented, "For us, Hispanic consumers are a very, very important target. We see it as a growth opportunity for the future" (Elliott, 2011).

FIGURE 9.7 *Walmart caters to its Hispanic clientele by using bilingual signs throughout their stores (Source: Alamy).*

ACCULTURATION

Acculturation is the change that occurs when people of different cultures interact. Meaning that when a person moves or visits a foreign country, that person absorbs the behaviors and cultures of people in that country while sharing his or her native culture with people in the new country. Typically, the guest adopts a larger share of the host culture's values, beliefs, and language but Hispanics influence non-Hispanics in a variety of ways. The U.S. environment and culture is diverse and because Hispanics have a low rate of acculturation, they earn lower wages and salaries. Strong indicators of acculturation include language and computer ownership and skills. Language is more predictive of consumer buying behaviors. As a group, Hispanics own fewer computers and as a result, have a deficiency in computer skills. The acculturation rate among Hispanics is expected to remain about the same due to the steady immigration rate and the tendency of some Latinos to become fluent in English (Mintel).

SHOPPING HABITS

As the largest minority consumer group with growth that surpasses African American and Asians, Latinos' spending is following suit. Education, food, and apparel are the highest categories of spending for Hispanics. Latinos spend a great deal of time shopping because shopping is viewed as inexpensive entertainment. Because of this and their cultural tendency to live in multigenerational households, they shop and consume in groups; however, Hispanics from Puerto Rico and Cuban exhibit buying patterns closer to those of non-Hispanics. Extremely acculturated Hispanics display buying behaviors more like average U.S. citizens.

Hispanics view appearance as a sign of success and therefore enjoy being fashionable and trendy. This is evident in the fact that Hispanic women spend an average of $717 on apparel per year, more than non-Hispanic women, who spend $582 per year. As a group, Hispanics are the least practical when it comes to purchasing. However, mass merchandisers are preferred by Hispanics and they are likely to shop at fast-fashion stores. Hispanics like stores with bilingual signs and loyalty programs and they do not frequent warehouse club-type stores. Hispanics like merchandise that is tied to supporting a cause and are very receptive to advertising with a culturally pertinent message. Latinos make high-ticket purchases without research, which is tied to their lack of computer skills, hence an aversion to shopping online.

Hispanics buy large amounts of children's clothing because they are a young population with a lot of children. Latinos buy more tops because tops are an affordable way to update one's wardrobe. Lots of jeans are purchased because many Hispanics work in blue-collar jobs where jeans are appropriate. Hispanics are fans of garments with visible designer logos since appearance is important to this group and logos are status symbols (Mintel).

Asian Consumers

DEMOGRAPHICS

The Asian cohort is the fastest growing racial minority in the United States and Asian households are larger than the U.S. average, second only to Hispanics. The 32–43 age group, or Gen X, is the largest for Asians but it is the female gender that is experiencing the most rapid growth. Chinese is the largest Asian American group followed by Asian Indians, Filipinos,

FIGURE 9.8 *Top six nationality/ancestral groups in Asia in population and percentage to the total Asian population (Source: Mintel).*

Nationality/ancestral group	Population	% of Asian Population
Chinese (excluding Taiwanese)	2,998,849	22.4
Asian Indian	2,495,998	18.6
Filipino	2,425,697	18.1
Vietnamese	1,431,980	10.7
Korean	1,344,267	10.0
Japanese	710,063	5.3

Vietnamese, and Koreans (Figure 9.8). Forty-seven percent of Asian Americans live in the West and the Bureau of Labor Statistics reports that 99.3 percent of Asian Americans live in metropolitan areas. Asians are very family oriented and most marry and stay married more than the average U.S. citizen.

According to Mintel, Asians are the most affluent of any demographic group, earning roughly double the median income of African Americans and Hispanics and about 25 percent more than the median income of Whites. Forty-five percent of Asian households earn more than $75,000 per year and are twice as likely as the national average to have a household income of more than $150,000. Japanese, Indians, and Filipinos are the largest earning groups of Asians with a median income of $70,000. Furthermore, Asian women earn more than White, African American, or Hispanic women, with their median weekly incomes being 5 percent higher than White women, 22 percent higher than African American women, and 46 percent higher than Hispanic women. Asian American purchasing power is $509 billion and is expected to continue to rise through 2013.

Asians value professional success and are twice as likely as other Americans to have master's degrees and professional degrees, and almost three times as likely to have a doctorate. Forty-three percent of Asians have college degrees and 6.5 percent have a law, medicine, or doctorate degree. When compared to the total U.S. statistic of 27.6 percent of all U.S. adults aged 25 or older that had a minimum of a bachelor's degree in 2008, the Asian emphasis on education is apparent. Approximately 26 percent of Asians work in sales, operations, and support jobs while about 24 percent work in blue-collar jobs.

ACCULTURATION

Asians are the most acculturated minority in the United States. As a group, Asians take on the American culture and way of life while preserving their native traditions. Even Asians born in the United States uphold their original culture in the household while maintaining the American lifestyle. Asian Americans possess excellent English-speaking skills that allow them to succeed in professions where the lack of English skills prevents the success of other minority groups. In fact, the Japanese are more likely to speak only English in their homes (Mintel).

SHOPPING HABITS

Mintel reports that it is likely that the Asian demographic made a purchase in 2009. Asians seek out high-quality products and prefer brand names and remain loyal to favorite brands.

FIGURE 9.9 *Eileen Fisher advertisement featuring an Asian model (Source: Eileen Fisher).*

Asians shop at a variety of retailers for bargains and deals, and more often than not, they shop in groups. They are proficient with computer technology and use the Internet for shopping, socializing, entertainment, staying abreast of current events, and conducting product research. Sixty-five percent of Asians use the Internet for product research. Asian men and women use the Internet to purchase their personal preferences. Asian men purchase entertainment items like DVDs, music, and video games whereas Asian women buy books and fashion. Asians are sensitive to promotional efforts featuring Asian models and those companies that join efforts with humanitarian causes. Eileen Fisher seized an opportunity to tap into the potential of the Asian demographic segment by offering expensive clothes in ads featuring Asian models and campaigning for a humanitarian cause (Figure 9.9).

International Consumers

Fashion is important to the citizens of the world; it generates revenue, creates profit streams, and employs millions of people. Sixty-seven percent of the people in the world report that they enjoy shopping for clothes. India leads the pack in the love of shopping, followed by Brazil, Columbia, Italy, Turkey, Japan, China, Germany, Great Britain, Thailand, and the United States. In 2009, total fashion revenues produced totaled $2.9 billion including sales in textiles, apparel, and accessories. Fashion took a hit during the 2008/2009 recession and many fashion-related businesses suffered. However, industry forecasts show growth between 2009 and 2014 bringing the industry to $3.9 billion by 2014. Industry growth will occur domestically and globally as more and more firms take their brands into new international venues (Datamonitor). When firms expand into foreign countries globalization occurs. Globalization is a hot topic for all industries and is defined from an economic fashion perspective as the connectivity of countries through international trade. When taking a brand global, firms discuss how to work across cultures and the impact of taking a brand global.

The three major players in the international fashion scene include Europe, Asia-Pacific countries, and the United States (previously discussed). An examination of each of these regions yields information about fashion attitudes, buying power, and the importance of fashion to each economy. An analysis of each noteworthy country within each region sheds light on the contributions and significance of each country.

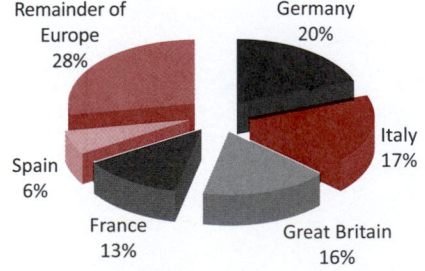

FIGURE 9.10 *The market segmentation of the European retail apparel industry.*

Europe

Europe is a continent rich in diversity reflected in lifestyles, food, and of course, fashion. The fashion industry contribution to the European economy is great. Several countries, Germany, Italy, United Kingdom, France, and Spain, lead Europe with approximately 72 percent of the apparel sales with the remainder of Europe producing about 28 percent of apparel sales. The pie chart in Figure 9.10 depicts the segmentation of the European retail apparel industry (Datamonitor, 2009).

GERMANY

Germany is not the first European country one might connect to fashion. However, Germany sells more apparel than any other European countries: It represents 20 percent of apparel sales in Europe. In 2009, total apparel income in Germany was $75 million with slow growth predicted. Women's wear is the top category of business (56 percent), followed by menswear (30 percent), and children's wear (14 percent). The fashion industry plays an important role in Germany because of the employment and revenue produced (Datamonitor, 2009).

Germany has a long and contentious history with fashion. As far back as the mid-eighteenth century, French fashion was the yardstick by which all fashion was measured and upper-class German women took note by filling their closets with French clothing. German women loved French fashion so German designers traveled to Paris to see the shows, buy prototypes, and take the pulse of the French fashion scene, bringing home these looks to their German consumers. Several German leaders throughout history sought to stop the influx of French fashion into Germany, including Frederick the Great, who ruled the leading German state of Prussia from 1740 to 1786. Frederick the Great attempted to stop this trend by promoting Prussia's domestic textile industry and instating corporal punishment for women caught wearing French fashions. Hitler also decried French fashion while also declaring that German women should be the best-dressed women in Europe. Since the reunification of Germany in 1989–1990, German designers and brands, such as Jil Sander, Escada, Hugo Boss, and Wolfgang Joop (Figure 9.11), have seen success in the global fashion industry.

FIGURE 9.11 *Wolfgang Joop, one of Germany's premier fashion designers (Source: Alamy).*

ITALY

The Italian fashion industry includes clothing, leather, textiles, leather processing, and shoes. The fashion industry has suffered, like the United States, from the outsourcing of production, mainly to China. Also, the skyrocketing price of leather has been detrimental to the Italian fashion business. Italy represents 17 percent of apparel sales in Europe with sales of $67 million in 2009 (Datamonitor, 2009). Women's wear is the most fruitful classification of business, followed by menswear and children's wear (Datamonitor). Figure 9.12 depicts the segmentation of Italy's retail apparel market.

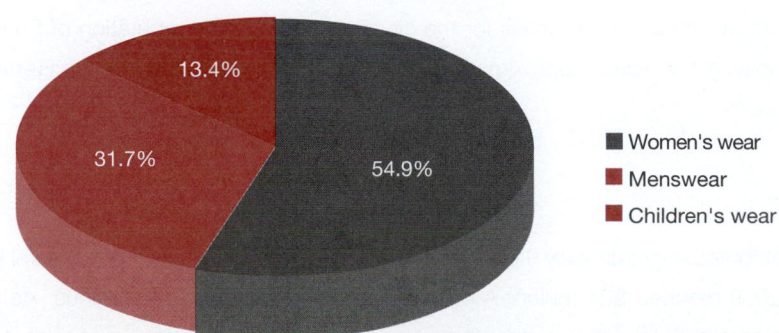

- 13.4%
- 31.7%
- 54.9%

■ Women's wear
■ Menswear
■ Children's wear

FIGURE 9.12 *Italy's retail apparel market segmented by classification.*

THE UNITED KINGDOM

The United Kingdom's retail apparel industry is also weakening. Total revenue in 2009 amounted to $63 million, a decrease from 2008. Slow growth is predicted between 2009 and 2014, with sales likely to reach $67 million by the end of 2014. As with Germany and Italy, women's wear is the most sales-producing classification, with menswear and children's wear rounding out second and third place. Approximately 16 percent of retail apparel sales in Europe occur in Great Britain (Datamonitor, 2009).

FRANCE

The French, known for fashion, produce fewer retail apparel sales than Germany, Italy, or the United Kingdom, creating sales of $49 million in 2009 or 13 percent of total European sales. This is a surprising discovery given the reputation of Paris and the well-known love of fashion by the French. Furthermore, the industry has been declining since 2008. Retail apparel sales will remain relatively flat, topping out at $50 million by the end of 2014. Women's wear accounts for over 50 percent of the retail apparel sales in France (Datamonitor, 2009).

Fashion in France became dominant in Europe in the mid-seventeenth century during the reign of Louis XIV (as discussed in Chapter 1). The government owned and operated the clothing industry, including production and sales. Throughout the turbulent times of World War I and World War II, Paris maintained its reputation as the fashion capital of the world. During the nineteenth century, Paris was the center of all things in good taste, including fashion and art. The nineteenth century also saw the creation of trade associations and a hierarchy for those involved in the production of clothes, the backbone of the French fashion industry. It was during the latter half of the nineteenth century that haute couture was born (see Chapter 1).

In 1973, the French organized the "Fédération Française de la Couture, du Prêt-à-Porter des Couturiers et des Créateurs de Mode." The "Fédération," as it is known, serves to maintain the integrity and culture of the French fashion industry. The 1980s brought prêt-à-porter (or ready-to-wear), a new level of business to French fashion that supplemented the small couture business. Designers used the couture shows to elevate the profitable and desirable ready-to-wear shows. Licensed products, such as accessories and fragrances, also benefited and profited from the elite and extravagant shows.

French fashion and other luxury goods remain crucial to the survival of the French economy. Furthermore, luxury products, like fragrances and cosmetics, are highly desired and sought after, globally enhancing French exports. Designers from all over the world seek to show in Paris to legitimize and strengthen their place in the world of high fashion. Likewise, the Paris shows mean big business for the city and enhance the reputation of Paris as the fashion capital of the world. Approximately 200,000 people are employed in the French luxury goods industry.

SPAIN

Spain contributes approximately 6 percent of the sales in the European retail apparel industry. Sales in 2009 reached $24 million. A decline in sales is expected to continue. As with the other European countries discussed, women's wear is the leading category of sales, trailed by menswear and children's wear (Datamonitor, 2009).

Fashion is an important industry to Spain and efforts exist to encourage its growth with private and public sectors working to see success in the industry. The Spanish government supports fashion with publicity campaigns. In addition, Barcelona and Madrid sponsor the Cibeles and 080 fashion shows for young designers. Several companies have become global fashion leaders in the early twenty-first century. Mango and Zara (Figure 9.13) offer trendsetting fashion at affordable prices in a retail venue called "fast fashion." Though endeavors to elevate Spanish fashion indicate signs of achievement, globalization of other fashion brands and the deregulation of the Spanish market in 2005 that enabled Chinese-made products to flood Spain, caused a decline in the Spanish fashion textiles and apparel markets.

FIGURE 9.13 *Zara, a Spanish retailer, is a global retailer of "fast fashion." (Source: Dreamstime).*

Asia-Pacific

The Asia-Pacific region is the largest retail market in the world, a designation that is unlikely to change with population growth of almost 5 percent between 2005 and 2009. Analysts predict that retail sales in the region will surmount retail in Europe and North America in the next two years and be the second-largest economy in the world by 2035. China, Japan, India, and South Korea lead the region in retail sales supplying 92 percent of sales. Within this group, China and Japan are the heavy hitters at 39 percent and 37 percent respectively, leaving India and South Korea at a combined 17 percent of the total. However, India is a market that cannot be disregarded. The combined remaining countries in the region contribute 8 percent. Asia-Pacific retail apparel sales totaled $264 billion in 2009, a 3 percent increase over 2008. Sales increases will continue through 2014 where sales expectations exceed $307 billion. The category of women's wear is 48.5 percent of total sales, followed by menswear at 35 percent, and children's wear at 17 percent. The saturation of women's wear is lower than in European countries where the average is over 50 percent of sales (Datamonitor, 2009).

CHINA

China, with 1.4 billion people, is the largest market in the region. It is a retail hotbed with three massive retailers, Tesco, Walmart, and Carrefour, doing business there. The Chinese enjoy shopping in a wide variety of retail venues including department stores, which saw a rise in shoppers in 2009. The Chinese prefer to shop in brick-and-mortar stores as seen in the slow start to online shopping. Part of the reason for this is that fewer Chinese people use credit cards, but as credit card usage increases, so does online purchasing. China is a country of savers and using credit cards is directly opposed to the Chinese culture. MasterCard is betting that China will exceed the United States in credit card usage by 2020 because of the country's rapid urbanization. According to Cotton Incorporated's Lifestyle Monitor, Chinese consumers value selection in apparel more than price. Likewise important to the discussion of fashion in China is a change in attitude regarding shopping by the Chinese. As a communist country, capitalism and consumption had evil connotations, but recently their attitudes have changed and shopping is viewed as a pleasurable

FIGURE 9.14 *Grand opening of a Louis Vuitton store in Zhengzhou City, China, January 2011 (Source: Newscom).*

and acceptable experience. According to Linda Lee, "China's fundamental value shift from communism to capitalism to consumerism has unleashed a new consumer with preferences towards brands." Additionally, the Chinese value appearance and feel that fashion is a way of communicating to the world their status in life.

The booming Chinese luxury market is a testament to price as a secondary consideration when purchasing and the rising number of people with a high net worth can afford luxury merchandise. "Wealth is being created in China at a rate exceeding anywhere else," according to Howard Davidowitz, chairman of retail consultancy and investment banking firm Davidowitz & Associates. "Today's newly rich luxury shoppers are young and eager to show off their social standing and prosperity in China. This is a youthful nation with a majority population between the ages of 25–40 years. They aspire to have more and better global designer brands as a symbol of social status, wealth, and style," according to Linda Lee's paper *Wrapped in Fur: China's Luxury Consumer*, 2010. This group has a voracious appetite for luxury goods, creating seemingly unstoppable growth. The Chinese market for luxury goods, is so lucrative that Prada made the controversial decision to launch an initial public offering (IPO) in Hong Kong instead of its home city Milan. The Chinese enthusiasm for luxury products is credited with saving the luxury goods industry during the economic downturn that began in 2008. Additionally, because the Chinese market proved itself to be profitable, many luxury retailers have expanded to China. Cotton Incorporated's Lifestyle Monitor reports that 53 percent of new luxury goods locations have opened in the last three years in China. Armani, Hermes, Chanel, and Valentino expanded beyond the top-tier markets in China to second- and third-tier markets in China. Figure 9.14 is a photograph of the grand opening of the Louis Vuitton store in Zhengzhou City, China, in January 2011.

Collectivism (an idea that decisions are made for the good of the group rather than the individual) and culture play a large part in the decision-making process of Chinese consumers. Collectivism and conformity go hand in hand and influence Chinese consumers to relegate individual tastes and conform to the masses. For many in China, it is more important to "save face" and present one's self with honor than to "lose face" and suffer disgrace. In recent years, however, 74.5 percent of urban Chinese residents surveyed reported that they wanted apparel and accessories that projected their personal tastes indicating a loosening of conformity. If a society's foundation is conformity, it is important to consider collectivism with regards to consumer behavior in China and other Asian countries when planning assortments and advertising efforts.

China led the way in GDP for the region in 2010, posting a 10 percent rise in GDP and a 35 percent rise in imports and there are no signs that China's economy is slowing down. Imports to the United States continue to rise with a value of $34 billion in 2011 ("Trade in goods," 2012). China's GDP is forecasted to grow by 10 percent and China will overtake Japan as the number-one economy in the region. In addition to GDP, China's population increased by just over 2 percent from 2005 to 2009, taking China's population to 42 percent of the world's total population, and according to Cotton Incorporated's Lifestyle Monitor, two-thirds of Chinese people enjoy shopping (Datamonitor, 2009).

JAPAN

Japan is the largest economy in the Asia-Pacific region. Seventy percent of Japanese people report that they "like" or "love" shopping according to Cotton Incorporated's Lifestyle Monitor. However, in recent years Japan has experienced lethargic economic growth and forecasted growth is lackluster. Growth is inhibited by huge debt incurred through government spending that hovers around 200 percent of GDP. Japan is counting on exports to stimulate its economy and boost consumer confidence. Yet, Japan's export trade is dependent on Europe whose financial footing is precarious. Furthermore, the Japanese population is contracting.

The Japanese apparel industry sales slightly declined from that of 2008 to $97 million in 2009, a trend seen for several years now. Women's wear is the overwhelming producer of sales, representing 66 percent of the total industry. Menswear and children's wear follow at 23 percent and 11 percent, respectively. The outlook for apparel sales in Japan is bleak, and because of increased competition of low-priced operators, prices are projected to fall (Datamonitor, 2009).

INDIA

India is on the brink of becoming a global economic power but governmental restrictions have prevented global retail growth, and unless the government sees fit to relax regulations, progress will remain impeded. But India does not seem to be concerned with global economic growth as seen in its refusal to export cotton, causing the increase in cotton prices worldwide with far-reaching effects throughout the fashion industry. Even so, India has a 6 percent share in the U.S. apparel and textile import market (Ellis, 2011a).

India's retail apparel sales totaled $28 million in 2009, a healthy growth of 9 percent over 2008. Projections have retail apparel sales in India reaching $40.5 million by 2014. Unlike any other country discussed in this text, India's primary category of retail sales is menswear. Menswear represented 42 percent of retail apparel sales in 2009, followed by women's wear at 36 percent and children's wear at 22 percent. India enjoys a healthy economy and a growth of 8.5 percent is expected. Likewise, India experienced the largest population growth of all Asia-Pacific countries between 2005 and 2009 with 7.5 percent growth (Datamonitor).

India has 5,000 years of tradition behind its fashion industry, and through globalization and industrialization, India has managed to remain true to its heritage, even as it incorporates modern fashion trends. A dichotomy of style exists as garments are made from indigenous textiles using centuries-old techniques but combining other-worldly influences as well, displaying clearly that past and present harmoniously coexist in Indian fashion. Beautiful and superbly crafted Indian textiles remain, after agriculture, the country's largest source of employment.

In 1947 when India attained independence, women could be classified as being traditional and Westernized from the way they dressed. Fashionable women wore saris (like the one pictured in Figure 9.15), a trend validated by Indira Gandhi, who for 35 years was photographed wearing saris. In the 1960s, casual wear became acceptable and Jackie Kennedy's fashion influence

FIGURE 9.15 *Woman wearing a traditional Indian sari (Source: Shutterstock).*

infiltrated India, as it did the rest of the world. In the 1970s, Western influences gained popularity once again and blue jeans topped the list of wanted items. During this time, men and women wore garments in tie-dyed fabrics and grew their hair long. In the 1980s, a series of International Festivals of India in the United States, the United Kingdom, Europe, and Japan promoted Indian textiles and emphasized India's extraordinary legacy of beauty and craftsmanship. Furthermore, the government recognized the capacity of the textiles industry to improve economic conditions in India during a time of recession and drought. The mid-1990s ushered in a more broadminded era and many foreign brands entered India's market, causing remarkable changes in Indian fashion. Satellite television exposed the Indian audience to MTV and other Western television shows and enticed Indian consumers with advertisements for Western products, creating an increasing demand for Western dress while ethnic dress declined in popularity. Indian fashion has managed to maintain its own identity and remain true to the heritage and tradition of its amazing textile industry, while the country has also recognized the potential of their textile industry to make India a force in the global fashion industry (Tyabji, 2007).

SOUTH KOREA

Apparel at retail produced $15 million in revenue in South Korea in 2009. Women's wear accounted for 48 percent of the revenue with menswear and children's wear at 39 percent and 13 percent, respectively. Retail apparel sales were strong in 2009 showing a 3 percent increase; however, the growth slowed from 2006 to 2009. The pattern of smaller sales increases reflects South Korea's declining economy (Datamonitor, 2009).

Attitudes about fashion and dressing have evolved for hundreds of years in South Korea. Missionaries and Western workers working in Korea introduced Western dress to the country in the mid-1870s. As South Korea modernized, women took on public roles and in the early 1900s women's dress began to change. Between 1910 and 1915, the Japanese took over and settled in South Korea and the way people dressed changed; many adopted Western styles while others wore standardized Japanese-styled clothes. Acceptance and popularization of Western fashion spread rapidly after emancipation in 1945. In 1956, Korea saw its first fashion show featuring creations from designer Nora Noh, which changed the idea of dressing for many women. During this time, stylish men wore suits made of imported English fabric in black or dark blue with white shirts. The revolution in 1960 prompted the government to develop the economy and work on its relations with Japan. The new economic plan was successful and saw exports hit $1 million. In the mid-1970s, foreign fashion became more accepted and encouraged with fashion design becoming specialized. It was during this time the Korea Federation of Textile Industries (KOFOTI) and Korea Fashion Association (KFA) were formed and universities increased the number of apparel and textile programs (Kim).

Korean society is ecofriendly and that philosophy carries into fashion. The Korean design is characterized by simple lines and refinement in off-white colors free of embellishment. The idea of Korean fashion is frugality and restraint. Layering is an important aspect of Korean dress (Kim).

Examining consumers by country is insightful when looking at the macroeconomic marketplace. But, dividing consumer groups into smaller sections yields a deeper understanding of smaller consumer groups within larger groups. Customer/market segmentation is examined in the next section.

Customer/Market Segmentation

Customer/market segmentation is the process of dividing a market based on customer need, grouping those with similar needs and demands and thus, allowing better service for customers. Segmentation permits a firm to define the competition and their position in the marketplace as well as their own. Segmentation improves a company's competitive position and is useful for making better use of a firm's resources.

For segmentation to prove useful, the segments must be definable, sizable, reachable, relevant, and homogeneous. By following this blueprint, firms better understand the target market and are able to fine-tune the product's message. The information gained by segmentation is beneficial in designing products that meet the needs in the marketplace, determining promotional strategies that drive sales in a cost-efficient manner, allowing for the analysis of the competition and their market position, and shedding light on marketing strategies.

Segmentation is a useful tool when managed correctly, but there are shortcomings. It is difficult to measure a customer's emotions, which change often and hinder brand loyalty. Besides the fickle nature of customers, other drawbacks exist as well. Segmentation is expensive and the usefulness of the added cost must be weighed against the derived benefits. Segmentation is also a major commitment for corporations; it is not a short-term endeavor. Lastly, segmentation paints a composite portrait of customers rather than specific individual profiles.

There are various forms of segmentation such as demographics, geographics, and psychographics. The topic of segmentation is several generations old, and several theories and methods exist. The chapter later examines Geert Hofstede™, VALS™ profiles, and Claritas PRISM™.

Demographics

Demographics studies human populations and their vital characteristics from a statistical point of view. The U.S. Census collects demographic information every ten years. Updated information is reported for certain locales between each census. Demographical information includes the population by area, and for the entire United States, age, gender, race, household and family income, the number of households, and household size. Population, race, gender, and age projections demonstrate trends and changes in the composition of citizens in the United States. Demographics reveals to fashion companies shifts taking place that influence the merchandise offered. Figure 9.16 illustrates the numerous demographic groups in the United States. As previously discussed, the Hispanic group is the fastest growing group in the United States. It is incumbent on astute fashion firms to plan for and react to this information. They must ask themselves how this shift changes product offerings, size ranges, and color selections, to name a few.

FIGURE 9.16 *Demographical statistics in the United States include race, national origin, age, occupation, and income (Source: Alamy).*

Geographics

Geographics studies a population based on physical attributes or local. It is an easy division of markets and an important tool since where people live impacts their buying behaviors. For example, because of climate, people living in New England purchase more outerwear than people living in the Southeast, a critical factor for outerwear manufacturers and retailers. Apparel retailers often allocate merchandise to stores based on geographical location to ensure that the proper types and quantities of merchandise arrive in the appropriate stores. **Geodemographics**, the fusion of demographics and geographics, examines where people live, what they do for a living, their education levels, ethnic background, and age.

Psychographics

The study of **psychographics** started in the late 1960s and early 1970s. Psychographics uses lifestyle, social class, values, attitudes, and other psychological attributes to figure out what people believe, think, and the values they hold as a portal to predicting customer behavior. The psychological, sociological, and anthropological information gleaned determines how the market is segmented by groups within the market and the decisions they make about a product, person, or ideology. Marketers use psychographics to understand current and potential customers because psychographics enlightens marketers about product use—who is using the product and how the product is used. The use of psychographics helps a marketer identify target markets, understand consumer behavior, develop strategic marketing plans, and minimize risk in the marketplace. Psychographic data is difficult and expensive to collect and everyone does not agree about its usefulness or validity.

VALS™

In the 1960s, consumer futurist Arnold Mitchell sought to explain the fragmentation of society and its impact on society and the economy. His work led to the present-day **VALS™** survey. "VALS™ identifies the psychological motivations that predict consumer differences. VALS™ uses proprietary psychometric techniques to measure concepts that researchers have proved empirically to correlate with consumer behavior" (About VALS, n.d.). The VALS™ survey segments adults in the United States into eight groups by using psychological traits and demographic information to explain consumer behavior. It further categorizes customers based on primary motivations and resources (education, intelligence, income, health, self-confidence, eagerness to buy, and energy level). Primary motivations include ideals, achievement, and self-expression. Individuals motivated by ideals seek guidance from knowledge and principles. Achievement-oriented people look for status symbols and other signs to prove their success to peers. Consumers driven by self-expression pursue physical and social activity, variety, and risk. Resources certainly include financial means and education; however, intelligence, innovativeness, impulsiveness, leadership, energy, leadership, and vanity fall into the resources category as well. "Resources enhance or constrain a person's expression of his or her primary motivation" ("US framework and vals types," n.d.). VALS™ is used to develop new products, create product positioning strategies, target new markets, design ad campaigns, and predict trends.

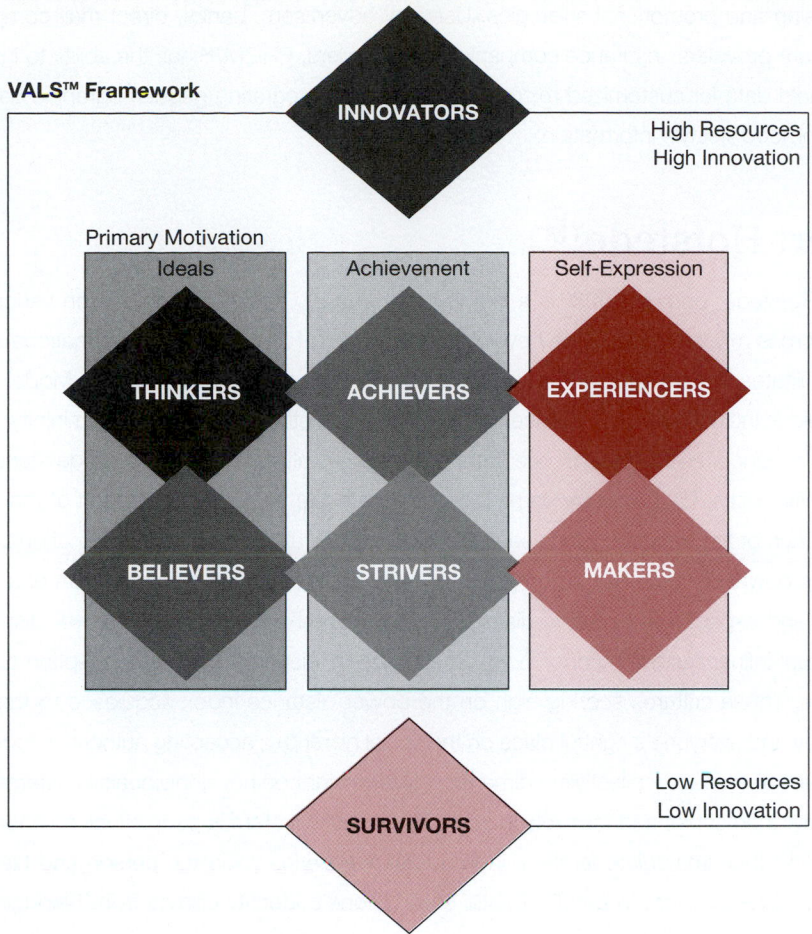

INNOVATORS

High Resources
High Innovation

Primary Motivation

Ideals

Achievement

Self-Expression

THINKERS

ACHIEVERS

EXPERIENCERS

BELIEVERS

STRIVERS

MAKERS

Low Resources
Low Innovation

SURVIVORS

FIGURE 9.17 *The VALS™ framework includes eight segments each with distinctive characteristics that segment the marketplace for a better understanding of consumers (Source: Strategic Business Insights/VAL).*

The VALS™ framework (Figure 9.17) contains eight segments, each with distinctive characteristics. The segments include innovators, thinkers, achievers, experiencers, believers, strivers, makers, and survivors. For innovators, image is important as these are successful, take-charge people with high self-esteem. Thinkers, motivated by ideals, look for practicality and functionality when making purchases. Motivated by image with a strong desire for achievement describes achievers. Self-expression and impulsiveness define experiencers. Believers are conservative and predictable, choosing familiar products and established brands. Strivers are trendy and driven by the approval of others and see shopping as a social activity. Makers are "do-it-your-selfers," suspicious of new ideas and big business. Survivors have few resources, and because of that, they are cautious consumers ("US framework and vals types," n.d.).

Claritas PRIZM™

In 1974 Jonathan Robbing developed the theory behind the **PRIZM™** segmentation now owned by Nielsen Claritas, Inc. The PRIZM™ method provides useful information for understanding neighborhood types, and therefore market segments. The organization of PRIZM™ is 40 neighborhood types with distinctive boundaries, values, and consuming habits, in all covering 66 segments. The information provided by PRIZM™ allows companies to understand customers' product preferences, helps in choosing locations, and offers insight when designing advertising and promotional strategies. Used by advertisers, banks, direct mail companies, healthcare providers, insurance companies, and retailers, PRIZM™ has the ability to integrate household data for customized microsegmentation by integrating geodemographic data with neighborhood lifestyle information.

Geert Hofstede™

Geert Hofstede, born in 1928, is a Dutch psychologist. Through his study on various cultures across modern nations, he developed the Model of Five Dimensions of national culture that facilitates understanding in basic value differences among cultures. The Model of Five Dimensions includes power distance, individualism/collectivism, masculinity/femininity, uncertainty avoidance, and long-term orientation of national culture that helps to understand basic value differences. Each country earns a score on a scale of 0 to 100 for each of the dimensions. Each of the five dimensions seeks to explain cultural differences among nations.

The power distance dimension is the extent to which less powerful members of a society accept and expect that power is distributed unequally. Recognizing that power distribution is unequal influences the manner in which authority is dispersed and the reception authority receives. Those cultures scoring high on the power distance index acquiesce to the social hierarchy and everyone's rightful place on the social hierarchy, accepting authority accordingly.

The individualism/collectivism dimension gives insight on how individuals in different societies view themselves and their role in that society. Individualism is people looking after themselves and their immediate families. Individualistic societies value the person and his or her need for differentiation. In a collectivistic society, one's identity comes from belonging to a social network and conforming to a larger group.

The masculinity/femininity dimension describes the dominant values of a culture. In a masculine culture, the prevailing values are success and achievement with an emphasis on status. Societies scoring low in masculinity value status less and prefer a more service-oriented nation. In a feminine culture, the principal values are caring for others and quality of life.

The uncertainty avoidance dimension explains the extent to which people feel threatened by uncertainty and ambiguity, and try to avoid these situations. Societies scoring high in uncertainty avoidance need rules, formality, and structure. Low-scoring cultures seek results and want as few rules as possible.

The long-term orientation dimension contends that there is no one truth. Cultures with high scores for long-term orientation accept change, have high degrees of perseverance, live thrifty lives, and pursue peace of mind. On the contrary, for cultures scoring high on short-term orientation, spending is more important than saving.

summary

Summary

Retailers and manufacturers of fashion goods compete in the domestic and global marketplace. The key to success lies in understanding the consumer in both venues. Domestically, the racial and ethnic complexions as well as other important demographical information like age, income, and education point those in the fashion industry to their target markets. Competing globally adds the additional challenge of culture that varies with each country. There are ways of identifying the customer, their likes, dislikes, and other preferences. VALS™ and PRIZM™ are two methods that expose the consumer from the different angles of psychology and geography for ascertaining predilections.

Key Terms

Review Questions

1. Define acculturation and give two examples.
2. Explain the differences in demographics, geographics, and psychographics.
3. Which group is the fastest growing racial/ethnic group in the United States? Which group is the slowest growing racial/ethnic group in the United States? Why is the growth rate of a particular ethnic group important?
4. Which country leads Europe in retail apparel sales?
5. Which country is the largest retail apparel market in the Asia-Pacific region?
6. In which country are designers all over the world opening stores in primary and secondary markets? What is the appeal of this country from a retail perspective?

Critical Thinking

1. Name the eight VALS™ profiles and give examples of the types of stores each profile shops and the types of merchandise purchased.
2. Name five characteristics for each race/ethnic group. Discuss the differences between each group.
3. Look up the demographics for your city. Summarize the data. What trends do you see? Describe the changes projected for the city.

Internet Activities

1. Visit the VALS™ website (http://www.strategicbusinessinsights.com/vals/presurvey.shtml) and take the VALS™ profile. What did you learn about yourself? Do you agree or disagree with the VALS™ assessment? Why or why not?
2. Visit the PRIZM™ website (http://www.claritas.com/MyBestSegments/Default.jsp) and conduct a search of your hometown zip code. In which segment did you grow up? Describe the segment.
3. Using the Geert Hofstede™ website (http://www.geert-hofstede.com/), conduct a search for one of the following countries: United States, Germany, Italy, France, Great Britain, Spain, China, Japan, India, or South Korea and summarize your findings on how the country scores on the Model of Five Dimensions.

Bibliography

About vals. (n.d.). Retrieved from http://www.strategicbusiness insights.com/vals/about.shtml

Blythe, J. (2006). *Marketing*. Thousand Oaks, CA: SAGE Publishing Inc.

Cahill, D. (2006). *Lifestyle market segmentation*. New York, NY: The Haworth Press.

Cho, H. J., Jin, B., and Cho, H. (2010). An examination of regional differences in China by socio-cultural factors, *International*

Journal of Market Research, 52(5), accessed March 26, 2011, http://web.ebscohost.com.proxy.library.vcu.edu/ehost/pdfviewer/pdfviewer?hid=14&sid=dbe40f0e-96f8-44b7-9917-7c5cfd35d4a2%40sessionmgr13&vid=28

Connor, Kim. (1995). *What is cool?: Understanding black manhood in America*. New York: Crown Publishing Group.

Datamonitor Apparel Retail in Asia-Pacific Reference Code: 0200-2005 Publication Date: December 2010, accessed March 27, 2011, http://web.ebscohost.com.proxy.library.vcu.edu/ehost/pdfviewer/pdfviewer?hid=14&sid=dbe40f0e-96f8-44b7-9917-7c5cfd35d4a2%40sessionmgr13&vid=28

Datamonitor Apparel Retail in Canada Reference Code: 0070-2005 Publication Date: May 2010, accessed March 27, 2011, http://web.ebscohost.com.proxy.library.vcu.edu/ehost/pdfviewer/pdfviewer?hid=14&sid=dbe40f0e-96f8-44b7-9917-7c5cfd35d4a2%40sessionmgr13&vid=31

Datamonitor Apparel Retail in China Reference Code: 0099-2005 Publication Date: December 2010, accessed March 27, 2011, http://web.ebscohost.com.proxy.library.vcu.edu/ehost/pdfviewer/pdfviewer?hid=14&sid=dbe40f0e-96f8-44b7-9917-7c5cfd35d4a2%40sessionmgr13&vid=32

Datamonitor Apparel Retail in France Reference Code: 0164-2005 Publication Date: May 2010, accessed March 27, 2011, http://web.ebscohost.com.proxy.library.vcu.edu/ehost/pdfviewer/pdfviewer?hid=14&sid=dbe40f0e-96f8-44b7-9917-7c5cfd35d4a2%40sessionmgr13&vid=33

Datamonitor Apparel Retail in Germany Reference Code: 0165-2005 Publication Date: May 2010, accessed March 27, 2011, http://web.ebscohost.com.proxy.library.vcu.edu/ehost/pdfviewer/pdfviewer?hid=14&sid=dbe40f0e-96f8-44b7-9917-7c5cfd35d4a2%40sessionmgr13&vid=34

Datamonitor Apparel Retail in India Reference Code: 0102-2005 Publication Date: December 2010, accessed March 27, 2011, http://web.ebscohost.com.proxy.library.vcu.edu/ehost/pdfviewer/pdfviewer?hid=14&sid=dbe40f0e-96f8-44b7-9917-7c5cfd35d4a2%40sessionmgr13&vid=38

Datamonitor Apparel Retail in Italy Reference Code: 0171-2005 Publication Date: May 2010, accessed March 27, 2011, http://web.ebscohost.com.proxy.library.vcu.edu/ehost/pdfviewer/pdfviewer?hid=14&sid=dbe40f0e-96f8-44b7-9917-7c5cfd35d4a2%40sessionmgr13&vid=39

Datamonitor Apparel Retail in Japan Reference Code: 0104-2005 Publication Date: May 2010, accessed March 27, 2011, http://web.ebscohost.com.proxy.library.vcu.edu/ehost/pdfviewer/pdfviewer?hid=14&sid=dbe40f0e-96f8-44b7-9917-7c5cfd35d4a2%40sessionmgr13&vid=40

Datamonitor Apparel Retail in South Korea Reference Code: 0117-2005 Publication Date: December 2010, accessed March 27, 2011, http://web.ebscohost.com.proxy.library.vcu.edu/ehost/pdfviewer/pdfviewer?hid=14&sid=dbe40f0e-96f8-44b7-9917-7c5cfd35d4a2%40sessionmgr13&vid=51

Datamonitor Apparel Retail in Spain Reference Code: 0180-2005 Publication Date: May 2010, accessed March 27, 2011, http://web.ebscohost.com.proxy.library.vcu.edu/ehost/pdfviewer/pdfviewer?hid=14&sid=dbe40f0e-96f8-44b7-9917-7c5cfd35d4a2%40sessionmgr13&vid=52

Datamonitor Apparel Retail in the United Kingdom Reference Code: 0183-2005 Publication Date: May 2010, accessed March 27, 2011, http://web.ebscohost.com.proxy.library.vcu.edu/ehost/pdfviewer/pdfviewer?hid=14&sid=dbe40f0e-96f8-44b7-9917-7c5cfd35d4a2%40sessionmgr13&vid=55

Datamonitor Apparel Retail in the United States Industry Profile Reference Code: 0072-2005 Publication Date: August 2009, accessed March 27, 2011, http://web.ebscohost.com.proxy.library.vcu.edu/ehost/pdfviewer/pdfviewer?hid=14&sid=dbe40f0e-96f8-44b7-9917-7c5cfd35d4a2%40sessionmgr13&vid=56

Datamonitor Apparel Retail in the United States Reference Code: 0072-2005 Publication Date: December 2010, accessed March 27, 2011, http://web.ebscohost.com.proxy.library.vcu.edu/ehost/pdfviewer/pdfviewer?hid=14&sid=dbe40f0e-96f8-44b7-9917-7c5cfd35d4a2%40sessionmgr13&vid=61

Datamonitor Global Textiles, Apparel & Luxury Goods Reference Code: 0199-1016 Publication Date: March 2010, accessed March 27, 2011, http://web.ebscohost.com.proxy.library.vcu.edu/ehost/pdfviewer/pdfviewer?hid=14&sid=dbe40f0e-96f8-44b7-9917-7c5cfd35d4a2%40sessionmgr13&vid=27

Economy watch. (n.d.). Retrieved from http://www.economywatch.com/world_economy/usa/

Elliott, S. (2011, April 5). A growing population, and target, for marketers. *The New York Times*, p. B3.

Ellis, K. (2011a, February 1). *Wwd.com*. Retrieved from http://www.wwd.com/business-news/asias-rising-tigers-3455895

Ellis, K. (2011b, March 8). *Wwd.com*. Retrieved from http://www.wwd.com/menswear-news/inflation-looms-over-apparel-industry-3544612#/article/menswear-news/inflation-looms-over-apparel-industry-3544612?page=1

Ellis, K., Casabona, L., Friedman, A., & Tran, K. (2011, January 10). *Wwd.com*. Retrieved from http://www.wwd.com/menswear-news/inflation-looms-over-apparel-industry-3544612#/article/menswear-news/inflation-looms-over-apparel-industry-3544612?page=1

Feitelbeg, R. (2010, November 2). *Wwd.com*. Retrieved from http://www.wwd.com/markets-news/nyc-rolls-out-plan-to-boost-fashion-industry-3368899

Geert Hofstede. (n.d.). Retrieved from http://www.geerthofstede.nl/

Hallwarad, J. (2007). *Gimme! The human nature of successful marketing*. Hoboken, NJ: John Wiley & Sons, Inc.

Independent retailer.com. (2011, February 15). Retrieved from http://independentretailer.com/2011/02/15/reports-says-u-s-apparel-sales-were-up-in-2010

Kahle, L., & Chiagouris, L. (1997). *Values, lifestyles, and psychographics*. Mahwah, NJ: Lawrence Erlbaum Associates Publishers.

Kotkin, J. (2010, August). The changing demographics of America, *Smithsonian Magazine*. Retrieved from http://www.

smithsonianmag.com/specialsections/40th-anniversary/The-Changing-Demographics-of-America.html?c=y&page=1

Lee, L. (2010). Wrapped in fur: China's luxury consumer, Unpublished Paper.

Lockwood, L. (2011, March 23). Hispanics seen as key market. *WWD*. Retrieved from http://www.wwd.com/markets-news/hispanic-buying-power-a-desirable-force-3562337#/article/markets-news/hispanic-buying-power-a-desirable-force-3562337?page=1

McGauran, A. (2001). Retail is detail: Cross-national variation in the character of retail selling in Paris and Dublin, *International Review of Retail, Distribution & Consumer Research*, 11(4), 437–458, doi:10.1080/09593960110073304, accessed March 27, 2011, http://web.ebscohost.com.proxy.library.vcu.edu/ehost/detail?hid=14&sid=dbe40f0e-96f8-44b7-9917-7c5cfd35d4a2%40sessionmgr13&vid=79&bdata=JkF1dGhUeXBlPWlwLHVybCxjb29raWUsdWlkJnNpdGU9ZWhvc3QtbGl2ZSZzY29wZT1zaXRl#db=bth&AN=5253953

Miller, P. (2005). *What's black about it?* Ithaca, NY: Paramount Market Publishing.

Miller, R. K., & Washington, K. (2011). Buying influences. In *Consumer behavior* (pp. 48–52). Richard K. Miller & Associates. Retrieved from EBSCOhost, Accessed March 27, 2011, http://web.ebscohost.com.proxy.library.vcu.edu/ehost/detail?hid=14&sid=dbe40f0e-96f8-44b7-9917-7c5cfd35d4a2%40sessionmgr13&vid=71&bdata=JkF1dGhUeXBlPWlwLHVybCxjb29raWUsdWlkJnNpdGU9ZWhvc3QtbGl2ZSZzY29wZT1zaXRl#db=bth&AN=58591670

Mooij, M. (2004). *Consumer behavior and culture consequences for global marketing and advertising*. Thousand Oaks, CA: SAGE Publications.

Ranieri, C. (2010, March 29). *Wwd.com*. Retrieved from http://www.wwd.com/footwear-news/italian-leather-firms-look-to-china-3016083

Song, K., & Fiore, A. (2008). Tradition meets technology: Can mass customization succeed in China? *Journal of Advertising Research*, 48(4), 506–522, doi:10.2501/S0021849908080586, accessed March 27, 2011, http://web.ebscohost.com.proxy.library.vcu.edu/ehost/detail?hid=14&sid=dbe40f0e-96f8-44b7-9917-7c5cfd35d4a2%40sessionmgr13&vid=86&bdata=JkF1dGhUeXBlPWlwLHVybCxjb29raWUsdWlkJnNpdGU9ZWhvc3QtbGl2ZSZzY29wZT1zaXRl#db=bth&AN=35651369

The new consumer. (2011). *Sphere Trading*. Retrieved from https://www.inforummichigan.org/sites/default/files/uploads/Inforum%20-%20The%20New%20Consumer.pdf

Tyabji, L. (2007, October). Fashion in post-independence India. *Outlook*, Retrieved from http://www.bergfashionlibrary.com.proxy.library.vcu.edu/view/bewdf/BEWDF

US framework and vals types. (n.d.). Retrieved from http://www.strategicbusinessinsights.com/vals/ustypes.shtml

U.S. Census Bureau. (2010). *State and county quick facts*. Retrieved from http://quickfacts.census.gov/qfd/states/00000.html

U.S. Census Bureau, Foreign Trade. (2012). *Trade in goods with China*. Retrieved from http://www.census.gov/foreign-trade/balance/c5700.html

Wasserman, T., & O'Leary, N. (2010). Report shows a shifting African-American population. *Brandweek*, 51(2), 6.

Weinstein, A. (1994). *Market segmentation using demographics, psychographics, and other niche marketing techniques to predict and model customer behavior*. Chicago, IL: Probus Publishing Company.

THE ECONOMIC
IMPACT OF INTERNATIONAL
FASHION CENTERS

OBJECTIVES

After reading this chapter, you will be able to:

- Understand the importance of fashion centers
- Identify and explore the purpose of a fashion center
- Discuss the four top fashion centers in the world
- Examine fashion shows, their importance, and cost
- Investigate the economic impact of fashion shows locally and globally

A fashion that does not reach the streets is not a fashion.
—COCO CHANEL

Introduction

Fashion centers throughout the world produce and promote fashion. This chapter identifies the four major fashion centers in the world and examines the history that led to their significance in the global fashion industry. Fashion centers hold **fashion weeks** that feature fashion shows biannually. Through these shows, the press, retailers, manufacturers, and fashionistas view the latest trends for the upcoming seasons. Everyone loves a fashion show, but as this chapter demonstrates, the shows are more than entertainment. They serve an economic purpose that impacts the local, and consequently, the global economy. In this chapter, we begin with the definition of a fashion center and then go on to examine the economic impact of international fashion centers.

Fashion Centers

A fashion center, or fashion city, is a city where fashion is produced and sold. Fashion centers have a long past as a place where raw materials, producers, and buyers congregate in an interdependent way to promote and advance the consumption of fashion goods and its interrelated businesses. Fashion centers throughout history have contributed to the solidification of fashion as a cultural and economic element of society, especially in Western cultures where fashion follows urban life. Prominence in the fashion industry adds to the cultural cache of a city. Cities use their fashion reputations to promote tourism, and traditional art institutions, like museums and galleries, have accepted fashion as an art form expressing the overall creativity of a city.

Many fashion centers are old and established, while others, because of globalization, are emerging in countries where the fashion industries are beginning to take hold. International negotiations that take shape in the form of trade agreements (more about trade agreements in Chapter 12) link global fashion centers. The countries that enter such agreements realize the symbolism and cultural significance of fashion as an art form and its economic importance through consumerism. Eager to protect and promote their cities as "fashionable," cities form councils and boards that oversee fashion. New York, Paris, Milan, and London comprise the four major fashion centers and, while there are others, the focus of this text is on these four.

New York

Immigrants played a pivotal role in the rise of New York as a major fashion center by providing labor and specialized skills required for the production of apparel. In the earliest days of the fashion industry in New York, Park Avenue was the location of choice. However, some in the Park Avenue neighborhood had a vision for an elegant street, like those seen in Paris and London, so a movement began to get the garment businesses and workers out of the neighborhood. On July 25, 1916, a zoning law, the first of its kind in the United States, was passed. By the fall of 1916, 95 percent of all apparel-related industries moved from Park Avenue, settling between Ninth Avenue and Broadway between 34th and 42nd Streets. This became, and remains, the garment center, and 10 years later it became the fastest growing area in the city. Refer to Figure 10.1 for a map of the New York Garment Center. Production of apparel in the garment center was so prolific that it was responsible for producing approximately 75 percent of ready-to-wear dresses and coats worn by American women.

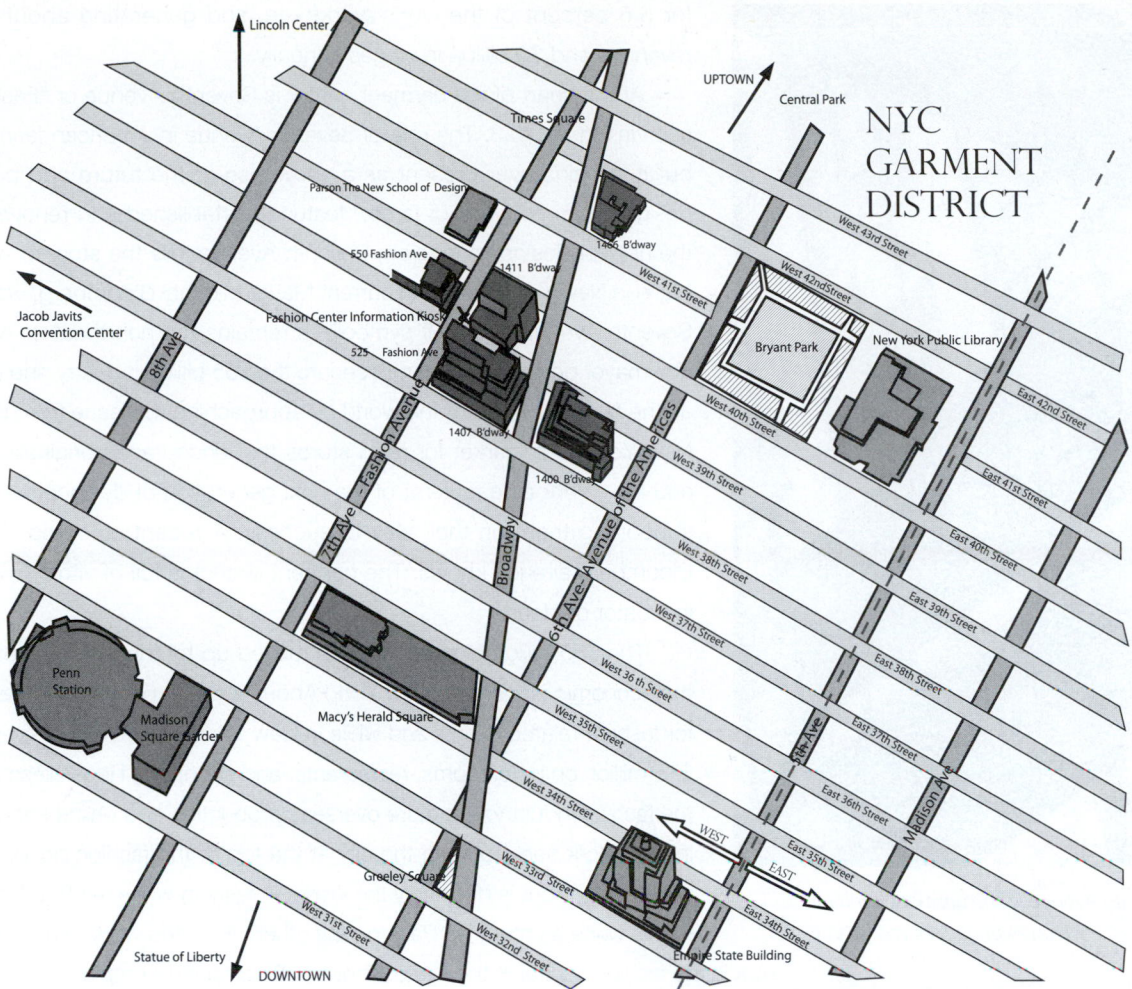

FIGURE 10.1 *The garment center in New York City in 2011 (Source: Hawa Stwodah).*

In the 1930s, the fashion industry was the largest industry in New York and the fourth largest in the United States. The German occupation of Paris and World War II propelled New York into the stratosphere of the "capitol of fashion." Mayor LaGuardia saw the potential of New York as fashion capitol and he also realized the economic perils should the industry fail; so he, along with union and industry leaders, formed the **New York Dress Institute** to promote the fashion industry in New York. What LaGuardia and the others had not counted on was the change in the way American women dressed. In the early 1950s, women began to favor sportswear because of its mix-and-match ease. The photograph in Figure 10.2 typifies the type of sportswear worn by women in the 1950s. Manufacturing these garments did not require the same skills as required for producing tailored coats and dresses, and manufacturers began to seek places where goods could be produced with lower labor costs. Other areas of the United States provided not only the labor pool needed to lower costs but also facilities for lower rents. This change cost New York 22,000 jobs; although New York was affected by the change, the United States did not suffer economically as the jobs moved elsewhere in the country. At its peak in the 1950s, the New York apparel industry employed 300,000 people. Today, the number of employees has decreased, but apparel jobs still amount to 28 percent of the city's manufacturing jobs. Furthermore, 90–95 percent of the clothing sold in the United States was made in New York (Feitelberg, 2010). In 2010 there were 165,000 jobs in the fashion sector, accounting

FIGURE 10.2 *Women began wearing sportswear in the 1950s. A typical outfit consisted of a cardigan sweater and a skirt or slacks (Source: Alamy).*

FIGURE 10.3 *Seventh Avenue in the garment center in New York is known as Fashion Avenue (Source: Alamy).*

for 5.5 percent of the city's workforce, and generating about $2 billion in tax revenues and $9 billion in wages annually.

At the heart of the garment center is Seventh Avenue or "Fashion Avenue," as seen in Figure 10.3. The role of Seventh Avenue in American fashion has changed but it remains ever present as a showcase of the future and past for American design. From its "walk of fame," featuring established and renowned designers to the newest designers in town, Seventh Avenue tells the story of American fashion. Many in New York, including current Mayor Michael Bloomberg, want to ensure that Seventh Avenue and all it symbolizes remains the heartbeat of American fashion. The mayor developed a plan to secure the $55 billion industry and solidify New York as the fashion capitol of the world by approaching the issue from two perspectives: New York as a market for retail stores that encourages originality and innovation, and New York as a fosterer of the next generation of designers and merchants by supporting them on their way to success. A recent study confirms what Mayor Bloomberg already knows: The garment district is full of vitality with a future as an incubator of ideas.

The $55 billion in sales revenue racked up by the fashion industry is the tip of the economic iceberg for New York. About 600,000 people visit New York each year for fashion-related events and while in New York, these visitors spend approximately $15 million on hotel rooms, restaurants, and shopping. Regardless of the changes in the fashion industry, like more overseas production and online shopping, the leaders in New York seek to keep the city at the top of the fashion heap. If numbers alone count, New York is decidedly the leader in fashion with over 900 fashion companies; that is twice as many as Paris or any other city in the world, substantiating that New York is the fashion capital of the world. Those 900 companies employ 175,000 people including designers, merchants, merchandisers, account executives, craftspeople, and distributors with a payroll of about $10 billion, making fashion the second-largest industry in New York. According to Mayor Bloomberg, the real value is in the intellectual property created by the talented individuals in the fashion industry.

Paris

Fashion is an integral part of French history, culture, and customs. Paris fashion epitomizes originality, vitality, elitism, and street fashion dominating the world fashion scene. Paris fashion includes clothing, accessories, and beauty products displaying the names of famed French fashion designers like Christian Dior, Chanel, and Yves Saint Laurent, all giving credence to the luxury and aspirational nature of French fashion. Designers from other parts of the world yearn to be a part of Paris fashion with many, from England, Ireland, Japan, and Korea, to name a few, launching their collections in Paris every year. Paris has scores of resources supporting the art and business of fashion including fine textiles, stylists, trend spotters, fashion show producers, and the press. The strength of the Parisian fashion scene is, and has always been, women's apparel design.

In the late seventeenth century, Paris emerged as the foremost fashion city in the world. In the eighteenth century, Europe was the economic and artistic leader for the world and European fashion was no exception. The French dominated women's fashions and the British led in men's fashions. Around the mid-eighteenth century, young aristocrats discovered French fashion, and it is through their patronage that couturiers gained reputations for design and extremely high-quality garment production. Couturiers, like Rose Bertin, encouraged their reputations by promoting themselves and Paris as the mecca of fashion. Rose Bertin became famous during the eighteenth century as the dressmaker for Marie Antoinette. She developed a distinct style that pleased her highbrow clientele by using the vast array of superior materials and products available in Paris. In addition to wonderful design, textiles, and trims, Paris was home to brilliant craftspeople that formed the foundation for Paris couture and the basis for Paris becoming the beacon of fashion for the world.

In 1940, during World War II, the Nazis' occupation of Paris threatened the Parisian fashion industry's existence. Hitler wanted to move the haute couture industry to Berlin, but the efforts of the **Chambre Syndicale** prevented this from happening. The Chambre Syndicale, which began in 1868, embraced very strict rules that invitees agreed to in order to gain membership. After the war, piece goods and clothes rationing created shortages in materials. Designers were forced to figure out how to create fashion worthy of the Parisian reputation while reusing and repurposing textiles. The result was utilitarian and mannish apparel. After the war, in 1947, Christian Dior's "New Look" (Figure 10.4), which consisted of an A-line shape, nipped in at the waist, worn with a short jacket, and a belt, came into being. Dior's decidedly feminine "new look" had women all over the world clamoring for the style and Paris was once again in the spotlight of women's fashion.

FIGURE 10.4 *After World War II, women were clamoring for Christian Dior's decidedly feminine "new look" (Source: Alamy).*

The Chambre Syndicale, the French fashion trade association, was organized to oversee and maintain the couture and **prêt-à-porter** (ready-to-wear) aspects of French fashion. The **Fédération Française de la Couture, du Prêt-à-Porter des Couturiers, et des Créateurs de Mode**, an offshoot of the Chambre Syndicale, was founded in 1973. The Fédération, the executive body for each of the specific Chambre Syndicale, is tasked with implementing policies that promote the growth of the French fashion industry. Haute couture, ready-to-wear, and menswear each have their own Chambre Syndicale. The chart in Figure 10.5 illustrates the French trade associations. The three trade associations combined have around 100 global brands including a few from Japan, Italy, and Belgium, a manifestation of the increasing globalization of fashion. The Chambre Syndicale de la Haute Couture strengthens the world presence of Paris fashion and enables the Parisian fashion industry to shine among the tough competitors of New York, Milan, and London.

London

London is the capital of the United Kingdom, the largest city in Britain, and without a doubt, the hub of London's fashion industry. London is one of the most vibrant and creative fashion cities in the world. Fashion in London signifies the city's global status and is an important contributor to the culture of the city. The city is the venue for London Fashion Week and the British Designer of the Year awards. London's prestigious shopping areas offer products with designer names like Armani, Burberry, Gucci, Louis Vuitton, Dior, Paul Smith, and Vivienne Westwood. Top Shop, Harvey Nichols, and Liberty of London are among the retailers and boutiques that

The Fédération Française de la Couture, du Prêt-à-Porter des Couturiers, et des Créateurs de Mode
1. The Chambre Syndicale de la Haute Couture
Didier Grumbah - Presides
Membership limited to those companies authorized as Haute Couture Houses. Membership is reviewed annually.
2. The Chambre Syndicale du Prêt-à-Porter des Couturiers et des Créateurs de Mode
Guillaume de Seynes of Hermes - Presides
Membership includes Couture houses and fashion designers that produce women's ready-to-wear
3. Fédération Française de la Couture, du Prêt à Porter, des Couturiers et des Créateurs de Mode
French Federation of Fashion Designers

FIGURE 10.5 *The three French trade associations governed by the Fédération Française de la Couture, du Prêt-à -Porter des Couturiers, et des Créateurs de Mode.*

characterize London's fashion scene. Prominent retailers flock to London with good reason as the city accounted for over a quarter of retail spending on fashion products in the United Kingdom. The number of major retail flagship stores in London is second only to New York, outranking Paris, Milan, Tokyo, and Los Angeles. London accounted for over a quarter of retail spending on fashion products in the United Kingdom and around a third of spending in England.

Without high-fashion corporations or a large base of manufacturing firms, London is at a competitive disadvantage when compared to New York or Paris. However, London's reputation for innovation, talent, diversity, and style is significant from a symbolic and cultural perspective, if not an economic one. London also hosts highly regarded fashion educational systems in its universities that breed, encourage, and cultivate the creativity and innovation that are trademarks of London's fashion.

London's fashion reputation began with menswear. As far back as the seventeenth century, **Savile Row** turned out elegant menswear. "Savile Row" is the term for London's **bespoke** or custom-made garments. In the nineteenth century, London catered to elite and middle-class clients and provided the United Kingdom with fashion information and world class shopping. Holding true to its expertise and reputation for menswear, designers and dressmakers during the nineteenth century looked to Paris for trends and fashion information for women's wear. After World War I, a few designers tried to establish couture houses, like those in Paris, but were unable to find success.

Britain's Incorporated Society of London Fashion Designers began in January of 1942 and was comparable to the Chambre Syndicale in France. The society had three objectives, all intended to maintain, develop, promote, and protect British fashion. In the early days of its inception, the society was successful in increasing Britain's export figures and global coverage of British fashion events, but the society closed in 1970 after a couple of decades of dismal results. In 1948, the London Model House Group represented 14 ready-to-wear companies by planning shows and promoting exports. In 1958 the group's name changed to the Fashion House Group of London and got to work planning biannual fashion weeks in London. Cohesiveness was short-lived and in 1965, because of disputes about the development of ready-to-wear in Britain, the group split. The British Fashion Council, founded in 1983, continues to represent British fashion design. The council organizes London Fashion Week and the British Fashion awards. In addition, the British Fashion Council works with designers, helping them through mentoring and education.

London's status as the home of expert men's tailors remained known by the beginning of World War II. After the war, fashion departments were established in art colleges throughout

Britain where students from all socioeconomic levels could attend because of state-funded grants for further education. Around the mid-twentieth century, London's couturiers found themselves in a conundrum: They possessed excellent skills and a keen understanding of their market but insufficient funding, and a lack of confidence stifled the innovation needed to show groundbreaking styles. They painted themselves into a box with their assessment that London fashion hung on couture and high-end ready-to-wear.

It was not until the 1960s that London blossomed into an international fashion city when a large influx of young people that worked in the arts, including fashion, moved into London neighborhoods. With one-third of London's population being under the age of 20, fashion change was inevitable. These fashionable young people created the "Swinging London" phenomenon of the mid-1960s. Designer Mary Quant led the way with miniskirts, knee boots, and baggy sweaters representing a new design aesthetic for London. The photo in Figure 10.6 shows models wearing the latest from Mary Quant in 1971. Quant's boutique on King's Road stimulated the opening of trendy stores

FIGURE 10.6 *Models wearing the latest Mary Quant designs in 1971 (Source: Alamy).*

on King's Road and Carnaby Street, giving a new meaning to ready-to-wear in London. In the mid-1980s, a combination of inspired forces came together and the London fashion scene captured international attention. The 1990s saw another surge of eclectic, artful expression when young people moved into the East End of London and opened boutiques.

The late twentieth century saw changes in production and only 14 percent of clothing producers in the United Kingdom worked in London. Distribution methods changed when many wholesale companies closed because retail buyers started working directly with overseas factories. Besides production and distribution, the retail landscape transformed when designers and retailers, seeking lower rents, opened shops in economically depressed areas. Carnaby Street once again became the street of hip, young, avant-garde stores.

London's fashion industry may not have the global economic impact seen by New York or Paris, but it is a substantial contributor to the economy of the United Kingdom. Research shows that the direct value of the London fashion industry to the overall UK economy is about £21 billion and the wider impact, or "**spillover**," is estimated at more than £16 billion. "Spillover" refers to the money spent when people visit London on fashion industry-related business and, while in London, spend money on hotels, restaurants, and other entertainment. A minimum estimate of tourism spending is £98 million in 2009. The fashion industry's total economic impact equals over £37 billion or about $57 billion. Direct and indirect sales revenues are joined by other factors that emphasize the importance of the fashion industry in London. There are over 800,000 people employed in London's fashion industry that create, innovate, produce, design, and sell fashion, making it the fifteenth largest employer in the country.

Milan

Milan is a relatively new fashion center, taking the title from Florence in the 1980s. Milan, as a fashion center, demonstrated to the world that Italy recognized the ready-to-wear industry. Attitudes about fashion switched from viewing fashion as art to viewing fashion as a modern industry and as an expression of quality and good taste. In the 1960s, Milan was in economic

crisis due to a slowdown in the oil and industrial industry. It was fashion that led the charge to economic recovery. The Italian fashion industry remains a vital component of the Italian economy. Sales in 2009 reached £56.5 billion, the equivalent of $78.5 billon. Fashion is credited as a key player in the prolonged time of economic growth in Italy called the "**Italian miracle**."

The success of prêt-à-porter in the eighties catapulted Milan's reputation for fashion and a new fashion capital was born. First seen in the seventies, Milanese prêt-à-porter combined the need to produce large quantities of merchandise with fashion designer cooperation and bearing fashion designer names. This combination met with exceptional success in the eighties and offered consumers the opportunity to buy garments with labels boasting "made in Italy." The wearable clothes, manufactured with high-quality materials, and with excellent workmanship, directed the success of Italian fashion. Milan's atmosphere of experimentation and open-mindedness was a catalyst for the success of prêt-à-porter. Creativity and design defined Milan, and, as home to many artists and people working in the field of art, there existed an understanding and an appreciation for art in its many forms, including fashion.

In addition to prêt-à-porter and the cosmopolitan ambience of Milan, the textile industry played an important role in the success of Milan as a fashion center. Milan has long been known for fine textiles, and the textile producers in Northern Italy sponsored Italian clothing manufacturers for hosting shows in Milan. Also notable to Milan's success as a fashion center is that since 1961, *Vogue Italia* has been published in Milan. Furthermore, Milan is geographically ideal, located in the center of the industrial areas, especially considering that production concepts like flexible specialization and vertical integration were part of Milan's industrial model. The combination of an artistic community, a reputation for modern product design, a well-regarded textile industry, the publication of the most respected fashion journal in Italy, and an ideal geographical location contributed to Milan's current status as a city of fashion leaders.

Milan's main attraction is shopping but it also has a strong presence on the wholesale side of the business. There are in excess of 3,000 fashion companies and 600 showrooms in Milan. Besides that, there are public relations firms, advertising firms, photographers, and production companies. Milan is also home to the National Chamber for Italian Fashion (CNMI) and hosts many high-profile fashion events like Milano Collezioni, MIPEL (International Leather Goods Market), MICAM ShoEvent (International Footwear Fair), and Milano Unica (Italian Textiles Fair).

Each of the four major fashion centers is the home of the most glamorous shows in the world. Attended by the press, retail buyers, and celebrities, the shows set the tone for the upcoming seasons featuring the world's best designers.

The Fashion Show

History

The fashion show is as much a part of the landscape of fashion as designers and retailers. The true origin of the fashion show is unknown, but its roots are French couture. The evolution of the fashion show began with sending fashion dolls (Figure 10.7) to the Royal Court, which transitioned to an exclusive, invitation-only haute couture design house presentation that eventually became biannual productions featuring haute couture and ready-to-wear. The shows themselves are largely invitation only, but in today's technological world, especially with the Internet, the average consumer sees the runway, sometimes simultaneously, to the actual show. The media coverage surrounding the shows is huge, covering everything from the designer to the

FIGURE 10.7 *Fashion dolls were sent to the Royal Court in the nineteenth century to present a designer's creations (Source: Hawa Stwodah).*

people in attendance. Through media coverage, more consumers are aware of couture and high-end designer ready-to-wear. Designers and models are celebrities in their own right and Hollywood stars attending the shows add to the allure and excitement.

In the mid-1800s, Charles Frederick Worth, the "Father of Haute Couture," became the first couturier to use live models, called **mannequins** (refer to Chapter 1), enabling a potential customer to visualize the garment on a live person by seeing the movement, fit, and construction in a dynamic, rather than a static way. By the end of the century, several designers, inspired by Worth, began using live models. After the couture shows in Paris, haute couture shows sometimes made their way to the United States. Around 1910, American department stores started holding fashion shows. Beginning in 1910, film companies showed fashion reels prior to movies in movie houses as part of their weekly newsreel production. The film documentation of fashion shows started in 1913 when a New York-based film company documented the biannual fashion shows in New York. During World War I, fashion shows traveled across the nation raising money for the war effort. By 1918, the Parisian couture industry planned two major shows for foreign buyers traveling to Paris. Jean Patou was instrumental in the organization of biannual press shows that originated from his special preview showings that were full-dress rehearsals attended by the press. By the mid-1950s, fashion shows became common in department stores and in many cases used as a backdrop to charity events. Fashion parades aptly describe the preferred fashion show style in the 1930s, 1940s, and 1950s. Shows had an order and sequence about them, like the customary wedding dress (Figure 10.8, seen at the end of the show).

In the late 1950s, big changes in fashion shows occurred because of the growth of the ready-to-wear market. With more manufacturers and designers in the ready-to-wear business, the 1950s witnessed an increase in the number of fashion shows, and in order to stand out, the scale and

FIGURE 10.8 *The traditional end-of-show wedding dress seen at the end of the Chanel Fall/Winter Haute Couture show, 2003 (Source: Alamy).*

grandeur of the shows increased. The increase in ready-to-wear fashion shows changed the purpose of the haute couture shows, becoming more about the press and buyers, than private clients. The 1960s marked the beginning of the fashion show as a marketing tool. In the 1970s, to attract the press, dazzling antics became the norm. Japanese designer Kenzo demonstrated excess when the catwalk became a stage performance complete with dancing and acrobatics. Kenzo's show changed the rules of the fashion show to "there are no rules." Fashion shows in the 1970s and 1980s became supersized spectacles, the enormity of which increased the public's appetite for fashion shows.

In 1980, Elsa Klensch joined CNN and brought runway shows into the homes of Americans on Saturday mornings, feeding the curiosity and enthusiasm for fashion in America. The show called, *Style with Elsa Klensch*, ran from 1980 to 2001 and spawned similar shows. It was not long until the fascination with the designers behind-the-scenes activities bled over into an interest in the models and the term **"supermodel"** was coined. Throughout the 1980s, shows continued to morph into major productions in some fantastic venues, like the Louver in Paris, with thousands in attendance. Thierry Mugler's 1984 anniversary show at the Zenith drew an audience of 6,000. Shows changed gears again in the nineties when a minimalist era of style surfaced, but by the twenty-first century, over-the-top presentations became fashion

FIGURE 10.9 *In 1915 the U.S. economy began a 44-month expansion and hemlines went up for the first time (Source: Alamy).*

shows' style of choice. In the early 1990s, the heyday of the super-model, the public began to pay more attention to fashion and fueled by the Internet, fashion weeks popped up from Mumbai to Sao Paulo.

Historically, the catwalk has seen a correlation between hemlines and economic growth. The "**hemline index**" is a theory from the 1920s attributed to economist George Taylor. His observations suggested that when stocks were up, so were hemlines, and conversely, when stocks dropped, hemlines followed suit. During World War I, in 1915 hemlines went up for the first time (refer to Figure 10.9) at the same time the U.S. economy began an expansion that lasted 44 months. This change is noteworthy because skirts and dresses were shoe length. According to the National Bureau of Economic Research, in December of 1914, the U.S. economy began an expansion that lasted 44 months. The 1960s, synonymous with the miniskirt, saw a 106-month growth in the U.S. economy with hemlines reaching an all-time high. In the late 2000s, the hemline index did not always prove true and the parallel between the runway and the economy was blurred.

Another economic theory with roots in the fashion industry is the "**lipstick theory**." The lipstick theory surmises that when the sales of lipstick increase, consumer confidence is decreasing. Women pur-chase lipstick when they want to treat themselves but are not feel-ing good about the economy. Leonard Lauder was the first to voice this theory after the September 11 terrorist attacks in 2001 when he noticed that lipstick sales were on the rise. Kline Consumer Products Research Practice confirmed that during hard economic times, lipstick sales increase (Ladurantaye, 2011).

Importance of Fashion Shows

Fashion shows are a key component in today's fashion industry and have encouraged the growth and development of the industry throughout the twentieth and twenty-first centuries. The primary purpose of a fashion show is to sell merchandise and to that end, the fashion show is a marketing tool. The visual presentation of merchandise on a live body, styled to bring out the best of a garment, in an environment that is interactive for the audience while creating a mood for the clothing, is instrumental for the designer in conveying the message of the products including clothing, accessories, cosmetics, and fragrances. When the message is received by the audience, magic happens. An excitement and enthusiasm for the designer's creations builds and people begin to visualize themselves as consumers of the products and acquire an appreciation for the talent of the designer.

The relationship of fashion shows to body image, conspicuous consumption, and con-sumerism is undeniable but it is the consumerism part that interests those in the fashion indus-try. Selling product is what keeps this vital, dynamic, and large contributor to the economy afloat and in turn employs millions throughout the world. Shows are planned and produced with special effects and lighting to create brands, promote brand recognition, and sell clothing and other designer accoutrements.

Types of Fashion Shows

There are four basic types of fashion shows: **production shows**, **formal runway shows**, **informal shows**, and **multimedia production shows**. The type of show is determined by the audience, the merchandise, the venue, and the desired result.

Production shows are theatrical and dramatic and require detailed planning and organization. Typically, a production show is produced for couture, evening wear, bridal, and in some cases, ready-to-wear.

A formal runway show, sometimes called a fashion parade, is similar to a parade with garments shown on the runway in an orderly and systematized manner. An overall theme defines a formal runway show with choreography, music, lighting, and in some cases, commentary planned to accentuate the garments and reinforce the theme of the show. Models walk the runway in the Marc Jacobs Spring 2011 show in Figure 10.10.

An informal fashion show works well for charity events, often held in a restaurant or tea room setting. Lighting, music, props, and runways are unnecessary for this type of show. The models meander throughout the room and distribute information regarding the outfits they are wearing and talk with the attendees about the garments. Some preparation is necessary for an informal show, but not on the same scale as a production or runway show.

A multimedia show is based on technology like video or Internet allowing accessibility for the runway show, product instructions, or trends to be easily dispersed. The purpose of this type of show is to present opportunities for consumers to purchase wherever and whenever they wish. Burberry put technology to work in its first fashion show in China. The show had no runway. Instead Burberry used a digital presentation using avatars in conjunction with live models. The high-tech, hologram-projected models wore Burberry trench coats and interacted with the live models (Karen Videtic, personal communication).

FIGURE 10.10 *Models walking the runway for Marc Jacobs Spring 2011 show (Source: Newscom).*

Cost of a Fashion Show

As previously established, the purpose of a runway fashion shows is selling and promoting fashion. Fashion shows attract press, which promotes the designer's line and generates sales. Many believe that, in fashion, there is no better marketing tool when it comes to exposure, promotion, and the buzz that is created, than the runway. However, the runway is expensive and many designers and brands conduct cost/benefit analyses to see if the expense of the runway is money well spent.

How much does it cost to produce a runway show in a fashion center? Costs vary widely but the low end of the scale is tens of thousands of dollars with some shows exceeding $1,000,000. Yves Saint Laurent spent more than $1,000,000 to stage a show in a tent behind the Musee Rodin. Rock and Republic, a designer jeans brand, spent as much as $2.5 million on a show. Keep in mind that the average New York Fashion Week show presents 25 to

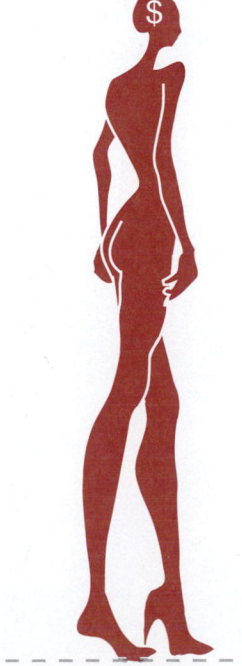

45 "looks" in only 15 minutes. The audience sees a beautiful show with special effects and lighting, but is generally unaware of the costs involved in producing the glamorous spectacles.

Spending for the venue is the largest expense in producing a fashion show. Before New York fashion week moved from Bryant Park, the tents cost up to $50,000. New York Fashion Week is now held at Lincoln Center because larger show spaces accommodate more people. Tents at Lincoln Center are reported to cost $26,000 to $50,000 but some report that staging a runway show at Lincoln Center ranges from $500,000 to $750,000 for 120,000 square feet of space. It's not cheap to show. "It's a fortune—$28,000 just for the tent!" exclaims Mara Hoffman, 31, who created memorable frocks for *Sex and the City*. "It totals maybe $70,000 for everything. It's nuts" (Puente, 2008). The price of a tent at Lincoln Center is outrageous but choosing an out-of-the-way venue costs more because of the extra equipment needed to prepare the location for a show.

In addition to the expense of the venue, there are costs for models, music, lighting, hair, makeup, stylists, public relations people, invitations, flowers, and just about anything else one can think of to create a mood and an atmosphere for the collection being shown. Models cost anywhere from $250 each for a lesser-known, to $50,000 each (plus a 20 percent agency fee) for more famous models. Music directors or DJs earn fees between $6,000 and $10,000. Lighting designers are about $65,000. One designer requested a lighting change so that a celebrity modeling in the show would look younger, and the cost was $20,000.

Of course, no show would be complete without clothing or hair and makeup, so stylists are hired to make sure each model and every garment represents the vision of the designer. A basic hairstylist is about $3,000, but those with reputations or celebrities in their own right charge $5,000 to $10,000. Stylists charge as much as $5,000 to $10,000 a day, with a four-day minimum. Well-known stylists charge higher fees, closer to $20,000 per day. Makeup artists collect large fees and in addition to paying the artist, the makeup purchased costs tens of thousands of dollars. "Right before fashion week, there are orders of at least 20,000 shadows—and that's just for the eyes," says John Demsey, global president of MAC cosmetics. "Multiply [that figure] by 25 to 30 makeup artists per show, with at least 45 shows going on. To re-stock a makeup artist's makeup box costs at the very least $2,000. The cost can really start to escalate" (Prabhakar, 2007).

Catering costs another $400 to $600 a day during the month leading up to the show. A surprising expense is the payment of celebrities to attend the show. Designers will pay as much as they can afford to have the right people sit in the front row. Some celebrities and their publicists collect fees up to $50,000 per show to sit in the front row, wear the designer's clothes, and say positive things in interviews. Designers hire public relations firms to send invitations and complete seating charts. In 2003, Sean "Diddy" Combs is rumored to have spent $75,000 on his invitations plus another $150,000 a day to rent New York hot spot Cipriani as his venue. Gucci spent $25,000 flying roses from South America for a show in Milan.

The enormous expense of producing runway shows is leading designers and others in the industry to rethink the way their lines are shown. The Council of Fashion Designers of America suggested that designers combine fashion shows and share costs. IMG, which organizes New York Fashion Week, is thinking of changing one of its tents to a presentation space for designers that prefer that format. **Presentations**, featuring models posing like mannequins instead of walking down a runway, offer a less expensive alternative to the catwalk. Italian fashion house Marni showed its fall 2009 menswear collection presentation style rather than on a traditional runway. Many designers favor this because it cuts down significantly on costs, particularly the venue expense. Many buyers and editors prefer the presentation style because it allows them to get a closer look at the clothes. Designer Carmen Marc Valvo has considered a presentation style show because the cost would be significantly less than the $250,000 typically spent to produce a runway show. A few designers use their boutiques as a stage, which reduces the price of producing their shows by several hundred thousand dollars. However, a presentation show is not always less costly to stage.

A few designers turned to virtual shows to defray the costs of a runway production. New York designer Marc Bouwer presented a webcast show that cost $140,000 less than a live runway show. In September 2008, Dutch design duo Viktor & Rolf gave up Paris Fashion Week to stage their spring 2009 show in their Amsterdam studio and to present it on their website. London designer Alice Temperley has taken an approach similar to Viktor & Rolf's, presenting shows four times a year that will save her upward of $100,000. This approach is appealing in a technological world where a runway show can cost in excess of $1 million to stage, while an online show costs virtually nothing. In 2010, no ticket was required to view Calvin Klein's latest fashions on the runway during fashion week. Calvin Klein and Marc Jacobs streamed their shows live. A few designers use social media to communicate to consumers during fashion week. Tommy Hilfiger used Facebook to stream his fashion show, allowing consumers to post questions, which would be answered the following day. Bloggers attend fashion weeks to report on the runway. Tumblr, a well-known blogging website, sent 24 bloggers to New York Fashion Week. Brands such as Kate Spade and Oscar de la Renta use Tumblr to connect with consumers.

The exchange of catwalk shows for less expensive presentation style or virtual shows is directly related to the cost of a catwalk show. However, it is important to remember that runway shows are marketing tools for designers and brands. The press and editorial coverage gleaned from a show is paramount to the amount received when shows are scaled down or seen in formats other than the runway. Besides, runway shows are popular with buyers, editorial press, consumer press, bloggers, and celebrities. Designers and brands look at the big picture in relationship to the cost of a runway show; if the hype generated from a show garners international sales, new sales outlets, or an increase in online sales, it could be said that the expense of a show is money well spent. Most designers see the runway as an investment and worth the payback in brand recognition, knowing that in the long term, runway shows increase sales and consequently profit.

Each fashion center holds fashion shows during fashion weeks. The calendars are carefully planned to ensure that many buyers, members of the media, and celebrities attend. The economic impact of fashion weeks for the fashion centers and the worldwide fashion industry are explored in the following section.

Fashion Weeks

"Fashion week" is the conventional name for biannual fashion shows held in various cities throughout the world. It is during fashion week that high-end designers present their collections for the following season. Fashion weeks attract designers, high-end brands, buyers from major retailers, luxury specialty stores, celebrities, and the press. The mainstream press includes fashion editors from *Women's Wear Daily*, major fashion magazines like *Vogue*, consumer magazines like *Good Housekeeping*, and newspapers like *USA Today* and *The Wall Street Journal*. In the digital age, bloggers and online journal fashion editors cover the shows as well.

As fashion became more accessible through television, the interest in fashion exploded. Fashion designers and models became celebrities and the press responded by covering the shows in print, on television, and online.

European sociologists Joanne Entwistle and Agnés Rocamora have said that fashion weeks are "the field of fashion materialized" (Skov, 2006). Excitement, anticipation, and sheer exhaustion define fashion weeks. In New York City fashion a typical fashion week in February or September finds tents of high fashion at Lincoln Center and buyers from all types of stores pounding the pavement up and down Broadway, Seventh Avenue, and the streets between 34th and 42nd. Manufacturers show their lines in showrooms with models sashaying about in offerings for the next season. Lunches, cocktail parties, dinners, and goody bags await buyers and celebrities as the vendors work to entice them to buy their merchandise. Buying offices host members for meetings discussing vendors, and style and color trends. When the fashion week is over, the dismantling of tents, catwalks, and showroom rigs takes place, returning the garment center to its usual tempo.

In January and July, 10 to 30 haute couture lines and 40 menswear collections hit Paris runways. Due to the rising costs incurred with runway shows, the number of haute couture shows has declined from 106 in 1945 to 10 in 2005. Additional fashion weeks in March and October present 150 women's ready-to-wear lines over eight days. Industry insiders, fashion aficionados, and celebrities flock to Paris to see the shows. Fashion week show schedules, organized by the Fédération, are distributed to 2,000 French and international journalists and buyers. Great care is taken so that those visiting Paris for fashion week are able to see as many shows as possible in the various venues throughout Paris.

The future of fashion cities and fashion weeks is uncertain. Fast fashion and the Internet play by less conventional rules. Zara and H&M produce, distribute, and sell fashion long distances from their consumers without the expense and hassle of a runway show. The Internet allows virtual shows that are seen at the convenience of the viewer and has the potential to replace the need for shows since trends are seen online as they happen. Without question, it is harder to get an overview of the key trends without sitting through all of the shows. The translation of the cut, color, drape, and fit is lost in a one-dimensional medium. Regardless of the disadvantages of digital fashion show, it is gaining traction in New York. Many designers are expanding their audiences using virtual shows. Many designers like Michael Kors, Dolce & Gabbana, and Alexander McQueen choose to use live streams of shows online. This trend of live streaming of shows is predicted to be adopted by more designers and brands in the days to come.

Economic Impact

New York Fashion Week started in 1943, and in 1993, the venue moved to Bryant Park where it remained until 2010 when it moved to Lincoln Center. Semiannual fashion weeks infuse large amounts of cash into the host city's economy. The 232,000 visitors to New York City spend about $460 billion toward fashion week events. Half of New York's visitors say shopping is their primary activity during their stay. Shopping in fashion cities is alluring and an important aspect of tourism. With numbers like these, city officials understand that the fashion industry is critical to New York City's future and its economy.

In addition to the twice-a-year influx of cash, New York's fashion industry and its related business employ 175,000 people that inject $10 billion into the economy every year. The business generated during the fashion weeks in New York City is of great importance. The spending in local fashion industry businesses accounts for $1.6 billion in taxes. In 2010, when the New York Fashion Week moved from Bryant Park to Lincoln Center, the businesses around Lincoln Center saw a surge in their business traffic.

The economic impact is felt in fashion centers around the globe. In London, fashion week contributes around £100 million to London's economy. London's fashion industry is worth £21 billion to the economy of the United Kingdom, supporting 1.31 million jobs, 80,000 of which are in London. The fashion industry in Great Britain is credited with influencing the contribution of over £37 billion to the country's economy. In Great Britain, the British Council estimates that fashion week attendees spend £20 million ($37.7). The shows employ over 270,000 people and produce orders for over £18 billion ($28 billion). The Camera della Moda, an Italian fashion body, reports that in 2009 the estimated sales from fashion week were £56.5 ($75.7). Currently, the percentage of fashion that contributes to the global economy is about 2 percent per year and growing.

Summary

This chapter looked at the history and characteristics that make the four major fashion centers vital to the fashion industry. Each city, New York, Paris, London, or Milan, has a rich fashion history and continues to thrive and innovate in a changing, international fashion arena. Each fashion center hosts fashion weeks where many thousands of visitors come to see the latest designs, trends, and fashion standouts. It is evident that the catwalk is the center of fashion weeks, and the economic power goes beyond creating demand for apparel and accessories. There is great strength in the economic power of the spillover effect into the community and the world economy.

Key Terms

bespoke 256
Chambre Syndicale 255
fashion center 252
fashion week 252
formal runway shows 261
Fédération Française de la Couture, du Prêt-à-Porter des Couturiers, et des Créateurs de Mode 255

hemline index 260
informal shows 261
Italian miracle 258
lipstick theory 260
mannequins 259
multimedia production shows 261
New York Dress Institute 253
presentations 262

prêt-à-porter 255
production shows 261
Savile Row 256
spillover 257
supermodel 259

Review Questions

1. What role did Mayor LaGuardia play in New York's history as a fashion center? What steps did Mayor Michael Bloomberg take in securing New York's future as a fashion center?

2. Describe the responsibility and function of the Chambre Syndicale.

3. How does London's fashion scene differ from those of New York, Paris, and Milan?

4. What facilitated Milan's rise as a fashion center?

5. What was Charles Frederick Worth's contribution to fashion shows?

6. What caused the increased number of fashion shows in the 1950s?

7. Who is credited with the "hemline index" theory? Give two examples of the theory.

8. Who is credited with the "lipstick theory"? Explain the theory's significance with regards to the economy.

9. What are the components of a fashion show and the estimated costs associated with these components?

10. Why is fashion week an economic asset to the host city?

Critical Thinking

1. As mentioned in the chapter, some designers are forego- ing runway shows, opting instead to use the Internet and other mediums. What are the advantages and disadvan- tages of runway shows? What are the advantages and disadvantages of other mediums? In your opinion, will the Internet eventually replace the runway show? Please explain.

2. In addition to the four major fashion centers discussed in the chapter, name three emerging fashion centers and discuss the economic impact of fashion weeks on those cities.

Internet Activities

1. Visit the Tommy Hilfiger website at usa.tommy.com to view the latest runway show. Write a review of the show including the overall theme, silhouettes, colors, fabrics, music, and so on.

2. Choose any three designers of your choice and review their fashion shows (from the same season) online. Note the trends seen in each show with regard to color, silhouette, fabrics, and so on and then compare and contrast the shows.

Bibliography

Breward, C. (2010, September). Fashion cities. In *Berg Encyclopedia of World Dress and Fashion*, Volume 10, Global Perspectives. Retrieved April 28, 2011, from http://www. bergfashionlibrary.com/view/bewdf/BEWDF-v10/EDch10030.xm

Breward, C., & Gilbert, D. (eds.) (2006). *Fashion world cities*, 1st ed. New York: Berg.

Burkitt, L. (April 14, 2011). *To lure young, burberry goes high- tech*. WSJ, http://blogs.wsj.com/chinarealtime/2011/04/14/ to-lure-young-burberry-goes-high-tech/?KEYWORDS= fashion+show

Conti, S. (2010, September 16). *British fashion industry worth over $30b*. WWD, http://www.wwd.com/markets-news/ british-fashion-industry-worth-over-30b-3277671

Craik, L. (2009). *Evening Standard*. Retrieved from Dow Jones Factiva, http://global.factiva.com.proxy.library.vcu.edu/ha/ default.aspx

Deprez, E. E. (2010, September 8). *NYC's biggest fashion week ever to generate $385 million for city economy*. Bloomberg, http://www.bloomberg.com/news/2010-09-08/ new-york-s-biggest-fashion-week-to-bring-385-million-to- city-mayor-says.html

Ehrman, E. (2010, September). London as a fashion city. In *Berg Encyclopedia of World Dress and Fashion*, Volume 8, West Europe. Retrieved April 29, 2011, from http://www. bergfashionlibrary.com/view/bewdf/BEWDF-v8/EDch8048.xml

Elzingre, M., & Hodgson, P. (September, 2010). Paris as a fashion city. In *Berg Encyclopedia of World Dress and Fashion*, Volume 8, West Europe. Retrieved April 28, 2011, from http://www.bergfashionlibrary.com/view/bewdf/ BEWDF-v8/EDch8037.xml

Evans, C. (2001). The enchanted spectacle fashion theory. *The Journal of Dress, Body, & Culture*, http://www. bergfashionlibrary.com.proxy.library.vcu.edu/view/nlm-j/ FT_5-3/1362704017789601865.xml

Feitelberg, R. (2010). *Garment center study looks to the future*, June 2, WWD, http://www.wwd.com/markets-news/garment- center-study-looks-to-the-future-3094065 http://books. google.com http://proxy.library.vcu.edu/login?url=http://search.ebscohost. com/login.aspx?direct=true&AuthType=ip,url,cookie,uid&db= oih&AN=58693483&site=ehost-live&scope=site http://www. bergfashionlibrary.com/view/bazf/bazf00232.xml

Feitelberg, R. (2010, September 9). *Mayor Bloomberg on fashion and shopping*. WWD, http://www.wwd.com/ business-news/mayor-bloomberg-on-fashion-and- shopping-3242454

Feitelberg, R. (2010, November 2). *NYC rolls out plan to boost fashion industry*. WWD, http://www.wwd.com/markets-news/ nyc-rolls-out-plan-to-boost-fashion-industry-3368899

Feitelberg, R. (2010, November 3). *City hall makes fashion a priority*. WWD, http://www.wwd.com/fashion-news/ city-hall-makes-fashion-a-priority-3370772

Finamore, M. (2005). Fashion shows. In *A–Z of fashion*. Retrieved April 29, 2011, from http://www.bergfashionlibrary.com.

proxy.library.vcu.edu/view/bazf/bazf00232. xml?q=finamore fashion shows&isfuzzy=no#highlightAnchor

Kazakina, K. (2010). *At fashion week hemlines are up and down, just like markets*, September 13. Bloomberg, http://www. bloomberg.com/news/2010-09-13/at-fashion-week-hemlines-are-up-and-down-just-like-the-markets.html

Laudurantaye, S. (2011, June 7). *Lipstick theory bodes Ill for U.S. retail*. Retrieved from http://license.icopyright.net/user/viewFeedUse.act?fuid=MTMxMjg0ODI%3D

LFW (2011, February 24). *£100 million to London's economy,* http://www.fashionunited.com/fashion-news/fashion/lfw:-l100-million-to-londons-economy-20112402486874

Lolley, S. (2010, August 31). *New York fashion week makeover*. Pittsburgh Post Gazette, http://www.post-gazette.com/pg/10243/1083823-314.stm?cmpid=lifestyle.xml

Milano Fashion Institute website, http://www.milanofashioninstitute.it/en/formazione/milano_moda.php

Mode à Paris Fédération Française de la Couture du Prêt-à-Porter des Couturiers et des Créateurs de Mode Paris Fashion Week, http://www.modeaparis.com/spip.php?rubrique6#toppage6

Montero, G. (2008). *A stitch in time*. New York: Fashion Center Business Improvement District, http://www.fashioncenter.com/about/publications/district-history

Pasquarelli, A. (2010, April 29). *Fashion week to add more show space*, CrainsNewYork.com, http://www.crainsnewyork.com/article/20100429/SMALLBIZ/100429795

Prabhakar, H. (2007). Cost of producing a fashion show. *Forbes Magazine*, http://www.forbes.com/2007/08/30/style-fashion-backstage-forbeslife-cx_hp_0831fashionpak.html

Prabhakar, H. (2007, February 2). Price of admission. *Forbes*, http://www.forbes.com/2007/02/01/price-of-admission-forbeslife-cx_hp_0202price.html

Puente, M. (2008, September 6). *Fashion week meets the weak economy*. Retrieved from http://abcnews.go.com/Business/story?id=5737974&page=1

Reinach, S. (May). Milan as a fashion city. In *Berg Encyclopedia of World Dress and Fashion*, Volume 8, West Europe. Retrieved

April 28, 2011, from http://www.bergfashionlibrary.com/view/bewdf/BEWDF-v8/EDch8044.xml

Relaxnews International. (2011). Retrieved from Dow Jones Factiva, http://global.factiva.com.proxy.library.vcu.edu/ha/default.aspx

Schnurnberger, L. (1991). *40,000 years of fashion. Let there be clothes*. New York: Workman Publishing.

Siegel, M. (n.d.). *Berg fashion library, A-Z of fashion*, http://www.bergfashionlibrary.com.proxy.library.vcu.edu/view/bazf/bazf00509.xml?isfuzzy=no#highlightAnchor

Sherman, L. (2009, Novermber 2). Fashion sees the end of the runway. *Forbes*, http://www.forbes.com/2009/02/11/fashion-week-downturn-lifestyle-style_0211_runway.html

Skov, L. (2006). *Snapshot: Fashion Week*, http://www.bergfashionlibrary.com.proxy.library.vcu.edu/view/bewdf/BEWDF-v10/EDch10031.xml?isfuzzy=no#highlightAnchor

Tan, C. (2008, December 2). *Lunchtime snap: Will fashion shows survive the economy?* WSJ, http://blogs.wsj.com/runway/2008/12/02/lunchtime-snap-will-fashion-shows-survive-the-economy/

"Top-dollar time at NYC Fashion Week", *USA Today* Section: Life, p. 01d, http://web.ebscohost.com.proxy.library.vcu.edu/ehost/detail?vid=4&hid=13&sid=21f79b62-ae17-41f7-9652-28c96e2795c8%40sessionmgr14&bdata=JkF1dGhUeXBlPWlwLHVybCxjb29raWUsdWlkJnNpdGU9ZWhvc3QtbGl2ZSZzY29wZT1zaXRl#db=a9h&AN=J0E091777698408

Value of Fashion Report (2010, September 16). *London fashion week*, http://www.londonfashionweek.co.uk/news_details.aspx?ID=229

Weston, N. (2007, February 5). *The real cost of an NYC runway show*. Luxist, http://www.luxist.com/2007/02/05/the-real-cost-of-an-nyc-runway-show/

What's Up at the Milan 2011 Fashion Week. (2010, June 20). *Reuters*, http://economictimes.indiatimes.com/Backpage//articleshow/6069360.cms

Zargani, L. (2011). Growth stokes mood in Milan. *WWD: Women's Wear Daily*, 201(39): 8. Retrieved from EBSCOhost.

INTERNATIONAL
FASHION
ECONOMICS

OBJECTIVES

After reading this chapter, you will be able to:

- Understand the international organization of the fashion industry
- Gain knowledge about the growth of the fashion industry compared to the growth of the nation's economy
- Understand the difference between fair trade and free trade
- Obtain knowledge of the meaning and impact of intellectual property rights
- Understand the foreign exchange market
- Acquire a basic understanding of foreign fashion markets
- Gain an understanding of trade agreements
- Examine trade preference programs
- Explore trade support programs and agencies

It has been said that arguing against globalization is like arguing against the laws of gravity.

—KOFI ANNAN (Ghanaian diplomat, seventh secretary-general of the United Nations, 2001 Nobel Peace Prize)

From Paris to New York and the cities in between, the world of fashion exists on a global scale. Globalization has enabled fashion to become an international business. Globalization is one of the most talked about topics today, whether by a business discussing how to work across cultures or a company discussing the impact of taking a brand global. According to the World Bank, "globalization is sometimes used in a much broader economic sense, as another name for capitalism or the market economy."

In the fashion world, it takes many companies in the supply chain to bring a product to market. The opening up of free markets is important to the development of the apparel and textile business by contributing to a country's employment. As seen in Chapter 9, most of the demand for apparel comes from the United States and Europe. In the development of a fashion line, many companies located throughout the world bring the creation of the line to fruition. For instance, a product is designed in New York, manufactured in India, and sold to consumers from a boutique in Spain. Through design, manufacturing, distributing, or promotional activities, such as a fashion week hosted by a major city, many countries have a hand in the production process.

Many retail and wholesale companies today seek to build their brands through distribution outside of their home country. For example, Zara, based in Spain, looks forward "to grow its global footprint between 8% and 10% a year through 2011." Although Zara focuses on its growth in the Indian market, it nevertheless, seeks to have an online presence in the United States and Europe (Stovall & Bjork, 2010). The fashion industry is truly an interdependent business as countries are specializing in different aspects in the process of producing fashion. Specializations include cutting, sewing and packaging, dyeing, printing, and weaving of fabric.

The business of fashion transpires 24 hours a day, seven days a week throughout the world. With globalization through the implementation of trade agreements, it is becoming easier to conduct business in foreign countries, and cities other than Paris, Milan, London, and New York are gaining fashion reputations. It is easier today than it was 20 years ago to cross borders to increase efficiency and lower costs to the consumer, by using production facilities with new technology systems, selling fashion to foreign consumers, and accessing lower labor costs.

Globalization dates back to the infamous "Silk Road," which was the routes used for trade between Asia, China, and Europe thousands of years ago. Examples of commodities traded among the routes included tea, silk, gold, and ivory. Besides trade, conversation about art, philosophy, and newly discovered innovations occupied the routes. Figure 11.1 depicts the trade routes intertwined throughout Europe and Asia. This type of trading went on for many years until countries built up their **infrastructures** and became more economically independent.

Countries were isolated and the two world wars inhibited the growth and development of trade among nations. After World War II, trade resumed at a faster pace when the manufacturing of fashion started to move offshore because of President Richard Nixon. "President Richard Nixon's trip to China in 1972 ended twenty-five years of isolation between the United States and the People's Republic of China and resulted in the establishment of diplomatic relations between the two countries in 1979" (Nixon Library). At the time of the agreement, products manufactured in China had a reputation of being inexpensive and of low quality, while fashions imported from Europe were high fashion and of outstanding quality and status. As fashion began to be mass-produced, the United States sought ways of lowering the cost of production. As a result, manufacturing today takes place in various countries around the world. China is the leader in offshore

Silk Trade Routes

Mongolia

China

South China Sea

Tibet

Himalaya

Bay of Bengal

Delhi

Arabian Sea

Saffayid Persia

Persian Gulf

Caspian Sea

Black Sea

Red Sea

Mediterranean Sea

FIGURE 11.1 *Map—depicts the trade routes intertwined throughout Europe and Asia (Source: Hawa Stwodah).*

production followed by India. See the front inside cover for a map depicting those countries that participate in the manufacturing and distribution of textiles and apparel.

In 2009, 97 percent of all apparel was imported into the United States (Personal communication, Nate Herman, Trade Specialist, American Apparel and Footwear Association). The U.S. government requires labels to be placed in garments. The country of origin rules and regulations require that a label contain the following information: "the fiber content, the country or origin, the manufacturer or dealer identity, and the care instructions" (OTEXA). The country of origin today is not an issue for the majority of fashion consumers; however, there are consumers that buy American-made products only.

The world is a **global village***, a belief that the world's nations have no borders. As such, the production, marketing, and retailing of goods and services are on a global scale. This means that with the adaptations of the products and services, companies are reaching across borders to connect with producers and consumers, which at times creates conflicts culturally, and problems with efficiency and communications. All are barriers to economic global growth.*

Furthermore, this chapter examines the importance of trade agreements and trade preference programs. The United States negotiates trade agreements to break down trade barriers and encourage trade among nations. "Forty-one percent of U.S. goods exports went to FTA partner countries in 2010, with exports to those countries growing at a faster rate than exports to the rest of the world from 2009 to 2010, 23% versus 20%" (Export.gov). Additionally, the chapter discusses the resources that aid importers and exporters in the United States and internationally.

Economic Growth of Nations

A nation's economic growth relies on supply factors, demand factors, and efficiency. The growing demands of a consumer can be satisfied only if the country has the ability to increase the quantity produced by using the combination of its natural resources, capital goods, and technology. The demand factors, in turn, increase the supply factors used to meet demand. According to the World Bank, "growth of the developing countries output and trade—and of their share of world output and trade—has accelerated over the past five years." Worldwide, textiles and clothing exports accounted for 2.6 percent of the world's exports, which equates to 316 billion dollars (WTO).

During the 1990s, in order to compete, clothing manufacturers moved manufacturing offshore into low labor-cost countries. According to a report by the United Nations titled "Globalization, the Changed Global Dynamics of the Clothing and Textile Value Chains and the Impact on Sub-Saharan Africa," Gereffi and Memedovic (2003, cited in Barnes and Morris, 2008) declared:

> This move began with Japan in the 1950s and 1960s followed by the East Asian Tigers (Taiwan, Republic of Korea and Hong Kong) in the 1970s and 1980s, and then South-East Asia in the 1990s, with China emerging as the biggest player. Other emerging, second level suppliers included India, Malaysia, Philippines, Indonesia and Sri Lanka.

Refer to Figure 11.2 for the World Trade Organization's list of the top ten clothing exporters for 2009. As of the writing of this text, world trade is in a recovery mode, having survived the global recession of 2007–2009 when, according to the World Trade Organization, world trade dropped 11 percent. The decline continued into the third quarter of 2009 with a 29.4

FIGURE 11.2 *Top ten clothing exporters.*

1	China
2	European Union
3	Bangladesh
4	Turkey
5	India
6	Vietnam
7	Indonesia
8	United States
9	Mexico
10	Thailand

percent decrease. The WTO notes that this is a difficult measurement, but places emphasis on the drop in overall world exports. In 2010 there was evidence of a global recovery. Refer to Figure 11.3 for a synopsis of the fastest growing export market.

Another important factor in a nation's economic growth lies in the development of its infrastructure, the physical structures such as roads, communication systems, electrical systems, and sewage. Because of an improved infrastructure, companies are able to take advantage of a nation's resources to increase output. Improvements in the infrastructure of countries like Vietnam, Guatemala, and India have facilitated globalization of the fashion industry and likewise provided a competitive edge in the global market. Global competition is inclined to restrain wholesale and retail prices from increasing drastically.

Globalizing a Brand

Companies take brands global to increase profits, but success is dependent on the product taking hold with its foreign consumer base. That means working harder and faster to meet demand both domestically and internationally. The advancement of technology through the development of a country's infrastructure has helped to increase the speed at which apparel manufacturing plants can produce. While labor costs remain low throughout the world in developing and less developed countries, the quality of workmanship has improved since the 1970s. Some countries, like China, have an advantage over other countries due to developed infrastructure.

FIGURE 11.3 *The chart is from the Office of Textile and Apparel and shows the growth of exports in dollar amounts of the top ten countries excluding Mexico and the Caribbean Countries. The countries have at least a 25 percent or more growth of exports in textiles and apparel (Source: http://otexa.ita.doc.gov/exports/fastgrow.htm).*

Country	2010	2011	YTD 1/2011	YTD 1/2012	% CHANGE	YE 1/2011	YE 1/2012	% Change	% Share
Colombia	123,748	165,252	12,278	13,658	11.24	128,884	166,631	29.29	0.74
Argentina	56,013	67,936	3,576	9,564	167.45	56,273	73,924	31.37	0.33
Taiwan	93,522	126,083	9,061	8,782	−3.08	96,623	125,804	30.20	0.56
South Africa	43,644	54,814	3,475	4,405	26.77	44,477	55,744	25.33	0.25
Poland	25,805	32,479	2,302	3,941	71.21	26,243	34,119	30.01	0.15
Ecuador	27,918	34,753	2,332	3,931	68.58	28,464	36,352	27.71	0.16
Angola	26,054	36,059	2,130	2,883	35.35	26,809	36,812	37.31	0.16
Sweden	33,115	47,008	2,336	2,636	12.83	32,971	47,308	43.48	0.21
Sri Lanka	21,146	29,160	2,316	2,005	−13.43	21,134	28,849	36.51	0.13
Uruguay	9,246	15,194	660	1,868	183.13	9,013	16,402	81.99	0.07

Note: YTD - Year to Date; YE - Year End

Free Trade versus Fair Trade

Free trade advocates believe that a system that invites trade and builds relationships among countries leads to a reduction in poverty. The argument is that those countries that are less developed do not have sufficient infrastructure and therefore cannot compete against the other global players, in other words, **developed countries**. The debate continues about what exactly free trade is among nations. Free trade refers to trade among nations without any restrictions such as government intervention, duties, or tariffs. Many studies have shown that international trade promotes economic growth among nations, contributing to a nation's wealth and economic development. **Fair trade** is trading among nations and adhering to trade agreements and trade acts set by governments to ensure that trade among nations is restricted to the agreements set up by the governments between nations. Chapter 11 covers Free Trade Acts in more detail.

Comparative and Absolute Advantage

Global competitive countries have a **comparative** or an **absolute advantage**. For China and other Asian countries, examples of comparative advantage include low labor costs, use of technology, skilled labor, and shorter lead times. If a country successfully competes in one or more of those areas, it has a comparative advantage over another country. For example, when sourcing for production, a buyer may choose one country over the other to get the shortest lead time to receive the product faster than the competition.

A country may choose to specialize in a specific area, such as speed of production. This in turn increases output. Production is faster, contributing to the overall economy of the country and the world. The downside is that once demand for the specialty no longer exists, the country must take time to retrain workers and possibly invest in new technology, necessitating the slowing and or stopping of the specialization as it seeks to find new ways to compete.

When one country has a lower opportunity cost of production than another, it has a comparative advantage. For example, India can produce either coats or hoodies, but the production is equal to increments of 200 coats for 200 hoodies. If India decides to produce 100 more coats, it must give up producing 100 hoodies. The production of 100 hoodies is an opportunity cost for India. Now, the scenario is the same for the United States. Why should the U.S. fashion companies seek to produce in India when they can produce the product in the United States? The answer is the cost of production in India is cheaper; therefore, India has the comparative advantage. The differences in the domestic opportunity costs necessitate that countries specialize, each according to a comparative advantage. Each country can achieve an increased output of resources and together countries can use their scarce resources more efficiently. The comparative advantage is pointless unless the country can produce efficiently at the lowest cost. *Absolute advantage* is often confused with comparative advantage. Absolute advantage is when a country produces products at a lower cost using the least amount of resources. When foreign governments subsidize industries, as Vietnam does to their fashion industry, it is difficult to assess whether or not the country truly offers comparative or absolute advantages. An advantage for a foreign country seeking to do business with the United States is speed of production. As fashion retailers operate with lower inventory levels, the speed and timeliness of deliveries is critical.

Nations specialize in the production of a particular area of the fashion supply chain; therefore, in economic terms, each nation is selling its service and output for money to the benefit of both nations involved. Economists note that when a country specializes in the production of one particular area, workers benefit because they become skilled in the specialization and consumers benefit because they end up with a product that has a value attached to it.

Barriers to Free Trade

Import quotas protect the domestic industry of a country. Quotas set limits to restrict the number of specific goods allowed into the country for a specific period of time, usually a year. Some quotas are worldwide while others are for specific foreign countries. For example, the North American Free Trade Agreement established trade preference limits on cotton or manufactured fiber wool apparel, wool apparel, fiber fabrics and made-ups, and cotton or manufactured fiber yarns (HTS Section XI Additional U.S. Notes). Established by presidential proclamation or legislation, quotas are either **absolute** or **tariff-rate**. Absolute quotas limit the quantity of goods allowed to enter the United States. Reaching the limit means that no additional goods of that type may enter the country until the quota period ends. For example, in 2002 there was a quota on 100 percent cotton and cotton blend denim jeans manufactured in China. Before the all-important back-to-school selling season, most manufacturers had reached their cotton denim quota; therefore, many of the jeans ordered by retailers were held in customs, leaving selling floors understocked in the jeans classification for back-to-school. This created a financial burden on the manufacturers of the jeans as well as the retailers, and the needs of the customers were left unsatisfied.

Tariff-rate quotas set a limit on the amount of goods that may enter the United States at a reduced rate of customs duty during the quota period. The quantity of goods that may enter is unlimited; however, quantities in excess of the quota limit are subject to a higher duty. In other words, a certain number of goods may enter at the lower rate before customs raises the rate on additional goods. A tariff-rate quota increases prices in the marketplace as manufacturers recover the cost of the tariff by adding the tariff to the wholesale cost of the goods. The president proclaimed most tariff-rate quotas under agreements negotiated under the Trade Agreements Act (www.customs.gov).

A **tariff** or **duty** is a tax imposed by the government on certain imported products it wants to restrict and thereby promote the competitiveness of the domestic product. Tariffs give a price advantage to locally produced goods over similar goods, which are imported, and they raise revenues for governments (World Trade Organization Tariffs). Many fashion goods, such as leather, genuine fur, faux fur, overcoats, sleepwear, skirts, and trousers (to name a few), are subject to tariffs based on the skins, yarns, and fabrics used in production. The amount of the tariff varies, but it is usually a percentage of the first cost. **First cost** is the wholesale price of merchandise in the country of origin.

Intellectual Property Rights

Intellectual property refers to creations of the mind: inventions; literary and artistic works; and symbols, names, images, and designs used in commerce. According to U.S. **Immigration and Customs Enforcement (ICE)**, **intellectual property rights** (IPR) violations involve the illegal use of trademarks, trade names, and copyrights. Copying designs and then selling them

TABLE 11.1

These are the top commodities seized by the U.S. Customs and Border Protection. The table shows statistical information comparing the monetary values from year to year. Notice that footwear has the highest value based on dollar amount and percentage.

	FY 2010	FY 2011
Number	19,959	24,792
Domestic value (in millions)	$188.1	$178.3
MSRP (est. in millions)	$1,413	$1,110

(*Source:* http://www.cbp.gov/linkhandler/cgov/trade/priority_trade/ipr/ipr_ communications/seizure/ipr_seizures_fy2011.ctt/ipr_seizure_fy2011.pdf)

for a profit is common in the fashion industry. The display of the innovation and creativity of the fashion industry puts the property of the companies into a community where selling knocked-off designs generates profit. Known as **style piracy**, the copying of original work is an international problem. The following are some facts from the International Anti-Counterfeiting Coalition:

- Counterfeiting costs U.S. businesses $200 billion to $250 billion annually.
- Counterfeit merchandise is directly responsible for the loss of more than 750,000 American jobs.
- Since 1982, the global trade in illegitimate goods has increased from $5.5 billion to approximately $600 billion annually.
- U.S. companies suffer $9 billion in trade losses due to international copyright piracy.
- Counterfeiting poses a threat to global health and safety.

Regulating counterfeiting and seizing property is often debated. Prosecuting piracy is not uniform due to different laws in different parts of the world. One fact that is consistent, and not up for debate, is that counterfeiting is illegal and costs the economy billions of dollars per year. Table 11.1 shows a comparison of the top commodities seized in 2010 versus 2011. The 19,959 seizures the Immigration and Customs Enforcement (ICE) reported in 2010 totaled more than $188.1 million in counterfeit and pirated goods, a 34 percent increase in domestic value over the 14,841 seizures in 2009. Refer to Figure 11.4 for a graphic comparison of IPR seizures versus

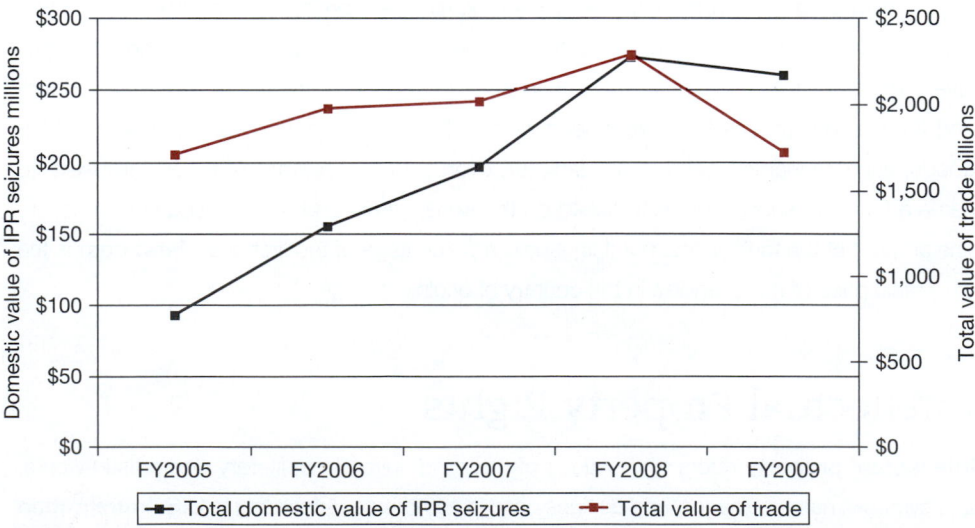

FIGURE 11.4 *Comparison of intellectual property rights (IPR) seizures versus total imports (Source: Public Domain from U.S. Customs and Border Protection).*

TABLE 11.2
U.S. trading partners' contributions to domestic value of seizures

Country	2011	2010
China	62%	66%
Hong Kong	18%	14%
India	3%	4%
All others	17%	16%

(*Source:* Public Domain from U.S. Customs and Border Protection)

total imports. Goods from China accounted for 66 percent of all seizures in 2010. Refer to Table 11.2 for details of U.S. trading partners' contribution to the number of seizures.

The list includes several fashion categories such as footwear, wearing apparel, and hand-bags/wallets/backpacks. Footwear was the top commodity seized in 2010 with a domestic value of $46.7 million, which accounted for 24 percent of the entire value of infringing goods. Counterfeit trade is booming and designer handbags have long been a sought-after counterfeit item. The idea of owning a Louis Vuitton bag for $50 rather than $1,500 appeals to a consumer who wishes to own a Louis Vuitton bag but cannot afford one. Consumers with little disposable income see knockoffs as a bargain and are willing to accept lower quality for a lower price. Figure 11.5 displays two Louis Vuitton bags, one original (Figure 11.5a) and one counterfeit (Figure 11.5b). Distinguishing the real from the fake is not easy. There are no recorded sales of counterfeit Louis Vuitton bags, but sales estimates on the bags are nearly a billion dollars. In addition to Louis Vuitton, other popular brands that are often counterfeited include Nike, The Northface, Chanel, Burberry, Dooney & Bourke, and Gucci, to name a few.

Well-known retailers sometimes fight allegations of copying the products and designs of recognized designers. Forever 21, Inc., a well-known cheap-chic retailer, is often embroiled in court battles fighting such charges. *Women's Wear Daily* reported in May 2009 that Jin Sook Chang, cofounder of Forever 21, testified in court against charges by Trovata that Forever 21 had copied the designs of Trovata. While the similarities are striking, Chang stood firm that the sweater designs in question were not unique to Trovata. This case is one of the more than 50 cases brought against Forever 21 in the last three-and-a-half years by companies such as Diane von Furstenberg, Anna Sui, Anthropologie, and Bebe. Out-of-court settlements ended most cases (Brown, 2009).

Designers and brands take their trademarks seriously. Using their names in an unapproved and inappropriate manner is illegal and unappreciated. On June 15, 2009, Chanel took out a full-page ad in *Women's Wear Daily* chastising what they called "mis-users" of the Chanel name. The ad describes what Chanel "was" and "is." Other designers have taken similar action to inform the public and protect the brands they have worked tirelessly to build.

The Foreign Exchange Market

The fashion industry, like all international businesses, must be concerned with the function of money in the global economy. The primary issue is that the money firms pay for goods and services and the money received for goods

FIGURE 11.5 *Louis Vuitton bag (Source: Alamy).*

and services will constantly change. This happens because in an international transaction at least one party is not dealing with its own currency, an element of risk that does not occur in a domestic transaction. Therefore, the foreign exchange rate becomes part of the risk of doing business in other countries and the aspects that manage and mitigate that risk are examined. A **foreign exchange rate** is the price of one currency in terms of another. If the exchange rate between the U.S. dollar and the Euro is $1.36, every Euro purchased costs $1.36. There are different delivery dates for exchange rates. A **spot exchange rate** takes place immediately. **Forward rates** are rates for transactions that take place sometime in the future, but seldom for more than 90–180 days. For example, a buyer of forward Euro agrees to pay $2,800 in 90 days. In 90 days, the buyer is obligated to take delivery of the Euro and pay the agreed-upon rate regardless of the current spot rate of the Euro. The difference in the spot rate and the forward rate is relative to the country's interest rate. In 90 days if the Euro is higher, the buyer realizes a profit; conversely if the Euro is lower, the buyer incurs a loss.

The rise or fall in value of a foreign currency affects an international company's ability to compete. When a currency rises in value, it is more expensive to buy goods priced in that currency and vice versa. Because the fashion industry operates as an "order today but take delivery sometime in the future" type of business, understanding exchange rates is vital to understanding the true cost of the goods. This is a converse relationship. Fashion businesses buy goods abroad and fashion businesses sell goods abroad; therefore, knowing how much is due at the time of delivery has dual impact. For example, a buyer for a chain of men's shoe stores bought Italian leather shoes from a company in Italy with delivery in 90 days. The buyer of the shoes now has two choices: take a spot rate at the time payment is due or lock in a 90-day forward rate. The buyer decides to lock in a 90-day forward rate. The shoe delivery transpired in the timeframe promised and the Italian manufacturer sent an invoice for the shoes to the store. The retailer renders payment to the manufacturer in Italy and the manufacturer's bank converts the dollars to Euros based on the current exchange rate. If the current rate is higher than the forward rate, the buyer made a wise decision to reserve the Euro at a forward rate but if the rate is lower than the current rate, the buyer will pay more than intended for the shoes. At this point, depending on the spot rate, the retail price of the shoes may require reevaluation.

The U.S. dollar is the most widely traded currency in the world. U.S. currency is the benchmark for most of the world's currency due to the economic power of the U.S. economy; therefore, when the supply of the U.S. dollar increases, the "price" falls globally based on demand of foreign currency; conversely, when the supply of the U.S. dollar decreases, the "price" increases globally based on the demand for foreign currency. Based on supply and demand, a shift in the supply of the dollar affects exchange rates (Figure 11.6).

Going Global

A fashion company competes and is able to expand by offering products that create a need among consumers for those products. **Market saturation** is the point at which the quantity of products in use in the marketplace is close to or at its maximum and further growth requires product improvements, market share gains, or a rise in overall consumer demand. Market saturation can mean the demise of a product and as the market saturation occurs, companies look for new avenues to market products. Many fashion companies expand the life cycle of an item by selling the goods internationally. Expanding into the global marketplace where customs, cultures, and currency are different is more difficult than conducting business domestically, but there are many positive reasons to invest internationally.

$1.00 EQUALS €.74

As of October 8, 2011,
one US dollar was equal to .74 Euro

€1.00 EQUALS $1.34

As of October 8, 2011,
one Euro was equal to one
US dollar and thirty four cents

FIGURE 11.6 *Worth of apparel in dollars by country.*

Fashion companies have to create competitive advantages to compete overseas. Advantages include economies of scale, superior knowledge or technical expertise, cost reductions, foreign subsidies, and diversification of assets. A company characterized by economies of scale has the ability to operate more efficiently, with lower cost structures. This gives the firm an advantage over smaller firms with higher costs per unit. In addition, bringing a product to market is sometimes dependent on local production because of trade barriers. Superior knowledge or technical expertise speaks to a company's proficiency in research and development or marketing skills. Both production and marketing capabilities can offset the cost of investing in overseas operations and can provide a competitive advantage that allows for a profitable venture even if the cost structure is higher.

Taking a company global can also result in cost reductions on raw materials and labor. In some firms, global expansion is critical to obtaining necessary raw materials for production. Overseas expansion primarily occurs because of lower labor costs. In the fashion industry, as previously mentioned, China has become a leading producer of fashion-related products because of its low labor costs. Subsidies like special tax treatment, tariff protection, or below-market financing entice companies to invest abroad. Foreign governments often offer subsidies to attract technology, jobs, and foreign exchange. Diversifying a company's portfolio has many advantages abroad as it does domestically (Bruner et al., 2003).

Analyzing all the risks is crucial before investing in business overseas. The first factor to consider, whether a firm is domestic or global, is the customer. Products may not be attractive to foreign customers and require adaptations before bringing the products to market. The second factor is the culture of the country and their business practices. **Culture** is the fundamental determinant of a person's wants and behavior. Practices that are a normal part of the American culture may be offensive in other countries. Additionally, understanding foreign regulations is a risk, as a lack of understanding will result in unexpected costs and delays in bringing product to the marketplace. Furthermore, finding talented managers with international experience is difficult and placing managers without the experience may prove to be expensive and detrimental to the entire venture. Lastly, conducting business overseas is fraught with political risks including revolutions, the expropriation of foreign property, devaluation of currency, and changes in laws. After evaluating the risks, the process of how to market the product begins.

Marketing begins with the consumer, and assessing products carefully and thoughtfully from the perspective of the consumer in the intended country is critical. To ensure that the product appeals to the target customer in a particular country and of a certain culture, adaptations, or modifications of the product in terms of color, size, or style may be necessary. In many big cities, because of globalization, clothing worn does not differ dramatically from that in the United States. However, differences do exist. For example, in India, wedding dresses are traditionally red, whereas in the United States wedding gowns are white or some variation of white. Therefore, the cultural acceptance of a color is an important delineation for a U.S. apparel manufacturer that desires to expand globally. After establishing adaptations and modifications, the next step is to determine the price.

Price, in the currency of the destination country, is set, but not without research and careful planning. Price is a significant determinant of whether or not the product will be accepted. Price is a delicate balance of earning as much profit from an item as possible and keeping the price on the item desirable for the target customer. The value placed on products by consumers is not constant internationally; therefore, knowing what the market will bear on the products brought to a new marketplace cannot be overemphasized. Distribution decisions follow once an acceptable price point is established.

What is the most effective distribution channel for the product? Is a brick-and-mortar store required? Is this an Internet business? Are licensing and/or franchising part of the marketing plan? What are the transportation needs? These questions are complicated and difficult to answer, requiring a great deal of research and planning. Companies worldwide answer these questions in various ways. Fashion companies such as Ralph Lauren, Nike, and Coach operate brick-and-mortar stores all over the world while maintaining websites where merchandise is available for purchase. Zara also has stores worldwide and they too have a website. However, Zara does not allow customers to purchase goods from their website. The Zara website is informational in its use. Some companies, like Benetton, are franchises. These companies made the decision about how they would conduct business in a global environment. The commonality shared by all is a strong brand.

According to *The Apparel Wars*, by A. T. Kearney, "The transition from labels to true brands calls for merchandising and marketing skills that do not typically exist in a retail environment. Yet the build out to these competencies can be managed in states beginning with education and developing processes for private label goods that will eventually lead to a full-blown brand building." Branding a product is an important step before taking a product global. The American Marketing Association defines a **brand** as "a name, term, sign, symbol, or design, or a combination of them, intended to identify the goods or services of one seller or group of sellers and to differentiate them from those of competitors." Brands identify the source of products and allow consumers to associate those brands with a particular manufacturer. To consumers, brands denote quality and dependability. Brands have the ability to satisfy wants and needs and in the process reduce the risk that the consumer will purchase a product he or she will consider substandard. Branding is all about creating differences between one product and another even when the products are identical.

International companies' marketing programs vary from standardized and low cost to highly adapted, to adjust to each local market, and expensive. Most companies find a marketing program between these two extremes. Obviously, not all marketing plans that work in the U.S. market would be appropriate in every overseas market. Companies sometimes learn marketing lessons the hard way and make adjustments as they go, as Nike had to do in Europe. One of Nike's most successful ad campaigns, "Just Do It," encouraged the average person to reach for the stars and chase his or her athletic dreams. The ads were perfect for the American market and consumers responded to the message of self-empowerment and the all-American "can do" attitude. When Nike took the message to Europe, the Europeans found the ads aggressive, and rather than seeing Nike as an activewear company, they saw Nike as a fashion company. Nike took a new approach and began associating its shoes with well-known athletes familiar to the European consumer, like the Brazilian soccer team that won the World Cup in 1994. By 2003, Nike's overseas revenues surpassed U.S. revenues for the first time (Kotler and Keller, 2008).

International Fashion Markets

Markets are where goods are produced and sold at wholesale. Fashion buyers attend markets to purchase goods for retail stores. There are two types of markets: **domestic markets** are markets in one's own country and **foreign markets** are markets outside one's own country. France was once the only foreign fashion market and highlighted French haute couture designs, the most prestigious of all fashion; but now, markets are seen all over the world. In the 1960s, the ready-to-wear market appeared in Italy and then in France. Now fashion markets are seen in Great Britain, Italy, Germany, Scandinavia, Canada, Mexico, China, and Japan (to name a few). Many retail fashion buyers visit foreign markets twice a year to stay abreast of global trends, seek new items, and search for up-and-coming designers. Foreign markets give retailers a competitive advantage by offering products from vendors that are not available domestically, adding an element of exclusivity to the retailer's assortment. Each country's market is unique to that country. For example, France connotes high fashion; Italy is arguably superior in knitwear, leather, and accessories; and Great Britain was first famous for men's wear and now for innovative, cutting-edge design. Another facet of globalization is the developing countries that are becoming important in the fashion arena, particularly in providing raw materials and undertaking production.

U.S. Textile and Apparel Free Trade Agreements

The General Agreement on Tariffs and Trade (GATT) makes negotiating trade agreements possible (WTO). GATT formed the **World Trade Organization** after World War II with the purpose of monitoring trade, settling trade disputes, and operating a system of trade rules. With the formation of the WTO, trade has grown "22 times the level since 1950" (WTO). The main function of the WTO is to facilitate the flow of goods among countries without interruption. WTO is a liaison in the resolution of unfair trade practices among countries. It is a protective agency designed to help consumers, businesses, and countries involved in international trade. Currently there are 153 countries that belong to the WTO. Trade statistics, published monthly by the International Trade Administration, show imports and exports from countries all over the world. With no boundaries between nations, trade agreements and trade preference programs ensure fair trade among nations and their trading partners and thus encourage their trade with one another. When the conditions of the trade agreements are met, generally the tariffs or duties are lowered. At times, duty rates have maximum shipments requirements but once the requirement is fulfilled, the duty is reduced. It is a win/win situation for all parties involved. Figure 11.7 demonstrates in percentages what apparel is worth by country.

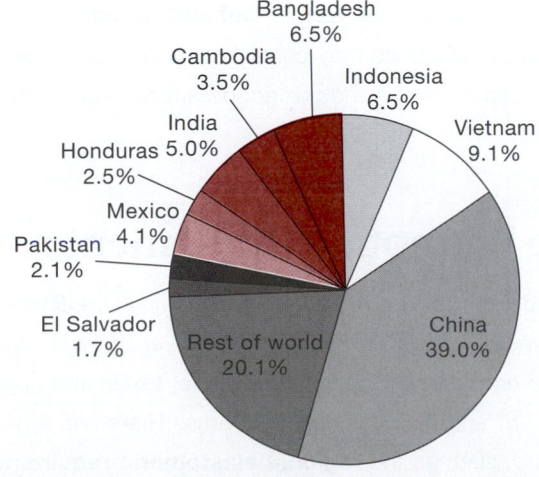

FIGURE 11.7 *The pie chart demonstrates the worth of the apparel industry by country.*

The following sections review current U.S. textile and apparel free trade agreements, including the **North American Free Trade Agreement (NAFTA)** and agreements with Dominican Republic-Central America (CAFTA-DR), Peru, Chile, Australia, Singapore (USSFTA), Oman, Bahrain, Israel, Jordan, and Morocco. As you read about each trade agreement, find the country or countries associated with the trade agreement on the map located on the inside front cover.

North American Free Trade Agreement (NAFTA)

The North American Free Trade Agreement, or NAFTA, states that qualifying textile and apparel will be classified as duty-free when exported to Canada and Mexico. To qualify as duty-free, these products must first be produced in the United States, either entirely of NAFTA products or with foreign products that have undergone a sufficient amount of processing within the United States. There are some exceptions; one is the **tariff preference levels (TPLs)**. TPLs are allowances made for specified nonoriginating products like yarns, fabrics, apparel, and premade textile goods that do not qualify as duty-free products, but meet the requirements for a preferential duty depending on the product and NAFTA partner.

Dominican Republic-Central America Free Trade Agreement (CAFTA-DR)

The Dominican Republic-Central America Free Trade Agreement, or CAFTA-DR, includes seven countries, the United States, Costa Rica, Dominican Republic, El Salvador, Guatemala, Honduras, and Nicaragua. CAFTA-DR surpasses the Caribbean Basin Trade Partnership Act (CBTPA) by allowing for further trade and business opportunities within the CAFTA-DR market.

Qualifying U.S. textile and apparel products are classified as duty-free when exported into the CAFTA-DR region by meeting the requirements of the textile and apparel rule of origin, which is commonly known as the **yarn-forward standard**. This standard requires that the yarn production and all operations from fabric production to apparel assembly must occur in either the United States and/or the CAFTA-DR region. There are some exceptions to the yarn-forward rule of origin, such as the **"Cut and Assemble" Rule of Origin**, which states that some yarns and fabrics may come from countries outside of the CAFTA-DR region as long as the fabric is cut and the goods are assembled in one or more of the CAFTA-DR countries.

Peru Trade Promotion Agreement

Under the **Peru Trade Promotion Agreement**, qualifying U.S. fibers, yarns, and apparel products can be exported into Peru duty-free. The yard-forward standard is in effect, which means that to enter the U.S. market duty-free, textile and apparel products must be made by using U.S. and regional Peruvian yarns. There are some exceptions to the yard-forward standard, such as the **regional elastomeric requirement**, which requires all elastomeric materials to be sourced from the regional suppliers to be eligible for duty-free entry. Other exceptions that are entitled for duty-free entry consist of those products that are required for production but are not commercially accessible in the region. There are also special textile safeguards in place that are subject to **most-favored-nation (MFN)** rates if a surge in imports is causing, or threatening to cause, serious damage to domestic industry.

Chile Free Trade Agreement

Under the **Chilean Free Trade Agreement**, duties on textile, apparel, footwear, and travel goods imported into Chile are exempt. To qualify, these goods must either be processed in the originating countries, the United States or Chile, or be made up of a specific amount of material initially processed in the United States or Chile.

All goods made exclusively of materials from the United States or Chile will automatically qualify for duty-free status. However, goods containing materials from other countries qualify if they meet specific criteria, such as the yarn-forward standard.

The yarn-forward standard requires that the yarn production and all further processes that make up for the completion of the product must occur in either the United States and/or Chile. However, the fiber may be sourced from any country, unless there are exceptions that require **fiber-forward** or **fabric-forward** standards.

If an item does not meet the yard-forward standard, it still may quality for duty exemption if all nonoriginating fibers and yarns make up less than a **de minimis** (7 percent) of the total weight of the product. Special provisions also apply to textile and apparel goods that are for retail sale.

Australia Free Trade Agreement

Under the **Australia Free Trade Agreement**, duties on qualifying textile and apparel goods imported into Australia are exempt. Travel goods and footwear exported from Australia, excluding 17 specific rubber/fabric and plastic/protective footwear items, are duty-free. The 17 exceptions will also qualify for duty-free entry on January 1, 2014.

To qualify for duty-free entry, all goods must be made of a specific amount of materials originating from the United States or Australia, or have been processed in the originating countries. All goods made exclusively of materials from the United States or Australia will automatically qualify for duty-free entry. However, goods containing materials from other countries may still qualify if they meet specific criteria, such as the yarn-forward standard that requires that the yarn production and all further processes that make up the completion for the product must occur in either the United States and/or Australia. However, the fiber may be sourced from any country, unless there are exceptions that require fiber-forward or fabric-forward standards.

If a product does not meet the yard-forward standard, it still may qualify for duty exemption if all nonoriginating fibers and yarns make up less than a de minimis (7 percent) of the total weight of the product. Special provisions also apply to textile and apparel goods that are for retail sale. Box 11.1 is an promotional material about Claudia Chan Shaw knitwear, a company in Australia with a niche in the marketplace. The company would qualify for duty exemption should it seek to go global.

Vivian Chan Shaw

Worn by discerning women around the world, Australian label Vivian Chan Shaw specializes in hand loomed women's knitwear. Called the "Queen of Australian Knitwear" by Harpers Bazaar, Vivian Chan Shaw creates designs that are flowing, soft, and easy and range from separates to divine two-pieces you could wear to a gala premiere.

{ *"A master of knit who would rival the Missinis."*
Sportswear international

Every garment is hand loomed in Australia, with each design knitted into shape—not cut and sewn. Each garment is therefore truly individual. (Think Missoni meets Yohji with a twist.)

The label was started in 1972 by designer, Vivian Chan Shaw and today the company is run by mother and daughter team, Vivian and Claudia Chan Shaw. Vivian and Claudia now share the design role.

One of Australia's ground breaking early fashion exporters, the Vivian Chan Shaw label, with its flagship store in Sydney's Queen Victoria Building, is sold around Australia, and over the years has exported to the United States, Germany, Switzerland, the United Kingdom, and New Zealand.

Chelsea Clinton has stopped at the Vivian Chan Shaw store. Sally Jessy Raphael is a fan. Randy Crawford drops by when she's in town.

The hand loom gives Vivian Chan Shaw the freedom to create knitted shapes that flow and drape—shapes that cannot be achieved with commercial knitting. The result is a light-weight, gossamer fine knit—the perfect travelling companion, which rolls into ball in your suitcase and arrives unwrinkled at the other end; in a range of fibres including blends of wool, cotton, silk, mohair, and manmade fibres. The yarns used are all dyed to the Vivian Chan Shaw specifications and are ingeniously blended.

Vivian Chan Shaw is internationally recognized as a master of knit. The label's signature draping and fluid lines are distinctive and original.

A label of timeless elegance, Vivian Chan Shaw is represented in the permanent collection of the Powerhouse Museum, Sydney.

The handmade product had become sought after around the world, and is riding high on the claim that the designs are truly individual. To see a Vivian Chan Shaw design is to recognize that this claim is indeed true.

Note: An exquisite range of costume jewellery has been added to the Vivian Chan Shaw collection. The designs, featuring gem stones, jet, Venetian glass beads, and cinnabar are all personally created by the designer. Not surprisingly, every earring and necklace in the collection is handmade.

HEAD OFFICE : 139 DOWLING STREET
WOOLLOOMOOLOO NSW 2011
AUSTRALIA

T: +61 2 9356 3700 F: +61 2 9358 1617
E: claudia@vivianchanshaw.com
W: www.vivianchanshaw.com

Singapore Free Trade Agreement (USSFTA)

According to the rules of the **Singapore Free Trade Agreement**, all eligible textiles, apparel, footwear, and travel goods imported into Singapore from the United States will qualify for duty-free entry. Textiles and apparel coming from Singapore to the United States will be exempt from duty as well.

To qualify for duty-free entry, all goods must be made of a specific amount of materials originating from the United States or Singapore, or have been processed in the originating countries. All goods made exclusively of materials from the United States or Singapore will automatically qualify for duty-free status. However, goods containing materials from other countries may still qualify if they meet specific criteria, such as the yarn-forward standard, which requires that the yarn production and all further processes that make up the completion for the product must occur in either the United States and/or Singapore. However, the fiber may be sourced from any country, unless there are exceptions that require fiber-forward or fabric-forward standards. Some exceptions to the yarn-forward standard include such goods as brassieres, as well as silk and linen apparel products that are made from fabric that is cut, knit, sewn, and/or finished in the United States or Singapore. If an item does not meet the yard-forward standard, it may qualify for duty exemption if all nonoriginating fibers and yarns make up less than a de minimis (7 percent) of the total weight of the product.

Oman Free Trade Agreement

Under the **Oman Free Trade Agreement**, duties on footwear and travel goods imported into Oman are exempt. Additionally, a specific amount of apparel goods that do not meet the yarn-forward standard receive a **preferential tariff rate**. These preferential tariff rates for apparel, or tariff preference level (TPL), are set at 50,000,000 square meters for cotton and all human-made fibers that are used in the production of apparel goods. Any apparel goods exceeding the TPL will be subject to MFN rates of duty.

After the TPL expires, the remainder of goods imported into Oman must adhere to the yarn-forward standard, which requires that the yarn production and all further processes that make up the completion for the product, must occur in either the United States and/or Oman. If a good does not meet the yard-forward standard, it may still qualify for duty exemption if all nonoriginating fibers and yarns make up less than a de minimis (7 percent) of the total weight of the product. Special provisions also apply to textile and apparel goods that are for retail sale.

Bahrain Free Trade Agreement

According to the rules put forth in the Bahrain Free Trade Agreement, all eligible textiles, apparels, and footwear and travel goods imported into Bahrain from the United States will be exempt from duty. To qualify for duty-free status these goods must be made of a specific amount of materials that originated from, or were processed in, the United States or Bahrain.

Goods made exclusively of materials from the United States or Bahrain will automatically qualify for duty-free entry; however, goods containing materials from other countries may still qualify for duty-free status if they first meet specific criteria, such as the yarn-forward standard. The yarn-forward standard requires that yarn production, and all further processes that make up the completion for the product, must occur in either the United States and/or Bahrain; however, the fiber may be sourced from any country.

The agreement also states that a specific amount of goods made with cotton or human-made fiber textiles that do not meet the yarn-forward standard will receive a preferential tariff rate. These preferential tariff rates for apparel, known as TPL, are set at 65,000,000 square meters. Any goods exceeding the TPL will be subject to MFN rates of duty. The TPLs are also applicable to Bahrain exports to the United States.

Israel Free Trade Agreement

Under the **Israel Free Trade Agreement**, duties on qualifying textile, apparel, footwear, and travel goods imported into Israel are exempt. Some exceptions will still be subjected to customs fees and taxes and the agreement does not cover exports to the West Bank or the Gaza Strip.

To qualify as duty-free, all goods entering into Israel must be produced or manufactured entirely in the United States. If goods are not exclusively made of, or produced in, the United States they will still qualify for duty exemption if they have a specific U.S. or Israel content to qualify for country of origin under the terms of the agreement. According to the agreement, that amount of value-added requirement is 35 percent, where the garment is required to be partially or fully assembled and finished in Israel.

Jordan Free Trade Agreement

Under the **Jordan Free Trade Agreement**, tariffs on the majority of textile, apparel, footwear, and travel goods were phased out in stages and most qualifying goods are now eligible for duty-free entry.

To qualify as duty-free, goods must be imported into Jordan directly from the United States and be made of at least 35 percent U.S. materials. If the product also contains materials from Jordan, up to 15 percent of the material can be counted toward the 35 percent requirement.

All goods made exclusively of materials from the United States automatically qualify for duty-free status; however, goods containing materials from other countries may still qualify if manufacturing or processing in the United States has substantially transformed them.

Morocco Free Trade Agreement

Under the **Morocco Free Trade Agreement**, duties on the majority of textile and apparel goods imported into Morocco are exempt, and the remainder of all qualifying products are to become duty-free by January 1, 2015.

The agreement contains a special allowance for U.S. and Moroccan industries to use cotton fibers from the least-developed sub-Saharan African countries. All apparel goods that do not meet the yarn-forward standard, which requires that the yarn production and all further processes that make up the completion for the product occur in either the United States and/or Morocco, will receive a preferential tariff rate. These preferential tariff rates for apparel, referred to as TPL, are set at 30,000,000 square meters for yarn and fabric that are used in the production of apparel goods. Any apparel goods exceeding the TPL will be subject to MFN rates of duty.

If a good does not meet the yard-forward standard, it still may qualify for duty exemption if all nonoriginating fibers and yarns make up less than a de minimis (7 percent) of the total weight of the product. Special provisions also apply to textile and apparel goods that are for retail sale. Figure 11.8 shows apparel imports ending January 2011.

Trade Preference Programs

The following section discusses the current trade preference programs, which consist of the African Growth and Opportunity Act (AGOA), The Andean Trade Promotion and Drug Eradication Act (ATPDEA), The Caribbean Basin Trade Partnership Act (CBTPA), and the Haitian Hemispheric Opportunity through Partnership Encouragement Act (HOPE).

FIGURE 11.8 *Apparel Imports: YTD January 2011 (Millions of dollars and units).*

Country	Dollars millions	SME millions	% Change dollars	% Change SME
World	**6,109**	**1,983**	**22.4**	**17**
China	2,385	8.5	20.9	10.4
Vietnam	557	185	19.8	21.7
Bangladesh	396	149	54.1	49
Indonesia	399	120	16.3	22.4
Cambodia	211	86	40.7	36.5
India	303	85	22.2	7.6
Honduras	150	77	23	18.5
Mexico	248	68	8.3	9.7
Pakistan	127	54	36.6	25.6
El Salvador	103	51	22.6	18.6
Rest of World	*1,230*	*303*	*19.8*	*16.1*
CBI	481	205	24.6	24.2
CAFTA – DR	449	190	18.2	17.3
South Asia	946	318	34.4	26.7
ASEAN	1,418	470	21.6	23.7
OECD	201	20	19.6	11.1

The African Growth and Opportunity Act (AGOA)

The **African Growth and Opportunity Act (AGOA)** allows for duty-free trade of apparel, textile, footwear, and travel goods between the United States and sub-Saharan African countries. Figure 11.9 is a list of countries and trade preference programs showing the dollar amounts through January 2011 of the apparel imports into the countries.

To qualify under the act, apparel is required to be comprised of yarns and fabrics originating from the United States, the sub-Saharan African countries, or from one or more of the designated lesser-developed countries. In addition, certain cashmere and merino wool sweaters, as well as hand-loomed, handmade, or folklore articles and ethnic printed fabrics are also eligible for duty-free trade. The lesser-developed beneficiary countries will also qualify for duty-free access for apparel made from fabric originating anywhere in the world.

The limitation for the amount of apparel goods imported into the United States from the sub-Saharan African countries is measured in SME (square meter equivalents). Currently this amount cannot surpass 7 percent. Those goods coming from the lesser-developed beneficiary countries cannot exceed three and a half percent of the total amount of apparel goods being imported into the United States.

All footwear and nontextile travel goods from the AGOA countries are duty-free, as long as they meet the rule of origin, where the product must contain a regional value content of at least 35 percent of the appraised value of the product. This percentage can be comprised of a combination of inputs from different AGOA countries, and no more than 15 percent of the total value can come from the United States.

Apparel products assembled in sub-Saharan Africa that contain the presence of some fibers or yarns not wholly formed in the United States, or beneficiary

Oil price volatility and the resulting currency swings aside, the single most important driver of US import growth is stronger demand for goods and services by our recovering economy.

Total US Imports and Exports Oil price spikes pushed imports up 23.4% in January to an unexpected $168 trillion. Other major import categories were autos, food, capital goods, and industrial supplies. Exports increased 21% to $111 trillion, due primarily to machinery, technology and energy products, and automobiles. Since imports are a much bigger number than exports, the deficit rose 28% to a staggering $57 billion.

International Trade Statistics	% Change	Jan	Dec	Jan
$MM - % Chng from PY	vs LY	2011	2010	2010
Total US Imports	23.4	168,504	168,544	136,509
Total US Exports	21.3	111,401	118,013	91,862
Total US Deficit	27.9	57,103	50,531	44,647
Apparel Imports	27.1	7,000	6,050	5,506
Apparel Exports	17.2	365	369	312
Apparel Deficit	27.7	6,635	5,681	5,194
Textile Imports	15.8	1,857	1,744	1,604
Textile Exports	19.2	969	897	813
Textile Deficit	12.3	888	847	791
App & Text as % of Tot Def		13.2	12.9	13.4

Apparel Imports and Exports Imports surged 22% in dollars and 7% on a unit basis compared to last January. Unit costs rose because of rising raw material and labor costs, which manufacturers have at least partially passed on to their US retail and wholesale customers. All major apparel categories grew in both dollars and units. Women's and men's tops were the largest import categories, but sweaters, men's tops, and women's lingerie were the fastest-growing. Exports rose 17% to $365 million, buoyed by trade with Canada, which consumes over a third of our apparel exports, and growth in shipments to Mexico, the UK, Belgium, and El Salvador.

sub-Saharan African countries, will still be eligible for duty-free access as long as the total weight of all foreign fibers and yarns does not exceed 10 percent of the total weight of the product.

A certificate of origin is required for each shipment. In order for countries to be eligible, they must first have an effective visa system with enforcement and verification procedures in place to prevent illegal transshipment and use of counterfeit documentation.

The Andean Trade Promotion and Drug Eradication Act (ATPDEA)

The **Andean Trade Promotion and Drug Eradication Act (ATPDEA)** provides duty-free trade between the United States and Bolivia, Colombia, Ecuador, and Peru for certain apparel, textile, and footwear products manufactured in Colombia and Ecuador.

To qualify for duty-free access under the act, apparel must be sewn or assembled in Colombia, Ecuador, or the United States, and foreign findings and trimming, such as sewing thread, hook and eyes, snaps, buttons, decorative lace trim, elastic strips, and zippers, may be used up to 25 percent of the cost of the product. Fabrics, or fabric components, wholly formed or knit-to-shape in the United States from yarns wholly produced in the United States, Colombia, or Ecuador, will only qualify if all dyeing, printing, and finishing of the fabrics is done in the United States.

Footwear assembled in Colombia and Ecuador must contain 35 percent regional value content from either United States or Colombia and Ecuador to qualify for duty-free access. Apparel and textile products not wholly formed in the United States, Colombia, or Ecuador may still qualify for duty-free access if the total weight of the foreign-used fibers or yarns is not more than 7 percent of the total weight of the product. A **certificate of origin** is required for each shipment of apparel and textiles to qualify for duty-free treatment under the ATPDEA.

The Caribbean Basin Trade Partnership Act (CBTPA)

The **Caribbean Basin Trade Partnership Act (CBTPA)** officially began on October 1, 2000, and is in effect until September 30, 2020. Under the act, Antigua and Barbuda, Aruba, Bahamas, Barbados, Belize, Costa Rica, Dominica, Grenada, Guyana, Haiti, Jamaica, Montserrat, Netherlands Antilles, Panama, St. Kitts and Nevis, St. Lucia, Saint Vincent and the Grenadines, Trinidad and Tobago, and the British Virgin Islands benefit from duty-free access on qualifying apparel, textile, and footwear products.

In order to qualify, the product must contain fabrics and yarn that was wholly formed and cut in the United States and assembled into apparel in one or more of the beneficiary countries in the Caribbean Basin Region. Apparel that has undergone further processing, such as embroidery, stone-washing, enzyme-washing, acid washing, perma-pressing, oven-baking, bleaching, garment-dyeing, or screen printing, can also qualify for duty-free treatment.

Foreign fibers, yarns, and findings and trimming, such as sewing thread, hook and eyes, snaps, buttons, and decorative lace trim, may be used as long as the total weight of the fibers and yarns does not account for more than 7 percent of the total weight of the product and the findings and trimming do not exceed 25 percent of the cost of the product. However, if the fabric is wholly from the United States and is cut and sewn in a CBTPA beneficiary country, U.S. thread must be used for sewing.

Footwear assembled in the CBTPA region must contain 55 percent regional value content, which can be wholly from the United States or CBPTA beneficiary countries or a combination of both to qualify for duty-free treatment. A certificate of origin is required for each shipment of apparel and textiles to qualify for duty-free treatment under the CBTPA.

The Haitian Hemispheric Opportunity through Partnership Encouragement Act (HOPE)

In addition to the CBTPA, the **Haitian Hemispheric Opportunity through Partnership Encouragement Act (HOPE)** ensures that Haitian-manufactured textile and apparel products are eligible for additional duty-free treatment. In order for apparel to receive the

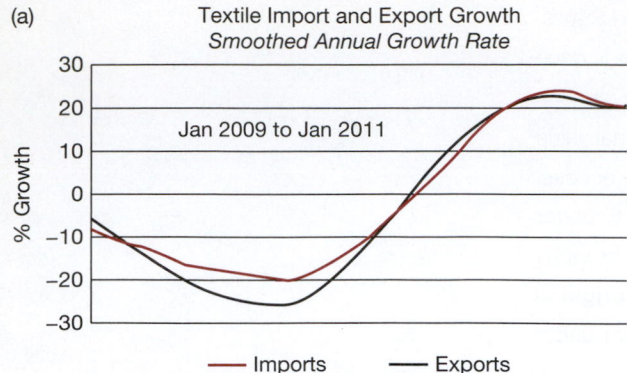

(a)
Textile Import and Export Growth
Smoothed Annual Growth Rate

Jan 2009 to Jan 2011

— Imports   — Exports

(b)
Textile Imports
Millions of Dollars

■ 2009   ■ 2010   ■ 2011

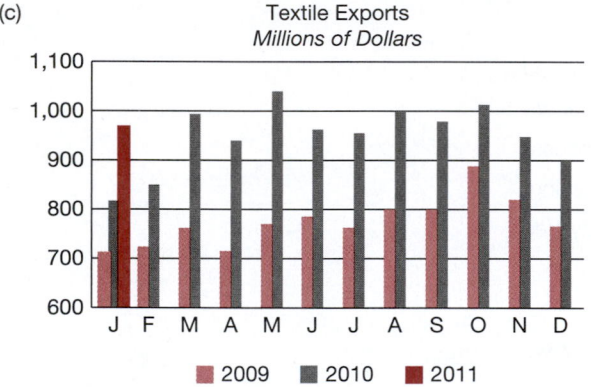

(c)
Textile Exports
Millions of Dollars

■ 2009   ■ 2010   ■ 2011

FIGURE 11.10 *Textile import and export growth in dollars and percent (Source: Apparel Strategist).*

additional treatment under HOPE and HOPE II, the apparel must be wholly assembled or knit-to-shape in Haiti and imported directly from Haiti or the Dominican Republic.

The limitation for the amount of apparel goods imported into the United States from Haiti or the Dominican Republic countries is measured in square meter equivalents (SME), with the total amount not to exceed 1.25 percent of the aggregate trade of the previous year. Certain apparel must meet applicable value-added requirements, which can range from 50 percent to 60 percent depending upon the applicable one-year period. A valid, original textile visa issued by the Government of Haiti is required for each shipment of apparel and textiles to qualify for duty-free treatment.

Resources Available to the Exporter

Office of Textiles and Apparel (OTEXA) is part of the International Trade Administration of the U.S. Department of Commerce. OTEXA is dedicated to helping those that work in the industry of textiles, apparel, and footwear to solve any problems that may arise with issues relating to importing, exporting, regulations, and classifications of a product or any other problem that may be more complex (OTEXA).

Export.gov is designed to help U.S. companies export their products. They provide four essential resources: (1) export assistance, (2) trade data and analysis, (3) relevant webinars and industry papers, and (4) assistance by industry market leads (export.gov).

International Monetary Fund (IMF) is made up of 187 countries. The purpose of the IMF is to provide assistance as needed to help the world's economies. IMF provides information about a country's economy, the world economy, statistical information on world trade, and the world economic outlook.

Export-Import Bank of the United States is designed as "the official export credit agency" for companies and people who want to get their products and services into the international marketplace. In existence for over 70 years, they provide many services including capital, loans, special initiatives, insurance, and lease guarantees. They have provided over 400 million dollars of services to U.S. exports to various international markets (Export-Import).

U.S. Customs and Border Protection is a department of Homeland Security. Their major focus is to protect the borders of the United States while ensuring that trade, travel, import, and export of goods flow freely among the borders by enforcing rules, regulations, policies, and laws. They keep the borders free from "terrorists and their weapons." In 2011, U.S. Customs assisted in over "$2 trillion legitimate trade" while working with all government agencies involved with trade issues (U.S. Customs). Figure 11.10 exhibits the textile import and export growth in dollars and percent.

Summary

This chapter explored the global fashion business by discussing the economic growth of nations and the globalization of brands. The distinctions in free trade and fair trade were examined along with comparative and absolute advantage. We learned that part of doing business in foreign countries and with other nations involves quotas, tariffs, duties, and trade agreements. Through our study of intellectual property and counterfeiting, we illustrated the significance of the problem and the detrimental effects counterfeiting has on local, national, and global economies. We looked at foreign markets and currency exchange to gain a broader understanding of the implications of doing business abroad. Lastly, trade agreements, trade preference programs, and agencies that aid in the trade process were studied.

Key Terms

absolute advantage   274

absolute quota   275

African Growth and Opportunity Act (AGOA)   287

Andean Trade Promotion and Drug Eradication Act (ATPDEA)   288

Australia Free Trade Agreement   283

Bahrain Free Trade Agreement   285

brand   280

Caribbean Basin Trade Partnership Act (CBTPA)   289

certificate of origin   289

Chilean Free Trade Agreement   283

comparative advantage   274

culture   279

"Cut and Assemble" Rule of Origin   282

de minimis   283

developed countries   274

domestic markets   280

Dominican Republic-Central America Free Trade Agreement (CAFTA-DR)   282

Export.gov   290

fabric forward   283

Export-Import Bank of the United States   290

fair trade   274

fiber forward   283

first cost   275

foreign exchange rate   278

foreign market   280

forward rates   278

free trade   274

global village   272

Haitian Hemispheric Opportunity through Partnership Encouragement Act (HOPE)   289

Immigration and Customs Enforcement (ICE)   275

import quotas   275

infrastructure   270

intellectual property   275

intellectual property rights   275

International Monetary Fund   290

Israel Free Trade Agreement   286

Jordan Free Trade Agreement   286

market saturation   278

Morocco Free Trade Agreement   286

most-favored-nations (MFN)   283

North American Free Trade Agreement (NAFTA)   282

Office of Textiles and Apparel (OTEXA)   290

Oman Free Trade Agreement   285

Peru Trade Promotion Agreement   282

preferential tariff rate   285

regional elastomeric requirement   282

Singapore Free Trade Agreement   284

spot exchange rates   278

style piracy   276

tariff/duty   275

tariff preference level (TPL)   282

tariff-rate quota   275

U.S. Customs and Border Protection   290

World Trade Organization   281

yarn-forward standard   282

Review Questions

1. Why does globalization have so many meanings? What is the meaning of globalization from a fashion economic perspective?

2. How can trade be restricted? Why would anyone want to restrict trade?

3. Explain how President Richard Nixon's trip to China has impacted world trade.

4. Discuss the economic growth of nations. How is it measured?

5. Read the proverb from Thomas L. Friedman's book, *The World Is Flat*. What is the relevance of the proverb to the fashion industry?

6. What is the difference between free trade and fair trade? How does that affect the fashion industry?

7. Explain two of the free-trade agreements. Explain two of the trade preference programs.

8. Why is intellectual property an economic threat to all nations?

9. What is the difference between a trade agreement and a trade preference program?

10. Explain the purpose of the World Trade Organization?

11. What three countries are involved in NAFTA? What does NAFTA stand for?

12. Explain the yarn-forward standard?

13. What is the exception to the yarn-forward standard?

14. Explain the difference between the Chile Free Trade Agreement and the Australia Free Trade Agreement?

15. Explain why all goods imported into Singapore are eligible for duty-free status? How can goods qualify as duty free for importation into Israel?

16. Explain the Trade Preference Program African Growth and Opportunity Act?

17. What is the difference between the Andean Trade Promotion and Drug Eradication Act (ATPDEA) and the Caribbean Basin Trade Partnership Act (CBTPA)?

18. What does OTEXA stand for? Why is it important?

19. List two resources for exporters and explain what they can do for them?

Critical Thinking

1. You are the product developer for Guess jeans, after sourcing the new denim line for the company; you decide where to produce the jeans. You have narrowed your choices to two countries, China and India. China's labor is lower, but you are very concerned about the human rights issues faced by Chinese laborers today. You know that the factory is clean and the final production is outstanding, but you know that child labor is being used. If you go to the factory in India for production, there is no child labor being used, and the quality is equal to the Chinese factory, but the cost of production is higher. In which country would you prefer to produce? Your decision and decisions like these help a country's economy.

2. Explain what you think would happen to the world economy if there were no tariff or import quotas in place.

3. You have decided to go into business for yourself and start a costume jewelry line. You cannot afford to open up a brick-and-mortar store, so you are going to sell as a wholesaler in the United States and one other country. What resources are you going to decide to sell and to which country?

4. Now that you have decided to sell your jewelry line in a country other than the United States, list the steps that you are going to go through to secure leads and find leads for potential distribution of your jewelry using the resources discussed in the chapter. You may use the website http://fibre2fashion.com to help find leads under industry leads.

Internet Activities

1. Visit the website for the Office of Textiles and Apparel (OTEXA) and answer the following questions: (1) Why are the imports from Vietnam being monitored as they assess into the World Trade Organization? (2) Explain what information would be useful to a buyer found on the OTEXA site.

2. Select one of the countries listed in the chapter. Profile the country to determine whether it is suitable for conducting business in terms of something fashion related whether it is manufacturing, retail distribution, importing product, and so on. Research the following information and then report your finding to the class: Population, average discretionary income, location, average age of consumer, global fashion products sold in the country, Internet access, and also a current article about the state of the country's economy. Have a classmate or your instructor make a chart on the board and fill in with the information that you as a class have collected about various countries. Which country, based on research, would be the best to conduct business. Why?

3. Access the website for the Office of Textiles and Apparel (OTEXA). You will find on the website statistics for trade. What five countries have the highest dollar import to the United States? What kind of economies do these countries have? Do you think based on the data that economies of these countries benefited from imports into the United States? Why or why not? Lastly, do you think the balance of imports coming into the United States based on this report are fair or free trade? Why?

Bibliography

About the IMF. (2011). 11 April 2011. Retrieved from http://www.imf.org/external/about.htm

Barbour, E. (2010, June 29). [Web log message]. Retrieved from http://international-trade-reports.blogspot.com/2010/07/trade-law-introduction-to-selected.html

Barnes, J., & Morris, M. (2008). *Globalization, the changed global dynamics of the clothing and textile value chains and the impact on Sub-Saharan Africa*. Vienna, Austria: Vienna International Centre, United Nations Industrial Development Organization.

Brown, R., & Riley-Katz, A. (2009, May 27). Mistrial in trovata, Forever 21 copying case. *Women's Wear Daily*.

Bruner, F., Eaker, M., Freeman, R., Spekman, R. R., Teisberg, E., & Venkataraman, S. (2003). *The portable MBA*, 4th ed. Hoboken, NJ: John Wiley & Sons.

Export-Import Bank of the United States. (2011). 11 April 2011. Retrieved from www.exim.gov

http://www.ice.gov/news/releases/1103/110316washingtondc.htm

http://www.ice.gov/doclib/news/releases/2011/110316washington.pdf

Kotler, P., & Keller, K. (2008). *A framework for marketing management*, 4th ed. Upper Saddle River, NJ: Prentice Hall.

Office of Textiles and Apparel. (OTEXA). (2011, April 11). Trade preference programs. Retrieved from http://www.otexa.ita.gov

Office of Textiles and Apparel. (OTEXA). (2011, April 11). Trade Agreements. Retrieved from http://www.otexa.ita.gov

Stovall, S., & Bjork, C. (2010, March 17). [Web log message]. Retrieved from http://blogs.wsj.com/source/tag/pablo-isla/

United States Export.gov. (2011, April 11). Retrieved from http://www.export.gov/

U.S. Customs and Border Protection. (2011). Department of Homeland Security, April 11, 2011. Retrieved from http://www.cbp.gov

World Trade Organization. (2011). *The multilateral trading system—past, present and future.* Retrieved from http://www.wto.org/english/thewto_e/whatis_e/inbrief_e/inbr01_e.htm

12

TRENDS IN
FASHIONOMICS

OBJECTIVES

After reading this chapter, you will be able to:

- Gain an understanding of what an economic trend is and how it evolves
- Examine the impact of economic trends in the fashion industry
- Evaluate current economic trends and their impact on the future of the fashion industry

The state of the economy has taken its toll on youth culture industries, but at the same time, it's organically incubated and created these veins of new market opportunities.

—TOM WALLACE, president of Label Networks

12

The common thread of this textbook is the focus of fashion economics and the con-nection between economics and the fashion industry. Whether it is the consumer of fashion, the designer of fashion, or the distributor of fashion, an understanding of the economics of the industry is necessary to create synchronization so that each level has the ability to make a profit. Therefore, it is vital to examine the trends that will enable the fashion industry to answer the three basic economic questions discussed in the beginning of the text: What to produce? How to produce? For whom to produce? Throughout this chapter, the future trends discussed relate in one way or another to those basic economic questions.

You now realize that fashion is a business, a driving economic force in the world today. It begins and ends with the needs and wants of the consumer, the force that enables the fashion industry to work at a rapid pace to produce those goods that meet their needs and wants. This chapter focuses on identifying economic trends and answering the questions: Where does a trend begin? And what are the resources of the basic trends? The discussion explores and discusses the top trends affecting the fashion industry today: **globalization**, *social media, technology, radio frequency identification, sportswear and technology,* **cross-merchandising** *of brands, growth of the luxury market, demographic changes, the changing American physique, the green movement, the impact of fashion designers and celebrities on apparel stores, and the conservative consumer.*

Economic Trends and the Impact on the Fashion Industry

An **economic trend** is the general direction of business conditions. The impact of economic trends is that they affect the decision making of a business, such as, is the time right for expansion, or should vertical integration be considered to lower the cost of the supply chain, or should underperforming stores be closed. Economic trends have a domino effect on the fashion trends and make a difference in business decisions. An economic trend is a graphical representation of the behavior of a financial position with respect to time. In simple terms, it is the expansion or contraction of a country's economy from one period to the next, typically represented over the course of the quarter, a year, or even decades.

The fashion industry embodies any product that is described as apparel, wearable acces-sories, or home fashions. According to Christopher, Lowson, and Peck (2009), the "fashion industry typically encompasses any product, services or market where there is an element of style and form that is likely to be short lived, if not constantly changing, with trends." Since fashion is characteristically in a state of constant flux, changing from one season to the next, year after year, the commercial success or failure of the fashion industry is determined not only by internal factors, such as an organization's marketing strategy, but by external factors, such as the global economy. For example, during the recession of 2007, consumers either refrained from purchasing new fashion items or began shopping in places known for lower prices. In the beginning of the first quarter of 2010, sales of fashion items hit an all-time low, with a marginal increase at the end of the quarter driven by new spring fashions. Purchasing fell back for the second and third quarters, to once again rebound in the fourth quarter with back-to-school spending. After experiencing several seasons of restraint, the retail industry eventually saw a 7 percent sales gain in the last two months of 2010.

A recent example of an economic trend, in regards to growth, has been in motion since the late nineteenth century with the increase of the standard of living of people in the developed world. North America, Western Europe, and Japan have seen a gradual growth in both GDP and per capita GDP. An example of the opposing economic trend is the sharp decline of the U.S. economy during the Great Depression. A current example of the opposing economic trend is the global recession that occurred in the latter part of 2007. Linked to the reckless lending practices of U.S. financial institutions and the growing trend of securitization of real estate mortgages, the global recession of 2007 earned the moniker the "**great recession**."

The major trends described below affect the fashion industry through marketing, business practices, inventory management, manufacturing, and assortment planning. Understanding these trends enables firms in the fashion industry to react to current conditions, keep their business plans relevant, and plan for the future.

Trend 1—Globalization

Though globalization is mentioned numerous times throughout this text, it is an ongoing trend that has occurred in the fashion industry, especially in the last 50 years. Globalization has enabled the world to open new markets, share resources, connect countries and people, and build relationships. The global demand for cheaper goods has spurred the growth of the globalization of the fashion industry, necessitating the production of fashion to grow tremendously in various countries around the world. There are positive and negative sides to globalization. Globalization has devastated the apparel and textiles industry in the United States with the Southern states getting hit the hardest. Numerous textile mills in the southern United States, such as Burlington Industries, Malden Mills, and Guilford Mills, filed for bankruptcy. Pillowtex Corporation, maker of Fieldcrest, Cannon, and Charisma bed linens, and Royal Velvet towels, is out of business altogether.

Also important to globalization are the evolving consumer markets in various countries throughout the world. More disposable and discretionary income is available to spend on fashion and retailers are eager to move into these markets. Retailers will enter the global markets by first testing through pop-up stores, the Internet, and catalogs, before making a more permanent move with a brick-and-mortar store or by licensing and franchising global partners.

Economic flows intertwine the U.S. economy with the economies of other nations. The **goods and services flow**, also known as trade flows, is the process adopted by the United States to export goods and services to other countries and import goods and services from them. **Capital and labor flows**, or resource flows, describe the establishment of production facilities by the United States in foreign countries and foreign firms establishing production facilities in the United States. As a result, labor also moves between nations when foreigners immigrate to the United States to work and Americans move to other countries to work. The **information and technology flow** involves the transmission of information from the United States to other nations about U.S. products, prices, interest rates, and investment opportunities. Conversely, the same information flows back to the United States from other countries. Additionally, firms in other countries use technology created in the United States and U.S. firms use technology developed abroad. **Financial flows** occur upon the transference of money between the United States and other countries for the purpose of paying for imports, buying foreign assets, paying interest on debt, and providing foreign aid (McConnell and Brue, 2008).

Through globalization, the Internet has the ability to bring brands to people through websites, live streaming of fashion shows, advertising on Facebook, or even simply Tweeting about a new product.

Trend 2—Social Media

Social media is in its beginning phases, with popular websites such as Facebook, Twitter, and MySpace. These social networking sites, typically used to connect with friends, now connect consumers to fashion firms as well. By "liking" the page of a favorite fashion company or "friending" the company, companies interact with consumers through these popular social platforms. Companies create "customer loyalty, raising brand awareness, spreading advertising messages, creating online communities, communicate directly with customers, and in many cases, driving sales" (Apparel).

Social networking has changed the shopping habits of consumers and the ways companies now communicate with them. Although, it is clear that the consumer reads, and participates, in online reviews, the reaction of the consumer, whether positive or negative, remains undetermined. "Forty-nine percent of shoppers read reviews, but don't write their own. Twenty-one percent read and contribute reviews," said Sarah Rand, senior director of NRF.

Retailers are making more of an effort to invest in the social media even though, according to a Forrester Survey, 62 percent are not clear as what their returns on investment are (Retailer). The potential Internet consumer will always be invisible to the retailer and as a result, it will be difficult to measure the rate of return on investment in social media.

Trend 3—Technology

Advances in technology touch our lives every day in numerous ways. We see news as it happens, we pay for goods and services with the swipe of a card, we can purchase the latest runway creations or red carpet styles within 24 hours of their debut, and we can buy virtually anything with the click of computer mouse. Technology touches every phase of the fashion industry from raw materials to the cash register.

Computer Aided Design (CAD) is a computer program that allows designers to manipulate their designs easily. Sketchpads and pencils are still important tools but with CAD, a designer can make color decisions without samples. CAD allows for testing and three-dimensional contouring of objects by simulating folds, textures, and creases so that the 3D created garment will drape properly. Pattern making ensues once the design is complete. The process reduces the number of samples, which are costly to produce.

Computer-integrated manufacturing (CIM) is the linking of computers within a manufacturing company from the design through to the production process. Once linked, these computers provide information internally, to suppliers, and even to retailers across the country and around the world.

There are other cutting-edge technologies used, such as the reversal of the typical concept to consumer method of product development, **Product Lifecycle Management (PLM)**, and **Programmable Logic Controller (PLC)**. Product Lifecycle Management (PLM) is a software that deals with the entire lifecycle of a product, from conception, through design and manufacturing, to use and disposal. A technology-based platform allows all suppliers in the fashion supply chain to have access through restricted rights from PLM platforms anywhere in the world; a solution to an ongoing way of conducting business. Fashion companies have been slow to come on board because of the expense and time involved for installation. What fashion companies fail to realize is that PLM is not a one-size-fits-all business model; it is adaptable to all types of companies. In the future, as companies begin to manage their own supply chain through vertical integration, it will be an important tool to keep track of the processes of manufacturing products. Gerber and Lectra, two of the brand leaders in PLM, are making companies more efficient and productive through their platforms, while at the same time developing software to run on the platforms.

The Programmable Logic Controller (PLC) is a digital computer used for automation. The PLC has many facets from the plotting and cutting room where the software helps to save money on materials used by controlling the plotting and marker combinations for efficient cutting of the material.

Additionally, Lectra and Gerber developed software that improved the efficiency in design. Lectra recently developed the software programs Easy Grading and Modaris 3D Fit, and both these programs are accepted as industry standards for their ease of use and efficiency. Easy Grading software ensures increased productivity, precise grading, and high-quality results. The Modaris 3D software has created innovative and significant improvements in CAD technology. "Passing 2D information between fashion designers, pattern designers, pattern makers, pattern graders, product developers, product developers, product managers, and marketing teams has been complex and prone to errors" (white paper, Lectra). The Modaris 3D software increases efficiency by allowing several people to work together even when thousands of miles apart. This collaboration reduces the number of prototypes needed for new styles.

By reversing the concept to consumer method, the consumer, through a body scanner, has his or her own measurements on file with a manufacturer or designer and special orders merchandise for custom fit. TC2, a developer of a body scanner on the market (Figure 12.1), explains that the idea behind the body scanner is to condition consumers to expect custom-fitted clothing, delivered fast and inexpensively, an idea that could make American-based apparel manufacturers more competitive with overseas manufacturers who are less equipped to respond quickly to American fashion trends (TC2).

OptiTex™ created 3D models naming them Adam and Jamie. The unique ability of OptiTex™ 3D Runway fashion software is a realistic cloth simulation/cloth modeling software system based on accurate CAD patterns and real fabric characteristics. Using OptiTex™ 3D Garment Draping and 3D Visualization software system, designers, pattern makers, and retailers can visualize any pattern modifications instantly.

Other noteworthy technological advances are the ways in which companies are testing products such as **Second Life**, which is a virtual world on the Internet created by its residents. Each person created is an **avatar**. Fashion designer Giorgio Armani, who recently opened a shop in Second Life modeled after his flagship location in Milan, has his own avatar. Armani's avatar went to the grand opening of the virtual store. Other fashion designers are selling products in Second Life as well. Some are even using it as a testing ground prior to the launch of a new product.

FIGURE 12.1 *TC2 body scanner offers consumers the option of custom fit clothing (Source: [TC]2, Cary, NC—www.tc2.com).*

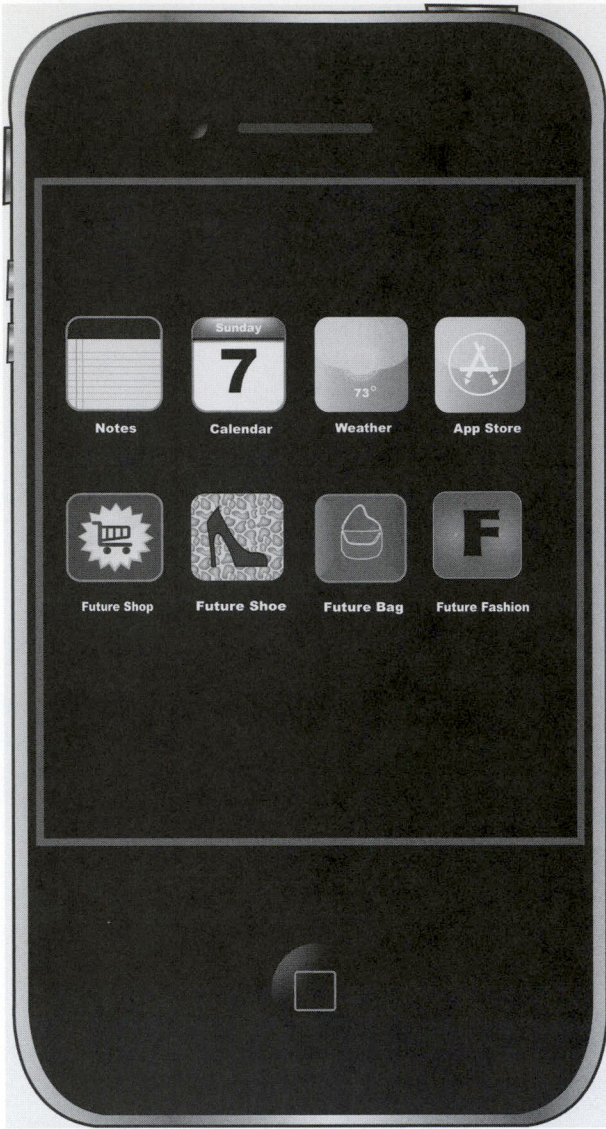

FIGURE 12.2 *Smart phones, such as iPhones, offer consumers new shopping options (Source: Hawa Stwodah).*

The personal computer fits in a pocket and enables the user to do almost anything from hand-held device. Smart phones and tablet computers have changed the way society thinks about staying in touch and shopping. The new technology offered by these devices is another layer of ideas, options, and alternatives for retailers. Fashion firms must decide which technology is beneficial to the marketing and promotion of merchandise and the convenience of consumers. Applications, or "apps" as they are better known as, are software programs. At the point of your finger on a smart phone (Figure 12.2), a consumer can open an app from his or her favorite store, or an app to see where the latest sales are happening, or even check the price of a product using a scanner built into the phone. The phrase "there's an app for that" is true of almost anything one can think of.

With the speed at which fashion moves, the supply chain of fashion has also implemented several technologies throughout the years including bar codes, scanners, and symbol placements. A universal technological system is on the forefront of linking all the supply chains together, thus saving time and money. The Uniform Code Council published a handbook titled *UCC Placement Guidelines,* which can be found at http://www.allbarcodesystems.com/pdf/uccbarcodeguide.pdf. This free book details information about label placement for the suppliers, which is important to scanning the product and the containers of the product. Even more important, as a student of fashion, the guidelines are a great starting point for understanding the bar code system.

The lines that are on the bar code are a zone. The bar code comes in the form of tags placed on the product with a hang tag or sewn into the label. The handbook gives examples for hanging the tag properly for more efficient scanning. The primary factor in the effectiveness of this technology is the speed at which suppliers are involved in scanning the product for a quick response from manufacturing to consumer.

As companies strive to work across borders, technology simplifies the solutions to problems such as low inventories, reorders, consumer demands, and substitutions. Since shorter lead times give a competitive advantage, technology provides solutions that address consumer demands in a matter of days, or even hours. Technology is the future of business models. Figure 12.3 illustrates technology trends.

Trend 4—Radio Frequency Identification (RFID)

Radio frequency identification (RFID) is a unique automatic identification system of tracking product using radio waves and governed by the Federal Communications Commission (FCC). RFID needs an antenna, a transceiver or reader, and a transponder referred to as a tag and sometimes called a smart tag. Embedded microchips containing data allow for the easy tracking of merchandise. There are, however, different levels of this type of technology and not all fashion companies have the desire or the **capital** to venture into this area.

Companies who have implemented the RFID system have seen a reduction in costs, specifically in inventory. Updating tags for new items with information when they enter the supply chain is easy. The negative side to RFID is that other retailers could intercept the information. Since there are no standards and policies regulating RFID, the implication

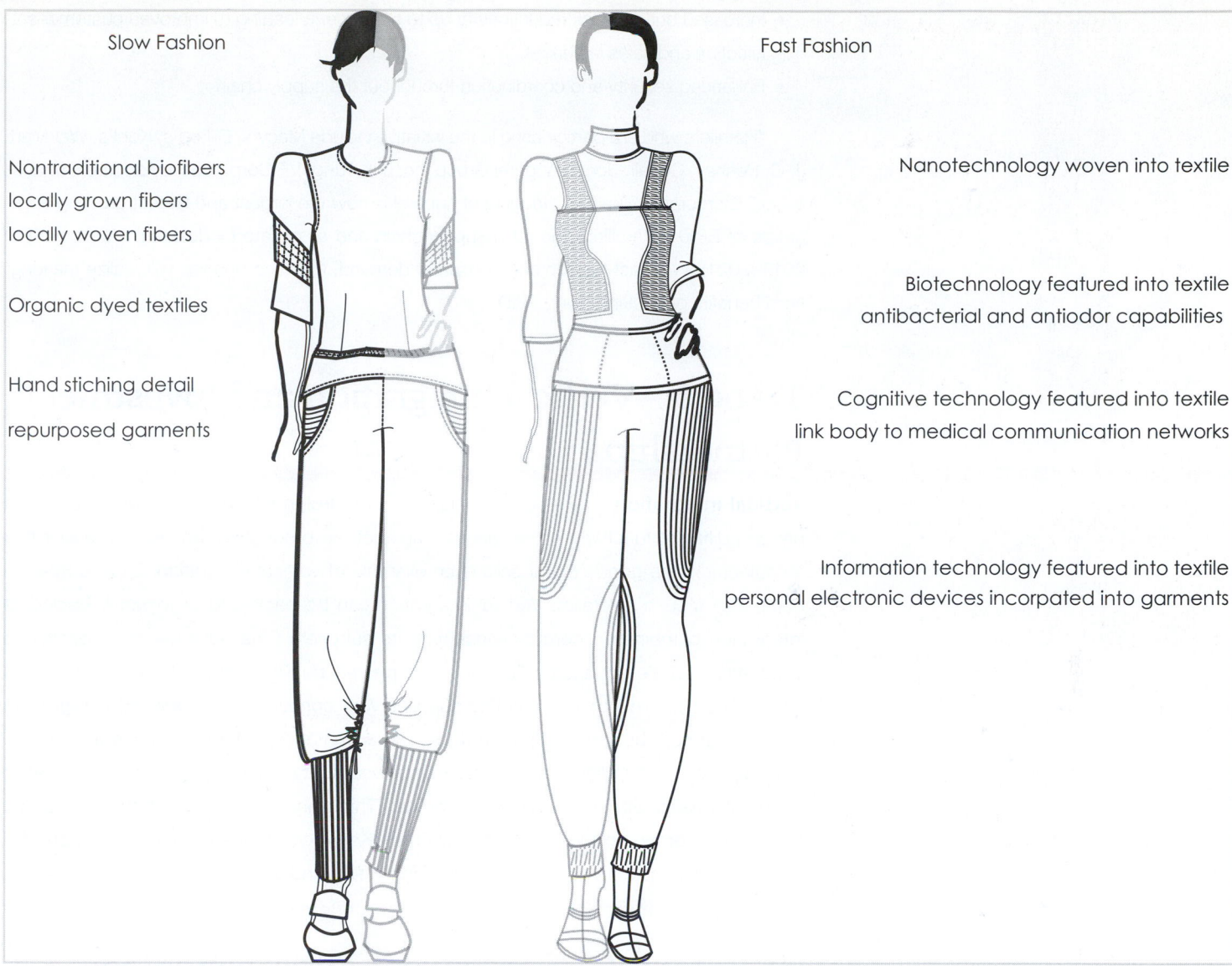

Slow Fashion

Nontraditional biofibers
locally grown fibers
locally woven fibers

Organic dyed textiles

Hand stiching detail
repurposed garments

Fast Fashion

Nanotechnology woven into textile

Biotechnology featured into textile
antibacterial and antiodor capabilities

Cognitive technology featured into textile
link body to medical communication networks

Information technology featured into textile
personal electronic devices incorpated into garments

FIGURE 12.3 *Fashion of the future (Source: Hawa Stwodah).*

is that Company B can access information about Company A with only a tag attached to a garment.

Major retailers are beginning to implement RFID, as its use is beneficial to accessing and correcting inventory problems. The idea is to have RFID installed on all merchandise or boxes of merchandise to ensure that nothing is lost in distribution. As a tracking system, it is very accurate once it is in place. Most retailers and suppliers will start on a smaller scale and then move forward once the implementation has taken place. Some European fashion companies, such as Britain's Marks & Spencer, have had great success with RFID. Sales have increased from 10 to 20 percent.

According to a study from the University of Arkansas, RFID introduced an initiative in November 2010 to direct the RFID adoption in retail with the following results:

- Improved inventory accuracy rates of more than 95 percent, up from an average of 62 percent
- Ability to count 5,000 items per hour using RFID versus 200 items per hour using barcodes, a time savings of 96 percent

- Increased out-of-stock reductions of up to 50 percent, leading to improved customer satisfaction and sales increases
- Enhanced security and coordination throughout the supply chain

"Retailers who are participating in the initiative include Macy's, Dillard's, Kohl's, Wal-Mart, J. C. Penney, Conair, Jones Apparel Group Inc. Li & Fung, VF Corp., Jockey and Levi Strauss & Co." (Corcoran). "The RFID tagging of apparel is now the largest and fastest growing application of RFID in retailing, the retail supply chain and associated industries" (Apparel RFID 2011–2021). With fast fashion and consumer demand, more companies will realize the long-term benefits of tracking using RFID.

Trend 5—Vertical Integration and Investment Partnerships

Vertical integration is a style of management control in which a firm owns plants that perform different functions in the various stages of the production process—a retailer that manufactures the goods that it sells is an example of vertical integration. Zara, a Spanish company, is such a retailer. Vertical integration can be backward or forward. Backward integration combines a core business with its suppliers. The advantages of backward integration include advantageous pricing, improved quality, availability of supplies, and efficiencies achieved by coordinating supplies with consumption. **Forward integration** combines a core business with its buyers. The advantages of forward integration include eliminating competing suppliers, providing improved ability to reach end users, and offering better information about the ultimate consumer. This gained momentum in the 1990s, and continues to grow, so that companies such as Kellwood, Jones Apparel Group, and Liz Claiborne are constantly working and reworking their brand and product mix.

Trend 6—Sportswear and Technology

High-tech sportswear offers technology to monitor your body for health as well as performance, all the while keeping the consumer looking fabulous. Innovation continues to seek ways to put harmony in touch with the athlete, through comfort, fit, resiliency to weather, and performance enhancement.

One of the leaders in high-tech sportswear is Textronics, Inc., a company that developed electro textiles. The fabric has circuitry, sensors, and functional components woven in that render the material capable of enabling electronic devices such as cell phones, providing heat for the wearer, or sensing external changes such as shifts in temperature. Textronics, Inc., currently manufactures a sport bra under the NuMetrex brand with built-in sensors that monitor the wearer's heart rate and communicate that data to a wrist monitor (Figure 12.4). The bra retails for about $99 (including a combination wrist monitor/watch), and dispenses with the wearing of a separate heart monitor (Plunkett, 2008).

In July 2006 Nike revealed the Nike iPod Sports Kit, an informational tool that allows communication to a runner about speed, distance, and calories burned. It works off of the Apple's iPod portable music player. The user places a sensor in the Nike shoe and wears an earphone connected to the iPod.

FIGURE 12.4 *A sports bra by NuMetrex includes a built-in heart monitor (Source: NuMetrix/Adidas).*

Manufacturers have been working to incorporate personal electronic devices into clothing. Items such as notebook computers, cell phones, MP3 players, and other gadgets factor into the design and manufacturing of garments (Global Foresight, Inc., 2006).

Technology is evident in the textiles segment of the industry as well. New fabrics feature **nanotechnology**, biotechnology, cognitive technology, and information technology. These fabrics have characteristics that link one's body to medical and communication networks. Fabrics will also have antibacterial and antiodor capabilities as well (Global Foresight, Inc., 2006).

The future for these technologies is bright, with more personal electronic devices incorporated into garments. Predictions hold that by 2015, washers and dryers will be able to read care instructions on chips placed within clothing (Global Foresight, Inc., 2006).

"Nanotechnology" is a term used that describes many small technologies that are going on in various industries of the world today. The name comes from the concept that nanotechnology is anything smaller than microtechnology. The fashion industry is experimenting with using nanotechnology in fibers and the textile industry, producing textile finishes using nano-size structure and techniques.

Stain-resistant and wrinkle-free clothing is pioneered by companies like Levi Strauss & Co.'s Dockers brand and Liz Claiborne, Inc., and marketed by a growing number of retailers, ranging from mass-market chains like Walmart Stores, Inc., to upscale merchants such as Paul Stuart. The start of the trend in 2004 began with fabric technology from companies such as Greensboro, N.C.-based Nano-Tex, LLC, whose customers include Eddie Bauer, Gap, Old Navy, and Perry Ellis (nanotech-now.com).

There have been many advances, such as Under Armour's partnership with Cotton, Inc., in the creation of **Charged Cotton**, which is a traditional cotton fabric with attributes like softness, but wicks away moisture and dries five times faster. The "**Hug Shirt**," which "gauges body temperature, pressure and heart rate," was developed by CuteCircuit. According to Francesca Rosella, creative director at CuteCircuit, "Wearers hug themselves, then using Bluetooth technology and their cell phone they can send someone else wearing a Hug Shirt that simulates the feeling of the hug" (Voigt).

Trend 7—Cross-Merchandising of Brands or Brand Extension

Cross-merchandising of brands is a business strategy used by fashion companies to build their brands. Most fashion companies today use cross-merchandising through licensing agreements, which, if profitable, are renewable. The trend in licensing is moving toward home fashions through products for the home and personal items for bath and body, creating a breadth of products beyond apparel that a retailer can market for incremental sales.

The building of brands is more than product. It is the creation of a lifestyle. For example, Ralph Lauren is more than just jeans, towels, shoes, or luxury goods. Ralph Lauren represents a classic and refined American lifestyle and its sales promotion reflects the image and iconic style of Ralph Lauren. Martha Stewart is another example of a lifestyle brand. "Martha Stewart Living Omnimedia Inc. (MSLO) is a leading provider of original 'how-to' information, inspiring and engaging consumers with unique lifestyle content and beautifully designed, high-quality products" (MarthaStewart.com). The focus of the Martha Stewart

FIGURE 12.5 *Martha Stewart pioneered the concept of lifestyle brands (Source: AP Wideworld Photos).*

brand is the home and her products are centered on home-making and living a gracious and elegant life (Figure 12.5).

Walt Disney has moved into the bridal business with a line of wedding dresses and accessories inspired by Disney princesses including Cinderella, Sleeping Beauty, Ariel, Belle, Jasmine, and Snow White. See Figure 12.6 for a photograph of a Walt Disney wedding gown. Designer Kirstie Kelly, a bridal designer for more than 10 years, unveiled the gowns in April of 2007 (DisneyBridal. com) with prices ranging from $1,500 to $3,000.

Trend 8—Growth of the Luxury Market

The luxury market in the United States has been robust for several years and the forecasts point to continued growth. The main luxury categories include home, personal (fashion included), and experiences. An opportunity exists for fashion companies to increase their luxury segments and to focus on higher price points for the United States as well as the international consumer. This is particularly true of consumers in China and India where there has been an increase in personal income.

Luxury is expanding its reach online. High-fashion Internet sites featuring various brands of apparel and accessories are flourishing. YOOXSpA (www.yoox.com) is an Italian site that offers more than 250,000 items from Chloe, Dolce & Gabbana, Jean Paul Gaultier, and Prada. Another haute couture site is Net-A-Porter. com, which was launched in 2000 and offers 120 brands online (Plunkett, 2008).

Haute couture companies such as Dior, Louis Vuitton, and Bottega Veneta are also operating websites that are proving to be profitable. For Dior, its website www.dior.com is becoming one of the company's fastest growing points of sale. Websites offer the benefit of reduced expenses: no exorbitant rent, no expensive staff, no posh store design, and no customer perks (Plunkett, 2008).

Trend 9—Demographics

Baby boomers are people born between 1946 and 1964, and within that group those aged 55 or older are the fastest growing demographic group in the United States (Plunkett, 2008). This demographic group is growing so fast that every 7 seconds a baby boomer turns 50 somewhere in the United States. That means that approximately 10,000 boomers turn 50 every day, 365 days a year. Boomer consumers over 50 are a new demographic segment with vast reserves of disposable income that they are willing to spend on products and services (Thornhill and Martin, 2007).

FIGURE 12.6 *Picture of a wedding gown from the Walt Disney collection (Source: AP Wideworld Photos).*

The boomer phenomenon is not new. They have been a driving force in the economy since they came of age in the 1970s. This is the period of time when they made up the majority of the 18–49-year-old demographic, and since then, they have been the focus of virtually all marketing and advertising. The year 1996 brought change to this group when over half of them reached the age of 50. Now they are at the peak of their earning years, and are spending more money annually on consumer goods and services than any other generation, some $2.3 trillion annually, about $400 million more than any other demographic group. Boomers are not a demographic to be ignored by the fashion industry (Thornhill and Martin, 2007).

Trend 10—The Changing American Physique

The plus-size market generally refers to women's sizes 14 and up. There is also a larger set of sizes, 14W to 24W; the W stands for "woman" and sizes extend further to include 24W to 34W. This is a strengthening market with sales in the United States reaching approximately $30 billion in 2009. Sales predictions are that the segment will grow to about $33 billion by 2001, according to the research firm Mintel. Weight gain is affecting many Americans—women, men, and children alike. Roughly two-thirds of American adults are overweight or obese (Flegal). However, this category has not been a slamdunk for retailers. This merchandise is more expensive to produce; from the fabric and thread costs to the costs associated with changing equipment, creating new patterns, and training employees the expenses are high.

Retailers must find solutions and figure out how to effectively market to these consumers. Product placement, store layout, departments exclusively for plus-sizes, larger fitting rooms, and inviting environments appear to appeal to this important market segment. Store design and layout are not the only issues; it is also about style and fit. Many stores such as J. Crew and Ann Taylor sell plus-size clothing online. Saks Fifth Avenue offered sizes up to 16 and 18 upon request in some of their designer lines in fall 2010 (Marsh).

The plus-size customer is not willing to give up fit for style or vice versa. This customer wants to dress like her size-six counterparts in youthful and chic clothing. She is tired of muu-muus and tents and of hearing that she cannot dress a particular way because of her size. However, it is not always possible to have all designs and fabrications work in a plus-size garment, but designers must work to create clothing that is exciting, fashionable, and great fitting for this consumer.

As more Americans have moved into the "overweight" category (women from size 12 to 16 and men from size 40 to 46), manufacturers have adopted vanity sizing. What was once a women's size 10 is now a size 6. Some men's pants in size 32 are actually 33 inches in the waist. Several clothing companies have adjusted the fit of their garments based on the SizeUSA study. Jockey updated the fit of its bras and Liz Claiborne altered the sizes of all 42 of its brands. Victoria's Secret and Gap are offering styles suited for different body types.

Trend 11—The Green Movement

A growing awareness of the environment and the evidence that how we consume and dispose of product impacts the economy is making an impact in the fashion world. As more consumers make a conscious decision to care for the environment through the purchases they make, more fashion companies have begun to create apparel using organic and sustainable materials. Brands like Levi's, Mavi, Loomstate, J. Jill, H&M, and Topshop are just a few that are producing organic products.

The organic movement is becoming organized and the Organic Exchange is one example of a resource for consumers and companies interested in organic cotton. The Organic Exchange, a nonprofit website, lists the brands and apparel companies that produce and/or sell organic cotton fashions. Companies like Nike, Timberland, Patagonia, Eileen Fisher, and Levi Strauss are all using organic cotton for some of their apparel offerings.

"According to the *Organic Cotton Market Report 2009* released by Organic Exchange in May 2010, global sales of organic cotton apparel and home textile products reached an estimated $4.3 billion in 2009. This reflects a 35 percent increase from the $3.2 billion market recorded in 2008" ("Organic Trade Association," n.d.).

The **Sustainable Technology Education Project (STEP)** educates designers and students on the importance of "eco-fashion." STEP defines "eco-fashion" as the following:

- Eco-fashion is about making clothes that take into account the environment, the health of consumers, and the working conditions of people in the fashion industry.
- Eco-clothing is made using organic raw materials, such as cotton grown without pesticides and silk made by worms fed on organic trees.

- The clothing does not involve the use of harmful chemicals and bleaches to color fabrics.
- Garments are often made from recycled and reused textiles. High-quality garments can be made from second-hand clothes and even recycled plastic bottles.
- Apparel is made to last, so that people keep the articles of clothing for longer periods of time.
- All materials are fair trade, that is the people who make them are paid a fair price and have decent working conditions.

Trend 12—Impact of Fashion Designers and Celebrities on Apparel Stores

It is no secret that the red carpet is a fashion runway for designers. It is a venue for designers to have their clothing worn, noticed, and talked about. Bombarded with clothing choices for awards shows, celebrities enjoy the indulgence of selecting from the best of the best. While on the red carpet, celebrities appear in television interviews fielding questions about their clothing and jewelry (Figure 12.7). The next day, knockoffs of the best of the red carpet appear in various stores and online at discounted prices. In a study of 2,000 women conducted by People StyleWatch, 74 percent said that celebrities give them style ideas, but sometimes they do not recognize it; 76 percent said the celebrities have more impact on fashion today than at any other time; and 61 percent look to celebrities for style rather than models (Lockwood).

Some celebrities have entered licensing agreements to produce lines and others have their own collections. Victoria Beckham has a

FIGURE 12.7 *While celebrities walk the red carpet they are typically asked about their clothing and jewelry (Source: Shutterstock).*

line of sunglasses and high-end denim sold at Saks Fifth Avenue and Henri Bendel. M by Madonna was a huge success at H&M debuting in March 2007, featuring glamorous apparel inspired by Madonna herself. Mango, a Spanish fashion chain, partnered with Penelope and Monica Cruz to create a 25-piece clothing line for September 2007. Other celebrities who have been successful with their own lines include Jessica Simpson. Jennifer Lopez and Marc Anthony created a fashion lifestyle brand for Kohl's. Beyonce Knowles, Mary Kate and Ashley Olsen, Sarah Jessica Parker, and Gwen Stefani have designed and produced apparel lines in recent years.

Hip-hop recording artists such as Sean Diddy Combs, Russell Simmons, and Jay–Z have created apparel lines that reflect their tastes and lifestyles. The impact of hip-hop on fashion began in the mid-1980s. Hip-hop is one of the most influential cultural movements to transpire in the United States and shows no sign of losing its grip on young, hip American fashion.

Trend 13—The Conservative Consumer

The recession of 2007 brought about unemployment, credit crunches, homelessness, less discretionary income, and in general, a shift toward more needs from the consumer and less wants in terms of goods and services. The "normal" way of shopping changed for many people. Some retailers survived and some did not.

Because of the 2007 recession, fashion consumers became conservative in the way they shop and what they purchase. They are concerned with the cost of gasoline and the time spent shopping, making the Internet an attractive shopping venue. The post–2007 recession consumer is not embarrassed to shop at a thrift store, seeking a treasure such as a designer dress or jacket. Consumers are beginning to believe that fashion is an investment and they understand the value of a good piece of apparel that will last for five years as opposed to five pieces that last for one season. Bargain shopping has not gone out of style, but they are reluctant to replace what is already in their wardrobe, such as a pair of khakis or white shirt. Retailers are wise and they know that exclusive products that the consumer does not already own will make the post–2007 recession consumer purchase again.

Summary

Your learning for *Fashionomics* ends with an understanding of how to interpret an economic trend as well as the impact a trend will have on apparel manufacturing and retailing. You have gained knowledge of the 12 leading trends impacting the future of fashion.

You began by reading about globalization and ended with the knowledge of the trend of conservative consumers. In between, you read about the greening of the consumer and the impact technology has on sportswear and apparel.

Key Terms

Review Questions

1. Why are economic trends important to the fashion industry?
2. What is the World Trade Organization and how did it come into existence?
3. What did China gain when it joined the WTO?
4. Explain how globalization ends up on the runway.
5. List and compare two economic flows.
6. What drives global inflation? How does it impact the textile and apparel industry?
7. List and define two technology trends related to the fashion industry.
8. Why are investment partnerships important?
9. What is cross-merchandising? Why is this business strategy becoming more important to the fashion industry?
10. Explain the statement "Baby boomers are a driving force of the economy."

Critical Thinking

Predict a future fashion trend. Base your prediction on current economic and fashion trends. Use various resources to support your prediction. Write a one-page summary of your prediction and read it to the class. Led by your teacher, discuss the predictions and have the class vote on which predictions they think will occur and why.

Internet Activities

Currently there is a movement in fashion that is labeled in various ways such as ecofriendly, green movement, and green clothes. The green movement's new name is "slow fashion." Using the Internet, research the "slow fashion" movement and explain what the movement of "slow fashion" based on ecofriendly clothing means. In your answer discuss who is designing clothing with green fashion in mind.

Bibliography

Christopher, M., Lowson, R., & Peck, H. (2009). *Creating an agile supply chains in the fashion industry*. Retrieved December 11, 2009, from http://martin-christopher.info/wp-content/uploads/2009/12/creating-agile-supply-chains-in-the-fashion-undustry.pdf

Corcoran, C. (2010, November 1). *RFID gets industry support*. Retrieved April 15, 2011, from http://www.wwd.com/business-news/rfid-gets-industry-support-3368849

2008 Corporate Fact Book. (2008). *The drive to differentiate*. Retrieved September 19, 2008, from http://www.macysinc.com/investors/vote/2008_fact_book.pdf

Flegal, K. M., Carroll, M. D., Ogden, C. L., & Curtin, L. R. (2010). Prevalence and trends in obesity among US adults, 1999–2008. *JAMA*, pp. 235–241, http://jama.ama-assn.org/content/303/3/235.full

Kirstie Kelley for Disney fairy tale weddings. Retrieved December 12, 2008, from http://www.disneybridal.com/about.html

Lipke, D. (2010, November 18). Jennifer Lopez and Marc Anthony to unveil Kohl's deal. *Women's Wear Daily*.

Lockwood, L. (2011, May 18). People StyleWatch: The celebrity link. *Women's Wear Daily*.

Marsh, L. (2010). Posts by Lisa Marsh. *Stylelist*. Retrieved July 28, 2011, from http://www.stylelist.com/

McConnell, C., & Brue, S. (2008). *Economics principles, problems, and policies*. New York: McGraw-Hill.

Organic Trade Association. (n.d.). "Organic cotton facts," n.p. Retrieved March 18, 2012, from http://www.ota.com/organic/mt/organic_cotton.html

Ozersky, J. (2011, May 18). Fine food and fat: Are chefs to blame for obesity? Retrieved June 10, 2011, from http://www.time.com/time/nation/article/0,8599,2072127,00.html

Plunkett, J. (2008). *Plunkett's apparel & textiles industry almanac 2008*. Houston, TX: Plunkett Research, Ltd.

Reuters. (2007, July 18). *New York tops list of world's fashion cities*. Retrieved September 15, 2008, from http://www.reuters.com/articlePrint?articled=USN1724237520070718

Stone, E. (2008). *The dynamics of fashion*. New York: Fairchild Books.

Thornhill, M., & Martin, J. (2007). *Boomer consumer*. Great Falls, VA: Linx.

Mintel. (n.d.). http://academic.mintel.com.proxy.library.vcu.edu/sinatra/oxygen_academic/search_results/show&/display/id=393566/display/id=496289#hit1

MoneyTerms. (n.d.). *Vertical integration*. Retrieved September 19, 2008, from http://moneyterms.co.uk/horizontal-vertical-integration/

Wiredberries. (2007, September 18). *High-fashion hippie?* Retrieved December 12, 2008, from http://www.com/organic_living/2007/09/highfashion_hippie.asp

index

Note: Locators followed by 'f' and 't' refer to figures and tables respectively.